CHINA'S FOREIGN RELATIONS

THE MACMILLAN COMPANY
NEW YORK · BOSTON · CHICAGO · DALLAS
ATLANTA · SAN FRANCISCO

MACMILLAN & CO., Limited
LONDON · BOMBAY · CALCUTTA
MELBOURNE

THE MACMILLAN COMPANY
OF CANADA, Limited
TORONTO

China's Foreign Relations

1917–1931

BY

ROBERT T. POLLARD, Ph.D.

Assistant Professor of Oriental Studies
University of Washington

New York
THE MACMILLAN COMPANY
1933

SET UP BY BROWN BROTHERS LINOTYPERS
PRINTED IN THE UNITED STATES OF AMERICA
BY THE FERRIS PRINTING COMPANY

33 - 5409
11-4-54

TO
MY FATHER
AND
MY MOTHER

PREFACE

THE well-known work of Dr. H. B. Morse on the International Relations of the Chinese Empire divided the history of China's modern contact with the Western world into three periods. Of these the first was the Period of Conflict, which lasted until 1860. It was followed by the Period of Submission, extending to 1894 and was succeeeded by the Period of Subjection. A fourth period, which might be called the Period of Recovery, began in 1917. In that year China entered the World War on the side of the Allies, and Russia threw off the yoke of the Tsars. One result of China's formal participation in the war was the abrogation of her treaties with Germany and Austria-Hungary. The Russian Revolution provided the Chinese with an opportunity to terminate a second group of treaties providing for special political rights in China. Thus the foundations of the treaty régime were badly shaken, and a step was taken toward the realization of China's ambition to be mistress in her own house.

If the year 1917 marked the opening of a new era in China's foreign relations, perhaps the year 1931 marked the end of that era. On the night of September 18, 1931, an attempt was made to dynamite a section of the Japanese-owned South Manchuria Railway, just north of the city of Mukden. Careful students are not yet prepared to say whether the damage, not very great in any case, resulted from a Chinese or a Japanese plot to damage the railway. The incident marked the climax, however, of a long series of irritations produced by Japan's peculiar interests in Manchuria and the resentment of Chinese Nationalists against the political aspects of those interests. Acting swiftly, and without waiting for advice from the cabinet

vii

in Tokyo, the Japanese military authorities seized the city of Mukden, expelled the native authorities, and launched expeditions against all Chinese forces in the vicinity who, left without leaders, could conveniently be branded as "bandits." During the next three months, Japanese armies overran the whole of Manchuria as far north as the Chinese Eastern Railway, taking over all of the principal cities and practically all of the railways with the exception of the Chinese Eastern in which Soviet Russia held a half interest. Thereafter Manchuria, including the province of Jehol, was declared to be independent of China, and a puppet government was set up dominated by Japanese advisers and dependent for support upon the Japanese army.

Japanese diplomacy since the beginning of the Nationalist movement in China has had to keep two objects in view. One was the protection of Japan's vested interests in Manchuria, whether resting on treaty sanction or not. The other was the preservation and expansion of Japan's profitable trade with China proper. Raw materials from Manchuria were vitally important to the economic life of Japan. Of equally vital importance was the Chinese market for Japanese goods. Statesmen might have foreseen the logical consequences of violent action in defence of Japan's special interests in Manchuria. Military rather than civil authorities were in control of the situation, however, and the Tokyo Foreign Office had perforce to accept the rôle of inventing high moral principles to justify non-moral conduct. The natural result of military aggression in any case was a Chinese boycott which virtually destroyed the continental market for Japanese goods. Thus while Japan's so-called vital interests in Manchuria were safe for the nonce, her trade with China, which was equally vital, was utterly ruined.

In an effort to break the Chinese boycott, and at the same time to demonstrate that Japan "would stand no nonsense" from revolutionary China, the Japanese naval commander at Shanghai landed forces on January 28, 1932, ostensibly for the purpose of protecting Japanese lives and property. The landing force, anticipating apparently as little effective resistance as had been offered in Manchuria, extended the scope of its operations from the International Settlement into Chapei. There it met with determined resistance, the result being a battle of the first magnitude which, in spite of the efforts of representatives of the neutral powers to mediate, lasted for over a month and caused enormous damage to property and great loss of life.

Doubtless some sort of international conference, similar in scope perhaps to the Washington Conference, will be necessary before the situation in the Orient is finally liquidated. Even superficial observers are now convinced that the question of China's relations with Japan is bound up most intimately with the larger question of peace or war in Eastern Asia. Continued political uncertainty in the Pacific area must necessarily affect most vitally whatever prospects exist for the success of the Disarmament Conference now being held at Geneva, and may also, according to views expressed by Secretary of State Henry L. Stimson, affect the attitude of the American Government toward the naval limitation program agreed upon at the Washington Conference. Whatever may be its policy with regard to Manchuria, even the Japanese Government has tacitly acknowledged that the powers have a direct interest in the re-establishment of order in the Shanghai area.

In prosecuting the present study of a critical period in China's diplomatic history, the author has had generous aid from a number of persons to whom special thanks are due. Professor Harold Scott Quigley, of the University of Minnesota, originally suggested the study and offered numerous and valuable criticisms of the work as it progressed. To him belongs much of the credit for what is meritorious in the work without any of the blame for its shortcomings. Miss Mildred Logg, of the University of Washington, has been of great help in checking a considerable number of the references. Mr. Charles G. Gates, of the University of Minnesota, read and criticized one chapter, and came nobly to the rescue of the

Preface

author one critical night when there was great need of haste in completing the original manuscript. But for unintended mis-statements of fact as well as errors of judgment, the author himself must be held solely responsible.

R. T. P.

Seattle, Washington.
July 2, 1932.

CONTENTS

CHINA'S FOREIGN RELATIONS

CHAPTER I

INTRODUCTION

CHINA at the close of the nineteenth century had lost, by successive treaties and agreements with various foreign powers, many of the distinctive attributes of a sovereign nation. Foreigners resident in the country, who were steadily increasing in number, enjoyed extraterritorial rights which removed them from the jurisdiction of Chinese courts. Over residential areas set apart for the use of foreigners, the Chinese Government had only nominal control. Chinese tariff rates, fixed in the treaties, could not be modified without the unanimous consent of the powers concerned. Foreign governments even stood at times between Christian converts and their own native officials.

When the scramble for concessions finally indicated the apparent determination of the predatory powers to partition the country, Chinese resentment took the form of violence. The Boxer Movement represented an attempt to rid China of foreign control and influence by the simple expedient of driving all foreigners into the sea. The resort to force, however, had disastrous consequences. The harsh and humiliating terms of the Final Protocol of 1901 testified to what lengths the powers would go when their interests were menaced. Violence having failed, there remained apparently only one avenue of escape from the network of treaty arrangements which crippled the government's freedom of action. The system of internal administration would have to be reformed along lines suggested if not dictated by foreign example. For such a huge and unwieldy empire, steeped in the traditions of past cen-

1

turies, the pathway leading to ultimate recovery promised to be very long and very thorny. Nevertheless, since it was the only pathway left open, the rulers of China set out cautiously to tread it with what courage they could muster. By grappling energetically with the vexatious problems which confronted them on every hand, the Manchus might yet save the nation and at the same time restore their rapidly waning prestige.

Three of the powers gave platonic approval to several aspects of the new reform movement. On September 5, 1902, a year after the completion of the Final Boxer Protocol, was signed the Mackay Treaty with Great Britain.[1] By Article VIII of this convention, the Chinese Government agreed to take steps to abolish the *likin* system of taxation on goods moving in domestic trade. In return for such reform, which was to be completed not later than January 1, 1904, Great Britain consented conditionally to certain changes in the Chinese tariff. A surtax not to exceed one and one-half times the rates leviable under the Final Protocol of 1901 might be imposed on all imports. A similar surtax on native goods exported was not to exceed seven and one-half per cent *ad valorem*. It was agreed also that the Chinese Government might recast the export tariff—the rates of which were still those of 1858—with specific duties as far as practicable on a scale not exceeding five per cent *ad valorem*. These provisions were not to be effective, however, unless all of the powers entitled to most-favored-nation treatment consented to their enforcement.

The necessary consent was forthcoming from two of the powers. Provisions substantially similar to those written into the Mackay treaty appeared in the Japanese treaty of October 8, 1903, and the American treaty signed the same day. The remaining Treaty Powers, however, were slow to follow suit. Subsequent negotiations revealed that the concessions desired by China would have to be paid for in each case by some *quid pro quo*. The negotiations thus terminated with no imme-

[1] J. V. A. MacMurray, *Treaties and Agreements with and concerning China, 1894-1919.* 2 vols., New York, 1921. Vol. I, p. 342.

diate prospect that the increased tariff rates promised conditionally in the British treaty would become effective.[2]

The British treaty set the pace also with a declaration of policy relative to consular jurisdiction. Article XII of that agreement, the substance of which was duplicated in the subsequent Japanese and American treaties, provided that

"China having expressed a strong desire to reform her judicial system and to bring it into accord with that of western nations, Great Britain agrees to give every assistance to such reform, and she will also be prepared to relinquish her extraterritorial rights when she is satisfied that the state of the Chinese laws, the arrangement for their administration, and other considerations warrant her in so doing."

The judicial and legal reforms desired by the foreign powers were radical indeed, involving not merely the drafting of new laws, but the reorganization as well of the entire political system of China. The existing legal code, the *Ta Tsing Liu Li*, dating from 1641, was in reality not much more than a criminal code, its civil provisions covering little beyond questions of marriage and succession.[3] Its harsh provisions relating to punishment for crime reflected none of the changes which had taken place during the nineteenth century in criminal codes of the West, although they compared not unfavorably with the laws of seventeenth century Europe which were in force when the *Ta Tsing Liu Li* was promulgated. The judicial system, unchanged for centuries, was linked inseparably with the administrative system. Justice, both civil and criminal—although little enough of the former—was meted out by the same magistrate of the *hsien* who was responsible for all of the other multifarious details of local government. The prisons were little better than pest houses, places to be avoided at any cost.

Noncommital as was the pledge contained in the British treaty, it reflected in a general way the views of Western Powers, namely, that domestic reform must precede any recon-

[2] H. B. Morse, *The International Relations of the Chinese Empire,* Vol. III, pp. 370, 372.
[3] M. T. Z. Tyau, *China Awakened,* New York, 1922, p. 247.

sideration of existing treaty limitations. The Chinese Government did what seemed necessary under the circumstances. The year 1902 saw the creation by Imperial Mandate of a Commission on Judicial Reform. The work of the Commission was placed in charge of Dr. Wu Ting-fang, who had studied Western law in England, and Mr. Shen Chia-pen, an eminent authority on Chinese law. A partial report of the Commission was ready for submission to the Throne in the spring of 1905. It referred to extraterritoriality as an encroachment on China's territorial sovereignty, recalled the provisions of the treaties of 1902 and 1903 relative to its surrender, and proposed the mitigation of rigorous punishments prescribed by the existing criminal law. The suggested changes received Imperial approval.[4]

Subsequently an Imperial Law Codification Commission undertook the work of drafting new criminal and commercial codes, as well as codes of civil and criminal procedure. The work of the commissioners received a setback in 1906, however, when the Throne rejected the draft code of criminal procedure on the ostensible grounds that it failed to harmonize with Chinese traditions or meet distinctively Chinese needs. In protest against the Throne's action, Dr. Wu Ting-fang resigned from the Commission. Shen Chia-pen remained at his post, however, and under his direction laws were drawn up during the next few years relating to bankruptcy, mining, the press, associations, nationality, police offenses, and transportation.[5] The new laws were semi-adaptations of Japanese legislation which in turn had been patterned after German models. Of these tentative drafts, only the criminal code, completed in 1909, was actually promulgated.[6]

Meanwhile hopeful beginnings were being made in other directions. In 1907 appeared the Law on the Organization of the Judiciary, providing for local courts to replace the old-fashioned magistrate's tribunals, and for a hierarchy terminat-

[4] Meribeth Cameron, *The Reform Movement in China, 1898-1912*, Stanford University, 1931, pp. 172-3.
[5] *Ibid.*, p. 173.   [6] Tyau, *op. cit.*, pp. 247-8.

ing in a national supreme court. Provision was made for a procurator's office to be attached to each district court, each provincial high court, and the national supreme court.[7] About the same time a nine-year program of preparation for constitutional government was drawn up which set forth, among other things, the steps by which the various grades of courts were to be established.[8] Meanwhile provision was being made also for the establishment of law schools to supply technically trained judges for service in these new tribunals.[9] Finally, a system of modern prisons was projected, and in 1908 in Peking construction was begun on the first of the new prisons.[10]

While a start had thus been made in the direction of judicial, legal, and prison reform, the work rested for the most part on a paper basis when the revolution broke out in 1911. With the discredited Ta Tsing rulers out of the way, it remained to be seen how well the Chinese themselves would be able to carry forward the work begun by their predecessors. The provisional constitution of 1912 [11] attempted to guarantee to citizens many of the personal rights which had counterparts in Western constitutional law. The rights, however, were those of citizens rather than persons, and there was no indication that they would be extended automatically to aliens resident in the country. The constitution also attempted a theoretical separation of powers among the three departments of government somewhat after the model of Montesquieu. In addition, an attempt was made to protect the judiciary against administrative and executive interference. The Manchu Court, partly owing to the shortage of technically trained judges, had been content in many instances to appoint old-style scholars to positions in the new judicial system. These half measures were now abandoned by the Republican rulers who early adopted the policy of ap-

---

[7] Cameron, *op. cit.*, p. 174.
[8] Pao Chao Hsieh, *The Government of China, 1644-1911*, Baltimore, 1925, pp. 355-8.
[9] E. T. Williams, *China Yesterday and Today*, New York, 1927, p. 452.
[10] Tyau, *op. cit.*, p. 253.
[11] Text, H. F. MacNair, *Modern Chinese History: Selected Readings*, Shanghai, 1923, pp. 729-34.

pointing only legally trained judges and procurators to posts in the modernized court system.[12] The Republican government decreed also that the draft criminal code, slightly amended in consequence of the destruction of the monarchy, should hereafter apply in all criminal cases. Simultaneously, a careful revision of that code was ordered.[13] The first revision was completed and approved toward the end of 1914. The Law Codification Commission, originally created by the Manchu government, was reorganized and its work continued by the new government. After 1914 Japanese and French advisers collaborated in the work of code drafting. Dr. Wang Ch'ung-hui, probably China's foremost modern jurist, was appointed in 1916 to be chairman of the Commission.[14] While the drafting of the codes proceeded, the work of extending the modern courts and of constructing modern prisons went slowly forward. All of the work of reform was seriously hampered, however, by the internal unrest which accompanied President Yuan Shih-k'ai's struggles with his enemies in Parliament and in the provinces, and by foreign complications resulting from Japan's aggressions in the years following 1914.

In 1917 China entered the World War on the side of the Allies. That fact worked a profound change in the international position of the country. In 1902 and 1903 three of the powers had expressed their readiness to forego the exercise of special privileges in China when the internal conditions which made those privileges necessary had been eliminated. The World War provided the Chinese Government with an opportunity to abolish some of these special rights without completing the work of domestic reform. The treaties with Germany and Austria-Hungary were abrogated, and for the first time the nationals of those countries became subject to Chinese laws and to the jurisdiction of Chinese courts. German and Austrian residential concessions reverted to Chinese control. Two of the great powers of Europe lost their right to be consulted with regard to Chinese tariff rates. Thus strands were cut in

[12] Tyau, *op. cit.*, p. 261.   [13] *Ibid.*, p. 248.   [14] *Ibid.*

the elaborate network of foreign control which dated back to the British Treaty of Nanking of 1842. During the years after 1917, other strands were destined to be severed from time to time, all without waiting for that complete modernization of the Chinese Government upon which the powers had insisted in 1902 and 1903.

CHAPTER II

CHINA IN THE WORLD WAR

CHINA was not concerned with the complicated issues which in 1914 plunged Europe into war. At first glance, there seemed to be little to choose between one and another of the warring powers, for each had its separate record of aggression in the Far East which hardly entitled it either to the sympathy or the whole-hearted respect of the Chinese. Officially, therefore, the government of China remained neutral during the first two and a half years of the conflict.[1] During the same period, unofficial opinion in the country, where it was not indifferent, tended to favor Germany rather than her enemies.[2] For among those enemies was Japan, whose aggressions in 1914 and 1915 at the expense of her weaker neighbor differed little from Austrian

[1] Twice during the early years of the war, President Yuan Shih-k'ai, who was deeply concerned lest Japan take advantage of the European crisis to establish her hegemony in China, considered the possibility of joining the Allies. Prior to August 15, 1914, the date of the Japanese ultimatum to Germany, the German representative in Peking discussed informally with Foreign Office officials the possibility of immediately returning Kiaochou to China. Japan pointedly warned the Chinese Government that the transfer would not be permitted. Yuan then considered declaring war on Germany and sending a Chinese army to coöperate with the Anglo-Japanese forces then preparing to attack Tsingtao. But the Japanese Minister informed the Foreign Office on August 20 that the matter of Kiaochou no longer concerned the Chinese Government which, he trusted, would remain absolutely passive with regard to it. Paul S. Reinsch, "Secret Diplomacy and the Twenty-One Demands," *Asia*, XXI, Nov., 1921, pp. 937-43. Thomas F. Millard, *Democracy and the Eastern Question*, New York, 1919, p. 95. Again in November, 1915, Yuan, seeking a way out of domestic entanglements, offered to join the Allies, and again Japan vetoed the proposal. Millard, *op. cit.*, pp. 97-100. Putnam Weale, *The Fight for the Republic in China*, New York, 1917, p. 311. See also "The Claim of China for the Abrogation of the Treaties and Notes concluded with Japan on May 25, 1915," presented by the Chinese delegation to the Paris Peace Conference, *Congressional Record*, LVIII, p. 3121. (July 24, 1919.)
[2] See E. T. Williams, *A Short History of China*, New York and London, 1928, p. 515. Weale, *op. cit.*, pp. 310-11. Millard, *op. cit.*, p. 85.

aggressions with regard to Serbia. Moreover, there were special grievances of a minor character against both Russia and France. In October, 1916, the Peking Government felt compelled to protest against the massacre by Russian Cossacks of 500 Chinese Mohammedans living near Kashgar, in Sinkiang. During the same month, the French authorities at Tientsin arbitrarily annexed a small area adjoining the French Concession, following their failure to secure the additional land by negotiation.[3]

In contrast with the attitude of these three Allied Powers, the German Government, through its representatives in China, lost no opportunity to cultivate Chinese friendship during the early years of the war. The task of these representatives was made easier by the fact that, according to common belief, German traders ordinarily showed a markedly greater disposition than the British, for example, to meet the Chinese people on a footing of social equality. It was remembered also that after 1905 the official German policy with reference to Shantung gave the government of China little cause to complain. Moreover, the army men of China were frank admirers of German military efficiency, and frequently expressed their belief that Germany would emerge victorious from the conflict.

The decision of the American Government to sever diplomatic relations with Germany introduced into this situation a new element whose ultimate consequences were far-reaching. The official German announcement that unrestricted submarine warfare would be resumed February 1, 1917, was communicated to the Chinese Minister in Berlin.[4] The announcement provoked no immediate resentment in Peking. On February 4, however, the American Minister to China, Mr. Paul S. Reinsch, acting on instructions from his government, notified the Waichiao Pu of President Wilson's determination to break off relations with Germany, and of his desire that the other neutral

[3] H. B. Morse and H. F. MacNair, *Far Eastern International Relations,* Shanghai, 1928, pp. 864-5.
[4] Zimmermann to Yen, January 31, 1917. Nagao Ariga, *La Chine et la grande guerre européenne au point de vue du droit international d'après les documents officiels du gouvernement chinois* (Paris, 1920), pp. 135-8.

powers, including China, should associate themselves with the
United States in taking similar action.[5] The Young China element in Peking immediately sensed the moral and political advantages which would result from China's association with her
powerful neighbor across the Pacific. President Li Yuan-hung
and his Premier, General Tuan Ch'i-jui, were disposed to proceed cautiously. President Li feared that an active foreign
policy, particularly if it should lead to war, would strengthen
the hands of the Chinese militarists. He inquired of Mr.
Reinsch, further, whether the United States would aid China in
bearing the responsibilities of the proposed step.[6] With regard
to the latter point, Premier Tuan was more specific. He pointed
quite frankly to the condition of the public treasury and intimated that although his government was disposed in principle
to heed the suggestion of President Wilson, it would not feel
safe in doing so "unless assured that it could obtain from
American sources such financial and other assistance as would
enable it to take the measures appropriate to the situation which
would thus be created." [7]

Mr. Reinsch hesitated at first to offer assurances of the sort
desired. Cable communications with Washington had been in-
terrupted, and as a consequence it was impossible for him to
know the mind of the State Department. A meeting of the
cabinet on February 6, however, revealed the reluctance of the
Chinese Government to take action without previous assurances.
A policy of extreme caution seemed to be dictated not only by
the existing financial stringency, but by the fear that a breach
with Germany would result in some additional impairment of
China's sovereign rights and of her power to dispose at will of
her own national resources. In particular, several members of
the cabinet voiced their conviction that precipitate action at
that time would furnish Japan with a convenient pretext for
reviving Group V of the Twenty-One Demands.[8]

Feeling that the situation called for heroic measures, Mr.

[5] MacMurray, *op. cit.*, Vol. II, p. 1368.
[6] Paul S. Reinsch, *An American Diplomat in China* (Garden City, 1922),
p. 245.
[7] *Ibid.*, p. 249.   [8] Reinsch, *op. cit.*, p. 252.

Reinsch decided not to wait for specific instructions from Washington. On February 7 he drew up a memorandum, the substance of which he communicated, on his own responsibility, to the Premier and the Foreign Office.[9] He had recommended to his government, he said, "that in the event of the Chinese Government's associating itself with the President's suggestion, the Government of the United States should take measures to put at its disposition the funds immediately required for the purposes you have indicated, and should take steps with a view to such funding of the Boxer Indemnity as would for the time being make available for the purposes of the Chinese Government at least the major portion of the current indemnity instalments. . . ." He declared further, however, that whatever specific arrangements were made would depend finally upon the decision of Congress and the various administrative organs concerned. Nevertheless, the American Minister felt warranted in assuring the Chinese Government that "by the methods you have suggested or otherwise, adequate means will be devised to enable China to fulfill the responsibilities consequent upon associating herself with the action of the United States Government, without any impairment of her national independence and of her control of her military establishment and general administration."

Meanwhile, the Premier was feeling quiet pressure from other quarters. Dr. John C. Ferguson and Dr. G. E. Morrison, respectively American and British advisers to the President of China, were using their influence in high official circles. The Young China Party, including among others Mr. C. T. Wang and Dr. Wang Ch'ung-hui, continued to urge immediate action.[10] Support for an active policy came also from Mr. Liang Ch'i-ch'ao, both a politician and an outstanding scholar, who had been called to Peking for consultation with Premier Tuan.

[9] Text, *ibid.*, pp. 249-50. When cable communications across the Pacific were reëstablished once more, Reinsch received from Washington belated instructions which seemed to imply that he had taken rather too seriously the circular letter of the State Department inviting coöperation on the part of the neutral powers. *Ibid.*, pp. 257-8.
[10] Reinsch, *op. cit.*, pp. 244, 247.

Despite the continued apprehensions of President Li, a protest was subsequently, on February 9, transmitted to the German Government through Admiral von Hintze, the German Minister in Peking. The note declared that [11]

"The new measures of submarine warfare inaugurated by Germany . . . constitute a violation of the principles of public international law at present in force; the tolerance of their application would have as a result the introduction into international law of arbitrary principles incompatible with even legitimate commercial intercourse between neutral states and belligerent powers.

"The Chinese Government, therefore, protests energetically to the Imperial German Government against the measures proclaimed on February 1, and sincerely hopes that with a view to respecting the rights of neutral states and to maintaining the friendly relations between these two countries, the said measures will not be carried out.

"In case, contrary to its expectations its protest be ineffectual the Government of the Chinese Republic will be constrained . . . to sever the diplomatic relations at present existing between the two countries. It is necessary to add that the attitude of the Chinese Government has been dictated purely by the desire to further the cause of the world's peace, and by the maintenance of the sanctity of international law."

On the same day, the Chinese Foreign Office notified the American Minister that [12]

"The Chinese Government being in accord with the principles set forth in Your Excellency's note and firmly associating itself with the Government of the United States of America, has taken similar action by protesting energetically to the German Government against the new measures of blockade. The Chinese Government also proposes to take such action in the future as will be deemed necessary for the maintenance of the principles of international law."

It had been a very long time since China had mustered the courage to address such a vigorous protest to one of the major powers. In a sense, the action thus taken marked "China's first independent participation in world politics." [13] And while the decision to act was frankly influenced by the example of the

[11] Wu Ting-fang to von Hintze, MacMurray, *op. cit.*, II, p. 1369.
[12] MacMurray, *op. cit.*, Vol. II, pp. 1368-9.
[13] Reinsch, *op. cit.*, p. 253.

China in the World War 13

American Government and by the personal activity of its official representative in Peking, it was nevertheless the decision of a government acting in accordance with a reasoned consideration of its own best interests.[14] The announcement that the Chinese Government intended henceforth to uphold the principles of international law had in it a note of genuine sincerity. The more far-sighted members of the Young China group perceived clearly that international law may sometimes serve the needs of weaker powers by restraining or modifying the conduct of the stronger powers. A second motive had its roots in the conviction that China would gain by associating herself with the United States. Had the suggestion which resulted in the protest of February 9 come from any of the Allied Powers, it would have raised the suspicion that ulterior purposes lay concealed behind it. Coming from the American President, however, the suggestion carried no such possible taint.[15] Moreover, even President Li was influenced by the probability that by associating herself with the powers allied against Germany, China would be entitled to an independent voice at the peace conference when the disposal of German rights in Shantung came up for consideration.[16] Finally, many Chinese in both official and unofficial circles entertained the hope, which grew stronger during the ensuing months, that by casting her weight into the scales against Germany, China might eventually bring the Allied Powers to reconsider the terms of some of the treaties which bore most heavily upon her, particularly the Boxer Protocol of 1901.

Having once been won to the support of an active policy

[14] The Allied representatives in Peking apparently influenced the decision only slightly, if at all; whatever cautious influence they did exert was unofficial. *Far Eastern Review*, XIII, Feb., 1917, p. 348. Reinsch, *op. cit.*, p. 254.

[15] Premier Tuan, immediately following the protest to Germany, addressed a telegram to the provincial governors which contained the following statement: "Our country has until now observed a strict neutrality and has done no injury to the interests of the belligerent nations. Germany, in putting into effect its new system of submarine warfare, interferes with neutral rights. The United States, an essentially neutral and pacific nation, has found intolerable this attitude of Germany, and protests against it. Why should we not do the same?" Ariga, *op. cit.*, pp. 146-8.

[16] Reinsch, *op. cit.*, p. 246.

against Germany, Premier Tuan, working in close harmony with his Foreign Minister, Dr. Wu Ting-fang, showed no disposition to turn back. A little more than a week after the protest of February 9, the Chinese Minister at Berlin, Dr. W. W. Yen, was instructed to press the German Government for a reply. The substance of that reply, which was oral and unofficial, was telegraphed by Dr. Yen to Peking on February 19. He had been informed at the German Foreign Office that there would be no change in Germany's program of indiscriminate submarine warfare in certain zones. However, every effort would be made to protect Chinese lives and property, and the Chinese Government was asked to regard the submarine policy as the inevitable result of Allied pressure and the last resort of a nation driven to extreme measures.[17]

Meanwhile, the Japanese Government was engaged in reconsidering its policy with regard to China. For two years Japan had vetoed attempts to bring China into the war on the side of the Allies. Now, however, the ascendency of American influence in Peking not only threatened the position of leadership in Chinese affairs which Japan coveted, but seemed likely, also, to bring China into the war as a protégé of the United States, quite regardless of Japanese views. The Tokyo authorities thereupon adopted a policy whose ultimate object was to enable China to enter the war without imperiling Japan's special claims and interests in Shantung or elsewhere in China. Being first assured that at the peace conference Great Britain would support the claims of Japan with regard to Shantung,[18] the Japa-

[17] *Far Eastern Review*, XIII, Mar., 1917, p. 386.
[18] On January 27, 1917, the Japanese Minister for Foreign Affairs, Viscount Motono, informed the British Ambassador at Tokyo, Sir William Conyngham Greene, of the desire of the Japanese Government to have assurances from the British Government concerning Shantung and the German islands in the Pacific north of the equator. The desired assurances were forthcoming in the note from the British Ambassador dated February 16. Meanwhile on February 10, the Chinese Minister to Tokyo, Mr. Chang Tsung-hsiang, acting on instructions from his government, informed Motono of the events leading up to the Chinese protest to Germany. Motono thereupon not only expressed his approval of China's action, but urged that she go one step further and join the Allied group. Carson Chang, "Inside History of China's Declaration of War," *Millard's Review*, V, Aug. 17, 1918,

nese Government, about the middle of February, sent Mr. Kamezo Nishihara to China bearing a confidential memorandum, presumably for circulation among the Allied Legations. Included in the memorandum were proposals that the Entente Powers should agree to the postponement of the Boxer Indemnity payments for a period of three years and should guarantee, further, that the German portion of the indemnity should be canceled; on condition that China should take steps to abolish the *likin* within ten years, her tariff rates on manufactured goods might be raised to an effective seven and one-half per cent and those on raw materials to an effective five per cent *ad valorem*. The export of such raw materials as cotton, wool, iron ores, and iron, was to be allowed without payment of duty. Finally, the Entente Powers should agree to use their good offices when negotiations concerning these matters took place between China and the other Treaty Powers.[19]

The next move, however, was made by China herself and not Japan. It had been assumed when the Chinese protest was dispatched to Germany that the United States would shortly enter

p. 463. Similarly the Japanese Chargé d'Affaires in Peking, Mr. Kenkichi Yoshizawa, informed President Li on February 11 that his government entirely approved of the Chinese note to Germany. *Japan Weekly Chronicle,* Feb. 22, 1917, p. 296. About the same time, the Japanese Minister, Baron Hayashi, then in Japan, stated in the course of a press interview that he thought China should have been induced to join the Allies soon after the outbreak of hostilities, *Ibid.,* p. 298.

The Japanese position was fortified still further by pledges exacted from the French and Russian Governments that Japan could rely on their support at the peace conference. The Italian Government, having less direct interest in the Japanese claims to Shantung, intimated that it would have no objections to whatever settlement might be made of them. The *quid pro quo* in the French note of March 1, to which the Japanese Government assented, was that Japan should lend its support "to obtain from China the rupture of its diplomatic relations with Germany" in addition to drastic measures directed against German subjects and interests in China. For the texts of the notes, which remained secret until the Paris Peace Conference, see *China Year Book, 1921-1922,* pp. 707-11.

[19] Carson Chang, "Inside History of China's Declaration of War," *Millard's Review,* V, Aug. 17, 1918, p. 463. Mr. Chang was a member of the War Commission and Secretary to President Feng Kuo-chang. It is hardly necessary to suggest that Japan would have benefited by the measures proposed, particularly the one relating to the free export of raw materials.

the war, and that China could then with safety follow in the wake of a powerful nation with a fixed war policy. As the United States delayed issuing a declaration of war, however, the Chinese Government apparently decided that American support was neither certain nor vigorous. Consequently, the Allied representatives in Peking were approached with a view to seeing what terms they were prepared to offer. On February 26, Mr. Lu Cheng-hsiang, acting as the personal representative of Premier Tuan, informed each of the Allied Ministers in turn that should China decide to sever diplomatic relations with Germany, she would find it necessary to take precautionary measures. In particular, she would have need of financial assistance. Mr. Lu, therefore, suggested that the powers agree to a revision of the Chinese tariff, and also to the postponement of the Boxer Indemnity payments.[20] Two days later the French Minister, M. Conty, acting on behalf of his six Allied colleagues, left at the Waichiao Pu a memorandum intimating that if and when China effectively severed relations with Germany and Austria-Hungary, the Allied Governments would be prepared to consider favorably the two proposals made on behalf of the Chinese Government by Mr. Lu.[21]

Some of the Chinese leaders, now convinced that China would gain most by entering the war without waiting for prior action by the United States, hoped to wring even greater concessions from the Allies. A telegram, drafted by Mr. Liang Ch'i-ch'ao for transmission to each of the Allied Governments, proposed that China's part in the war should consist in supplying labor and raw materials; on her part, China desired assurances that with regard to military assistance and whatever munitions she might need, she would be allowed full freedom of action; she desired, furthermore, the confiscation of the entire German portion of the Boxer Indemnity and a postponement of the other Indemnity payments for ten years; the Chinese

[20] Chang, *op. cit.*
[21] *North China Herald*, CXXII, Mar. 3, 1917, p. 447. The text of the note appears in *Far Eastern Review*, XIII, Apr., 1917, p. 402.

tariff should be increased to an effective twelve per cent; finally, all clauses in her existing treaties which conflicted with the principles of equality should be modified.[22] The telegram, however, was not sent. On March 3, the draft was presented to President Li for his official consideration. Although the President was personally opposed to a diplomatic breach with Germany, he had expressed his willingness to adopt the policy of the majority in the government. On March 4, however, Li informed the members of the cabinet that he objected to the terms of the proposed telegram and would refuse to affix his official seal to it. He insisted that since such a proposal meant a definite step toward war, it must have the prior approval of Parliament, which alone had the power to declare war. Premier Tuan thereupon charged the President with bad faith and, resigning his office, departed for Tientsin in an exceedingly angry frame of mind.[23]

The breach between President Li and his Premier was eventually healed through the mediation of the Vice-President, Feng Kuo-chang. On March 7, Tuan consented to resume office on the understanding that Li should cease to obstruct the execution of the policy upon which the cabinet had decided. It was agreed that the question of severing diplomatic relations with Germany should be referred to Parliament for final decision, and the President expressed his willingness to abide by the result.[24] On March 9 the Premier appeared before Parliament to explain his policy toward Germany. He declared that while the dismissal of the German Minister was dictated primarily by a desire to uphold the sanctity of international law, the Chinese Government had nevertheless been led to expect that more tangible and immediate benefits would follow the step. In particular, the Premier mentioned the probable increase in the

[22] Chang, *op. cit.*
[23] *Far Eastern Review*, XIII, Mar., 1917, p. 386. Throughout this entire controversy, President Li showed special anxiety to safeguard the Constitution by upholding the prerogatives of Parliament. Tuan on the other hand favored the concentration of executive power in the cabinet. He resented presidential interference and held Parliament in contempt.
[24] *North China Herald*, CXXII, Mar. 10, 1917, p. 503.

tariff rates and a modification of the Protocol of 1901.[25] The next day, the House of Representatives voted overwhelmingly in favor of the step demanded by the government, and the Senate took similar action on the day following.

On March 10, while Parliament considered the question of a diplomatic rupture, the German Government returned a reply to the Chinese note of February 9. Astonishment was expressed "at the threat made by the Government of the Republic of China in its note of protest." However, in consideration of the good relations which had hitherto subsisted between the two nations, the Imperial Government was "disposed to overlook the threatening terms which the Chinese Government has employed." Germany pleaded her inability to abandon unrestricted submarine warfare, but expressed a willingness to enter into negotiations "in order to arrive at a plan for the protection of Chinese lives and property. . . ."[26]

Feeling assured of the support of Parliament, however, the government felt safe in ignoring the German offer to negotiate. On March 14, Admiral von Hintze received his passports from the Waichiao Pu together with a note explaining the reasons for this action.[27] On the same day a presidential mandate was published announcing the severance of diplomatic relations with Germany and commanding the appropriate authorities to formulate regulations for the protection of German subjects "in accordance with the rules of international law." A further proclamation was issued at the same time explaining to the nation the reasons for the step.[28]

[25] *Asia*, XVII, June, 1917, p. 277. *North China Herald*, CXXII, Mar. 24, 1917, p. 634.
[26] Von Hintze to Wu Ting-fang, March 10, 1917. Ariga, *op. cit.*, pp. 142-3.
[27] Wu Ting-fang to von Hintze, *ibid.*, p. 149.
[28] MacMurray, *op. cit.*, Vol. II, p. 1369. The Minister of Public Instruction explained the significance of the government's action in an order to the educational authorities of the country. "This rupture [he declared] constitutes an act of the greatest importance for the foreign relations of China. The Chinese Government, in accord with the will of the entire nation, has taken the weighty responsibility for it in order to maintain the position of China among the nations of the world. . . . This event indicates that China aspires to be a nation in the family of nations." Ariga, *op. cit.*, pp. 196-7.

Under accepted rules of international law, as is well known, the suspension of diplomatic intercourse does not of itself terminate treaties in force between the nations concerned. The situation in China, however, was exceptional. Under the provisions of the Protocol of 1901, Germany possessed the right to maintain a legation guard in Peking and to share with the other powers in the work of policing the lines of communication between Peking and the sea. In addition, German Consuls had the right of extraterritorial jurisdiction in cases involving their nationals, as well as special powers of administration over the German Concessions at Tientsin and Hankow. It was not the contention of the Chinese Government that the agreements which provided for these and other German rights were abrogated by the termination of diplomatic relations between the two nations. A distinction was made, however, between the special political privileges enjoyed by Germany, and the normal legal rights of German subjects in China. According to the view adopted from the first by the Chinese Government, the private rights of Germans, concerning the protection of their lives, liberties, and property, remained substantially intact after March 14. A different view was held, however, with regard to the exceptional political privileges of the German Government. Concerning this point, it was evident that with the enforced withdrawal of all German consular authorities, a political vacuum was created which must be filled by the transfer of certain functions either to Chinese officials, or to the Minister of the Netherlands, who was now charged with the care of German interests in China.[29]

In the class of special political grants belonged the German rights of administration over the Concessions at Hankow and Tientsin. Immediately following the dismissal of the German Minister, the administration of these areas was taken over by the Chinese local authorities acting under instructions from the Peking Government.[30] The transfer of the Tientsin Concession

[29] Ariga, *op. cit.*, pp. 154-5, 247.
[30] *Ibid.*, pp. 234-6.

was accomplished without incident. At Hankow, however, the German consul protested against the transfer and declared that it was necessary to preserve all rights resulting from the action of the Chinese Government. He was assured by the local Commissioner for Foreign Affairs, however, that the security, liberty, and the protection for the lives and property of Germans in the area would be adequately safeguarded by the Chinese authorities.[31] On March 28, the Ministry of Interior published regulations for the government of the two Concessions.[32] A Bureau for the Provisional Administration of the Special Areas was created under a Chief of Bureau who was to assume all of the administrative functions formerly exercised by the local German consuls. Existing municipal regulations were temporarily to be continued in force, except those in conflict with the laws and regulations then in effect in China, and those which were considered unsuited to the treatment of residents within the areas.

The Chinese Government gave order to the local authorities that all members of Germany's armed forces in China were to be disarmed and either interned or allowed to quit the country.[33] Additional instructions were issued for the sequestration and, under certain conditions, the confiscation of all German property, whether publicly or privately owned, which might be used for military purposes.[34] In order to make these regulations effective, Chinese local officials were empowered to search both German persons and premises owned or occupied by them.[35] Orders were likewise given to the Inspectors-General of Maritime Customs and the Salt Gabelle to stop further payments to Germany of interest on loans and indemnities.[36]

[31] *Ibid.*, pp. 236-7.
[32] Text, MacMurray, *op. cit.*, Vol. II, p. 1370.
[33] Text, *North China Herald*, CXXII, Mar. 31, 1917, p. 710. The regulations included the provision that with reference to those who were interned, "the chief authority will, out of China's special regard for their officers' 'face' allow them to wear their military swords, so as to show high consideration."
[34] Text, *ibid.*, pp. 710-11.
[35] Text, *ibid.*, p. 711.
[36] *Ibid.*, CXXII, Mar. 24, 1917, p. 624.

While arrangements were thus being made for the suspension of the special political rights belonging to the German Government, the normal personal rights of German subjects in China continued without substantial change. To this general rule, however, there were several exceptions. On the day diplomatic relations were broken off, the Chinese military commandant at Shanghai took possession of six German merchantmen which had been tied up in the port since the early months of the war. The protest of the German Consul was not sufficient to prevent this sequestration.[37] Before the end of the month, other German ships at Amoy and Canton were likewise taken over by the Chinese authorities, following the receipt of instructions from Peking. It was claimed on the part of the Chinese Government that these seizures were necessary in order to safeguard the harbor facilities against the possibility that the ships would be blown up or otherwise injured. In April, also, official instructions were published forbidding vessels flying the German flag from navigating the inland waters of China, and withdrawing the licenses of German pilots.[38]

In other directions care was taken to insure no greater interference with German private rights than was required by particular circumstances. On March 14 the provincial authorities were cautioned to notice the distinction between the breaking off of diplomatic relations and the declaration of war, and to observe that with regard to Germany only the former step had been taken. Local officials were therefore to see that proper protection was accorded to all German subjects, as required by existing circumstances.[39] German employees holding positions under the Chinese Government, or in schools, hospitals, mines, and industrial plants having no special relation to the public

[37] Ariga, *op. cit.*, p. 229. At Shanghai the sequestration was carried out three hours before the publication of the official proclamation announcing the diplomatic break. *North China Herald*, CXXII, Mar. 24, 1917, p. 622.

[38] *North China Herald*, CXXIII, Apr. 14, 1917, p. 58.

[39] Text, *ibid.*, p. 63.

security, were to be left in office as before. Only in case of necessity were their functions to be suspended.[40]

For the guidance of local officials, the Peking Government promulgated a set of Rules for the Protection of German Merchants and Missionaries. Such individuals were to be permitted to reside where they were and to follow their professions without molestation, as in the past. But they were required to register with the appropriate local authorities and to observe at all times "the laws and orders which are now in force and which may be promulgated in the future." [41] Individuals who were guilty of violating the laws referred to or who had committed a breach of the peace, or "whose conduct is deemed to be detrimental to the interests of China," were subject to expulsion from the country. Under supplementary rules issued April 21, 1917, German merchants and missionaries were even permitted to travel in the interior, provided the necessary passports were first issued by the local Commissioners of Foreign Affairs.[42]

The German Government, in April, asked for some assurance that during the continuance of the war, its subjects in China would be secure against internment or general deportation from the country. The Chinese Government, however, declined to commit itself beyond promising that "its attitude in these matters will be in strict conformity with international law." [43] Later, in the same month, the Minister of the Netherlands entered a formal complaint against the Rules for the Protection of German Merchants and Missionaries, published in

[40] Decision of the cabinet, March 14, 1917, Ariga, *op. cit.,* p. 194.
[41] Text, Ariga, *op. cit.,* pp. 203-4.
[42] *Ibid.,* pp. 206-7. The Chinese Government regarded this permission to travel in the interior as an act of grace. At the beginning of the vacation season in 1917, the Commissioner for Foreign Affairs at Shanghai declined to grant permission to certain German subjects to go to the summer resorts at Kuling and Mokansan. Against this action the Netherlands Minister protested to the Chinese Foreign Office. Dr. Wu Ting-fang, replying June 9, 1917, insisted that the permission when granted was proof of the courtesy of the Chinese Government. When permission was refused, however, there was no resulting violation of the treaties, since the regulations plainly stated that the right might be suspended in case of necessity. *Ibid.,* p. 207.
[43] Wu Ting-fang to van Blokland, April 13, 1917. Ariga, *op. cit.,* p. 218.

March. The issuance of special regulations governing German subjects, he declared, was a violation of the most favored nation clause of the German Treaty of 1861. Particular exception was taken to that provision of the rules which seemed to subject German merchants and missionaries to the provisions of Chinese law.⁴⁴ In his reply, the Chinese Minister of Foreign Affairs, without touching directly on the continued validity of German treaty rights, declared simply that "all arrangements relative to the treatment of German subjects are based on the principles of international law." He was willing to state, however, that "the laws and orders to which allusion is thus made are only the *special* laws and orders governing German merchants and missionaries, together with the detailed regulations for their application. They do not signify at all the general laws and orders of the country." ⁴⁵

The judicial rights of German subjects following the departure from China of the German Minister and Consuls raised legal questions of considerable complexity. In a sense, these were special political rights which had, by treaty, been accorded to the German Government to be exercised by its representatives in China. As such, it was logical that the functions of the former German Consuls should simply be placed in charge of Chinese officials. There can be no doubt that China was sincerely desirous of assuming full jurisdiction over all Germans within her territory. On the other hand, the new judicial codes were still in process of preparation, and the organization of the judiciary, begun under the Empire and continued by Yuan Shih-k'ai, was not as yet completed. Under the circumstances, the Chinese Government perceived that if the arrangements made in the case of Germans did not meet with the approval of other foreigners resident in China, "the ultimate abolition of extraterritoriality by the other nations of Europe and America would be further delayed." ⁴⁶

⁴⁴ Van Blokland to Wu Ting-fang, April 30, 1917. Ariga, *op. cit.,* pp. 210-12.
⁴⁵ Wu Ting-fang to van Blokland, May 25, 1917, *ibid.,* pp. 212-13.
⁴⁶ Ariga, *op. cit.,* p. 241.

After a brief interval of evident uncertainty, the Chinese Government decided to compromise. The Provisional Criminal Code of 1909, as amended in 1912 and 1914, was then in force. A small beginning had been made in the work of organizing a modern court system, and there were some modern prisons scattered over the country. Consequently, orders were issued that where a German subject was accused of a crime punishable under certain specified sections of the Provisional Criminal Code, or where he was accused of an offense touching the peace and order of China for which as yet the Code made no provision, the case was to be handled by a Chinese modern court. Imprisonment, where necessary, was to take place only in the modern prisons.[47] The Minister and Consuls of the Netherlands, having taken over the care of German interests, were given jurisdiction in all other cases.

The Chinese Government desired to make it clear, however, that its action in vesting the Dutch authorities with consular jurisdiction over German subjects was one of favor and not of legal obligation. In transmitting a copy of the regulations to the Dutch Minister, the Chinese Minister for Foreign Affairs observed that the arrangement was made "despite the principle of international law which does not permit the delegation to another state of the exercise of rights of consular jurisdiction

[47] *Ibid.*, pp. 244-5. The responsibilities of the Chinese Government resulting from the disappearance of German consular jurisdiction doubtless hastened the promulgation by the President of a number of mandates touching judicial reform. On May 1 were issued "Rules and Regulations Governing the Formation of the District Court of Justice," and also "Rules for the Examination and Employment of Judges of the District Courts of Justice." *North China Herald*, CXXIII, May 12, 1917, p. 300. On October 18, following the abrogation of German and Austro-Hungarian extraterritorial rights, appeared the "Order Governing the Examination of Judicial Officials," and the "Order Governing the Examination of Legal Practitioners." *North China Herald*, CXXV, Oct. 27, 1917, p. 203. These mandates were followed on August 5, 1918, by a "Law Concerning the Application of Foreign Laws." Text, *China Year Book, 1921-22*, pp. 654-7. This law contained chapters relating to Persons, the Family, Succession, Things, and Forms of Juristic Acts. Article I laid down the general principle that "when according to these Rules a foreign law is to be applied, its application is nevertheless forbidden if it contravenes the public order or good morals of China."

based on the Sino-German treaties." [48] The Dutch Minister, however, denied that any cases whatever involving German subjects as defendants could legally be tried in Chinese courts. He insisted that the German Treaty of 1861 remained in full force despite the rupture of diplomatic relations, that German subjects must, therefore, in accordance with the provisions of that treaty be tried according to their own law and if guilty punished according to the provisions of that law, and that the enforcement of the regulations in question would "be a flagrant violation of the stipulations of the treaties" against which it was necessary to protest "formally and in the most energetic manner." [49]

In his reply to this note, Dr. Wu Ting-fang admitted freely that under the rules of international law, treaties existing between two countries were not affected by a diplomatic rupture. But, he contended,

"since international law does not sanction the delegation to a third Power of the exercise of consular jurisdiction, the application of the principle above mentioned to the question of consular jurisdiction cannot be recognized in practice, for the consular jurisdiction accorded by China to Germany is, according to international law, a sort of special right, and as the German consuls, having left China . . . are no longer able themselves to exercise the functions and the power which is conferred on them by the treaty, every case civil or criminal, concerning German subjects, should be judged exclusively by the Chinese authorities."

It was only because the Chinese Government was anxious to secure equitable treatment for German subjects that it consented, of its own will, to confer on the Dutch authorities qualified rights to exercise consular jurisdiction in cases involving Germans, as provided in the Regulations of March 31.[50]

While arrangements were thus being completed for the care

[48] Wu Ting-fang to van Blokland, March 31, 1917, Ariga, *op. cit.*, pp. 243-4.
[49] Van Blokland to Wu Ting-fang, April 11, 1917, *ibid.*, pp. 246-7.
[50] Wu Ting-fang to van Blokland, April 30, 1917, Ariga, *op. cit.*, pp. 249-50.

of German political rights as well as the legal rights of German subjects, the domestic situation in China was undergoing a series of rapid changes. It had seemed for a time as if the diplomatic break would be followed very shortly by a declaration of war, particularly in view of the overwhelming vote by which Parliament had expressed its approval of the government's policy.[51] A number of influential leaders urged this further step without awaiting prior action by the United States. It was argued in support of this view that a declaration of war would result in the return to China of the German Concessions at Tientsin and Hankow, and would also terminate the extraterritorial rights enjoyed by German subjects.[52]

Four influences, however, combined to delay this final action. The first of these was the change of heart on the part of certain members of Parliament, due to the failure of China to secure from her prospective allies diplomatic concessions of a material character. Many members of Parliament had been led to believe that immediately after the dismissal of the German Minister, the powers would take steps to redeem the pledges which, seemingly, they had made to the Chinese Government at the end of February.[53] However, on March 14, the day on which Admiral von Hintze received his passports, when

[51] The vote was 330 to 87 in the House of Representatives, and 158 to 37 in the Senate.

[52] See particularly the summary of Liang Ch'i-ch'ao's Memorandum to the Commission on Diplomatic Questions, *North China Herald*, CXXII, Mar. 31, 1917, p. 672.

[53] The noncommittal character of these Allied "pledges" is most apparent in the French text of M. Conty's Memorandum of February 28 to the Waichiao Pu: "S. E. M. Lou Tsêng-tsiang étant venu au nom du Président du Conseil demander officiellement aux Représentants des Gouvernements alliés les dispositions de leurs Gouvernements pour le cas d'une rupture entre la Chine d'une part et l'Allemagne et l'Autriche-Hongrie d'autre part, les Représentants des Gouvernements alliés ont l'honneur de lui faire savoir que leurs Gouvernements se sont mis d'accord pour réserver en principe un accueil favorable à ces demandes sauf à examiner avec les dispositions les plus amicales d'ailleurs les détails, les précisions et les modalités à adopter notamment en ce qui concerne la question des indemnités de 1901, étant bien entendu toutefois dans l'esprit des Gouvernements alliés que les concessions demandées supposent entre la Chine d'une part, l'Allemagne et l'Autriche-Hongrie d'autre part une rupture des relations diplomatique comportant toute l'extension nécessaire." *Far Eastern Review*, XIII, April, 1917, p. 402, note.

Dr. Wu Ting-fang opened formal negotiations with the Allied Ministers, they showed no disposition toward hasty action.

The Memorandum of the Chinese Minister of Foreign Affairs contained three proposals.[54] First, with a view to assisting Chinese finances, which were badly in need of assistance, the Entente Powers were asked to agree to the suspension for ten years of their respective shares of the 1901 Indemnity; thereafter the annual installments were to be resumed according to the original schedule without any additions of interest. Second, the Chinese Government desired permission to increase the existing import duties by two and one-half per cent; thereafter the customs tariff would be revised, and after revision a duty would be levied amounting to an effective seven and one-half per cent; as soon as the *likin* was abolished, this duty would be raised to an effective twelve and one-half per cent, in accordance with the provisions of the commercial treaties of 1902 and 1903. Third, the hope was expressed that the provisions of the 1901 Protocol that tended "to impede the effectiveness of precautionary measures of the Chinese Government *vis-a-vis* the Germans, e.g., respecting the inability of the Chinese troops to be stationed within the radius of 21 *li* of Tientsin and the presence of foreign troops in the Legations and along the railway" would be canceled. In return for these concessions, the Chinese Government was prepared to undertake with regard to the Entente Powers only two responsibilities: to supply primary materials, and to furnish assistance with respect to labor.

After considering the Chinese Memorandum, the Allied representatives, on the same day, presented Dr. Wu with an *aide-mémoire* containing the following specific questions: [55]

[54] Text, *ibid.*, p. 403.
[55] *Far Eastern Review*, XIII, April, 1917, p. 403. The French note of March 1 to the Japanese Ministry for Foreign Affairs, above referred to, indicated that the government of France hoped that, following the rupture of diplomatic relations between China and Germany, all German nationals would be required to leave Chinese territory, all German ships in Chinese ports would be sequestrated and ultimately placed at the disposal of the

1. Does the rupture of diplomatic relations extend to Austria-Hungary?

2. What is to be done with the secretaries of Legation and German Consuls, the German financial adviser, the German commercial attaché and other German officials?

3. What is to be done with the German Concessions?

4. How is China going to disarm the German troops?

5. What measures will be taken with regard to German and Austrian ships in Chinese ports?

6. What is to be done with German and Austrian employees in the service of China?

7. What treatment is to be accorded to German and Austrian civilians of military age, and to German commercial houses?

On March 20, Dr. Wu made the following reply to the Allied note: [56]

1. For the time being the breach of diplomatic relations extended only to Germany.

2. German diplomatic and consular officials would be given passports to return to Germany. They might, however, leave behind members of their respective staffs to look after archives and to assist the diplomatic and consular officials of the power having charge of German interests.

3. The German Concessions would be patrolled by Chinese police sent by the Chinese Government.

4. German troops would be disarmed within a specified time.

5. German ships had already been taken in charge by officers of the Ministry of Navy.

6. Germans in the employ of the Chinese Government would be dismissed or retained as the case might require.

7. German private individuals and businesses carried on by them would be treated according to international usage.

The Chinese reply was regarded by the Allied Ministers as the reverse of satisfactory. According to their view, the Chinese Government had asked much, and was willing in return to assume only nominal responsibilities as a belligerent power. Thus the negotiations from which the Chinese leaders had

Allies, all German commercial houses established in China would be sequestrated, and German rights in Concessions in Chinese ports would be forfeited. *China Year Book, 1921-1922*, p. 709.

[56] Text, *Far Eastern Review*, XIII, April, 1917, p. 403.

hoped much, ended in failure. Various members of Parliament believed that the Allied Powers were guilty of bad faith and that China would gain nothing by associating herself with them.[57]

The second influence tending to delay China's entrance into the war was the shadow cast by the unexpected revolution in Russia. As reports of recent happenings in Petrograd began to filter into China, speculation was rife concerning the possible effect of this new development on the military prospects of the Allies, particularly if Russia, as seemed not improbable, should conclude a separate peace with the Central Powers. And with Russia out of the war, it appeared not unlikely that Germany might yet emerge victorious.[58]

The third influence was that of the merchants. The war in Europe had stimulated Chinese trade, as it had the trade of other neutral nations. Now the merchants of many of the large cities, particularly in central and southern China, were apprehensive lest China's formal entry into the war would interfere seriously with both their domestic and their international transactions. The Shanghai Chamber of Commerce pointed to the danger that with her entrance into the war, China's food supplies would be drawn upon by the Allies. The result would be a shortage of foodstuffs in the country, higher prices for rice with corresponding popular disorders, and a depression in the internal trade of the country.[59]

Finally, the largest single party represented in Parliament, the Kuomintang, was not a unit in support of the government's war policy. The Young China group within the party, led by Dr. C. T. Wang, lent its full approval to that policy. The leaders of this faction were convinced that both material and diplomatic gains would result from China's association with

[57] *Asia*, XVII, June, 1917, p. 277. The views are those expressed by Putnam Weale in the Peking *Gazette*.

[58] *North China Herald*, CXXIII, May 5, 1917, p. 234. Translation from the Chinese press. See also the report of an interview with C. T. Wang, Kuomintang leader and Vice-President of the Senate, *ibid.*, June 2, 1917, pp. 486-7.

[59] *North China Herald*, CXXIII, Apr. 21, 1917, p. 115.

the Allies.[60] The note of February 9 and the subsequent action
of March 14 they regarded as being, in a sense, the nation's
declaration of independence and an earnest of its determination
to hold to the whole body of international sanctions upon
which that independence rested. Many of the older leaders of
the party, however, focussed their attention less on the international than on the domestic implications of the proposed step.
They questioned vigorously not only the wisdom of declaring
war, but the motives of the cabinet leaders who sponsored that
policy. Early in March, before Parliament had taken action,
Dr. Sun Yat-sen had sent a telegram to Premier Lloyd George
protesting that the Allied representatives in Peking were
"coercing China to join the Allies." Should China abandon
her neutrality, according to the Kuomintang leader, there was
danger not only of Mohammedan uprisings in the country, but
of widespread domestic anarchy with the prospect that the anti-
foreign elements in the population would seize on the opportunity to launch another Boxer movement.[61] Opposition came
also from the ex-viceroy, Tsen Ch'un-hsüan, who telegraphed
President Li and Premier Tuan denouncing China's entry into
the war, and from T'ang Shao-yi and Li Lieh-chun, both of
whom published long articles in the vernacular press voicing
their disapproval of a declaration of war.

The older Kuomintang leaders were fearful also that a
declaration of war would lead to the subversion of the constitution, the suppression of Parliament, and the fatal ascendency
of the militarists. These fears were not groundless. In April

[60] The sentiment of this faction of the Kuomintang is reflected in an
editorial appearing early in April in the Peking *Kuo Min Kung Pao.*
"Interest demands that China should associate herself with the Entente,
which represents the group of powers who will control the destinies of the
world. Germany can not help her nor harm her. If China is not with the
Entente, she will be isolated. Not only that, but she will have no voice
in the peace conference, which will adjust international interests in this
country as well as in other parts of the world. Without representation in
the peace conference, China may suffer further humiliation and perhaps
spoliation." Quoted in Patrick Gallagher, *America's Aims and Asia's Aspirations,* New York, 1920, p. 175.

[61] *North China Herald,* CXXII, Mar. 10, 1917, p. 504. Also *Far
Eastern Review,* XIII, April, 1917, pp. 404-7.

the tuchuns, or provincial military governors, met in conference in Peking. At first hostile to China's proposed venture
into world politics, the military leaders were won over by the
prospect that a declaration of war would be followed by foreign
financial assistance, an increase in the revenue from the revised
tariff rates, and the temporary cessation of the Boxer Indemnity payments. Henceforth the tuchuns were to be numbered
among the foremost advocates of the war policy.[62]

Early in May, Parliament began to consider the question
of declaring war. There was a disposition to prolong the debate
beyond what, perhaps, seemed needful under the circumstances.
Becoming impatient, the tuchuns took matters into their own
hands. On May 10, both houses of Parliament were surrounded
by a disorderly mob clamoring for war. While the police
looked complacently on, various members of Parliament,
notably those known for their opposition to the war policy,
were roughly handled as they attempted to enter or leave the
legislative halls. Troops had also been stationed about the
Parliament grounds. The House of Representatives declined
to consider the Premier's motion declaring war until both the
mob and the troops were withdrawn. Not until late at night
did the Chief of Police finally give orders for the dispersal of
the rowdy elements. And at a half hour after midnight, the
disgruntled legislators were permitted to leave the parliament
buildings in safety.

Two members of the cabinet, both Kuomintang adherents,
promptly resigned their offices, and it was reported that others
contemplated following suit. The rump cabinet which remained
was referred to contemptuously by Parliamentary leaders as "a
one man ministry" consisting of the Premier alone, and demands were made that Tuan Ch'i-jui resign. The Kuomintang
members of Parliament decided to refuse to attend further
sessions until guaranteed protection against mob violence and
intimidation. The Young China faction of the party, hitherto

[62] *North China Herald*, CXXIII, Apr. 28, 1917, p. 168. *Ibid.*, May 5,
1917, p. 231.

staunch supporters of the Premier's war policy, were now convinced that he must go, particularly in view of the apparent sympathy between him and the tuchuns.

The tuchuns were disappointed but not discouraged. After consultation they decided that under no circumstances was Premier Tuan to be allowed to resign.[63] It soon became clear, however, that the breach between Parliament and Tuan Ch'i-jui could not be healed. At a meeting of the lower House on May 19, a resolution was adopted branding as illegal the most recent message of the government urging action on the declaration of war, since the cabinet consisted for all practical purposes of only two members, the Premier and the Minister of Education.[64] Four days later President Li attempted to cut the Gordian knot by dismissing Tuan and appointing Wu Tingfang to act temporarily in his stead.

The question of declaring war now became bogged in the mires of factional politics. The tuchuns denounced the President for dismissing Tuan and demanded instead that he dissolve Parliament.[65] The serious character of the situation prompted the American Government, on June 6, to suggest to the Chinese Foreign Office that "the entry of China into war with Germany or the continuance of the status quo of her relations with that government are matters of secondary consideration," and pointing to the need for restoring internal harmony if China was to assume "that place among the Powers of the world to which [she] is so justly entitled, but the full

[63] An interesting commentary on the attitude of the militarists appears in an address said to have been made by Li Hou-chi, Tuchun of Fukien, at a tea given at the Waichiao Pu May 14 to the diplomatic representatives of the Allied Powers. Not only, he declared, must Premier Tuan be retained in office, but the declaration of war would assuredly be passed "as soon as Parliament has been persuaded to take the view of the Government." *North China Herald,* CXXIII, May 19, 1917, p. 369.

[64] *North China Herald,* CXXIII, May 26, 1917, p. 423.

[65] It should be remarked that the military opposition to Parliament arose not merely out of its refusal to be hurried into a declaration of war. The tuchuns had protested earlier against the almost complete draft of the new national constitution, certain provisions of which would have given Parliament greater control over the exercise of executive, including military powers than the tuchuns cared to see put into practice. Putnam Weale, "The Problem of Peking," *Asia,* XIX, April, 1919, pp. 315-22.

attainment of which is impossible in the midst of internal discord." [66]

The friendly advice of the American Government passed almost unheeded amid the domestic turmoil. The tuchuns, meeting at Tientsin, sent to Peking an ultimatum threatening to attack the capital unless Parliament were dissolved. Against his better judgment, President Li, fully aware that he would have to act without warrant in the constitution, but hoping to avert civil war, finally yielded to the demand. When the Acting Premier, Dr. Wu, declined to countersign the order for dissolution, he was replaced by a less scrupulous appointee in the person of the Commander of the Peking Gendarmerie. Under such dubious circumstances, the mandate dissolving Parliament was issued June 13. [67]

The consequences of President Li's action were two. The first was an open rupture between the North and the South. Following the dissolution of Parliament, its members fled to the cities of the seaboard protesting that the President had acted under the coercion of the rebellious tuchuns and that his mandate lacked legal validity. Subsequently the Southern or Constitutional Party set up an autonomous military government at Canton which declared its independence of the Peking authorities. Many members of the disbanded legislative body gathered there, attracted in some instances by the promise that the new government would find funds to continue their salaries.

The second consequence was the establishment at Peking of a military oligarchy. President Li, left without the support of either Parliament or cabinet, made overtures to the tuchuns at Tientsin. One of the most powerful, but least intelligent of these, General Chang Hsün, was called to Peking to mediate between the Chief Executive and the still truculent military governors. Instead of devoting himself to the task of mediation, Chang Hsün, on July 1, proclaimed the restoration of

[66] *U. S. Foreign Relations*, 1917, pp. 48-9.
[67] Text, *North China Herald*, CXXIII, June 16, 1917, p. 613.

the Manchu monarchy. The restoration lasted little more than a week, however, and on July 12 a coalition of nominally Republican forces led by General Tuan Ch'i-jui recaptured the capital. President Li, who was innocent of any share in the monarchical movement, retired from office in favor of the Vice-President, General Feng Kuo-chang.

With the return to power of the Northern militarists under the leadership of Tuan, the question of declaring war came once more to the fore. The members of the new government, all of whom were Northerners, were encouraged by the fact that the representatives of the Allied Powers made repeated inquiries concerning the matter.[68] Furthermore, the government leaders were no longer hampered by parliamentary opposition, and there was the additional fact that Li Yuan-hung, who continued to question the wisdom of joining the Allies, had ceased to be President. Consequently, early in August, the cabinet adopted a declaration favoring immediate action.[69] And on August 14 appeared a presidential proclamation announcing the

[68] The Japanese and French Ministers were especially active in this connection. Reinsch, *op. cit.*, p. 286. See also the report of an interview given by Foreign Minister Wang Ta-hsieh to a correspondent of the Shanghai *Shun Pao*, August 2, 1917, translation in *North China Herald*, CXXIV, Aug. 11, 1917, pp. 311-12. Although the American Government still held the view that China should not be pressed to join the Allies, its representative in Peking did not conceal his hope that a way might yet be found "to bring the war situation into harmony with justice to China." Reinsch, *op. cit.*, pp. 286-7. The Russian Minister, however, because of the special interests of his government in Manchuria, was less inclined than the other Allied Ministers to draw China into the circle of Entente Powers. Wang Ta-hsieh interview, *op. cit.* In connection with this entire matter, the following statement of Mr. Thomas F. Millard deserves to be quoted: "I am assured by a Chinese diplomat that at the time when China was being urged by the Allies *en bloc* to declare war on Germany, and when China very naturally wanted to obtain guarantees for her protection, some Allied diplomats in Peking denied that anything invidious to China existed in interallied war commitments and said that China could be sure of fair treatment." *Conflict of Policies in Asia*, New York, 1924, p. 57.

[69] The government's anxiety to enter the war at this time arose in considerable degree out of its urgent need for funds. The Minister of Finance, Liang Ch'i-ch'ao, declared early in August that the declaration of war should be made without further delay "as foreign money is urgently needed at the present moment." Mr. Liang said that while no formal negotiations for a loan from Entente banks had yet been opened, all preparations had been made to do so as soon as war had been declared. *North China Herald*, CXXIV, Aug. 11, 1917, p. 308. See also Reinsch, *op. cit.*, p. 292.

existence of a state of war between China and both Germany and Austria-Hungary. In consequence thereof, it declared,[70]

"all treaties, agreements, [and] conventions, concluded between China and Germany, and between China and Austria-Hungary, as well as such parts of the international protocols and international agreements as concern the relations between China and Germany and between China and Austria-Hungary are, in conformity with the law of nations and international practice, all abrogated. This Government, however, will respect the Hague Conventions and her international agreements respecting the humane conduct of war."

The proclamation deplored the necessity of the step at a time when "our people have not yet . . . recovered from the sufferings on account of the recent political disturbances," but expressed the hope that "our people will exert their utmost in these hours of hardship with a view to maintaining and strengthening the existence of the Chinese Republic, so that we may establish ourselves amidst the family of nations and share with them the happiness and benefits derived therefrom." No more momentous decision had been taken by the Chinese Government since the beginning of formal intercourse with the nations of the West. Through force of circumstances which were not of her own creation, but were rather the product of those same conditions of international rivalry which had worked to her disadvantage so often in the past, China seemed likely to regain at least a part of the rights of internal administration which, as it seemed after 1900, would be restored to her only after a long and arduous course of domestic reform.

Notice of the Chinese war declaration was communicated to the German Government through the Minister for the Netherlands, and to the Austro-Hungarian Government through its Minister in Peking. The Waichiao Pu's notification to Germany mentioned specifically the termination of the Treaty of September 2, 1861, the Supplementary Convention of March 31, 1880, and "all other treaties, conventions and agreements of whatever nature at present in force between China and Germany"

[70] Text, MacMurray, *op. cit.*, Vol. II, pp. 1361-2.

and in addition "all such provisions of the Protocol of September 7, 1901 and other similar international agreements as only concern China and Germany." [71] The note to the Austro-Hungarian Minister announced the abrogation of the Treaty of September 2, 1869, and the appropriate provisions of the Protocol of 1901 [72]

The formal announcement of China's action was communicated also to the Entente Ministers in Peking. To this note each of the Allied representatives replied, in effect, that

"my Government is pleased to take this opportunity to give to the Chinese Government the assurances of its solidarity, of its friendship and of its support. It will do all that depends upon it in order that China may have the benefit in her international relations of the situation and the regards due to a great country." [73]

The knowledge that China was now one of the Allied and Associated Powers was received by the nation "with almost

[71] Text, MacMurray, *op. cit.*, Vol. II, p. 1364. It is worth noting that the Chinese Government did not, at this time, mention specifically the Sino-German Convention of March 6, 1898, relating to the leasehold at Kiaochou and to mining and railway rights in Shantung.

[72] Text, *ibid.* The Austrian representative introduced a humorous element into the situation by attempting to question the legal validity of the Chinese Government's action. After receiving his passports, he transmitted to the Waichiao Pu a note in which he stated that "I cannot here enter into the arguments contained in the declaration of war, but feel bound to state that I must consider this declaration as unconstitutional and illegal, seeing that according to so high an authority as the former President Li Yuan-hung, such a declaration requires the approbation of both Houses of Parliament." The Chinese authorities considered the note to be an unwarranted piece of impertinence, and returned it forthwith to its author. *Far Eastern Review*, XIII, Sept., 1917, p. 647.

[73] Text, MacMurray, *op. cit.*, Vol. II, p. 1363. This harmless pronouncement was all that remained of a proposal originating with the American Minister, that in return for China's entry into the war, the powers should agree upon a statement which would fortify her sovereign rights and prevent the further growth of special privileges and spheres of influence. Reinsch had suggested that the Allied Governments declare it their policy to "favor the independent development of China, and in no way to seek in China, either singly or jointly, advantages of the nature of territorial or preferential rights, whether local or general." The Chinese desired in addition that the other governments pledge their assistance in helping China to "obtain the enjoyment of the advantages resulting from the equality of powers in their international relations." Reinsch, *op. cit.*, pp. 287-8.

pathetic indifference." [74] The autonomous government at Canton, however, soon took steps which seemed to indicate that regardless of how the nation might be divided over domestic questions, it was still a unit in regard to foreign affairs. On September 18, 1917, the Military Government inquired of what remained of the National Assembly gathered at Canton, whether it should recognize the existence of a state of war. On the 22nd, the Assembly resolved to recognize the reality, if not the legality, of the declaration of war, and the Military Government thereupon issued a proclamation to that effect, pledging itself to prosecute the war to the full extent possible. [75] Not until November 3, 1918, eight days before the armistice, was the war mandate ratified by the rival northern Parliament which met in Peking in August, 1918.

An immediate consequence of the declaration of war was the liquidation of German and Austro-Hungarian political interests in China. All members of the Austro-Hungarian military forces in the Legation Quarter in Peking, as in other parts of the country, were promptly disarmed and interned. The German caserne at Pehtaiho and the Austrian caserne at Taku passed into the hands of the Chinese. All Austro-Hungarian merchantmen in Chinese waters were seized. No immediate attempt was made to intern or deport the civilian subjects of the two enemy powers, but they were required to register with the local authorities, under whose protection they were placed. [76] The property of certain economic enterprises controlled by enemy subjects, including the powerful Deutsch-Asiatische Bank, was placed under sequestration. All Germans and Austro-Hungarians in the service of the Chinese Government were dismissed from office. German and Austrian teachers in Chinese schools, however, might be retained in their present

---

[74] Tyau, *China Awakened*, p. 299.
[75] Official statement from the Military Government to Reuter's correspondent, *North China Herald*, CXXV, Oct. 13, 1917, pp. 79-80.
[76] "Regulations for Treatment of Enemy Subjects," August 14, 1917. MacMurray, *op. cit.*, Vol. II, p. 1371.

positions, provided they were recognized to be entirely unconnected with the military affairs of their government. Similarly German and Austrian schools in the interior of the country might continue to operate.[77]

Of greater ultimate significance than these distinctively war measures were the steps taken to resume permanent control over the German Concessions at Hankow and Tientsin, to which was now added the Austro-Hungarian Concession at the latter port, and to terminate the extraterritorial rights hitherto enjoyed by subjects of the two enemy powers. On August 14, the Minister of the Netherlands was formally notified that Chinese courts would thereafter exercise full jurisdiction over such cases involving enemy subjects as had, since the diplomatic break with Germany, been handled by the Dutch Consular Courts.[78] A similar notification was communicated to the representatives at Peking of each of the Treaty Powers, whose Consuls were still, however, to retain jurisdiction in civil cases where German or Austro-Hungarian nationals were plaintiffs and their respective nationals were defendants.[79] In connection with these new responsibilities, the Peking Government instructed the appropriate local authorities that except for cases of rebellion and certain crimes connected with international relations and foreign war, the trials of enemy nationals were

[77] Instructions of the Ministry of Education to the Civil Governor of Kiangsu, *North China Herald*, CXXIV, Aug. 25, 1917, p. 424.

[78] Ariga, *op. cit.*, p. 295. At a meeting of the Peking Diplomatic Body on August 23, the Acting Doyen, Beelaerts van Blokland, raised a question as to the jurisdiction of the Shanghai Mixed Court over Germans and Austrians. The Dutch representative argued that German and Austrian subjects should not be placed on a plane with Chinese, but only with non-treaty foreigners. The French Minister, however, insisted that the declaration of war had terminated absolutely the extraterritorial privileges enjoyed by nationals of the Central powers. The Russian, Italian, and Belgian Ministers joined M. Conty in protesting against any proposal to place enemy subjects on an equal footing with non-treaty foreigners, and contended that they must be reduced to the level of the Chinese themselves. M. J. Pergament, *The Diplomatic Quarter in Peking: its juristic nature*, Peking, 1927, pp. 59-61. Subsequently, as indicated above, the Chinese Government adopted the view of the Dutch Minister.

[79] MacMurray, *op. cit.*, Vol. II, pp. 1372-3.

to be conducted in the modern courts and detention, where necessary, to be made in modern prisons.[80]

With regard to the former German and Austrian Concessions, the Bureau for the Provisional Administration of the Special Areas, first organized in March, was changed to a Bureau for the Municipal Administration of the Special Areas. On August 14, also, regulations were published determining the administrative organization of these special areas.[81] The Italian Minister in Peking apparently hoped to profit by the new situation. He requested not only that Italians should be employed to replace Germans dismissed from the Salt Gabelle Administration, but also that the former Austro-Hungarian Concession at Tientsin should be added to the adjoining Italian Concession.[82] When news of the negotiations leaked out, the Italian representative, Baron Aliotti, declared that only "requests" and not "demands" had been submitted to the Chinese Foreign Office. He insisted, further, that no demand had been made for the transfer to Italy of the Austro-Hungarian Concession; what was desired was merely a rectification of the boundary between the two concessions.[83]

One result of China's new association with the Allied Powers was the resumption of the negotiations of February and March concerning the benefits which she should receive from that association. In a collective note dated September 8, 1917 [84] the

[80] "Provisional Regulations Governing the Trial of Civil and Criminal Cases of Enemy Subjects," Aug. 14, 1917, MacMurray, *op. cit.,* Vol. II, pp. 1373.

[81] MacMurray, *op. cit.,* p. 1372.

[82] *Millard's Review,* II, Sept. 1, 1917, p. 5. The report appeared first in the usually reliable Peking *Daily News,* commonly recognized as the semi-official organ of the Waichiao Pu.

[83] *North China Herald,* CXXIV, Sept. 1, 1917, p. 476. It was doubtless in connection with these "requests" that Baron Aliotti refused his assent to the release to the Chinese Government of 2,000,000 taels of surplus customs funds, after the approval of each of the other interested Ministers had been given. This refusal was subsequently withdrawn. *Ibid.,* CXXIV, Sept. 8, 1917, pp. 537-8.

[84] MacMurray, *op. cit.,* Vol. II, pp. 1375-6. The note was signed by representatives of Belgium, France, Great Britain, Italy, Japan, Portugal, and Russia. The American Minister apparently was not a signatory.

Allied Powers expressed their willingness to agree to a postponement for five years of the annual Boxer Indemnity payments, Russia, however, consenting to forego only one-third
of her usual share. It was understood, according to the note,
that Germany and Austria-Hungary were not to benefit from
any future payments of the 1901 indemnities. China also was
to be allowed to increase her customs duties to an effective
five per cent *ad valorem.* Finally, the representatives of the
powers agreed to permit the temporary access of Chinese troops
to the reserved zone of Tientsin to the extent necessary to
exercise surveillance over Germans and Austrians.[85] In return
for these Concessions, the powers mentioned a number of
measures which they hoped would be taken by "China in its
own interests." These included the promulgation by China of

[85] The suspension of the indemnity payments to the seven Allied Governments became effective in December, 1917. *North China Herald,* CXXVI,
Jan. 12, 1918, p. 65.
  It should be noted that the agreement in regard to tariff revision was
less of a concession than appeared on the surface. Under the treaties, China
was entitled to collect an import duty of five per cent *ad valorem.* The
duties actually collected, however, were specific duties based on the average
values prevailing from 1897 to 1899. The Chinese Government had attempted on several occasions to get the consent of the powers for a revision
of the tariff schedule, so as to bring the rates up to an effective five per cent.
These attempts met with failure in every instance. It was estimated that
in consequence of the abnormal rise in prices during the early years of the
war, the Chinese treasury received only about three-tenths of the effective
five per cent tariff revenues to which it was properly entitled. A schedule
of five per cent duties based on the values prevailing in 1917 would have
increased the Government's customs revenues by approximately 70,000,000
taels for that year alone. *Far Eastern Review,* XIV, January, 1918, p. 15.
  The tariff conference, consisting of the representatives of the fourteen
interested powers and China met at Shanghai in January, 1918. Two months
elapsed after the first session before an agreement was finally reached concerning the rules of procedure. The delay was caused partly by the in-
capacity of the chief Chinese delegate, who lacked a knowledge of the English
language, and partly by obstructionist tactics on the part of the Japanese
representatives. *Millard's Review,* VII, Dec. 21, 1918, p. 110. *North China
Herald,* CXXVIII, July 6, 1918, p. 13. The Japanese textile manufacturers
had previously protested to their government against any revision whatever.
See issues of the *Japan Weekly Chronicle* for April 15, April 19, and
September 20, 1917. In May, the head of the Chinese delegation resigned
and was replaced by Admiral T'sai Ting-kan. The Commission did not
complete its labors until December, 1918. The new rates, providing for an
effective five per cent on the basis of average values during the years 1912-
1916, finally came into force August 1, 1919—twenty-two months after
revision was originally agreed upon. MacMurray, *op. cit.,* Vol. II, p. 1456.

a general tariff for all non-treaty nations; the prohibition of trading between Chinese and enemy aliens; the internment of such enemy aliens as were indicated by the Allied Legations; the sequestration and complete liquidation of German and Austro-Hungarian commercial firms; the reorganization of the former German and Austro-Hungarian Concessions in the form of international concessions; the transfer to the Allies, subject to payment, of enemy vessels interned in Chinese ports; and, finally, Chinese official coöperation, as complete and effective as possible, in the operations of the Allies.

The Chinese reply to the Allied note expressed gratitude that the representatives of the Allied Governments had agreed to the three measures desired by the Government of China.[86] There was ready acceptance of the Allied suggestions with regard to a tariff for non-treaty nations, the leasing of the former enemy merchantmen in Chinese ports,[87] and the proposal for coöperative action during the conduct of the war. Concerning other matters dealt with in the collective note, the Chinese Government expressed only qualified agreement. In the matter of trading with the enemy and the sequestration of enemy commercial firms, the promise was made that "where a Chinese

[86] Text, MacMurray, *op. cit.*, Vol. II, pp. 1376-7.

[87] In each of its official statements proclaiming the existence of a state of war, the Chinese Government had announced its intention of respecting the Hague Conventions and other similar engagements concerning the humane conduct of the war. After the Chinese seizure of the German and Austro-Hungarian ships in Chinese waters, the Minister of the Netherlands protested formally that under the Hague Convention, such ships could only be detained or requisitioned, and could not be confiscated. Van Blokland to Wang Ta-hsieh, September 17, 1917, Ariga, *op. cit.*, p. 315. A careful examination by Chinese officials of the Dutch note revealed a difference of opinion relative to the application to the question of the second Hague Convention. Eventually a Chinese Prize Court was set up which condemned each of the enemy vessels. It was contended that the second Hague Convention applied only to merchant ships which were surprised in the harbor of a belligerent power by the outbreak of hostilities, that the enemy vessels in question by remaining idle in Chinese ports since the beginning of the war had ceased to be bona fide merchant ships engaged in trade, and that they were therefore not covered by the provisions of the Hague Convention. Decisions in the cases of the *Sixta*, the *Keong Wei*, and the *Fortuna*, *Chinese Social and Political Science Review*, IV (1919), pp. 200-12. The ships were eventually turned over under charter to the British Government for use in the common interests of the Allied Powers.

inspection has shown that they (the enemy commercial and industrial establishments) should be closed, they will be closed and officials appointed to administer them." With reference to the protective measures against enemy subjects, it was agreed that "if plots are discovered, the plotters will be interned. . . ." In the matter of the former German and Austro-Hungarian Concessions, the Chinese Government showed its reluctance to meet Allied wishes.[88] As a substitute for the Allied suggestion in this connection the government promised that these areas would be reorganized as "Model Voluntarily Opened Sino-Foreign Trade Marts" in which the nationals of the different powers would enjoy all commercial advantages in addition to a special system of local government.

China's value as a co-belligerent was a distinct disappointment to her friends among the Allied and Associated Powers. About 175,000 coolies were recruited for service as laborers behind the Allied lines in Mesopotamia and Europe.[89] But with the exception of a military commission which was sent to France shortly after her declaration of war, China sent no troops to Europe. A War Participation Bureau, organized on paper in the fall of 1917 for the purpose of training an expeditionary force for service on the Western Front, had made only small beginnings in its work when the armistice was signed.[90]

[88] The proposal of the Entente representatives, it is obvious, would simply have transformed these areas into foreign controlled districts similar to the International Settlement at Shanghai.

[89] In a crisis these Chinese laborers sometimes participated in the actual fighting, the total casualties among them numbering approximately 2,000. Tyau, *China Awakened*, pp. 309-10.

[90] *Ibid.*, p. 305. The editor of *Millard's Review* in April, 1918, interviewed at random more than 100 soldiers and noncommissioned officers of the Chinese army patrolling the streets of a city in north China. A very small percentage of these men knew, apparently, that China was officially at war with Germany. They did know, however, that a great war was in progress. "Every Chinese soldier interviewed was outspoken in his admiration of the German system that had thus far been able to stand out against the whole world." *Millard's Review*, IV, May 17, 1918, p. 377. Dr. Reinsch was convinced, however, that only the difficulty of transportation prevented the sending of a Chinese military expedition to participate in the fighting on the Western Front. Reinsch to Lansing, April 30, 1918, *U. S. Foreign Relations*, 1918, p. 91. In September, 1918, the Canton Government sent Mr. C. T. Wang to the United States for the purpose of con-

Moreover, the Peking authorities, either indifferent or busy with matters of more immediate concern to themselves, took no effective steps to restrict the activities of German agents who, it was charged in Entente circles, continued to make of the country a hotbed of pro-German agitation. Representative business men in China of Allied sympathies finally reached the conclusion that the deportation from the country of all German and Austro-Hungarian subjects offered the only certain remedy for this situation.[91] Not until May 17, 1918, did the Peking Government issue regulations forbidding or greatly restricting trade between Chinese and enemy subjects, and these regulations were not enforced.[92] Only vigorous protests from the British and Japanese Ministers prevented the Chinese Government from negotiating a loan of £500,000 from a Danish corporation for purposes of wireless development in China; scarcely concealed behind the Danish company, it was alleged, stood German financial interests.[93]

In still other directions, it seemed likely that China's technical participation in the war might turn out to be not only a farce but a tragedy as well. The country continued to be torn with internal dissension which finally assumed the form of open civil war. Faced with the refusal of the southern provinces to recognize the authority of his government, Premier Tuan fell back on the policy of attempting to unify the country by force. With the enthusiastic assistance of the northern militarists, he launched repeated campaigns against the southern "rebels." The autonomists at Canton, however, continued to maintain their separate government which, because of the presence of many

ferring with the Allies relative to the dispatch of 30,000 Chinese—presumably troops—to Europe. Address delivered by Mr. Wang at Canton, January 18, 1920, *North China Herald*, CXXXIV, Jan. 24, 1920, p. 218.

[91] See particularly the petition of the foreign merchants of Shanghai, *North China Herald*, CXXVII, Apr. 20, 1918, p. 131.

[92] Text, MacMurray, *op. cit.*, Vol. II, pp. 1379-80.

[93] *North China Herald*, CXXV, Dec. 22, 1917, p. 710. For additional instances of pro-German sympathy among Chinese officials, see the quarterly report of the American Chargé in Peking, Mr. J. V. A. MacMurray, for the period July to September, 1918. *U. S. Foreign Relations*, 1918, pp. 127-8.

members of the dissolved Parliament, they declared to be the only legal government in the country.[94]

Far from using the opportunities provided by the war to improve the international status of the nation, the Peking authorities followed a policy which seemed likely to lower that status more than ever. For the military expeditions against the South were financed for the most part out of the proceeds of repeated Japanese loans, each of which carried with it some fresh lien on the natural resources of the nation.[95] Even more

[94] The Kuomintang leaders at Canton insisted that their aims were identical with those of the Allies, for they too were fighting to destroy military autocracy and to restore and preserve constitutional government. *North China Herald*, CXXVII, Apr. 20, 1918, pp. 132-3. Also "Manifesto of the Southern Government" signed by Wu Ting-fang, August 17, 1918, *North China Herald*, CXXVIII, Aug. 24, 1918, pp. 442-3.

[95] Apparently the loans were all made with the approval of the Japanese Government. Mr. MacMurray's quarterly report to the Secretary of State, covering the period from July to September, 1918. *U. S. Foreign Relations*, 1918, pp. 122-3, 130-33. Mr. Millard, in his *Democracy and the Eastern Question*, treats of this period under the chapter heading "The Corruption of a Nation." Belatedly, the American Government was prevailed upon by Minister Reinsch to interest itself in the ominous significance of these numerous Japanese loans. During his visit to the United States in the summer of 1918, Dr. Reinsch found the officials at Washington interested less in the financial needs of China than in the immediate problem of training and transporting troops to Europe. China entered the war after the law providing for financial advances to the Allied and Associated Governments was passed and was not, therefore, entitled to benefit from its provisions. Reinsch, *op. cit.*, p. 356. Secretary Lansing, however, feeling the importance of the matter, brought it to President Wilson's attention in a letter dated June 20, 1918, in which he stated that "China has expected some financial assistance from the United States. Japan has made her many loans recently. We have made none. It was at our invitation she entered the war, and it is to us that she is looking for some financial help to guard against possibilities now that the scenes of war are nearing her borders. The indications are that her disappointment at not receiving what she has felt she had reason to expect has made her somewhat resentful against this country. . . ." *U. S. Foreign Relations*, 1918, pp. 169-71. On June 21 the President gave his approval to a plan for a new consortium in the operations of which American banks would be encouraged to participate. Letter to Secretary Lansing, *ibid.*, p. 171. Thereafter Mr. Lansing conferred on June 26 with representatives of various New York and Chicago banking interests. The bankers expressed their willingness to coöperate in making necessary loans to China provided that any loans which might be concluded had the public approval of the government. In communicating this information to Ambassador Page in London, Mr. Lansing said that the Department of State had approved the formation of a four-power banking group "since all four powers are deeply interested in measures to strengthen China and fit her for more active part in the war. . . ." Telegram of July 11, 1918, *ibid.*, p. 176.

disquieting than this mortgaging of the country's resources was the apparent willingness of Peking officials to give Japan control over China's military and naval forces. With the situation created by the Treaty of Brest-Litovsk serving as a pretext, a Sino-Japanese military convention was signed May 16, 1918. The agreement provided that whatever forces might be sent jointly by the two powers against Russo-German troops operating in Siberia should be subject ultimately to the direction of Japanese commanders.[96] A convention providing for substantially the same type of Sino-Japanese naval coöperation was signed three days later.[97] A second military agreement supplementing the terms of that signed in May was concluded September 6, 1918.[98] And finally, on September 24, 1918, the Chinese Government agreed to an arrangement with the Japanese Government regarding Shantung which not only confirmed but extended Japan's economic and political influence in that province.[99] Although the actual terms of each of these agreements remained secret until the time of the Paris Peace Conference, rumors as to their sinister import stirred the student and merchant classes in China to a high pitch of indignation and despair.

The Austro-Hungarian peace note of September 14, 1918 served to remind Chinese officialdom of the rapidly moving course of events in Europe. With the end of the war apparently in sight, the Peking Government became acutely aware that a continuance of strife within the country might react to its disadvantage at the peace conference. In a message congratulating Mr. Hsü Shih-ch'ang on his inauguration, October 10, as the new President of the Republic of China, President Wilson took the occasion to urge that an end be made of domestic dissension and that the factional leaders should "unite in a determination

The war ended, however, before the bankers representing the four powers were able to iron out their differences. For a particularly trenchant criticism of American policy at this time, see Putnam Weale, *An Indiscreet Chronicle from the Pacific*, New York, 1922, pp. 25-29.
    [96] MacMurray, *op. cit.*, Vol. II, pp. 1411-12.
    [97] *Ibid.*, pp. 1412-13.
    [98] *Ibid.*, pp. 1413-14.   [99] *Ibid.*, pp. 1445-6, 1450-2.

to bring about harmonious coöperation among all elements of your great nation, so that each may contribute its best effort for the good of the whole, and enable your Republic to reconstitute its national unity and assume its rightful place in the councils of nations." [100]

In his reply, President Hsü pledged his best efforts to bring about a restoration of internal unity and to "meet the wishes of the people of the whole country that in coming councils of [the] family of nations our country may assume its rightful place and work with your country hand in hand toward the realization of the highest ideals." [101] The new chief executive was committed to conciliation as a means of terminating the desultory civil wars. The retirement of the Premier, General Tuan Ch'i-jui, on October 11, seemed to promise that the new policy might meet with success.

In an effort to quiet the discontent which quite evidently existed among the representatives of the Allied powers in Peking, President Hsü, on October 29, issued a proclamation reminding his countrymen of their participation in the war. After recalling that China had entered the war to uphold humanity and the sanctity of international law, the President declared: [102]

"More than a year has elapsed during which the soldiers and civilians throughout our country have unanimously done their respective parts in carrying out the object of the Government in declaring war: some, taking precautionary measures against enemy intrigues and plots, have maintained the peace and order of their localities; some by making generous donations to the Red Cross funds, have saved and relieved sick and wounded soldiers; some have permitted the departure of large numbers of Chinese laborers for Europe, thereby helping the works preparatory to a battle; some have devised means to assist in the purchase of raw materials, foodstuffs and cattle in the interior provinces; and some have built transport ships for,

[100] U. S. Foreign Relations, 1918, p. 111.
[101] Telegram of October 13, 1918. Ibid. Dr. Reinsch reported later that President Wilson's appeal for national unity "made a profound impression" and was "welcomed by leaders and the public as counsel inspired by true friendship." Telegram to Lansing, October 26, 1918, ibid., p. 115.
[102] North China Herald, CXXIX, Nov. 9, 1918, p. 328.

and sent supply ships and boats to our Allied countries. Whatever plans to confound the enemy that may seem to be beneficial to the cause of the Entente have all been energetically executed without fail. . . .

"(Now) the enemy forces are gradually becoming weak, and they have asked for peace. Thus, the final triumph of the Entente countries can be confidently expected. However, so long as the enemy troops have not been reduced to a position of complete surrender, so long must our Government and people not relax their duties in rendering every help to the Allied countries. Let the soldiers and people of our provinces each do their utmost to assist the representatives and subjects of the Entente countries in order to attain our common object in the war."

The Allied Ministers were not to be mollified by paper pronouncements. On the day following the publication of the Presidential mandate, the representatives of the seven Allied Powers presented the following note to the Chinese Foreign Office:

"It would appear that a clear understanding on the part of Chinese officials and other public men, of the manner in which the Chinese Government has fallen short of doing what could reasonably be expected of it as a co-belligerent, and of the result which a continuance of this condition would have upon public opinion among the Associated Powers and, therefore, upon the standing of China after peace is concluded, is requisite both in the interests of China and of the Powers with whom she is associated."

The Chinese Government was reminded that "instead of devoting its energies single-heartedly to performing in the fullest manner its duties towards its associates," it had "engaged its force almost entirely in internal affairs in an attempt, by military means, to solve the internal difficulties." The note then requested:

"the concentration of national resources and revenues upon constructive work, so as to enable China to give actual assistance to the Allied cause; also, within China such measures should be promptly carried through as will effectively protect the interests of the Associated Powers and put proper restrictions upon resident enemies; in connection with this, individual officials showing lack of energy or a positive bias favorable to the enemy, should be replaced by men in sympathy with the declared policy of the Chinese Government and ready to carry it out."

The memorandum went on to enumerate twelve grievances which the Allied Ministers desired to see redressed.[103] Intended less as an indictment of the Chinese nation than as a stern rebuke to the cynically minded clique then dominating the Government at Peking,[104] the note was nevertheless interpreted in many circles, both Chinese and foreign, as a frank warning that China's official inaction during the war would react to her disadvantage at the peace conference.[105] Indeed, a movement was already under way to deprive her of any voice whatsoever at that conference.[106]

The Peking Government took hasty steps to appease China's disgruntled associates. A presidential mandate finally, on November 17, ordered the cessation of hostilities on all domestic fronts as a measure preparatory to peace negotiations looking toward the reunification of the country.[107] At the instance of Japan, the Allied and Associated Ministers added their benediction to the peace movement in an *aide-mémoire* dated December 2 and delivered simultaneously to the authorities at Peking and Canton.[108]

Another development which met with the complete approval of Allied sympathizers was the recall, at the instance of the Chinese Government, of the Dutch Minister, Beelaerts van Blokland, whose zeal in caring for German and Austro-Hungarian interests during the war had left him with few friends in Allied circles. The Chinese Government also gave orders for the liquidation of German banking and commercial houses,

[103] The text of the note as given above appears in Tyau, *China Awakened*, p. 308. A summary of the remainder, translated from the Chinese press, is to be found in the *North China Herald*, CXXIX, Nov. 9, 1918, pp. 328-9.

[104] Reinsch, *op. cit.*, pp. 322-3.

[105] Tyau, *op. cit.*, pp. 308-9.

[106] T. R. Jernigan, "Observations," *Millard's Review*, VI, Oct. 26, 1918, p. 296.

[107] *Millard's Review*, VI, Nov. 23, 1918, p. 466.

[108] *U. S. Foreign Relations*, 1918, p. 134.

and finally for the "repatriation" of all enemy aliens in the country, including with a few exceptions both merchants and missionaries.[109] Orders had previously been given for the internment of a few of the more objectionable enemy residents.

In January, when official representatives of the North and South met in a peace conference at Shanghai for the purpose of composing their political differences, it seemed possible that despite her war record, China might yet win a hearing for her claims at another more important peace conference, the delegates to which were already gathering in Paris.

[109] The deportations were carried out during February and March, 1919.

CHAPTER III

VERSAILLES

DESPITE the unpromising tone of the Allied memorandum
of October 30, many elements in China, both official and lay,
hoped greatly that the approaching peace conference at Paris
would work a much desired change in the international position
of their country. President Wilson's public utterances, particularly those relating to self-determination and the rights of weak
nations, had left a deep impression in intellectual circles in
China, as in the rest of Asia. This interest was especially strong
after the military and political collapse of the Central Powers
had demonstrated the surprising force of those ideas.[1] Such
was the instant popularity of a low-priced edition of President
Wilson's collected war addresses, newly translated into Chinese,
that book shops in Shanghai found it impossible, for a time, to
supply the demand for copies.[2]

[1] The extravagant optimism fostered by the Wilsonian principles was
reflected in a conversation between a British resident of Shanghai and an
intelligent Chinese friend. The Chinese gentleman declared that all the
Chinese in the city were greatly excited over President Wilson's speeches
on the Fourteen Points on which peace was to be based, especially the one in
which "the President claimed that all territories alienated from their original
owners must be restored." Since China had been one of the Allies, "if
this principle is carried into effect, those parts of our territory taken from
us should be restored to us." The speaker mentioned Tsingtao, Hongkong,
and Formosa as being included in the list, together, perhaps, with Siam
and Burma. When it was suggested that President Wilson had referred
primarily to the situation in Europe, the Chinese gentleman replied, "But
the principle is there. The aim of the Conference is so to settle all questions
that there will be no root of unrighteousness left from which a fresh war
will spring." *North China Herald*, CXXIX, Dec. 21, 1918, pp. 749-50.
[2] The compilation was made by Mr. Carl Crow, the Shanghai representative of the American Committee on Public Information, and translated
by Dr. Monlin Chiang, one of China's foremost educators.
Not all Chinese, however, were familiar with the utterances of the
American War President. Toward the end of 1918, Sir John Jordan, then

The problem which attracted greatest attention in semi-official circles throughout the country was that of finance. The habitual penury of governmental units in both north and south China created a situation which, it was felt, must be remedied without further delay. As a consequence of foreign control over China's finances, and the treaty and other restrictions which limited the power of her government in finding remedies for the existing situation, the Peking Government had been compelled now for a considerable period of time to subsist mainly on the proceeds of foreign loans which served merely to bridge the interval between one financial crisis and another.[3] In many quarters it was felt that loans, coupled as they were in most instances with the grant of valuable rights for the exploitation of natural resources, constituted a grave menace to the territorial integrity of the country. Particularly sinister in their implications were the intimate relations between highly placed Peking officials who negotiated the loans and such Japanese financiers as Mr. Nishihara.[4] Not a few patriotic Chinese even voiced the fear that their nation might eventually share the fate of Korea.

Thoroughgoing and radical financial reform was necessary, therefore, to ward off the danger of a Japanese economic if not political protectorate, to avert national bankruptcy, and to preserve the continued existence of a central government. Three

British Minister in Peking, had a conversation with Duke Kung, the 76th lineal descendant of Confucius. Kung spoke freely about political conditions in his native province of Shantung, and commented bitterly on the foreign aggressions to which it had been subject during the previous two decades. Sir John then turned the conversation to the European peace terms which were then under discussion, and asked the Duke what he thought of President Wilson's Fourteen Points. "Who is President Wilson?" was his prompt and ingenuous reply. "Some Chinese I have Known," lecture delivered by Sir John Jordan at the London School of Oriental Studies, in *North China Herald*, CXXXVII, Dec. 25, 1920, pp. 885-90.

[3] The critical state of China's finances is set forth in "A Review of China's Finances in 1918," by Hollington K. Tong, in *Millard's Review*, VII, Jan. 25, 1919, pp. 272-76.

[4] Eventually, following the replacement of Viscount Terauchi's ministry by that of Mr. Hara, the Japanese Government, on December 3, announced that it would henceforth cease to lend its encouragement to further financial transactions between its bankers and the officials of the Peking Government. *Far Eastern Review*, XV, January, 1919, p. 33. Reinsch, *op. cit.*, p. 326.

measures were proposed for meeting the situation. It was hoped, in the first place, that the powers would agree to an outright cancellation of the remaining installments of the Boxer Indemnity. In January, 1919, a number of China's prominent educators deliberated over the advisability of appealing to President Wilson and the Allied statesmen for the total cancellation of the indemnity.[5]

In the second place, there was confident expectation that the new Consortium, with revived participation by the United States, would agree to make a large loan to the Chinese Government. This loan would serve to refund the numerous Japanese advances of the past several years, to make possible a complete reorganization on a solid foundation of the financial structure of the government, and to finance an elaborate program of railway construction and industrial development.

The third measure involved recognition by the Treaty Powers of China's full right to fix her tariff rates. The existing import tariff still rested on the rates fixed in 1902 [6] and the rates on goods exported were those provided for in the treaties of 1858. It was asserted that these schedules yielded a revenue insufficient to meet the current expenses of the government, that they made no distinction between luxuries and necessities, and that a perpetuation of treaty restrictions deprived the government of the necessary power to foster native industry.

The industrial and mercantile classes gave their hearty support to such political leaders as expressed themselves in favor of full tariff autonomy. Chambers of commerce in both Peking and Shanghai inaugurated movements designed to interest Presi-

---

[5] The Peking *Leader*, then the organ of Liang Ch'i-ch'ao, in its issue of January 4, 1918, made a plea for total cancellation of the Boxer Indemnity. The full amount of these payments, it was asserted, was a trifle compared with the colossal sums that the warring powers were then flinging to the winds. *North China Herald*, CXXVI, Jan. 12, 1918, p. 65. A similar plea was made in April, 1918, by Mr. Carson C. Chang, then private secretary to the President of China. *Millard's Review*, IV, Apr. 27, 1918, p. 305.

[6] As indicated above, the revision undertaken in 1918 did not come into full force until August 1, 1919, and the new rates were not fully effective until the last quarter of that year.

dent Wilson and other Allied statesmen in the cause of China's fiscal independence.[7] A Society for the Promotion of Tariff Reciprocity was organized, led by Mr. Chang Chien, nationally known as an industrial leader.[8] In January a joint telegram went to the Paris Conference signed by representatives of forty-six chambers of commerce throughout the country. It complained of the treaty restrictions on the nation's power to fix her own tariff, and declared that "this is unlike other independent sovereign states where a national tariff and not a treaty tariff is enforced as part and parcel of their inherent fiscal autonomy."[9]

Hopes were also expressed that the Paris Conference would take steps leading to the eventual removal of other foreign restrictions on China's sovereignty. Even in the puppet Parliament at Peking, lately organized by the northern militarists as a successor to the old body whose members sat at Canton, voices were raised in favor of the abolition of foreign extraterritorial rights.[10] Mr. C. T. Wang, one of the Chinese delegates to the Conference, intimated, however, that China would be satisfied with the gradual removal of extraterritorial rights.[11]

The Chinese delegation which was to represent these national aspirations began to arrive in Paris in January.[12] At the head of the delegation was Mr. Lu Cheng-hsiang, Chinese Minister for Foreign Affairs, who had represented his government at the peace conference at The Hague in 1907, but who more

[7] *North China Herald,* CXXIX, Dec. 14, 1918, p. 652. The telegram of the Peking body complained that "our Customs Tariff is a matter entirely fixed by other Powers," and asserted that "this item, if not rectified, will not only cause everlasting pain and shame to our four hundred million people and our future generations, but also make us poorer and weaker every day until our country is ruined and our race exterminated!"
[8] *Millard's Review,* VII, Dec. 28, 1918, p. 128.
[9] *North China Herald,* CXXX, Jan. 25, 1919, p. 240.
[10] *Ibid.,* CXXIX, Nov. 30, 1918, p. 512.
[11] *Ibid.,* CXXX, Feb. 1, 1919, Supplement, p. 78.
[12] The sum of $200,000 was appropriated for the expenses of the Chinese peace delegation. The almost hopeless state of the public treasury is evidenced by the fact that it was necessary to borrow this sum from one of the foreign banks. The appropriation was subsequently increased to $600,000. *Millard's Review,* VI, Nov. 30, 1918, p. 507. *Ibid.,* VII, Dec. 14, 1918, p. 56.

recently had been forced in 1915 to sign the Sino-Japanese notes and agreements resulting from the Twenty-One Demands. With Mr. Lu were associated Dr. V. K. Wellington Koo, Minister to Washington, Dr. Sao-ke Alfred Sze, Minister to London, and Mr. Ch'en-tzu Wei, Minister to Brussels. As evidence of its conciliatory attitude toward the South, no less than to preserve an outward appearance of national unity, the Peking Government readily added to the delegation Dr. Cheng-t'ing Thomas Wang, who at the time of the armistice was in the United States representing the interests of the Canton Government. Dr. C. C. Wu, the son and close political associate of Dr. Wu Ting-fang, was later added as a second representative of the South. Except for their leader, Mr. Lu, the principal members of the delegation were all representatives of the newer generation in China who took much of their inspiration as they had taken much of their education from the West. The entire delegation numbered fifty-two members, including seventeen technical experts and five foreign advisers. Among the latter were Sir John MacLeavy Brown, counsellor of the Chinese Legation in London; Dr. George E. Morrison, political adviser to the President of China, and M. Georges Padoux, adviser to the Law Codification Commission.[13] The Chinese Government declined to act on the Japanese suggestion that an adviser from the neighboring empire should be added to the mission.[14]

Originally, the Chinese Government had proposed to employ two American experts on international law to serve as official advisers to the Chinese peace delegation. When, however, it was intimated unofficially to the Peking authorities that the American Government was disposed to question the wisdom of this proposal, it was dropped.[15] The American Govern-

[13] Tyau, *China Awakened*, p. 315.
[14] The proposed Japanese adviser was apparently Dr. Nagao Ariga. Mr. Thomas F. Millard before the Senate Foreign Relations Committee, August 18, 1919, *Sen. Doc.* 106, 66 Cong. 1 Sess., p. 447.
[15] Testimony of Mr. Millard and Dr. John C. Ferguson before Senate Foreign Relations Committee, August 18 and 21, 1919, *ibid.*, pp. 430-2, 614-15. Early in March, 1919, when prospects for the success of the Chinese cause were anything but bright, Dr. Koo cabled Mr. Millard to come to

ment anticipated that the Chinese representatives at Paris would be somewhat in the position of wards of the United States, and that foreign advisers would therefore be unnecessary.[16] The United States had made no positive official pledges to protect China's interests at the Conference. At the same time, China had reason to believe that the United States would use its utmost efforts to protect those interests.[17] There was, in fact, the closest possible coöperation during all of the negotiations at Paris, between the Chinese delegation and the experts attached to the American Commission. Every step taken by the Chinese representatives was promptly communicated to their American friends.[18] Despite their conviction that the Lansing-Ishii Agreement of November, 1917, was a menace to China, the Chinese delegates, in their anxiety to avoid embarrassing the American President, resisted powerful pressure from American unofficial sources urging them to test the validity of that agreement at Paris.[19]

In the proceedings connected with the formal organization of the Conference, it was decided that most of the minor states, including China, must be satisfied with only two seats.[20] Chinese disappointment over this decision and Mr. Lu's inability to secure a reconsideration of it, was only partially assuaged by the general adoption of the panel system, which

Paris as an unofficial adviser. The American publicist accepted the invitation and reached Paris late the same month.
[16] Testimony of Mr. Millard, *op. cit.*, p. 431.
[17] Testimony of President Wilson before Senate Foreign Relations Committee, August 19, 1919, *Sen. Doc.* 106, 66 Cong. 1 Sess., p. 526. Even before either China or the United States had entered the war, the American Government had pledged itself to help in securing for China a seat at the peace table. Testimony of Dr. Ferguson, August 20, 1919, *op. cit.*, p. 581.
[18] Testimony of Mr. Millard, August 18, 1919, *op. cit.*, p. 450
[19] Gallagher, *America's Aims and Asia's Aspirations*, pp. 72-3.
[20] Japan, as a great power, was awarded five seats in the Conference. In addition, she was entitled to have two representatives on the Council of Ten. While she lacked direct representation on the Council of Four, formed in March to expedite the work of the Conference, Japan had direct access to that body when questions affecting the Far East were under discussion. China could appear before either council only by invitation and in the rôle of petitioner. R. S. Baker, *Woodrow Wilson and World Settlement*, Garden City, 1922, Vol. II, pp. 225, 231.

permitted the delegates representing Peking and Canton to take turn about during plenary sessions of the Conference.[21] China, however, was given fairly generous representation on the various committees of the Conference. Dr. Koo was elected as one of the five members representing the lesser states on the League of Nations Commission, Dr. Wang served on the International Ports and Waterways Commission, and Dr. Sze on the Economic Commission.[22]

The Chinese program at Paris embraced four more or less distinct projects. These were, first, the effort to dispossess Japan of all former German rights in Shantung, including particularly the leasehold of Kiaochou; second, the abrogation of all or part of the treaties and agreements resulting from the Twenty-One Demands imposed by Japan on her weaker neighbor in 1915; third, the liquidation of German and Austro-Hungarian economic and political interests in China; and finally, the general consideration with a view to eventual abolition of all special rights enjoyed in China by foreign powers and their nationals.

An opportunity for the presentation of China's claims in respect of Shantung arose in January during the discussion, in the Council of Ten, of the disposition which should be made of the former German colonial possessions.[23] At the morning session of the Council held on January 27, President Wilson suggested that a decision should first be reached relative to

[21] Gallagher, *op. cit.*, pp. 188-93. Tyau, *op. cit.*, p. 316. Since the usual diplomatic rule was adopted that all decisions must be unanimous, and since also the really important decisions of the Conference did not depend upon votes, the exact allotment of seats was of sentimental rather than actual significance. H. W. V. Temperley (ed.), *A History of the Peace Conference of Paris*, London, 1920-1924, Vol. I, p. 248.

[22] Tyau, *op. cit.*, pp. 328-9.

[23] Since the Sino-Japanese negotiations over Shantung might properly constitute the basis of a study distinct in itself, no attempt has been made in these pages to deal with the subject in any detail, except where such treatment has seemed necessary, as in the present instance, to preserve the sequence of events. For special studies of this phase of the subject, see W. Leon Godshall, *Tsingtao Under Three Flags*, Shanghai, 1929, and G. Zay Wood, *The Shantung Question: A study in diplomacy and world politics*, New York, 1922.

the applicability of the mandatory principle, for which he was contending, to the Pacific area. He proposed, therefore, that the Japanese claims should be heard that afternoon in the presence of the Chinese delegates. Over the objections of Baron Makino, who said frankly that he did not wish to discuss Japanese relations with Germany in the presence of the Chinese representatives, the proposal was adopted. That afternoon, therefore, Messrs. Wellington Koo and C. T. Wang attending, Baron Makino stated briefly that his Government felt justified in claiming from Germany the unconditional *cession* of "the leased territory of Kiaochou together with the railways and other rights possessed by Germany in respect of Shantung province." [24] The Chinese delegates, on asking if they might say a word in reply to Baron Makino, were told that their case would be heard later.

Early the next morning, the Chinese delegates received word that the Council of Ten was now prepared to hear a statement of their claims. Dr. Koo, after preparing hastily on such brief notice, appeared before the Council several hours later. China, he declared, desired the direct restitution to her of all former German rights in Shantung on two grounds, first, that China's entrance into the war had cancelled all existing agreements with Germany, and, second, that direct restitution was in accordance with the general principles which had been accepted by the present Conference. Baron Makino promptly challenged the soundness of the Chinese delegate's contentions. He desired, he said, to make one point clear. Japan was in actual possession of the territory under discussion. It had been taken by force from Germany. Before disposing of it, therefore, to "a third party" it was necessary first that Japan should have from Germany the free right of disposal. What should take place thereafter had already been made the subject of an interchange of views between the Japanese and the Chinese Governments. The Japanese representative then read pertinent extracts from previously unrevealed agreements, notably those of

[24] Baker, *op. cit.,* Vol. II, pp. 228-9.

September 24, 1918, which indicated that the two governments had already arrived at an amicable settlement regarding
the matter under consideration.[25] Dr. Koo next argued that
China's entrance into the war had completely altered her status,
and invoked the principle of *rebus sic stantibus* to support the
contention that China was by that fact no longer bound by the
agreements to which the Japanese delegate had referred.[26]
President Wilson suggested that, of course, the two parties
would be willing to make all such secret agreements available
for examination by the members of the Council. Dr. Koo assented to the suggestion without qualification. Baron Makino
intimated that prior to their publication it would be necessary
for him to consult telegraphically with his government.[27]

[25] Baker, *op. cit.*, Vol. II, p. 230. These agreements, taking the form
of notes exchanged at Tokyo between Baron Goto and the Chinese Minister,
Mr. Chang Tsung-hsiang—who was also the representative of the pro-
Japanese camarilla in Peking—related, first, to the negotiation of Japanese
loans for the construction of railways from Tsinanfu (Shantung) to Shun-
tehfu (Chihli) and from Kaomi (Shantung) to Hsuchowfu (Kiangsu);
and second, to the withdrawal of Japanese troops to Tsingtao, except for a
small detachment at Tsinanfu, and the abolition of the Japanese system of
civil administration in parts of Shantung, in exchange for the transformation
of the Kiaochou-Tsinanfu Railway into a Sino-Japanese enterprise, the property of which was to be policed by Chinese guards under the supervision of
Japanese instructors. Texts, MacMurray, *op. cit.*, Vol. II, pp. 1445-6,
1450-2.
[26] Baker, *op. cit.*, Vol. II, p. 231.
[27] Tyau, *op. cit.*, p. 317. Gallagher, *op. cit.*, pp. 273-4. There can be
no doubt that Lu Cheng-hsiang, as Minister for Foreign Affairs, had full
knowledge of these agreements before going to Paris. Not apparently until
January 26, however, did he see fit to reveal their contents to his colleagues on the Chinese delegation. Less than forty-eight hours later, Dr. Koo
was summoned to present the Chinese claims before the Council of Ten. Some-
time earlier he had prepared an elaborate argument on the subject which he
was now able to use only in part. Gallagher, *op. cit.*, p. 272. See also
Liang Ch'i-ch'ao, "Causes of China's Defeat at the Peace Conference,"
Millard's Review, IX, July 19, 1919, pp. 262-68. From this moment there
was dissension within the Chinese delegation. It was caused not only by the
delay in revealing the agreements of September, 1918, but by the suspicion
that Mr. Lu, while in Tokyo on his way to Paris, had entered into an understanding with Viscount Uchida which limited China's freedom of action
at the Conference. Gallagher, *op. cit.*, p. 272. On February 10, Mr. Lu
cabled to Peking his resignation, which was not accepted. In March he
pleaded illness as an excuse for going to Switzerland, and again cabled
his resignation. On April 5 he consented to return to Paris on condition
that henceforth his official relations with the other members of the
Chinese delegation should be conducted through his friend, the Chinese
Minister to Italy. *Ibid.*, pp. 263-4.

The next act in this Sino-Japanese drama was staged in Peking. On January 30, the Waichiao Pu received from its representatives at Paris a telegraphic account of the meeting before the Council of Ten. The next day, which was the eve of the Chinese New Year, the Japanese Minister, Mr. Torikichi Obata [28] notified the Waichiao Pu that urgent business required that he have an immediate interview with Mr. Ch'en Lu, the Acting Minister of Foreign Affairs. The request was declined because of the New Year holidays. Mr. Obata insisted, however, and on February 1, the Chinese New Year Day, he was received by the Acting Foreign Minister. The Japanese representative announced that he had received three telegrams from Tokyo complaining that the Chinese delegates in Paris were "adopting an unfriendly attitude and opposing Japanese interests too strongly." He demanded, therefore, that the Sino-Japanese agreements should not be made public without the approval of the Japanese delegates, and that the Chinese Government should telegraph its representatives instructing them to modify their attitude. Otherwise, declared Mr. Obata, "Japan would take what steps she deemed necessary to maintain her international position." [29]

When it was first known in Peking that the Chinese delegates in Paris had successfully crossed swords with the Japanese

[28] Mr. Obata is frequently referred to by Chinese newspaper writers as "the table thumper" for the vigorous rôle he played during the negotiations of 1915 concerning the Twenty-One Demands.

[29] Two versions of this meeting exist. That given above is based upon an interview given by Ch'en Lu to a representative of the Peking *Leader*, and to several delegates from the People's Diplomatic Society. *North China Herald*, CXXX, Feb. 15, 1919, p. 386. Tyau, *China Awakened*, p. 318. Mr. Obata's version was given to various press representatives who visited him February 4. It agrees substantially with the first account, except in the following respects: he declared he had received no instructions on the subject from Tokyo, but that the telegrams upon which his action was based had come directly from the Japanese delegation at Paris. He denied absolutely that Japan contemplated anything in the way of a military or naval demonstration to intimidate China. *Millard's Review*, VII, Feb. 15, 1919, p. 373. However, Dr. Tyau, who was apparently in close touch with the Foreign Office, states that it was casually suggested to one of the Waichiao Pu secretaries that "about a million Japanese soldiers and half a million tons of Japanese warships were then lying absolutely idle." *China Awakened*, p. 317. See also Reinsch, *op. cit.*, pp. 339-40.

spokesmen, a feeling of elation spread to all classes among the Chinese. The hope was even expressed that this would mark the "Year One" in the matter of the foreign treaties. Whatever might transpire thereafter, China had at least been given a sympathetic hearing before an international conference.[30] Later, when details of the Obata visit to the Waichiao Pu became known, this popular elation gave way before a fear that Japanese displeasure might lead to military intervention.[31]

The feeling of despair was speedily followed, however, by a widespread determination to support the Chinese delegation with evidences of popular approval—a tendency which contrasted significantly with the almost universal apathy which had accompanied vigorous action by various foreign powers in the past. On February 3, several hundred public-spirited Chinese met in Peking to draft telegrams to the delegation at Paris, to various public bodies over the country, and to the members of the internal peace conference meeting in Shanghai. The latest Japanese action was denounced as "an outrage against international decency and righteousness," and the Chinese representatives at Paris were urged to demand the unconditional abrogation of all Sino-Japanese contracts and agreements concluded since 1914.[32] Chinese students in many of the provinces obtained numerous signatures to a telegram to the Paris delegation urging its members to stand their ground. Mr. T'ang Shao-yi, the head of the southern commission negotiating peace at Shanghai, telegraphed President Hsü Shih-ch'ang to remain firm, and pledging him the support of a united country if he did so. Mr. Chu Ch'i-ch'ien, the chief of the northern commission at Shanghai sent a similar message in which he threatened to resign his post in case the government accepted the Japanese demands.[33]

At first the Chinese Government, evidently in a state of

[30] *North China Herald*, CXXX, Feb. 8, 1919, p. 325.
[31] *Ibid.*
[32] *Millard's Review*, VII, Feb. 15, 1919, p. 374.
[33] "Can Japan Successfully Gag China at the European Conference," *Millard's Review*, VII, Feb. 15, 1919, pp. 377-82.

acute alarm, telegraphed its Paris representatives not to publish the secret agreements, since they were not regarded as valid and their publication at that time might lend them a force otherwise lacking.[34] President Hsü and Premier Chien Nung-hsun favored supporting the independent stand of the Chinese delegates. The pro-Japanese elements within the cabinet feared, however, that the Japanese expression of displeasure presaged the end of further loans from Japanese sources.[35] A reconsideration of this early decision was forced by the unmistakable evidences of popular sentiment in all parts of the country. Thereupon the Chinese delegates received instructions to use their discretion regarding the publication of all secret documents covering past transactions between China and Japan.[36] Following a request from Mr. Lu Cheng-hsiang for a full list of existing agreements, the Waichiao Pu telegraphed the texts of four agreements relating to forestry, mining, and railway loans which were not then in the possession of the Chinese peace commission.[37]

Encouraged, apparently, by these evidences of official and popular support, the Chinese delegates at Paris pushed their claims with renewed vigor. In February the Chinese statements with regard to Kiaochou were amplified and reinforced in a memorandum formally submitted to the Conference.[38] The memorandum traced the history of German rights in Shantung and the ways in which Japan, since the beginning of her occupation there, had sought persistently for an extension of those rights. The agreements of September 24, 1918, were explained as being temporary arrangements made absolutely

[34] Reinsch, *op. cit.*, p. 340.
[35] *North China Herald*, CXXX, Feb. 15, 1919, p. 393.
[36] *Ibid.*, p. 411.
[37] *Ibid.*, Feb. 22, 1919, pp. 452-3. Subsequently, during March and April, the Chinese Government, in collaboration with the Government at Tokyo, published officially what purported to be a complete list of all Sino-Japanese agreements.
[38] "The Claim of China for Direct Restitution to Herself of the Leased Territory of Kiaochou, the Tsingtao-Tsinan Railway and Other German Rights in Respect of Shantung Province." Text, Tyau, *op. cit.*, Appendix B. *China Year Book, 1921-22,* 660-705.

necessary in order to quiet popular unrest by the withdrawal, at whatever cost, of the Japanese civil administration then functioning illegally in the interior of the province. China claimed restitution of the leased territory on the grounds of inherent sovereignty, national sentiment, and historical association. Moreover, Shantung Province was declared to possess the elements necessary to the economic and political domination of all northern China. The strictly legal arguments set forth in the memorandum were three in number. The Shantung agreement of 1915 was declared to be "in the view of the Chinese Government at best merely a temporary arrangement subject to final revision by the Peace Conference, because it dealt primarily with a question which had arisen from the war and which, therefore, could not be satisfactorily settled except at the final Peace Conference." China's subsequent entry into the war had so vitally changed the situation contemplated in the treaty that "on the principle of *rebus sic stantibus* it ceased to be applicable." In the second place, as a legal consequence of China's declaration of war, Germany had lost her leasehold rights, and now possessed "no rights in relation to Shantung which she [could] surrender to another Power." Finally, the lease convention which Germany signed in 1898 contained a clause which expressly denied her right to sublet any of the leased territory to a third power. Direct, rather than indirect, restitution was urged in the Chinese argument because, among other things, it would comport with "her national dignity and serve to illustrate further the principle of right and justice for which the Allies and Associates have fought the common enemy." [39]

The Chinese delegates were fully aware that the legal force of their arguments was weakened considerably by the existence of the Sino-Japanese agreements of May, 1915. Consequently, shortly after filing their first brief, they submitted a second asking for the abrogation of all of the treaties and notes signed

[39] For a critical appraisal of the legal arguments advanced by the Chinese, see H. S. Quigley, "Legal Phases of the Shantung Question," *Minnesota Law Review*, Vol. VI, pp. 380-94. (Apr., 1922).

following the presentation of the Twenty-One Demands.[40]
The Peace Conference was asked to cancel these agreements:

1. Because the treaties constituted "one entire transaction or entity arising out of the war and they attempt to deal with matters whose proper determination is entirely a right and interest of the Peace Conference."
2. "Because they contravene the Allied formula of justice and principles now serving as the guiding rules of the Peace Conference in its task of working out a settlement of the affairs of nations in order to prevent or minimize the chances of war in the future."
3. Because they tended to violate the territorial integrity and political independence of China as guaranteed in the series of conventions and agreements severally concluded by Great Britain, France, Russia, and the United States with Japan.
4. Because the negotiations were concluded under circumstances of intimidation and the threat of the Japanese ultimatum of May 7, 1915.

The Chinese statement pointed out that the Allied and Associated Powers had already taken action to nullify the Treaties of Brest-Litovsk and Bucharest, which were concluded during the war under duress. It was contended, also, that the Sino-Japanese agreements were lacking in finality, "being so regarded by Japan who sought to make them final by negotiating—before China was suffered to enter the war in association

[40] "The Claim of China for the Abrogation of the Treaties and Notes Concluded with Japan on May 25, 1915," *Congressional Record*, LVIII, pp. 3117-23. The southern section of the Chinese delegation insisted on raising the Shantung question in connection with the Twenty-One Demands and the 1915 treaties on the grounds that all of these matters represented a single transaction arising out of the war. The Peking delegates opposed this program, and as a result the Shantung question was presented to the Conference divorced from the Twenty-One Demands and exposed to the facile rebuttal of Japan on the basis of the secret pacts of September 28, 1918, and other interallied secret agreements. The Chinese case relative to the Twenty-One Demands alone was prepared with greatest care by one of the southern delegates, and then revised by a committee including Dr. Morrison, Sir John MacLeavy Brown, and M. Padoux. The Peking delegates led by Dr. Koo frustrated the formal presentation of this case to the Conference. The above statement embodying facts and arguments was submitted, but nothing was done to press the claim. Not until one of the southern delegates remonstrated were steps taken by the delegation to secure a formal acknowledgment of the filing of the claim. Eugene Chen, "From Versailles to Washington," *China Review*, I, Nov., 1921, pp. 287-90.

with the Allies and the United States—a set of secret agreements at variance with the principles accepted by the belligerents as the basis of the peace settlement." [41] It was the Chinese belief that these notes were no longer binding on the signatory powers for, with the entrance of China into the war on the side of the Allies, "the principle of *rebus sic stantibus* necessarily applies to them." The Chinese argument made no effort to question the validity of the 1915 agreements on the ground that they lacked the necessary approval of the Chinese Parliament.

From the point of view of political and moral principles, the Chinese had presented a strong case. On legal grounds, however, their position was open to attack. And the Japanese reply to the Chinese statement rested squarely and almost exclusively on a legal foundation. It was the Japanese contention that the 1915 agreements, no less than the supplementary understandings of 1918, were not only entirely legal, but were intended to be permanent. Even if "in consequence of China's declaration of war upon Germany, the Treaty of May 25, 1915, could have been nullified, the declaration could not, in any case, have the slightest effect upon the validity of the agreement of September 24, 1918, subsequent to that declaration. But that agreement itself would be inexplicable if one considered as null and void the Treaty of May 25, 1915, of which it is the sequel." With regard to the Chinese contention that the declaration of war by their government had completely terminated all Sino-German agreements, the Japanese reply expressed doubt as to whether such would be the effect on a lease treaty.

"Such a treaty differs from a treaty of cession pure and simple only in that it confers for a certain period of time the exercise of the rights of sovereignty, whereas a treaty of cession pure and simple

[41] Reference is here made to the understanding reached in February and March, 1917, between the Japanese Government and the Governments of Great Britain, France, Russia, and Italy, according to which Japan was to have the support of her allies when the disposal of German rights in Shantung came before the peace conference.

transfers it without any limitation of time. And it is universally recognized that a declaration of war does not abrogate treaties fixing frontiers and the territorial status of the belligerent powers. Moreover, in our particular case, there is no need to appeal to this juridical theory, for, if war abrogates certain treaties between belligerents, never does it abolish treaties between co-belligerents, that is to say, between allies." [42]

A considerable part of the Chinese argument had consisted of an attempt to apply the doctrine of *rebus sic stantibus* to their treaties and agreements with Japan. In regard to this matter, the Japanese statement declared:

"Jurists justly observe that the clause *rebus sic stantibus* may only be invoked with an extreme caution, lest it should at once reduce treaties into mere scraps of paper. The conditions of life [among] states are constantly changing, and to avail oneself of any modification in order to get rid of stipulations which no longer please one of the contracting parties would be to render all conventions vain. It would introduce a régime of perpetual instability into the interpretation and application of treaties whose object it is precisely to establish fixed rules and points in the ever-changing realm of international relations. The clause *rebus sic stantibus* can only be invoked when all the essential elements which had prompted the agreement having changed, it becomes evident that the terms of that agreement and the obligations which proceed therefrom do not correspond in any way whatsoever to the intentions and anticipations of the signatories. This is evidently not the case of the agreements under discussion. . . . It would seem that China wishes to take advantage of the presence of her delegates in Paris to evade, without any plausible reason, the fulfilment of the agreements already concluded." [43]

The Peace Conference took no action regarding these conflicting claims during the months of February and March. The Chinese delegation meanwhile was engaged with other matters. In early March, there was presented to the Conference China's suggested "Provisions for Insertion in the Preliminaries of Peace." [44] These provisions, which were proposed also for incorporation into the treaty with Austria, consisted

[42] Gallagher, *op. cit.*, pp. 305-6.   [43] Gallagher, *op. cit.*, pp. 304-5.
[44] Text, *Millard's Review*, July 17, 1920, Supplement, pp. 4-5.

of nine clauses. [In the preface to this statement, China expressed her desire to have restored to her "the territory, rights, and property which were originally obtained from her either by intimidation or by actual force, and to remove certain restrictions on her freedom of political and economic development."] The first of the nine clauses declared that the state of war between China and Germany having terminated all treaties, conventions, agreements, and contracts between them, "all rights, privileges, concessions, immunities, and tolerances granted therein . . . including notably the leasehold rights of Kiaochou Bay, the railway and mining concessions, and other rights and options in relation to the Province of Shantung, have reverted to China and/or ceased to exist." At the same time, China expressed her willingness, after regaining possession of Kiaochou, to open Tsingtao and "other suitable places in Shantung Province to foreign trade and residence."

In the second place, China desired Germany to accept "the principles of equality and reciprocity as the basis of a new treaty of commerce and general relations" to be concluded with China, and to relinquish therein on her part the principle of the "so-called most favored nation treatment." Prior to the conclusion of this new treaty, German trade with China should be subjected to "the tariffs, dues, and regulations which are or may be applied to the ships and merchandise of non-treaty powers. . . ." The third clause required Germany to renounce her claim to that portion of the Boxer Indemnity payments which became due after China's severance of diplomatic relations and before her declaration of war. The fourth specified that Germany should cede to China all German public property except that used for diplomatic and consular purposes, located in the Concessions at Tientsin and Hankow, and in other parts of Chinese territory, including the leasehold at Kiaochou. Except for the submarine cables at Tsingtao and other German property in Shantung, this portion of Clause IV became Article 130 of the Treaty of Versailles. China expressed her willingness to restore all private property of German citizens subject to the payment of any claims she might hold against their government. Clauses V and VI concerned Chinese compensation for losses, both public and private, arising out of the war. Clause VII called for payment by Germany of the expenses occasioned by the internment and maintenance of German soldiers and civilians in China, subject, however, to a reduction in this sum for similar expenses incurred by Germany. Germany would also be required to return the astronomical instruments and other works of art removed from China by German troops in 1900 and 1901. Aside from the reference to works of art, this clause became, substantially, Article 131 of the treaty. Finally, Germany would be required to put into operation the International Opium Convention signed June 23, 1912, at The Hague.[45]

While concentrating most of their energies on the effort to secure recognition of their claims to the German rights in Shantung and the cancellation of the Sino-Japanese agreements of 1915 and 1918, the Chinese delegation decided also to ask for a consideration of all special foreign rights in China. With this end in view, they presented to the Conference, in April, a lengthy memorandum entitled, "Questions for Readjustment."[46]

[45] Under Article 295 of the Treaty of Versailles, this provision was made binding on all states signatory to the treaty. The Chinese proposals made no mention of the stipulations incorporated as Article 132 of the treaty relating to the abrogation of the German leases for Concessions at Hankow and Tientsin. Presumably the Chinese delegates considered these matters to be satisfactorily covered by the general provisions of Clause I of their proposals. For obvious reasons, the Chinese statement omitted any recommendation for the transfer to the British Government of German public property at Shameen; this provision appeared in the treaty as Article 134.

[46] Text, *Chinese Social and Political Science Review*, V, No. 2, June, 1920. Soon after the armistice, the Chinese Foreign Office communicated to the American Legation at Peking a summary of the matters which China proposed to raise at the peace conference. The summary included requests for the abolition of all special rights enjoyed by foreigners or their governments in the country. The American Minister, who had recently returned from Washington, advised the Foreign Office officials that it would be wiser to restrict Chinese claims at Paris to the issues arising out of or directly touching the war, and to defer consideration of all other matters until a more suitable opportunity presented itself. To do otherwise, it was suggested, might complicate the situation to the disadvantage of China. *Mil-*

In its introductory statement, this memorandum pointed out that the progress of China since the opening of the century had been retarded by a number of hindrances of an international character, some the legacies of the past due to conditions which no longer existed, and some arising from recent abuses not justified in either equity or law. "Their maintenance," it was asserted, "would perpetuate the causes of difficulties, frictions, and discords. As the Peace Conference seeks to base the structure of a new world upon the principles of justice, equity, and respect for the sovereignty of nations, as embodied in President Wilson's Fourteen Points and accepted by all the Allied and Associated Powers, its work would remain incomplete if it should allow the germs of future conflicts to subsist in the Far East."

lard's Review, July 17, 1920, Supplement, p. 1. See also Mr. Millard's testimony before the Senate Foreign Relations Committee August 18, 1919, *Sen. Doc.* 106, 66 Cong. 1 Sess., pp. 431, 446-7. Mr. Gallagher states, however, that "in January, the Chinese and the American delegations were laboring hard upon many Far Eastern problems, such as railways, extraterritorial jurisdiction, abolition of foreign concessions, extinction of spheres of influence, the special Manchurian and Eastern Inner Mongolian issues, etc. That was in line with Mr. Wilson's specifically pronounced Chinese policy. The Chinese question was to be considered, *as a whole,* at the conference." The apparent coöperation between the American and the Chinese delegations relative to these matters worried both the British and the French authorities, and the French Government showed its extreme concern by calling from the Far East every available Oriental expert. *America's Aims and Asia's Aspirations,* p. 229. There can be no question of Dr. Reinsch's sympathy with the broader aspirations of the Chinese. It seems probable, therefore, that his post-armistice advice—if tendered at all—was tendered unofficially, and that the suggestion was motivated solely by his anxiety to have the Chinese delegates focus their energies exclusively on the task of securing an equitable settlement of the Kiaochou question. Dr. Reinsch, in his *American Diplomat in China,* makes no reference to the matter. Mr. J. B. Powell has suggested that Japanese officials even helped with the formulation of this broad program, knowing full well that the requests would never be granted, and hoping in consequence that the powers would turn a deaf ear to the more reasonable demands of the Chinese. *Millard's Review,* VII, Dec. 21, 1918, p. 84. In this connection, the Osaka *Mainichi* reported an unnamed "high Chinese official," evidently very friendly to Japan, as having said that his government would make the most of its opportunity at Paris to secure the removal of consular jurisdiction and the recovery of tariff autonomy, but that it had no intention of seeking to nullify the Sino-Japanese agreements of 1915 without previous consultation with the authorities at Tokyo. *Japan Weekly Chronicle,* Feb. 6, 1919, p. 192 However, in the light of the evidence of popular sentiment given at the beginning of the present chapter, it seems unnecessary to assume that these general proposals for treaty revision had their origin in Japan.

Seven specific grievances were then enumerated, together with the reasons why they should be redressed. First came spheres of influence or interest, based either upon agreements between the powers to which China was not a party, or agreements made by individual powers with China "under circumstances precluding the free exercise of her will." These spheres of influence, it was declared, hampered China's economic development, violated the principles of the Open Door, and were the source of international jealousies and frictions which threatened the peace of the Far East. Each power was asked therefore to make an independent declaration that it possessed no such sphere of interest, and that it was prepared to undertake a revision of such treaties, agreements, notes, and contracts as had conferred on it territorial rights or preferential advantages in any part of the country.

The withdrawal from China of all foreign troops and police was next asked. These troops included some which were there under the provisions of the Boxer Protocol, and some "whose presence is unwarranted." Complaint was made against the continuance of the exclusive Legation Quarter in Peking and against the legation guards maintained there. China asked, consequently, for the cancellation of Articles VII and IX of the Protocol of September 7, 1901 and for the withdrawal of legation guards and other troops stationed on Chinese territory in virtue of these provisions.

The third question dealt with foreign post offices and agencies for wireless and telegraphic communications. It was pointed out that the foreign post offices existed in China despite the absence in the treaties of any provision relating to the matter. Since the original establishment òf these foreign post offices, China had organized an efficient postal system of her own; she was, moreover, a member of the Universal Postal Union. Therefore, the Chinese Government now desired that "their own postal service should become the sole establishment of the kind carrying on postal work within the limits of the Chinese territory, as is the rule in every other independent country," and asked that the foreign post offices should be entirely withdrawn "on or before January 1st, 1921." Further-more, "the Chinese Government must demand that no foreign wireless or telegraphic installations of any kind shall be set up on Chinese territory and that all such installations as may have already been set up on Chinese territory shall be handed over forthwith to the Chinese Government upon due compensation being given." In this last statement there was more than a hint of impatience.

The fourth grievance was that of consular jurisdiction, the exercise of which, it was argued, was incompatible with the rights of territorial sovereignty. The system was admittedly a makeshift and was founded, according to the memorandum, not on international law but on the provisions of particular treaties. Reference was made to the "formal and explicit promise" concerning the eventual relinquishment of extra-territorial rights, made by "the several friendly Powers" in the Sino-British Treaty of 1902, the Sino-American Treaty of 1903, and the Sino-Japanese Commercial Treaty of the same date. "While we do not claim," it was said, "that the Chinese laws and their administration have now reached such a state as has been attained by the most advanced nations, we do feel confident to assert that China has made very considerable prog-ress in the administration of justice and in all matters pertain-ing thereto since the signing of the above-mentioned Commer-cial Treaties." As evidence of this improvement, the memoran-dum cited the National Constitution, with its provisions for a separation of powers and judicial independence, the five new codes, the new courts, the improvement in legal proceedings, the improved training for judicial officers, and the reform of the police and prison systems. China asked, then, that the system of extraterritoriality be abolished on the fulfillment of the following conditions: (1) the promulgation of the Crimi-nal, Civil, and Commercial Codes, the Code of Civil Pro-cedure, and the Code of Criminal Procedure; (2) the estab-lishment of modern courts in all localities where foreigners resided. The promise was made that these conditions would be met by the end of 1925, and the corresponding pledge was asked that with the fulfillment of the conditions named, the powers would relinquish their rights to consular jurisdiction and the use of special courts. The memorandum intimated that the entire country might thereafter be opened to trade and residence by foreigners.

Next the question of leased territories was taken up. The origin of the system of territorial leases was traced to German aggressions in Shantung, which had disturbed the balance of power in the Far East and led other powers to demand leases similar to that at Kiaochou. Since Germany was now eliminated, and since also a League of Nations was being founded "to prevent wars of aggression," it was evident that the system of territorial leases had lost its *raison d'être*. Consequently, the Chinese Government felt warranted in asking "for the restitution of these territories, with the assurance that in making this proposal, they are conscious of, and are prepared to undertake, such obligation as the relinquishment of control may equitably entail on them as regards the protection of the rights of property-owners therein and the administration of the territories thus restored to the complete control of China."

The restoration of all foreign concessions and settlements was likewise asked for. After reciting in some detail the historical origin of the system of foreign concessions, together with the abuses to which the system had given rise, the memorandum declared that China was willing to enter into negotiations for their restoration, which was to be fully accomplished by the end of 1924.

The last item in the list of grievances was that dealing with tariff restrictions. The conventional tariff then in force was condemned on four grounds: China lacked the power to negotiate reciprocity agreements with particular powers, the existing tariff made no distinction in rates between luxuries and necessities, the rates prescribed in the treaties provided revenue insufficient to meet the reasonable needs of the government, and there had been no revision of the original five per cent

over

rate since 1858. "To conform [therefore] to the aim and object of the League of Nations, it is urgently desired that the right of China to revise the existing tariff conventions should be recognized and agreed to by the friendly powers. The Chinese Government regard the Peace Conference as a unique opportunity because such revision requires the consent of all treaty powers, which is practically impossible to obtain under ordinary conditions." The powers were then asked to agree in principle that the existing tariff should be superseded two years hence "by the general tariff which is applied to the trade of non-treaty powers." [47] Meanwhile China agreed to negotiate trade agreements with particular powers "with a view to arranging new conventional rates for those articles in which they are specially interested" under the following conditions: a differential rate of duties, the rates applied to necessities to be not less than twelve and a half per cent, reciprocity in the granting of tariff rate concessions, and, finally, the recognition of a definite period after which China would be "at liberty not only to revise the basis of valuation, but also the duty rate itself." In return for these concessions, China pledged herself to abolish all *likin* taxation. In thus proposing tariff reform "and in placing China's case before the Peace Conference, the Chinese Government have behind them the voice of the whole country. It is to be hoped that the friendly powers will restore to China the same fiscal right as is enjoyed by all independent nations. . . ." [48]

[47] A new Chinese tariff covering trade with subjects of non-treaty nations was promulgated December 25, 1917. The rates were as follows:

Luxuries	30 to 100	per cent *ad valorem*
"Useless goods"	20 to 30	" " " "
"Useful goods"	10 to 20	" " " "
"Necessary goods"	5 to 10	" " " "

Far Eastern Review, XIV, February, 1918, p. 58.

[48] On April 11, 1919, the Chinese Foreign Office issued, at Peking, a surprisingly spirited official communiqué which was in part a supplement to the memorandum on "Questions for Readjustment" and in part a rejoinder to the Japanese statement published following China's formal request for the abrogation of the 1915 agreements. It declared that "the Chinese people know that their contribution to the war has been indeed small, although had wiser counsels prevailed it might have been large and important." Refer-

The memorandum was marked throughout by a high degree of moderation and by an evident disposition to pursue with the powers a coöperative policy in the adoption of remedies necessary to meet the conditions complained of. At the same time, the Chinese delegates were not too sanguine that the Peace Conference would turn its attention to the correction of these specific grievances. What was chiefly desired was a general declaration written into the treaty which would later form the background for a real constructive policy on the part of the powers toward China, and the eventual removal of all restrictions which interfered with her full administrative integrity.[49] The memorandum acknowledged that these questions did not arise primarily out of the World War. It was claimed, however, that the purpose of the Peace Conference was not merely to conclude peace with the enemy, but "to establish a new world order upon the foundation of the principles of jus-

ence was then made to the tens of thousands of Chinese laborers recruited by England and France whose numbers "could have been indefinitely increased without perceptibly affecting an inexhaustible man-power." China thus showed something "of the limitless possibilities her territories will offer when peaceful development and good fellowship have taken the place of foreign garrisons planted in her cities; when railways are no longer used as disruptive agencies; when . . . the policing of every district of her domains is confided to her own citizens and not given over to those who covet her potential wealth. . . . Since the Revolution of 1911 and the adoption of Western principles of government, China has been given no legitimate opportunity to develop herself either politically or economically." This circumstance was due in part to internal schisms, "often prompted by foreign influences." And if China now "claims that a complete mandatory [sic] be given her to regulate her own destinies, and to secure her true autonomy, it is because she is convinced that it is solely by this method that lasting peace and happiness can be brought to Eastern Asia and the ill-effects of the history of the past quarter-of-a-century totally expunged." Text, *North China Herald*, CXXXI, Apr. 19, 1919, pp. 144-5.
    [49] Testimony of Mr. Millard before Senate Foreign Relations Committee, August 18, 1919, *Sen. Doc.* 106, 66 Cong. 1 Sess., p. 447. Also letter dated April 24, 1919, from the London correspondent of the *North China Daily News*, in *North China Herald*, CXXXI, June 28, 1919, pp. 847-8. This fact explains why, among other reasons, Dr. Koo associated himself so strongly with the Japanese proposal for a racial equality clause in the League of Nations Covenant. In its amended form, as brought forward April 11 in the League of Nations Commission, this proposal called for the incorporation in the Covenant of a clause indorsing "the principle of the equality of nations and the just treatment of their nationals." Baker, *op. cit.*, Vol. II, pp. 234-5, 237-9.

74   *China's Foreign Relations*

tice, equality, and respect for the sovereignty of nations." And
the solemn warning was sounded that these questions, if neglected, "contain germs of future conflicts capable of disturbing
the world's peace again." [50]

The statement of China's broader national aspirations was
accorded a mildly sympathetic hearing. The delegates representing all of the minor nations were clamoring for special
consideration of a similar character. The Allied statesmen, on
the other hand, were anxious to finish the work of drafting the
Treaty. Of the greater statesmen, only President Wilson was
inclined to turn an attentive ear toward the Chinese petition.
In February he had already expressed to Dr. Koo his willingness to aid China in effecting a revision of her import tariff.[51]
On April 22, during a discussion of the proposed Shantung
settlement in the Council of Four, he declared "he had hoped
that by pooling their interest the several nations that had gained
a foothold in China (a foothold that was to the detriment of
China's position in the world) might forego the special position
they had acquired and that China might be put on the same
footing as other nations, as sooner or later she must certainly
be. He believed this to be to the interest of everyone concerned." [52] Neither M. Clemenceau nor Mr. Lloyd George,

[50] The memorandum contained no mention of China's desire for the
cancellation of the remaining payments of the Boxer Indemnity. This omission is explained by the fact that the question had already been discussed
before the technical commissions concerned, so that it was now a matter
for individual negotiations between China and the particular governments
concerned. Tyau, *op. cit.*, pp. 329-30.
[51] *Millard's Review*, VIII, Mar. 1, 1919, p. 16.
[52] Secret Minutes, Council of Four, April 22, 1919, Baker, *op. cit.*,
Vol. II, p. 252. According to Dr. Tyau, Mr. Wilson assured Mr. Lu and
Dr. Koo at this meeting of the Council of Four (Mr. Orlando being absent)
that "as soon as the proposed League of Nations is established, we will
give China all our assistance and aid her to remove all present inequalities
as well as restrictions upon her legitimate rights, so that the Republic
of China shall truly become a perfect, independent, sovereign, great state.
. . . Such sentiments, I am happy to state, are also shared by Baron
Makino." *China Awakened*, p. 328. Dr. Tyau's account of the Peace Conference is based, according to his own statement, on excerpts from the official
minutes of the Chinese delegates in Paris deliberating together, and on the
official summary submitted to the Peking Government of the work accomplished or attempted by its representatives.

however, indicated any willingness to give reality to this hope, although that morning Baron Makino and Viscount Chinda, for Japan, had informed Mr. Wilson that their government stood ready to abandon the special Japanese rights in China as soon as the other powers concerned were in a similar frame of mind.[53]

At most, China was given the promise that her grievances would be considered at some more appropriate time in the future. Acting on behalf of the Supreme Council, M. Clemenceau stated on May 14 that while the powers fully recognized the importance of the questions raised by the Chinese memorandum, unfortunately the immediate object of the Conference was to formulate the terms of peace with enemy countries and not to undertake the greater task of formulating a world peace. Hence no official action on the subject was possible at that time. The Supreme Council was of the opinion, however, that "these matters should be brought to the attention of the Council of the League of Nations as soon as that body is able to function." [55]

A solution still remained to be found for the knotty problem of the German rights in Shantung. In the Council of Foreign Ministers on April 15 and again on April 17, Mr. Lansing had urged strongly that as a compromise measure, the former German rights in Shantung should be ceded in trust to the five great powers for eventual restoration to China.[56] President Wilson also advocated the adoption of this plan in meetings of the Supreme Council. When it became apparent that Kiauchou

[53] Baker, *op. cit.,* Vol. II, p. 248.

[55] Tyau, *op. cit.,* p. 327. In a telegram of April 30 to Secretary Tumulty in Washington, giving details of the Shantung settlement, President Wilson stated, "I find a general disposition to look with favor upon the proposal that at an early date through the mediation of the League of Nations, all extraordinary foreign rights in China and all spheres of influence should be abrogated by the common consent of all the nations concerned." Text, Baker, *op. cit.,* Vol. III, pp. 315-16.

[56] *Ibid.,* Vol. II, p. 246. The proposition seems to have originated with Dr. James Brown Scott, who suggested that it might be found more acceptable to the Japanese than direct restitution of the rights in question to China. Testimony of Prof. E. T. Williams before Senate Foreign Relations Committee, August 22, 1919, *Sen. Doc.* 106, 66 Cong. 1 Sess., pp. 620-1.

was not to be restored directly to China, the Chinese delegates likewise became staunch advocates of the proposal.[57] The Japanese representatives, however, opposed it unqualifiedly. Equally unsatisfactory to them was the suggestion made by Mr. Lloyd George that Shantung should be assigned as a mandate under the League of Nations. Furthermore, Viscount Chinda bluntly told the Three on April 22 that the Japanese delegates "were under an express instruction from their Government that unless they were placed in a position to carry out their obligation to China [relative to the eventual restoration of Kiaochou] they were not allowed to sign the Treaty." [58]

Despite Premier Lloyd George's half-hearted proposal to transform Kiaochou into a mandated territory under the League of Nations, it was readily apparent that both he and M. Clemenceau were disinclined to nullify the secret agreements of February and March, 1917, whereby the Japanese were to have British and French support for their claims to the German rights in Shantung. It was likewise apparent that the Japanese representatives would continue to insist that the Sino-Japanese notes and agreements of 1915 and 1918 were absolutely valid. President Wilson, in the presence of the two Chinese delegates, admitted reluctantly that there was some truth in the Japanese contentions concerning this point. For while China's entrance into the war had cancelled all of her agreements with Germany, it did not, he said, "cancel the agreement between China and the Japanese Government which had been made before the war." [59] Chinese hopes for an application of the

[57] On April 23 the Chinese delegation proposed in writing to the Council of Four that as a compromise (a) German rights in Shantung should be ceded to the Five Principal Powers for eventual restoration to China; (b) Japan should evacuate Shantung and Kiaochou within a year after the conclusion of peace; (c) China should pay Japan the cost of the military and naval operations necessitated by the capture of Kiaochou; (d) China should create an international settlement and port at Tsingtao, to continue as long as other such settlements in China. *Millard's Review,* July 17, 1920, Supplement, p. 7.

[58] Secret Minutes, Council of Four, April 22, 1919, Baker, *op. cit.,* Vol. II, pp. 250-1.

[59] Baker, *op. cit.,* Vol. II, p. 253. In a subsequent statement, issued August 6 in reply to a pronouncement by Viscount Uchida four days before,

principle of *rebus sic stantubus* to their agreements with Japan were thus dashed to the ground.

Mr. Lloyd George finally suggested that the real question was whether the Chinese treaty with Japan was better for China than the transference to Japan of Germany's rights in Shantung.[60] The Chinese delegates, after withdrawing from the room for consultation among themselves, protested that it was quite unfair to ask them to accept either of these alternatives. Nevertheless, it was agreed among the Three to refer to the British, French, and American experts on the Far East the question as to whether it would be less injurious to China's interests to transfer Kiaochou directly to Japan, or to require the execution of the Sino-Japanese agreements of 1915 and 1918.

While the experts were deliberating, the Italian delegation deserted the Conference, and there were signs that the Belgians might follow suit. The threatened withdrawal of the Japanese also would have seriously hampered if not wrecked the work of completing the treaty, and with it the plan for a League of Nations. The situation was rendered more serious by the fact that the German representatives had already been summoned to Paris.

M. Clemenceau, President Wilson, and Mr. Lloyd George met April 25 to consider the recommendations of the Far Eastern experts. The report expressed the opinion that it would be less disadvantageous to China if Japan merely inherited the German rights in Shantung than if the settlement were based entirely on the Sino-Japanese agreements of 1915 and 1918.[61] This opinion of the experts formed the basis of Articles 156,

President Wilson declared with reference to the exchange of views in the Supreme Council meeting of April 30, "I felt it my duty to say that nothing that I agreed to must be construed as an acquiescence on the part of the Government of the United States in the policy of the notes exchanged between China and Japan in 1915 and 1918 and reference was made in the discussion to the enforcement of the Agreements of 1915 and 1918 only in case China failed to coöperate fully in carrying out the policy outlined in the statement of Baron Makino and Viscount Chinda." Text, MacMurray, *op. cit.,* Vol. II, pp. 1498-9.

[60] Baker, *op. cit.,* Vol. II, p. 255.
[61] Baker, *op. cit.,* Vol. II, p. 259.

157, and 158 of the Treaty of Versailles, transferring to Japan all former German rights in Shantung. On their part, the Japanese delegates, in response to questions by President Wilson, declared that [62]

"The policy of Japan is to hand back the Shantung peninsula in full sovereignty to China, retaining only the economic privileges granted to Germany and the right to establish a settlement under the usual conditions at Tsingtao.

"The owners of the [Kiaochou-Tsinan] Railway will use special police only to ensure security for traffic. They will be used for no other purpose.

"The Police Force will be composed of Chinese and such Japanese instructors as the Directors of the Railway may select will be appointed by the Chinese Government."

At the request of President Wilson, Mr. R. S. Baker went to the headquarters of the Chinese delegation on the evening of April 30 to inform them of the settlement and to express the hope of the American President that as soon as Japan and China met together as members of the League of Nations, the differences which separated the two countries would be composed. The Chinese delegates, however, were in no mood to trust the matter to an as-yet unorganized League. On May 1, Mr. Balfour, representing the Council of Three, communicated to them the main outlines of the settlement. The Chinese representatives expressed their keen disappointment and asked for copies of the minutes of the Supreme Council reporting the discussion of their problems. On May 4, Mr. Lu addressed a letter to the President of the Council of Three which stated that

"China, in coming to the Peace Conference, has relied on the Fourteen Points set forth by President Wilson . . . and the principles laid down in his subsequent addresses, and formerly [sic] adopted by the Powers associated against Germany. She has relied on the spirit of honorable relationship between states which is to open a new era in the world and inaugurate the League of Nations. She has relied, above all, on the justice and equity of her case. The

[62] Secret Minutes, Council of Three, April 30, 1919, *ibid.*, p. 263.

result has been to her a grievous disappointment. . . . The Chinese Delegation feel it to be their duty to register a formal protest with the Council of Three against the proposed settlement of the Kiaochou-Shantung Question." [63]

The reply to this protest, made by Mr. Balfour on May 9, merely inclosed a draft of the Shantung provisions of the treaty together with a copy of a statement issued by Baron Makino.[64] On being pressed for more definite assurances, the British Secretary for Foreign Affairs wrote the Chinese delegation on May 13 to the effect that his previous statements and the press statement of Baron Makino contained all that the Council of Three thought it necessary to say at the moment.[65] Meanwhile, on May 6, before the plenary session of the Conference where the text of the treaty was read, Mr. Lu had read a statement voicing China's disappointment over the provisions relating to Shantung and announcing that the Chinese delegates "have registered a formal protest with the Council of Three against the proposed settlement in the hope of having it revised, and if such revision cannot be had, they deem it their duty to make a reservation on the said clauses now." [66]

When the news of the Shantung decision reached China, there was widespread dismay and indignation. On May 4, several thousand students in Peking attacked the residence of Ts'ao Ju-lin, the Minister of Communications, who was accused of being the head of the corrupt pro-Japanese clique in the government. Ts'ao and his family fled for safety to a foreign hotel in the Legation Quarter. His house was completely wrecked, and Mr. Chang Tsung-hsiang, Chinese Minister to Tokyo, who chanced to be on the premises, fared so badly at the hands of the students that he was compelled to enter a hospital.[67]

[63] Text, MacMurray, *op. cit.,* Vol. II, pp. 1494-5.
[64] *Millard's Review,* July 17, 1920, Supplement, p. 11.
[65] *Ibid.*
[66] Text, MacMurray, *op. cit.,* Vol. II, p. 1496.
[67] For an excellent contemporary account of these incidents, see Rodney Gilbert, "Downfall of Tsao the Mighty," *North China Herald,* CXXXI, May. 10, 1919, pp. 348-9.

The popular movement begun by the students in Peking developed impressive proportions as it spread rapidly over the country. In practically all large cities, the students organized "Committees of Correspondence" to keep in touch with each other and to facilitate common action. Merchant strikes were added to student strikes, and a determined campaign was launched to boycott all Japanese goods.

The leaders of this popular movement demanded two things: first, that President Hsü should dismiss from office the three "pro-Japanese traitors"—Ts'ao Ju-lin, Minister Chang, and Lu Tsung-yu, the Director of the Currency Bureau—and, second, that the Chinese delegation at Paris should be instructed not to sign the treaty as it then stood. When the Government showed a disposition to defend the three culprits, a general strike was declared at Shanghai and in other cities.[68] On June 10, President Hsü finally accepted the resignations of the three officials. Several days later the entire cabinet resigned, and only extreme pressure, from both Chinese and foreign sources, prevented the resignation of President Hsü Shih-ch'ang himself.

The Chinese Government meanwhile had notified Mr. Lu at Paris not to sign the treaty without making a reservation concerning the three clauses relating to Shantung.[69] On May

[68] Apparently even the Thieves' Guild in the native city in Shanghai had a patriotic share in this popular movement. It was said that for several days after the call for the general strike went forth, neither thefts nor burglaries were reported from that section of the city. *Millard's Review*, IX, June 14, 1919, p. 59.

[69] These instructions reached Paris only after a period of evident vacillation on the part of the Peking authorities. On June 15, the Cabinet dispatched a telegram to the provinces declaring that "as we have tried in vain to obtain the consent of the Powers to sign it [the treaty] with a reservation, we consider it the best policy to sign it and thereby conclude a state of war against Germany." On June 17, the cabinet seems to have decided to telegraph Mr. Lu to sign the treaty without hesitation. *North China Herald*, CXXXI, June 21, 1919, pp. 760-1. Some days later the Acting Premier, Kung Hsin-chen, received a formidable delegation from Shantung after its members had been denied access to the President. At this time the Acting Premier stated that the United States, Great Britain, and France, through their representatives, had advised China to sign the treaty, and had guaranteed that Japan's oral promise to return Tsingtao would be carried out. "Consequently, the Chinese delegates have been instructed to do whatever circumstances require them to do." *Ibid.*, June 28, 1919, pp. 832-3. During this period of uncertainty, the Chinese delegation at

26, Mr. Lu informed the President of the Conference of these instructions.[70] Two days later, in acknowledging receipt of this communication, the Secretary-General of the Conference stated that it had been transmitted to the delegates of the nations represented on the Supreme Council.[71] On June 24, the Chinese delegation was informed, on behalf of the President of the Conference, that reservations in the text of the treaty could not be allowed "for want of a precedent." [72] Permission was next asked to make the reservation an annex to the treaty. This request was also denied.[73] Finally, on June 28, three hours before the time set for the ceremony at Versailles, the Chinese representatives proposed that before proceeding to Versailles, they be allowed to transmit to the President of the Conference a formal notification that

"In proceeding to sign the Treaty of Peace with Germany today, the undersigned, Plenipotentiaries of the Republic of China, considering as unjust Articles 156, 157, and 158 therein . . . hereby declare, in the name and on behalf of their Government, that their signing of the Treaty is not to be understood as precluding China from demanding at a suitable moment the reconsideration of the Shantung question, to the end that the injustice to China may be rectified in the interests of permanent peace in the Far East." [74]

Even this final proposal met with rejection, the Chinese being notified that "the Supreme Council had decided to admit no reservation of any kind in the text of the treaty, or separately,

Paris received approximately 7,000 telegrams from groups of their countrymen scattered all over the world, urging them not to sign the treaty without a reservation in regard to Shantung. *Far Eastern Review,* XV, August, 1919, p. 569. In many quarters, however, it was urged that unless she signed the Treaty of Versailles, China would forfeit her opportunity of belonging to the League of Nations. Rumors, undoubtedly of Japanese origin, circulated to the effect that the Covenant of the League was not to be included in the Austrian treaty which remained to be signed.

[70] Lu to Clemenceau, MacMurray, *op. cit.,* Vol. II, pp. 1496-7

[71] The Chinese plenipotentiaries had intended to write in the treaty over their signatures, "Subject to the reservation made at the Plenary Session of May 6 relative to the question of Shantung (Articles 156, 157, and 158)."

[72] Official statement of the Chinese Delegation to the press, June 28, 1919, MacMurray, *op. cit.,* Vol. II, pp. 1497-8.

[73] *Ibid.*

[74] Lu Cheng-hsiang and Chengting Thomas Wang to Clemenceau, June 28, 1919. MacMurray, *op. cit.,* p. 1497.

before it was signed, but that the Delegation could send [to the President of the Conference] a declaration after its signature." The Chinese delegates considered that the action suggested would be without legal value. Consequently, when the representatives of the nations assembled in the Hall of Mirrors at Versailles on June 28 to affix their signatures to the treaty of peace with Germany, the two seats reserved for the Chinese plenipotentiaries were vacant. The same day the Chinese delegation issued to the press an official statement declaring that

"The Peace Conference having denied China justice in the settlement of the Shantung question, and having today in effect prevented them from signing the treaty without sacrificing their sense of right, justice, and patriotic duty, the Chinese Delegates submit their case to the impartial judgment of the world." [75]

Although the Chinese plenipotentiaries withheld their signatures from the treaty,[76] its provisions relating to China were not without importance, especially since these were, with few exceptions, duplicated in the Treaty of St. Germain with Austria. Only such treaties between Germany and China, not inconsistent with the present treaty, as China desired to revive, were to continue in force, all others being abrogated (Article 289). Germany forfeited all benefits and privileges under the Protocol of 1901 and renounced her claim to any indemnities accruing thereunder subsequent to March 14, 1917 (Article 128). She likewise forfeited all advantages resulting from the Tariff Arrangement of August 29, 1902, and the arrangements of 1905 and 1912 relating to Whangpoo conservancy. Germany agreed to the abrogation of the leases under which the German Concessions at Tientsin and Hankow had been held, and China, "restored to the full exercise of her sovereign rights" in these areas, declared her intention of opening them to international trade and residence (Article 132). Germany also ceded to China all of her public property situated within those Concessions or elsewhere within Chinese territory. This

[75] *Ibid.*, pp. 1497-8.
[76] *Sen. Doc.* 348, 67 Cong. 4 Sess., pp. 3329 ff.

provision was subject, however, to three exceptions relating to (a) the German rights in Shantung which were transferred to Japan, (b) property used for diplomatic and consular purposes, and (c) German public and private property located within the Legation Quarter in Peking, which was not to be disposed of without the consent of the powers remaining signatory to the Protocol of 1901 (Article 130). German state property located in the British Concession at Shameen, moreover, was ceded to Great Britain, and the property of the German school in the French Concession at Shanghai was ceded conjointly to France and China (Article 134). Germany waived all claims against the Chinese Government arising out of the internment of German nationals in China or their repatriation (Article 133). She also renounced all claims resulting from the condemnation of German ships in Chinese ports, or the sequestration or liquidation of German property, rights, and interests in China since August 14, 1917 (Article 133). Within one year, however, the Reparations Commission might direct the German Government to acquire title to any rights or interests possessed by its nationals in any public utility undertaking or Concession in China, and to require the transfer of all such rights to the Commission (Article 260). Finally, the German Government was required to restore all astronomical instruments carried away by its troops in 1900 and 1901 (Article 131).[77]

Despite their refusal to sign the Treaty of Versailles, the Chinese delegates continued to participate in the work of the Conference. In connection with the Austrian Treaty, two questions arose which affected the interests of China. Of these the first concerned Italy's desire to take over control of the former

[77] Neither the Treaty of Versailles nor the Treaties of St. Germain and Trianon provided specifically for the abandonment of extraterritorial rights in China. The omission contrasted with the provision contained in Article 135 of the Treaty of Versailles whereby Germany recognized "that all treaties, conventions and agreements between her and Siam, and all rights, title, and privileges derived therefrom, including all rights of extraterritorial jurisdiction, terminated as from July 22, 1917." However, China, in her "Provisions for Insertion in the Preliminaries of Peace" made no mention of extraterritorial rights, and was content, apparently, with the mere abrogation of existing Sino-German treaties.

Austrian Concession at Tientsin. China's rights in the area were
ably championed by Dr. Wellington Koo, whose contentions
were upheld by the representatives of the United States, Great
Britain, and France. Withdrawing her claim, Italy then asked
that the Chinese Government administer the former Austrian
Concession so as not to prejudice the sanitary well-being of the
adjacent area under Italian control. Dr. Koo readily promised
that his government would without delay effect the necessary
sanitary improvements. This agreement was later confirmed by
an exchange of notes between Mr. Lu and the President of the
Peace Conference.[78]

The second question arising during the Austrian negotiations
concerned the Austrian request for a mitigation of the terms
of the treaty. The delegation representing Austria desired that
her share of the Boxer Indemnity should continue to be paid,
that compensation be allowed for all public property owned by
the former Austro-Hungarian monarchy in the Tientsin Concession, that Austrian citizens in China should continue to enjoy
most-favored-nation treatment, and that the old Sino-Austrian
commercial treaties should continue in full force. The powers
gave their full support to China by rejecting these proposals.[79]

With three exceptions, the Treaty of St. Germain duplicated
the provisions of the Treaty of Versailles relating to China.
The Boxer Indemnity payments were suspended as from
August 14, 1917, for China had not severed diplomatic relations with Austria-Hungary in March. Austria was not concerned with the Shantung settlement, nor was she required to
return any objects removed by troops during the Boxer intervention. The treaty was signed by Lu Cheng-hsiang and C. T.
Wang together with the representatives of other powers on
September 10, 1919. By her signature and subsequent ratification of this treaty, China became an original member of the
League of Nations. Dr. Koo subsequently signed the Treaty

[78] Tyau, *China Awakened*, p. 326. *Millard's Review*, IX, July 26, 1919,.
p. 310. *North China Herald*, CXXXII, July 26, 1919, Supplement, p. 446.
[79] *North China Herald*, CXXXII, Aug. 23, 1919, p. 471. *Ibid.*, Aug.
30, 1919, pp. 525, 531.

of Neuilly, with Bulgaria, although China had never declared war on that power, and the Treaty of Trianon, with Hungary. The latter treaty copied word for word the provisions of the Treaty of St. Germain relating to China. China refrained, however, from signing the treaty with Turkey, presumably because it provided for a continuation of the capitulations.[80]

Not until two and a half months after the signing by the other powers of the Treaty of Versailles, did China proclaim officially the conclusion of the state of war with Germany. On August 1 and August 2, the two houses of the Peking Parliament passed a resolution declaring peace with Germany. Thereafter, on September 15, 1919, a presidential proclamation appeared announcing that the war had ended. The proclamation included the statement: "Dissatisfied with the conditions embodied in three clauses relating to Shantung, this country refused to sign the Treaty. But it must be remembered that the other terms in the document are as acceptable to us as to other Associated Powers." [81] On September 18 a second presidential mandate was issued announcing the conclusion of peace with Austria. The proclamation declared, however, that "the rules and regulations promulgated in respect of German and Austrian subjects after our declaration of war, unless cancelled or revised in a formal manner, shall continue to remain in effect." [82] A subsequent mandate abrogated the temporary regulations issued during the war, but stated that "in future, law suits of German and Austrian subjects should be heard and decided in accordance with the regulations governing the trial of cases in which subjects of a non-treaty country are concerned." [83]

The net results of China's participation in the World War were disappointing and yet gratifying. She had been defeated in her diplomatic struggle to gain possession of Kiaochou. She had not managed to secure the abrogation of her agree-

[80] Tyau, *op. cit.*, p. 330.
[81] MacMurray, *op. cit.*, Vol. II, p. 1381.
[82] *North China Herald*, CXXXII, Sept. 27, 1919, p. 789.
[83] *North China Herald*, CXXXIII, Oct. 11, 1919, p. 77.

ments of 1915 and 1918 with Japan. The powers had laid aside her request for a general consideration of special foreign rights in China. True, they had at least taken note of the request and had promised to aid her in bringing these matters before the Council and Assembly of the League of Nations. But the League was still an unknown quantity. Originally Chinese officials and others had shown a pronounced interest in the plans for a comprehensive association of free and equal nations.[84] But after the announcement of the Shantung settlement, this early enthusiasm waned perceptibly.[85]

That China gained definite benefits from the World War, however, cannot be denied. The principles concerning self-determination and the rights of weak nations, which had aroused widespread popular interest during the war, may have been misapplied at Paris. But they were still weapons which China might use in future for purposes of both defense and offense. China, moreover, had participated in the most important international conference of the century, and had signed three of the five treaties resulting from that conference. Her request for the redress of her entire list of grievances had at least been noticed. And her very failure to secure a satisfactory settlement of the Shantung question gave her an unparalleled opportunity to present those grievances before the greater bar of public opinion in Western countries. With the termination of her treaties with Germany, Austria, and Hungary, a breach

[84] See *North China Herald*, CXXX, Feb. 15, 1919, p. 388. *Ibid.*, Mar. 1, 1919, p. 521. A telegram to the Chinese delegation at Paris from the Citizens Diplomatic Association on April 10 placed support of the League of Nations first in a list of seven demands which the Chinese delegates were asked to support. *Ibid.*, CXXXI, Apr. 19, 1919, p. 147.

[85] Mr. Millard prepared a memorandum for the Chinese delegation in which he observed (1) the ruling force in any league then constituted would "be the same major Powers that composed the Council of Five at Paris and which made the decision in the Shantung question"; (2) "It is not logical to assume that a League of Nations created by the same body as made the Treaty and in conjunction with the Treaty is designed to reverse the terms of the Treaty"; (3) "It is only the so-called weak nations that are asked to depend for justice and security upon the League of Nations, while the so-called Principal Powers decline to rest their own positions and security on the League alone and plainly regard its assurance to be insufficient." Millard, *Conflict of Policies In Asia*, pp. 79-80.

had been made in the unlovely structure of international servitudes to which she was subject. And it was evident that a breach had been made as well in the ranks of the European powers whose united efforts in the past had served to sustain that structure of foreign rights and privileges. Not only Germany and Austria-Hungary, but Russia as well, had ceased for the moment to be members in good standing of the European concert of powers. Finally, the war had generated in China a widespread and fairly intelligent appreciation of the humiliating position of the country in the family of nations, and a resolute determination in many quarters to work for an improvement in that position. It was not without significance that high officials in both the north and south of China declared that "from now on they would concentrate more attention on the international relationships of China and devote less time to internal politics." [86]

[86] Hollington K. Tong, "The Significance of China's Refusal to sign the Peace Treaty," *Millard's Review of the Far East,* IX, July 12, 1919, p. 219.

CHAPTER IV

CONFIDENT EXPECTATION

ON June 13, 1918, at Tokyo, there was signed a Treaty of Amity between China and Switzerland. The plenipotentiaries were M. Ferdinand de Salis and Mr. Chang Tsung-hsiang, respectively the Swiss and Chinese Ministers to Japan.[1] The treaty was brief. In substance, it provided merely for the reciprocal exchange of diplomatic and consular agents, each of whom was to "enjoy the same rights, privileges, favours, immunities and exemptions as are or may be conceded to the diplomatic and consular agents of the most favored powers." However, by a declaration appended to the treaty, it was agreed that Swiss Consuls in China should enjoy the right to exercise extraterritorial jurisdiction until such time as the other Treaty Powers agreed to abandon their rights in that regard. Furthermore, Swiss citizens in China were to have the benefit of most-favored-nation treatment.

The treaty with Switzerland marked the end of a period in Chinese diplomatic history. It was the last in which China conceded extraterritorial privileges to a foreign power. On April 28, 1919, the very day on which the Three decided at Paris to transfer the Kiaochou leasehold to Japan, the President of China issued a mandate [2] declaring that:

[1] Text, MacMurray, *op. cit.*, II, p. 1429. It should be noted that Minister Chang who signed the treaty on behalf of China was one of the three "traitors" who in May, 1919, was driven from office by the Peking students.

[2] Text, *North China Herald*, CXXXI, May 3, 1919, p. 269. The active campaign for treaty revision had really been commenced by the Chinese Government in 1918 when it sought to establish direct relations with the Vatican, and thereby modify the treaty arrangement for French protection over Roman Catholics in China. Diplomatic negotiations with this in view were first opened in July of 1918, and the Chinese Minister to Madrid, Mr. Tai Ch'en-lin, was instructed to act concurrently as Minister to the Vatican.

"Henceforth, all non-treaty countries wishing to enter into treaty relations with China should do so on the basis of equality. Those severing their connection with their parent countries and establishing independent new states should not be allowed to succeed to the rights and privileges secured in the treaties signed by their parent countries. The peoples of these races now living within Chinese territory in large numbers should all obey and respect Chinese laws and orders in all matters of taxation and litigation. If any Third Power should demand the privileges of protecting them, such demands, one and all, must be rejected. . . . Regulations for the control of such non-treaty subjects should speedily be framed for the guidance of all concerned."

Many mandates on a variety of subjects, each couched in words as brave as these, had appeared before in Chinese history. Too often, however, their actual importance had been literary rather than political and legal; they were rhetorical flourishes rather than solemn commands which must be obeyed with fear and trembling. From the first there were signs, however, that the mandate of April 28 was no mere rhetorical flourish. China's diplomatic defeat at Paris served to breathe life into the new policy, and the popular resentment provoked by that defeat assured the government leaders that they would not lack for support in breaking out into new paths. The principles enunciated in the wartime addresses of President Wilson were

About the same time, Monseigneur Petrelli was nominated as the first papal nuncio to Peking. The French Government immediately protested that this action was in contravention of the Sino-French Treaty of 1858 authorizing it to assume protection over Roman Catholics in China. The Chinese Government, however, claimed that the Treaty of 1858 did not prevent it from entering into diplomatic relations with the Vatican or any other power. In reality, the Chinese Government yielded to French pressure by declining to receive the newly nominated papal nuncio, ostensibly on the grounds of his intimacy with the former German Minister in Peking. At the same time, the Chinese Minister at Madrid was instructed to postpone the presentation of his credentials at the Vatican. Still later, China refused to accept a new papal nominee, Monseigneur Pizani, this time on the ground that he was notoriously pro-Austrian. Tyau, *China Awakened*, pp. 269-70; *North China Herald*. CXXVIII, Aug. 17, 1918, p. 381. In August, the Waichiao Pu gave the French Legation formal assurances that since the nuncios hitherto appointed had proved unacceptable, no representative of the Vatican would be received until after the war. Then a religious and not a political plenipotentiary of the Holy See might be invited to reside at Peking. (*North China Herald*, CXXVIII, Sept. 7, 1918, p. 556.)

accepted seriously throughout the whole of Asia; in China these new ideas had already taken deep root.[3] Altogether, it seemed likely that China would cease henceforth to be content with the crumbs dropped from the international conference tables.

The mandate of April 28, however, reflected merely one aspect of the new diplomatic policy, that with reference to the new nations of Europe. Another aspect, vastly more important, concerned the determination to all patriotic Chinese to see that no opportunity was neglected which seemed likely to hasten the end of foreign domination in China. The World War, among other things, had taught the lesson that nations wax and wane. As a result of circumstances over which the Chinese had little actual control, and in which, indeed, they took little active interest, two of the Great Powers had been compelled to abandon their special treaty rights in China. Other similar opportunities might be expected to present themselves in future. Whatever might happen to the nations of the West, China, with her four thousand years of continuous history, and her apparent genius for muddling through difficult situations, seemed likely to last forever. She would ultimately have the opportunity to rid herself of the network of foreign privileges if only she bided her time. Thus the Chinese policy toward foreign nations after 1919 was one of patient but confident expectation. It was a policy of opportunism, but its object never varied. That object was the elimination piecemeal, where opportunity offered, of Western political control in the country. There was a singleness of purpose about it which had been lacking before. It was not an aggressive policy; instead it rested upon a willingness to wait attentively for changes in the international situation of which China could take advantage. The policy called for patience. But the patience of the Oriental

[3] Professor W. M. McGovern once stated within the hearing of the writer that during his clandestine visit to Lhassa in 1922-3, he found even the Tibetans discussing self-determination. Because of the deficiencies of their language, it had been necessary to coin a new word to express the idea.

is equaled only by his persistence in the face of repeated dis-
couragement.

The international situation seemed to promise that the new
policy of the Chinese Government might meet with more than
a measure of success. The World War had revealed very clearly
that many of the apparently more powerful governments in
the West rested on foundations far less secure than outward
appearances seemed to indicate. In March, 1917, the proud
empire of the Tsars had collapsed in ruins; the upstart succes-
sors of the Romanoffs seemed quite unable to hold together
the vast Russian territories which stretched from the Pacific to
the Black Sea and the Baltic. Less than eighteen months later,
the last scion of the oldest reigning house in Europe was swept
from his throne by a revolution which replaced the Dual Monarchy by a number of new states. Shortly thereafter revolution
passed over Germany also, leaving political chaos in its wake.
And what military defeat and revolution had begun within the
Central Empires was completed by the provisions of treaties
imposed on them by the victors in the war. China had little to
fear, henceforth, from either Germany or what remained of
the old Hapsburg Empire. And even the victors in the war,
burdened as they were with mountainous loads of debt, and
wrestling desperately with problems of social and economic
readjustment arising out of the war, could hardly be expected
to pursue a strong policy, or even a particularly active policy,
in the Far East.

If the World War had laid bare the political instability of
Europe, it had likewise revealed the fact that European unity
was a scarcely veiled myth which need no longer frighten the
Chinese. The structure of foreign rights and privileges in
China, which patriotic Chinese were beginning to find intoler-
ably burdensome, had been created and perpetuated by the
common action of the Great Powers of the West. Now united
action by the powers seemed no longer possible. Russia had
been ostracized, Germany had been shorn of her colonial possessions and was temporarily in eclipse, and the Austro-Hun-

garian Empire had disappeared from the map. Moreover, the circumstances under which the American Senate declined to ratify the Treaty of Versailles, seemed to indicate that the North American republic intended in future to play a lone hand in world politics. For China, the significance of these unexpected developments was that the Doyen of the Diplomatic Body in Peking, whose voice had formerly been so authoritative, would henceforth be able to speak for only a few of the nations of western Europe.

Although the international situation was distinctly favorable to the success of China's new program for treaty revision, the domestic situation was far less so. One of the consequences of China's diplomatic defeat at Paris was the complete breakdown of the internal peace conference at Shanghai. Thereafter the North and the South went their several ways. In Peking, cabinets rose and fell, while the real power remained in the hands of tuchuns or military governors in the provinces. Sometimes the tuchuns coöperated to advance common ends. At other times, they made private war upon each other. Where peace existed in the country, it was a peace based on an armed truce between rival dictators backed by personal armies. Whatever successes China's diplomats managed to win, therefore, would have to be won in spite of the political situation within the country, and not because of it.[4]

Soon after the issuance of the mandate of April 28, 1919, the Peking Government adopted a program of action which, while moderate, left no doubt of its intention to make a distinction between non-treaty aliens and those enjoying special treaty rights. On May 23, regulations were promulgated governing the trial of criminal cases involving the subjects of non-treaty countries.[5] The new rules provided that with certain

[4] For a description of the confused political situation in the country during 1920, see "China in 1920," in *North China Herald*, CXXXVIII, Jan. 15, 1921, pp. 119-125.

[5] Text, *North China Herald*, CXXXI, May 31, 1919, p. 552. These rules were amended on October 30, 1919, so as to apply to all aliens not subject to foreign consular jurisdiction in China. *China Year Book*, 1924, p. 257.

specified exceptions, the first trial of all cases in which non-treaty nationals were concerned should take place in modern district courts of justice. In frontier districts, or in distant places where no such courts existed, the local authorities were to ask the Ministry of Justice for instructions regarding the procedure to be followed in each individual case. Criminals of non-treaty nations were to be imprisoned in modern prisons, or in a suitable building or room serving the same purpose. Chinese laws governing civil and criminal proceedings were to be applied in the trial of all non-treaty aliens.

The rules concerning the trial of cases involving the subjects of non-treaty countries were followed, on June 22, by a set of Regulations Governing Jurisdiction over Aliens of Non-Treaty Countries.[6] These regulations set forth the conditions under which non-treaty aliens might reside, lease houses, do business in the country, and travel in the interior. In most respects, the rights thus accorded were similar to those enjoyed by foreigners having the benefits of existing treaties. However, non-treaty aliens were forbidden to act as editors or publishers of newspapers or magazines, to become members of political societies, or to participate in meetings for political discussion. They were also to "be governed by the general laws and executive orders of the country in addition to the present regulations and other special laws and orders containing provisions for that purpose." Under regulations previously issued, on June 13, citizens of non-treaty countries had been subjected to the same fiscal imposts that the Chinese themselves were compelled to pay.[7]

Other executive decrees followed. In June the Minister of Finance and the Minister of Justice submitted to the President a plan for the creation of a system of modern courts which would cover the entire country. According to the plan, between 1920 and 1924, branch high courts were to be established in the old *tao* (circuits) of all the provinces, and district courts

---

[6] Translated by Hung Tzon-foh, in *Chinese Social and Political Science Review*, IV, No. 2, pp. 180-81. (June, 1919.)

[7] *Far Eastern Review*, XV, p. 569. (August, 1919.)

94   *China's Foreign Relations*

in all old *fu* (prefectures). Between 1925 and 1940, in addition, it was planned to set up district courts in all *hsiens* (districts). In approving the recommendations contained in the joint memorial, the President declared that "in twenty years properly constituted courts are expected to be established in all the districts." With reference to the proposed court system as well as the system of modern prisons, the President said further, "As it is now proposed to abolish the right of consular jurisdiction, more energetic effort should be made with a view to attaining perfection in this respect."[8]

More significant than this ambitious program for the creation of a modern judicial system was the completion and publication of the second revised draft of the criminal code.[9] For five years, a notable group of Chinese and foreign legal experts, headed after 1916 by Dr. Wang Ch'ung-hui, China's foremost jurist, had been engaged in the work of completing this draft.

Not only were non-treaty aliens required to observe the general laws and regulations of China; they were required as well to pay special customs duties, higher than those prescribed in the commercial treaties, on goods which they might import. On December 25, 1917, a Presidential mandate had prescribed the rates which the subjects of non-treaty nations were required to pay.[10] In September, 1919, the Superintendent of Customs at Shanghai was instructed that [11]

"In view of the fact that the fixation of our customs tariff by means of treaty with other Powers is a procedure both prejudicial to our national right and detrimental to our revenue receipts . . . you are hereby instructed to take note that with the exception of

[8] *North China Herald,* CXXXII, July 5, 1919, p. 13. It was estimated that in 1920 the system of modern courts in China included 44 high courts and procuratorates, 38 branch high courts and procuratorates, and the supreme court. Tyau, *China Awakened,* p. 252.
[9] Text, *Chinese Social and Political Science Review,* IV, pp. 144-179, 220-292. For comments on the Code by a jurist who aided in drafting it, see Lo Wen-kan, "Criminal Code of the Republic of China." *Chinese Social and Political Science Review,* IV, pp. 213-218.
[10] *Far Eastern Review,* XIV, p. 58 (February, 1918).
[11] *North China Herald,* CXXXII, Sept. 20, 1919, p. 725.

those cases in which we are bound to respect the treaty-fixed tariff, you are not to apply the tariff newly revised at Shanghai by agreement with other Powers when dealing with the imports in future from all non-treaty countries or from countries with which this country has broken off and cancelled all treaties; that is, you must understand that our country has full right and freedom to fix and impose a national tariff or duty on imports from those countries without let or hindrance. . . . This is very important, constituting as it does our first step toward the retrocession of our full right to fix and impose a national tariff of customs duty ultimately."

The Ministers in Peking of the several Treaty Powers objected to the application of the new national tariff to goods imported by their nationals from non-treaty and ex-treaty countries. It was their contention that in accordance with the most-favored-nation clause, all Treaty Powers were entitled to claim that only the duties specified in the treaty tariff should be imposed on goods imported into China by their nationals, regardless of the country from which such goods came; thus the national tariff should be applied only to goods originally manufactured in non-treaty countries and imported from such countries by non-treaty subjects.[12] To these arguments, the Waichiao Pu returned the answer that [13]

"If the procedure suggested by the Diplomatic Body . . . were to be followed, then the privileges gained by the treaty Powers through the treaty tariff would be given *in toto* to non-treaty Powers. This, it is feared, is contrary to the original purpose of the treaty, while the Chinese Government would have issued its nationally adopted tariff to no purpose at all."

The policy of imposing special duties on imports from non-treaty countries stimulated an immediate desire on the part of their governments for commercial treaties with China. During 1919, Czecho-Slovakia, Greece, and Siam made inquiries of the Chinese Government concerning the tariff rates which would be applied to their products.[14] Representatives of the Czecho-

[12] Tyau, *China Awakened*, p. 283.
[13] *Ibid.*, p. 284.
[14] *North China Herald*, CXXXIV, Jan. 10, 1920, p. 59.

Slovak Government approached Mr. Lu Cheng-hsiang, the head of the Chinese delegation to the Paris Peace Conference, with the suggestion that a treaty be concluded between their respective nations. The Czecho-Slovak representatives proposed that the two countries should exchange ministers and consuls; that China should accord Czecho-Slovakia most-favored-nation treatment, and grant her consuls in China the right to exercise extraterritorial jurisdiction; that a commercial treaty should be negotiated on the most-favored-nation basis; and that Czecho-Slovaks should be allowed to own property and rent houses in China. Mr. Lu consented to discuss proposals for the exchange of diplomatic and consular representatives; the other proposals he rejected entirely.[15]

In the following year, Chile asked for a commercial treaty which would grant extraterritorial rights and secure the admission into China of Chilean nitrates which were then excluded because of their use in the manufacture of munitions.[16] The Governments of Poland and Lithuania likewise desired commercial treaties which would include provisions for the exercise of consular jurisdiction.[17] These overtures, so far as they suggested any extension of the system of consular jurisdiction, met with the unyielding opposition of the Peking Government. The representative of the Greek Government, for example, was informed that while Greek citizens in China would be permitted to enjoy certain commercial privileges, China would never concede to them extraterritorial rights. The Waichiao Pu authorities declared that since China was then engaged in establishing a modern judicial system, it would be inconsistent for the government even to consider a request for the extension of the system of consular jurisdiction which its representatives at Paris

[15] *North China Herald*, CXXXII, Sept. 20, 1919, p. 728. Chinese press translation.
[16] *North China Herald*, CXXXVI, Sept. 25, 1920, p. 819.
[17] *Far Eastern Review*, XVI, p. 173. (March, 1920.) At this time, also, the Government of Afghanistan, for reasons of its own, desired to enter into treaty relations with China. British opposition prevented the negotiations from going beyond the preliminary stage. *Ibid.;* see also P. T. Etherton, *In the Heart of Asia* (Boston and New York, 1926), pp. 217-18.

were doing their utmost to have abolished.[18] In 1920, the Greek Government again opened negotiations for a commercial treaty which would include the grant of extraterritorial privileges; this second venture fared no better than the first.[19]

These, however, were merely negative victories for the new diplomacy. The first positive victory came with the signature, on December 3, 1919, in Tokyo, of a Treaty of Amity between China and Bolivia. The treaty followed exactly the terms of the Tokyo Treaty of 1918 between China and Switzerland, including the provision in Article II that the two countries should exchange diplomatic and consular agents, each of whom was to "enjoy the same rights, privileges, favors, immunities and exemptions as are or may be accorded to the Diplomatic or Consular Agents of the most-favored-nation." However, by a supplementary exchange of notes, the two plenipotentiaries agreed that the most-favored-nation clause of this article did not include the right to extraterritorial jurisdiction in China.[20]

[18] H. K. Tong, "Extraterritoriality and the New Nations," *Millard's Review*, X, Oct. 25, 1919, p. 315.

[19] *North China Herald*, CXXXVI, July 17, 1920, p. 146. Chinese jurisdiction over Greek citizens at this time was impaired by the willingness of French Consuls to extend protection to Greeks. In the late summer of 1920, a Greek resident of Harbin brought suit in a Chinese court against one of his countrymen who was registered with the French Consul. The registered Greek refused to heed the summons of the Chinese court to appear. Chinese court officers then attempted to compel the obstreperous defendant to appear by arresting him. The French Consul immediately interfered and forced the Chinese police to surrender their man. Although the action of the French Consul in this instance lacked justification with reference to any known treaty, he requested his diplomatic superior at Peking to lodge with the Waichiao Pu a "strong protest" against the conduct of the Chinese local authorities. *North China Herald*, CXXXVII, Oct. 16, 1920, p. 153.

[20] Text of the treaty, in *Treaties and Agreements with and Concerning China*, 1919-1929, published by the Carnegie Endowment for International Peace (Washington, 1929), p. 22. French text in *British Foreign and State Papers*, CXXI (1925). For a copy of the supplementary notes exchanged, the writer is indebted to Mr. Lawrence Tsang, formerly of the Ministry of Foreign Affairs, Nanking. Apparently the Bolivian envoy, Mr. V. Munos Reyes, hoped originally that the Chinese Government would concede the grant of extraterritorial rights. The Chinese representative, Mr. Tchuan King-ko, acting on instructions from Peking, declined to proceed with the negotiations on this basis, and Reyes then withdrew his proposal. H. K. Tong, "Extraterritoriality and the New Nations," *Millard's Review*, X, Oct. 25, 1919, p. 314.

Just six months later, the new diplomacy scored its second triumph. On June 1, 1920, General Isaac Khan Mofakhamod-Dowleh and Mr. Wang Kuang-ch'i, respectively Persian and Chinese Ministers to Rome, signed a Treaty of Friendship between their two countries.[21] Article IV of the treaty provided expressly that

"Subjects or citizens of either of the two High Contracting Parties residing or traveling in the country of the other Party shall be subject to the jurisdiction of the country—Persia or China as the case may be—in which they are residing or traveling, as regards legal proceedings, disputes, law-suits, or as regards crimes and offenses which they may commit."

Articles II and V, which provided for the establishment of diplomatic and consular relations, stipulated that the appropriate representatives of each country residing in the territory of the other were to enjoy the same privileges and immunities that were accorded to similar representatives of the most-favored-nations "except in regard to rights in connection with consular jurisdiction."

Meanwhile, on May 26, 1920, the House of Representatives of the Peking Parliament had ratified the Treaty of St. Germain by a vote of 203 to 1. The Senate by a vote of 90 to 1 took similar action three days later.[22]

The treaties with Bolivia and Persia had been new ones establishing regular relations between China and those countries where none had existed before. The agreement which was negotiated with Mexico in 1921 was, by contrast, an actual revision of a treaty already in existence, certain provisions of

[21] The official French text and an English translation are printed in *League of Nations Treaty Series*, No. 240 (1922) Vol. IX, p. 18; the English translation appears also in *Treaties and Agreements*, 1919-1929, pp. 26-27.

[22] *North China Herald*, CXXXV, May 29, 1920, p. 506; June 5, 1920, p. 571. On March 31, 1920, it had been announced in Peking that the government would henceforth place no obstacles in the way of Austrian citizens who desired to return to China. *North China Herald*, CXXXV, April 3, 1920, p. 9.

which were distasteful to both the Chinese and the Mexicans. In December, 1920, a Sino-Mexican commission was set up in Mexico City to study the situation arising out of the denunciation, by the Mexican Government, of the Treaty of December 14, 1919, with China.[23] On September 26, 1921, representatives of the two governments signed an agreement which was to serve as a *modus vivendi* pending the negotiation of a new treaty. The agreement stipulated that the treaty of 1899 was to continue in force until "a definitive and formal amendment of the said Treaty" had been made by the two parties "by the regular procedure as required by" their respective constitutions.[24] In order to meet the wishes of the Mexican Government relative to immigrant laborers, China agreed to the provision (Article II) that

"So long as the Mexican Government prohibits the immigration of foreign laborers, each of the two High Contracting Parties prohibits her citizens of the laborer classes to enter the national territory of the other."

In form, the clause was rendered palatable to the Chinese Government by the fact that it made no discrimination against Oriental laborers as such. Moreover, according to Article XII of the agreement, Chinese agricultural colonists were not to be considered as immigrant laborers. The Mexican Government in turn expressed its willingness (Article XIV) to incorporate in the new treaty, which would supersede that of 1899, a clause providing for the formal renunciation by Mexico of her right to exercise consular jurisdiction in China. The Chinese representative, Mr. Wang Chi-tseng, in taking note of this declaration, voiced the hope that the formal amendment of the treaty would "be made at the earliest possible date." [25]

The foregoing three agreements were all negotiated by Chinese representatives abroad, away from the artificial atmosphere

[23] *North China Herald*, CXXXVII, Dec. 11, 1920, p. 719
[24] Text, *League of Nations Treaty Series*, XIII, p. 201.
[25] Note to A. J. Pani-Rubrica, Sept. 26, 1921, *Ibid*.

which one former member of the Peking Diplomatic Corps has aptly called "le mirage de Pékin." [26] The next agreement, that with Germany, was to be concluded at Peking. As early as March, 1920, the Secretary of the Chinese Legation in Berlin received intimations from the German Government that it was desirous of seeing a resumption of commercial relations between the two countries. Learning of these overtures, the Waichiao Pu notified its representative in Berlin that it was not averse from resuming relations, provided Germany agreed to recognize Chinese rights under the Versailles Treaty. Meanwhile, the Chinese Government would raise no objection should Germany decide to send a commercial agent to represent German interests unofficially in China. [27] During the following month, the Peking Government published rules to govern the readmission of Germans into China. [28] Such German citizens as desired to enter the country were required to carry passports issued by Chinese Ministers or Consuls abroad. However, only the Ministry of Interior and the Waichiao Pu could grant permission for the return of such German nationals as had been expatriated following the armistice of November, 1918.

Negotiations between the Chinese and the German Governments were initiated by Dr. Wilhelm Solf, the newly appointed German Ambassador to Japan. In the summer of 1920, following the arrival of a German agent in the Chinese capital, these negotiations were transferred to Peking. Conversations extending over a period of six months resulted in a general under-

[26] Comte Sforza, *L'Enigme Chinoise* (Paris, 1928), Ch. XXI. The active interest of the Chinese Government in foreign affairs at this time is reflected in its decision, despite the ever-present financial stringency, to increase its diplomatic representation abroad. A program prepared by the Cabinet and approved by Parliament called for the appointment of a Chinese Minister to Mexico who was to act concurrently as Minister to Cuba. A Minister was likewise to be accredited jointly to Norway and Sweden, and a chargé d'affaires was to be sent to Bolivia. The policy of the Peking Government, according to one of its diplomatic representatives, was that of giving careful attention to the changing international situation. *Millard's Review*, XIII, July 24, 1920, pp. 419-20.

[27] *North China Herald*, CXXXIV, Mar. 20, 1920, p. 748. Chinese press translation.

[28] *North China Herald*, CXXXV, Apr. 24, 1920, p. 186.

standing on all points between the representatives of the two governments. An obstacle then arose through the insistence of the German Foreign Office that China assume responsibility for the redemption of certain Chinese railway bonds held by German nationals.[29] A second delay resulted from the Allied occupation of a number of German cities in the Rhineland.

The Chinese and German representatives finally agreed upon the text of an agreement which was signed in Peking on May 20, 1921.[30] The agreement was prefaced by a Declaration made by the German plenipotentiary. This Declaration included the statement that future relations between Germany and China "should be based on principles of complete equality and absolute reciprocity in accordance with the rules of international law." Germany declared also that "owing to the events of the war and the Treaty of Versailles" she had been compelled to renounce all of her rights and privileges in Shantung and was therefore "deprived of the possibility of restoring them to China." Germany consented also to "the abrogation of consular jurisdiction in China." Finally, she renounced in favor of China all rights which the German Government possessed "in respect of the 'glacis' appertaining to the German Legation at Pekin. . . ."

The agreement itself consisted of seven articles. In the preface, the two governments expressed their agreement that "the application of the principles of respect for territorial sovereignty, of equality and of reciprocity is the only means of maintaining good relations between peoples. . . ." Article I provided that the two parties should have the right to send to each other duly accredited diplomatic agents, each of whom was to enjoy "the privileges and immunities granted to them by international law." Provision was made in Article II for the exchange of consular agents who were to "be treated with the

[29] *Millard's Review*, XVI, Mar. 26, 1921, pp. 173-4.
[30] Texts of the German Declaration, the Sino-German Agreement, and the supplementary exchange of notes are printed in *League of Nations Treaty Series*, No. 261 (1922), Vol. IX, pp. 283-89.

consideration and respect granted to agents of the same category in the service of other nations." According to Article III, "The nationals of either of the two Republics residing in the territory of the other shall have the right, in accordance with the laws and regulations of the country, to travel, settle, and carry on commerce or industry in all places where nationals of any other nation are entitled to do so." And "in respect of their persons and property, they shall be subject to the jurisdiction of the local courts, and must comply with the laws of the country in which they reside. They shall pay no duties, taxes, or contributions in excess of those paid by the nationals of that country." Thus while German citizens in China were obliged to obey Chinese laws and to recognize the jurisdiction of Chinese courts, they were given only the same privileges of residence and trade in the interior of the country that nationals of the Treaty Powers enjoyed.[31]

By the fourth Article, the two parties recognized "that all matters relating to Customs shall be regulated solely by the internal legislation of the respective parties. Nevertheless, no duties higher than those paid by nationals of the country shall be charged on products, whether raw or manufactured, coming from one of the two Republics or from another country, when such products are imported, exported, or in transit." Article V stipulated that the German Declaration and the provi-

[31] At first sight, the provisions of Article III seem somewhat strange. Aside from missionaries who are covered by special clauses of the treaties, foreigners in China are restricted to the treaty ports as regards trade and residence; they have no legal right to enter the interior except with a special passport issued for the purpose by the Chinese authorities. Even if not rigidly enforced, these restrictions are doubtless necessary as long as alien residents of the country continue to enjoy immunity from Chinese laws and from the jurisdiction of Chinese courts. It has frequently been suggested, however, that the Chinese Government would be willing to open the entire country to foreign residence and trade whenever the foreign powers agreed to abandon their rights in connection with consular jurisdiction. But if the Chinese Government had consented in the present instance to open the whole of the interior to German trade and residence, it is obvious that the same right would have extended immediately, under the most-favored-nation clauses of the treaties, to other foreigners who still retained their extraterritorial rights.

sions of the present agreement were to be taken as the basis for the negotiation of a final treaty between the two countries.

Questions other than those dealt with in the agreement were adjusted by a supplementary exchange of notes which were given the same date as the more formal agreement. "In order to satisfy the Chinese demands for reparations," the German Government undertook to pay four million dollars in cash and the rest in Tientsin-Pukow and Hukwang railway debentures. This payment, the full amount of which was to be fixed by mutual agreement, was to approximate half the proceeds of the sale of German property in China already liquidated and half the value of the property sequestrated. Chinese movable and real property in Germany was to be restored *in toto*. China on her part promised to put an end forthwith to the liquidation of German property and, on receipt of the above-mentioned reparations payment, to hand over to their owners all proceeds of liquidation and all property still sequestrated. The assurance was given also that the Chinese Government would grant full protection to Germans in China in the peaceful exercise of their several professions, and that it would not again confiscate their property "save in accordance with the generally recognized principles of international law or the provisions of Chinese law," provided the German Government adopted the same policy with regard to Chinese nationals living in Germany. The German Government was assured, further, that "all law-suits in China in which Germans are involved will be decided before the newly established courts, with right of appeal." China consented also that German barristers and interpreters, officially accredited to the courts, might act as counsel during the proceedings. With regard to proceedings before mixed courts, in which Germans were plaintiffs or defendants, China promised to seek a solution which would be just to all parties. The rights of German owners of trade-marks were to be restored after they had been re-registered at the Maritime Customs Office.

As to the tariff, the Chinese Government announced that until the autonomous customs regulations came into general operation, German imports would be required to pay customs duties "as provided in the general Customs regulations." [32]

While the Chinese Foreign Office was thus engaged in building up a body of precedent favorable to the general reconsideration of her treaties with foreign powers, other opportunities presented by the international situation were not being neglected. One of the grievances of which the Chinese delegation to the Paris Conference had complained was the continued existence of foreign postal establishments in China. German and Russian post offices had already disappeared from the country by the end of 1920, when the Chinese Government inaugurated a movement for the withdrawal of similar establishments maintained by the other powers in the country. [33] The Chinese Government insisted that these foreign post offices had originally been established and still continued to operate without any sanction in the treaties. Moreover, they were being run in competition with the efficiently managed Chinese Post Office which had been admitted in 1914 to membership in the Universal Postal Union. Consequently, the Chinese delegate to the Congress of the Universal Postal Union which met at

[32] The Sino-German Agreement of 1921 was supplemented by two notes dated June 6 and 7, 1924, addressed by the Foreign Minister, Dr. Wellington Koo, to the German Minister in Peking, Dr. Boyé. The notes provided for the restoration of property belonging to the Deutsch-Asiatische Bank, for the final liquidation of Chinese claims against Germany and of German claims against China arising out of the war, and for the resumption of interest payments on certain bonds of the Chinese Government originally held in Germany. *Treaties and Agreements,* 1919-1929, pp. 144-147.
[33] At the outbreak of the World War, Germany had 17 post offices in China while Russia had 28. The Chinese Post Office ceased to have any relations with the German post offices after March 14, 1917, and they were forced to close. The last of the Russian postal system in China disappeared in September, 1920, after the Chinese Government ceased to recognize Prince Koudacheff, the representative in Peking of the defunct Tsarist Government. Of the remaining foreign post offices in the country, Great Britain maintained 11, France 15, the United States one (at Shanghai), and Japan 44. It was charged, apparently justly, that the many Japanese post offices in China were used to smuggle opium and other contraband into the country, and also to advance Japanese political ambitions there. *Far Eastern Review,* XV, Dec. 4, 1920, pp. 2-3.

Madrid October 1, 1920, was instructed to raise the question of their continued existence. The Chinese representative, Mr. Liu Fu-cheng, first approached the postal delegates of Great Britain, France, and the United States regarding the matter. While expressing sympathy with Chinese aspirations, the delegates of all three powers advised against bringing up the question at the moment. They pointed out that it would be difficult to secure proper consideration of the Chinese proposal by the delegates of more than sixty nations, most of which had no post offices in China and were therefore not directly concerned with the problem.[34] The American delegate, however, notified the Chinese representative that he was authorized by his government, "to say that the United States is sympathetic with the desire of the Chinese Government that all foreign Post Offices be withdrawn from its territories and would be glad to join in a unanimous action of all foreign countries to discontinue postal operations of all other nations within the territory of China." The American delegate also expressed the opinion that "the Postal Administration of your country is entitled to the approval and respect of the entire world in the matter of the efficiency of your postal operations.[35] The Congress itself reflected the opinions of the British, French, and American Governments by intimating that the problem of foreign post offices in China was one coming properly within the purview of the foreign offices concerned. However, a resolution was passed to the effect that only such foreign postal agencies could be considered as within the Universal Postal Union as were established in a foreign country not itself within the Union.[36]

[34] *Millard's Review*, XV, Dec. 4, 1920, p. 2.
[35] Otto Praeger, Second Assistant Postmaster General, to Liu Fu-cheng, Director General of the Chinese Posts, *Conference on the Limitation of Armaments*, p. 952.
[36] *Ibid.*, p. 942. Apparently Mr. Liu did not seek the advice of the Japanese delegate to the Madrid Congress. From Peking, however, came the report that the representative there of one of the powers—presumably Japan—defended the system of foreign postal agencies on grounds of military necessity. *North China Herald*, CXXXVII, Nov. 27, 1920, p. 589.

More serious than the grievance connected with foreign postal agencies was the system of consular jurisdiction. The Chinese statement at Paris dealing with the latter problem merely marked the beginning of a campaign of "popular education" in foreign countries designed to bring about the abrogation of the system. The subject of extraterritoriality was raised discreetly at many social gatherings in Peking attended by foreigners and by Chinese of the "returned student" class. Moreover, President Hsü Shih-ch'ang in his farewell audiences with various prominent Chinese about to leave for foreign countries, particularly those bound for Geneva, impressed upon them that they must campaign abroad for the abrogation of the humiliating extraterritorial clauses in the treaties.[37] Meanwhile the Chinese commission on the codification of laws continued steadily at work. And in May, 1921, it was reported that the Chinese Foreign Office had instructed its representatives accredited to Washington, London, and Paris, to approach those governments with a formal proposal for direct negotiations looking to the gradual abandonment of consular jurisdiction.[38] Chinese hopes in this direction were undoubtedly stimulated by the signature at Washington, on December 16, 1920, of a treaty between the United States and Siam. By this treaty, the American Government renounced, in effect, its rights to exercise consular jurisdiction in Siamese territory.

In the period immediately preceding the Washington Conference, three other developments tended to reveal the mettle of the Chinese Foreign Office and the trend of its policy. These were the protest against the renewal in its existing form of the Anglo-Japanese Alliance, the refusal to enter into direct negotiations with Japan for the settlement of the Shantung question, and the termination of the Sino-Japanese military and naval agreements of 1918 and 1919.

[37] Rodney Gilbert, "The Foreigner's Rights in China," *North China Herald*, CXXXVIII, Mar. 26, 1921, p. 822.
[38] Yee K. York, "China on the Way to Finding Herself," *Millard's Review*, XVI, May 28, 1921, p. 679.

The ten-year term for which the Anglo-Japanese Alliance had been renewed in 1911 was due to expire July 13, 1921. Thereafter the treaty might be denounced by either party. In the early spring of 1920, the Chinese Minister to London was instructed to make formal inquiries at the British Foreign Office concerning the matter, and to point out that "the treatment of China merely as a territorial entity in the written text of any such agreements would no longer be tolerated by the public opinion of the country and would, indeed, be viewed by all as an unfriendly act." [39] In response to his inquiries, the Chinese Minister received from the British Government a verbal assurance that the question of the renewal or termination of the Alliance had not yet come up for consideration; that inasmuch as the successive agreements between Japan and Great Britain dealing with the subject had been couched in the same language, it followed naturally that if the Alliance were renewed, it would be along lines similar to those adopted in the past. [40] In June, the Chinese Foreign Office made public a memorandum showing that the wording of the three Anglo-Japanese agreements differed, and that the agreement of 1911 clearly recognized the fact that certain changes had taken place. "In view, then," it declared, "of the fact that beneath the framework of what is on the surface a self-denying ordinance, vital and far-reaching changes have acquired the sanction of the high contracting parties, Chinese opinion is not unnaturally distrustful of any renewal of this agreement, all men holding that China has suffered enough from its operation during the World War in the matter of Shantung." It was pointed out, further, that since China had ratified the Austrian treaty and was therefore a member of the League of Nations, "which she assumes was created in good faith," she considered, "that a contract regarding her affairs between other members of the League cannot be entered into without her prior consent having been

[39] Waichiao Pu statement June 6, 1920, *North China Herald*, CXXXV, June 12, 1920, p. 642.
[40] *Ibid.*

obtained, Article 10 being a sufficient guarantee that her territorial integrity will be respected." [41]

Apparently recognizing the force of the Chinese contention that the Treaty of Alliance conflicted with the Covenant of the League, the British and Japanese Governments agreed upon a declaration, dated July 8, 1920, which recognized that the Treaty of 1911 was not entirely consistent with the letter of the Covenant, and that if it were renewed after 1921, it would have to be "in a form which is not inconsistent with that Covenant." [42]

Even this declaration regarding the purposes of the Japanese and the British Governments did not set entirely at rest the fears of the Waichiao Pu officials. In the spring of 1921, the Chinese Government launched a determined campaign to warn the British Dominions concerning the serious political consequences which might follow a renewal of the Alliance, and to enlist their support in the effort to have it terminated. In April, 1921, Dr. Wang Ch'ung-hui, Chief Justice of the Supreme Court of China, crossed Canada on his way to Geneva, where he was to participate with nine other delegates representing the nations of the world in the work of revising the Covenant of the League. On landing at Vancouver, Dr. Wang issued a lengthy statement of more than ordinary significance. [43] He declared that at the moment China had "three dread ene-

---

[41] Waichiao Pu statement, *op. cit.* The views of the Waichiao Pu regarding the Alliance were shared by many influential Chinese, especially in Shanghai. On the occasion of his departure for England, the British Minister to China, Sir Beilby Alston, was handed a memorandum subscribed to by eleven Chinese organizations in Shanghai, representing educators, bankers, industrialists, students, and foreign-trained Chinese. The memorandum declared that Japan had taken advantage of British activities during the war to violate the objects of the Alliance by imposing the Twenty-One Demands on China. China was diplomatically independent, and her people would resent any attempt to treat her as semi-dependent. As a member of the League, furthermore, China had a right to appeal the Shantung question to that body. Any renewal of the Alliance would indicate to the Chinese people that another attempt was being made to settle China's case out of court without her consent. *North China Herald,* CXXXVI, July 10, 1920, pp. 79-80. *Millard's Review,* XIII, July 10, 1920.

[42] *Treaties and Agreements,* 1919-1929, p. 29.

[43] Text, *North China Herald,* CXXXIX, May 14, 1921, p. 459.

mies." These were Article Twenty-One of the Covenant of the League, the Anglo-Japanese Alliance, and the Lansing-Ishii notes of 1917. The Chinese jurist stated that Article Twenty-One of the Covenant laid down "the untenable doctrine of regional understandings, which is not only a direct challenge to China's integrity because of its interpretation, but which is destructive of the League itself, since it permits all member powers to form private groups to exploit in their own interests the territories and waters of neighboring member powers." The Anglo-Japanese Alliance was criticized as an arrangement tending to provoke war in the Pacific in which China would be aligned with the United States against Japan and Great Britain. Dr. Wang declared that "China is determined to force these three issues to a satisfactory conclusion this summer, as she fully recognizes that so long as they remain in their present condition, so long will her progress and stability be menaced."

In addition to pointing out the danger of a Pacific war in case the powers continued to neglect China's problems, Dr. Wang revealed two other possible consequences of such neglect. He stated that "China, on March 18, communicated to the American representative of the consortium in the presence of the American Minister to Peking an important decision, which it is too soon to make public in detail, but which is practically the death knell of the consortium and the international program as decided at Paris unless very radical modifications in the present international situation speedily come." In veiled language, he then alluded to the possibility that further British mistakes in the Far East might breed conditions favorable to the growth of Bolshevist influence in China which would have a damaging effect on British interests there.[44]

---

[44] These arguments were supplemented by another, put forward in a telegram sent to the British Cabinet and Parliament on June 12, 1921, by eighteen commercial and other Chinese bodies in Shanghai. The message stated that "the relations between the Chinese and British people have always been of the friendliest nature, but since the conclusion of the Anglo-Japanese Alliance that friendship has been growing colder. There is not a single person in the Orient who does not see that the Japanese are trying to dominate the Far East. They are depending upon the Alliance for

The Chinese Chief Justice declared that in the settlement of such matters as these, China could no longer be ignored. "As the power possessing by far the greatest interests on the western littoral of the Pacific, she is now setting to work through the whole network of her international relations to preserve her rights. I believe that the Canadian Government, when it is put in possession of all the facts, will take a view identical to China's and become a very valuable factor in the inauguration of a new and proper policy."

During the next month, Dr. Wang and Mr. B. Lennox Simpson who accompanied him, lost no opportunity to educate the Canadian people and their government regarding the serious nature of the situation in the Pacific area. At Ottawa, Mr. Simpson, who was acting as an unofficial representative of the Chinese Government, managed to arouse the interest of the Candian Premier, Mr. Arthur Meighen, to whom he presented a memorandum setting forth China's views on the subject of the Anglo-Japanese Alliance.[45] Later, following his arrival in London, Mr. Simpson had interviews with various British officials on the same subject.[46] Publicly, he announced that before leaving Peking he had been informed by the Chinese Minister of Foreign Affairs that China would regard the renewal of the Treaty of Alliance as a formal ratification by Great Britain of Japan's policy toward China during the war, especially in the matter of Shantung.[47]

The problem thus presented, carrying with it the possibility that the British Dominions might be called upon to support

support. If the Alliance is renewed in any form whatever, our relations will become estranged, for not only will it injure our friendly relations, but it is sure to be detrimental to British commerce in China." Other telegrams of similar tenor were sent to the Governments of Canada, Australia, and India, to the American Congress, and to the Governments of France and Italy. For full texts of these telegrams, see *North China Herald*, CXXXIX, June 18, 1921, p. 791.

[45] Text, Putnam Weale (B. L. Simpson), *An Indiscreet Chronicle from the Pacific*, pp. 53-58.

[46] *Ibid.*, pp. 95 ff.

[47] *North China Herald*, CXXXIX, June 11, 1921, p. 724.

Japan's pretensions on the Asiatic mainland, was raised in an acute form in the British Imperial Conference which opened June 20. The British Government was placed in an embarrassing position when the Canadian Premier, on June 29, circulated a confidential memorandum declaring that if the Anglo-Japanese Alliance were renewed, it would not be binding upon Canada unless ratified by the Dominion Parliament.[48] Faced with Chinese and Canadian opposition, in addition to the known opposition of the United States to any renewal of the Alliance in its existing form, the British Government had reason to welcome President Harding's opportune call for an international conference on disarmament and Pacific problems. In consequence of the Washington Conference, the Anglo-Japanese pact was to be abandoned in favor of a Four Power Treaty signed by Great Britain, Japan, the United States, and France.

While the Chinese Government was thus voicing its opposition to any renewal of the unmodified Anglo-Japanese Treaty of Alliance, it was also being compelled to deal with the problem raised by Japan's desire to negotiate regarding the still unsettled Shantung problem. On January 20, 1920, immediately following the coming into force of the Treaty of Versailles, the Waichiao Pu received from Mr. Torikichi Obata, the Japanese Minister in Peking, a note indicating the willingness of the Japanese Government to open negotiations for the return of Shantung to China.[49] Several weeks afterward, President Hsü Shih-ch'ang circularized the officials of the provinces, asking their opinion regarding the proposal for direct negotiations with Japan. The answers to this circular telegram revealed that the provinces opposed such direct negotiations, and favored instead submission of the entire Shantung question to the League of Nations.[50] In April, the National Students' Federa-

[48] Weale, *op. cit.*, pp. 107-8.
[49] Statement of the Japanese Ministry of Foreign Affairs, June 15, 1920, *China Year Book*, 1921-22, p. 717.
[50] *North China Herald*, CXXXVIII, Jan. 15, 1921, p. 123.

tion sent an ultimatum to the Peking Government protesting vehemently against direct negotiations with Japan.[51]

Finally, on May 22, 1920, the Chinese Government returned an answer to the Japanese note of January 20.[52] The government took the position that since China had not signed the peace treaty with Germany, there was no need for negotiations based on the provisions of that treaty. Note was taken, however, of Japan's declared intention to restore Kiaochou, and the request was made that since the Japanese military establishments located along the Kiaochou-Tsinan Railway were no longer necessary, they should be withdrawn. China was intent on avoiding any action which might be construed as formal recognition by her of the objectionable clauses of the Treaty of Versailles. The resentment provoked in Tokyo by this refusal to enter into direct negotiations was plainly evident in Japan's next note.[53] The Japanese Government, noting that China declined to negotiate on the ground that her representatives had refrained from signing the treaty with Germany, pointed to the existence of "a formal agreement between the two governments as to the fundamental principle governing the settlement of the question. . . ." Furthermore, "it is a positive fact that all the rights and interests which Germany formerly possessed in Shantung . . . have been transferred to Japan in accordance with the Treaty of Peace. The Chinese Government having . . . pledged themselves beforehand to acknowledge and consent to this transfer, these rights and interests have of right come into the possession of Japan, irrespective of whether or not the Chinese Government have signed the Peace Treaty with Germany." The Japanese note suggested that China must bear the responsibility for the delay in settling the question at issue,

[51] *North China Herald*, CXXXV, Apr. 17, 1920, p. 121. The tone of this telegram to President Hsü and his cabinet is suggested by its opening sentence: "We have for a long time known that you are traitors." When the Peking Government continued to delay an announcement of its policy, the students issued a call for a nation-wide strike.

[52] Text, *China Year Book*, 1921-22, pp. 717-18.

[53] Text, *Ibid.*, p. 718.

and expressed the hope that the Chinese Government would reconsider its decision not to negotiate.

The Chinese Government, however, showed no inclination to modify its attitude. Instead, preparations were made to submit the question to the Council of the League. These preparations came to a halt when the Chinese delegates at Geneva learned as a result of preliminary inquiries that the British and French Foreign Offices still felt bound to support the spirit of their commitments made to the Japanense Government in February and March, 1917, until such time as the Shantung question had finally been disposed of to the satisfaction of Japan.[54] After making this discovery, the Chinese delegates in the first Assembly of the League, meeting from November 15 to December 18, 1920, bent their efforts toward securing for China a non-permanent seat on the Council. Despite the opposition of Japan, these efforts were successful.[55] Subsequently, on December 18, 1920, Dr. Wellington Koo, as the chief Chinese delegate, read before the Assembly a statement announcing that his government reserved the right at any time thereafter to bring China's case before the Council.[56]

In September, 1921, the Japanese Government made a second attempt to open direct negotiations with China for the retrocession of the Kiaochou leasehold. This overture fared no better than the one initiated in the previous year.[57] Toward the end of October, in spite of the fact that it had already accepted an invitation to attend the Washington Conference, the Chinese Government instructed Dr. Koo, its representative at the League, regarding the specific terms on which

[54] T. F. Millard, *Conflict of Policies in Asia*, p. 153.
[55] Millard, *op. cit.*, p. 154.
[56] *New York Times Current History*, XIII, Part 2, p. 13 (January, 1921).
[57] Statement of the Japanese Ministry of Foreign Affairs, *Japan Year Book*, 1921-22, pp. 339-345. For the Chinese reply to this statement, see *North China Herald*, CXLI, Nov. 5, 1921, p. 362; *Ibid.*, Nov. 12, 1921, p. 426.

China would agree to a final settlement of the Kiaochou dispute.[58]

If this exchange of correspondence revealed that the views of the two governments regarding Shantung were still far apart, negotiations in other directions were more successful. The Sino-Japanese military and naval agreements of 1918 and 1919, concluded ostensibly for the purpose of joining forces to combat the Bolshevist menace from Siberia, had never been popular in China. One of the demands made by the students during their strike of April and May, 1920, had been that the Peking Government bring these agreements to an end. On January 28, 1921, the objectionable agreements were finally terminated by an exchange of notes between the Chinese Minister for Foreign Affairs and the Japanese Minister in Peking.[59]

[58] *North China Herald*, CXLI, Nov. 5, 1921 p. 361. It is impossible to know whether these gestures of the Chinese Government in the direction of Geneva were made with serious intent, or whether they were merely a means of forcing a modification of the terms on which Japan agreed to surrender the Kiaochou leasehold. Their effect, in any case, was to compel the Japanese Government to modify very seriously its original proposals to the Chinese Government on the subject.

[59] Texts, *Treaties and Agreements*, 1919-1929, pp. 45-47.

CHAPTER V

THE LIQUIDATION OF RUSSIAN INTERESTS IN CHINA
1917–1921

THE revolution which broke out in Russia in 1917 had consequences whose ultimate effect on the structure of foreign
rights and privileges in China was only less important than
that produced by the World War. The collapse of Tsarist
authority in European Russia, culminating in the Bolshevist
coup d'état of November, 1917, had speedy repercussions in
the Far East. A long frontier separated Siberia from the territories belonging to China. As disorder spread across the Urals
into Asiatic Russia, this straggling land frontier, virtually un-
defended throughout much of its length, became the scene of
recurring border troubles. China's territorial sovereignty was
ignored more than once by bands of irregulars which crossed
and recrossed the frontier with little if any interference. Thousands of Russian aristocrats, fleeing before the Bolshevist hurri-
cane, found havens of refuge in the cities of Manchuria and
northern China. Thereafter, in comparative safety, they plotted
and intrigued for the restoration of the old régime in Russia.
Harbin in particular became a veritable hotbed of anti-Bolshevist intrigue.

It was at Harbin, also, that the Chinese Government was
compelled for the first time to deal with the situation caused
by the spread of Bolshevism to the Far East. Shortly after the
Bolshevist seizure of power in Petrograd, orders were sent to
Russian Workers' Delegates at Harbin to take over the control
of the Chinese Eastern Railway zone from General Horvath
who, as director of the Railway, maintained the pretense of
representing the defunct Kerensky Government. The members

115

of the foreign consular body at Harbin promptly informed Horvath that they would decline to recognize the authority of the delegates, and that they would support him fully in whatever steps he might take to preserve order within the railway zone.[1] When it became evident that General Horvath's authority over his railway guards was crumbling, the consular body, on November 22, 1917, drew up a formal program for Allied military intervention in case Chinese military police could not be procured in sufficient numbers to handle the situation.[2] Meanwhile, the delegates, their position strengthened by a personal telegram from Lenin, made formal demands on General Horvath that the administration of the railway zone should be turned over to them.

In the interval, the Chinese authorities had become aroused by rumors that the new Russian Government intended to conclude a separate peace with the Central Powers, and also that it contemplated the establishment in Harbin of a committee having power to control all trade across the Russian frontier. Consequently, on December 5, the local Taoyin, Sze Shaochang, informed the consular body that the Chinese Government would oppose Bolshevist participation in the administration of the railway zone, and that Chinese troops had been dispatched from Kirin to intervene if and when necessary.[3] Despite these precautions, the delegates, on December 12, assumed physical control of the railway administration, and six days later they issued an order dismissing from office General Horvath and various other railway officials. Thereupon the Chinese Government, prompted by the Harbin consular body, sent 7,000 troops to the region.[4] The local Chinese officials, however, were still hesitant, and the next few days were spent in negotiations between them and representatives of the Workers' Delegates. Finally, on Christmas Day, the British, French, Japanese, and American consular representatives called upon

[1] *Far Eastern Review*, XV, p. 298. (March, 1919.)
[2] *Ibid.*   [3] *Ibid.*
[4] *Ibid.;* Ken Shen Weigh, *Russo-Chinese Diplomacy* (Shanghai, 1928), p. 220.

the Chinese Taoyin to demand action. The next morning at dawn, Chinese military forces disarmed all Russian troops, who were showing distinct signs of Bolshevist leanings, and loaded them on trains for shipment across the frontier into Siberia.[5] Following this reassertion of Chinese authority in a region where it had long been suspended, the Chinese Government established military police throughout the Russian Settlement at Harbin, and set up customs stations there and at other cities along the railway. Bureaus for the examination of passports were likewise set up at Harbin and at frontier stations, and in spite of the protest of the Russian Minister in Peking,[6] an embargo was laid on exports from Manchuria into Asiatic Russia.[7] On January 2, 1918, the Peking Government, asserting a right which had not been exercised since 1900, appointed Kuo Hsiang-hsi, Civil Governor of Kirin, as President of the Chinese Eastern Railway.[8] In May, the Chinese Government notified the Russian Minister that it felt itself bound no longer by the terms of the Russo-Chinese Agreement of 1916 relative to restrictions on the liquor traffic along the Sungari River.[9]

Another immediate consequence of the Russian Revolution was the reassertion of Chinese authority in Outer Mongolia. In 1912, seizing the opportunity presented by the revolutionary upheaval in China, and relying on the promise of aid from Russia, the princes and rulers of Outer Mongolia had declared their independence.[10] Formal agreements between Russia and Mongolia, the first signed at Urga, November 3, 1912,[11] and the second at Kiachta on September 30, 1914,[12] provided in substance for a Russian protectorate over Outer Mongolia and for Russian preferential rights in the exploitation of the region's natural resources. Protracted negotiations between China and

[5] *Far Eastern Review, op. cit.; North China Herald,* CXXVI, Jan. 12, 1918, pp. 70-71; Weigh, *op. cit.,* p. 221.
[6] *China Year Book,* 1921-22, p. 624.
[7] *Far Eastern Review,* XV, p. 298. (March, 1919.)
[8] *Millard's Review,* III, Jan. 5, 1918, p. 161.
[9] *China Year Book,* 1921-22, pp. 624, 627.
[10] *China Year Book,* 1921-22, pp. 572-3.
[11] MacMurray, *op. cit.,* Vol. II, p. 992.   [12] *Ibid.,* p. 1178.

118   *China's Foreign Relations*

Russia regarding the matter resulted finally in the tri-partite Treaty of Kiachta, signed on June 7, 1915, by representatives of Russia, China, and Mongolia.[13] By the terms of this agreement, Chinese suzerainty over Mongolia was recognized to the extent that it did not conflict with Russia's political and economic rights there, or with the right of the Mongols to govern themselves without interference on the part of the Chinese authorities.

In 1917, Mongolian trade with Siberia, which had been greatly stimulated by the commercial treaty of 1912 with Russia, came virtually to an end in consequence of disturbed conditions in the latter area. Thereupon, the pro-Chinese faction among the Mongol princes began to agitate for a restoration of the old political and commercial relations between Mongolia and China. During the latter part of 1918, Chinese official interest in the former dependency was stimulated by reports from both the Chinese Resident at Urga and from the Tuchun of Chahar concerning Bolshevist intrigue in Mongolia.[14] Rumors spread also that Ataman Semenov, the youthful and unscrupulous commander of a band of Buriats waging guerrilla warfare against the radicals near Chita, was scheming to set up, presumably under Japanese protection, a Pan-Mongolian empire consisting of Inner and Outer Mongolia, Hulunbuir, Trans-Baikalia, and Tibet.[15]

By the terms of the Treaty of Kiachta (Article VII), the number of military guards which the Chinese Government was allowed to maintain in Mongolia for the protection of its four representatives there was not to exceed a total of 350 men. In spite of this restriction, the Chinese forces in Mongolia were materially strengthened during March, 1919. On April 3, the Russian Minister in Peking, Prince Koudacheff, protested that this military activity violated the provisions of the treaty of

[13] *Ibid.*, p. 1239; E. T. Williams, "The Relations between China, Russia, and Mongolia," *American Journal of International Law*, X, pp. 798-808 (1916).
[14] *North China Herald*, CXXIX, Oct. 5, 1918, pp. 20-21.
[15] *Millard's Review*, VIII, Mar. 29, 1919, pp. 157-60; *China Year Book*, 1921-22, p. 576.

1915.[16] Ignoring this protest, the Chinese Government, in July, took active steps to bring about a full restoration of its political authority in Outer Mongolia. The War Participation Bureau, which had been created for the ostensible purpose of organizing a Chinese expeditionary force to be used in France, was transformed into a Frontiers Protection Bureau, with General Tuan Ch'i-jui at its head.[17] As part of the new arrangement, General Hsü Shu-tseng, one of the most ambitious and least scrupulous of the Anfu militarists, was appointed Defense Commissioner for the Northwest Frontiers.[18]

During the summer of 1919, the Chinese Resident at Urga made repeated but unsuccessful attempts to persuade the Hutukhtu, or Living Buddha, and the Mongolian princes of the advantages to be gained by cancelling their declaration of autonomy which had been written into the tri-partite treaty of 1915.[19] By October, General Hsü was on the scene with 4,000 Chinese troops at his back. The methods of bribery which he used at first were no more successful than the persuasive arguments of the Chinese Resident had been. The Hutukhtu, the titular ruler of the country, refused to receive Hsü in audience, and sought to relieve the pressure on himself by asking the legislative body to consider the question as to whether Mongolian autonomy should be cancelled. The legislators voted against the proposition.[20] Thereupon General Hsü issued an ultimatum threatening that unless, within thirty-six hours, the Mongolians asked for a cancellation of their autonomy, the Living Buddha would be taken as a prisoner to Kalgan.[21]

The Mongolian leaders were thus left with only one choice.

[16] *North China Herald,* CXXXI, Apr. 5, 1919, p. 13. The Chinese Government had previously asked Koudacheff to restrain the activities of Semenov, and especially to put a stop to his intrigues in Mongolia. Chinese troops were dispatched following the Russian Minister's confession that he was unable to exercise any restraint over the forces of the Buriat leader. *Millard's Review,* VIII, Apr. 19, 1919, pp. 272-3.
[17] Presidential mandate of July 20, *North China Herald,* CXXXII, July 26, 1919, p. 209.
[18] *China Year Book,* 1921-22, p. 576.
[19] *China Year Book,* 1921-22, p. 577; Weigh, *op. cit.,* p. 190.
[20] *China Year Book,* 1921-22, p. 577.
[21] *Ibid.;* Weigh, *op. cit.,* pp. 190-93.

On November 16, 1919, the President of the Mongol Council of Ministers handed to General Hsü a petition containing the desired request.[22] The petition stated that "no good result has been obtained" from the treaties of 1912 and 1914 between Mongolia and Russia, and referred to the disorders in the country which had resulted from the movement of Red and White Russian armies and from the agitation of the Pan-Mongolian plotters. Consequently it declared that:

"Whereas the friendly feelings between China and Outer Mongolia have been gradually restored and the old time prejudices have disappeared, and, whereas, both sides are anxious to promote the welfare of the people and to secure for them permanent peace and tranquillity, we, officials, princes, and lamas, hereby declare the abolition of the Autonomy of Outer Mongolia, and the restoration of the relations subsisting under the late Tsing Dynasty. All Djazaks shall hereafter be subject to the control of the (Chinese) Central Government, which shall define uniformly all their rights and shall reform our internal administration and resist external invasions for us.

"In connection with foreign relations, we beg further to state that it was on account of the declaration of autonomy that in former days the Sino-Russo-Mongolian Treaty and the Russo-Mongolian Commercial Treaty were concluded and notes between China and Russia were exchanged. Since we are willing to renounce Autonomy, all these instruments become null and void automatically."

The Mongolian petition, which was addressed to the President of the Republic of China, was received in Peking November 17, 1919. Five days later there appeared a presidential mandate complimenting the Living Buddha, the princes and the lamas on their patriotism and declaring that "their petition is hereby granted. . . ."[23] At the same time, the Waichiao Pu addressed a note to Prince Koudacheff informing him of the cancellation of the Russo-Mongolian Commercial Treaty of 1912 and the Sino-Russo-Mongolian Treaty of 1915.[24] The

[22] *China Year Book,* 1921-22, p. 577. The text of the petition appears in *Millard's Review,* XI, Dec. 6, 1919, p. 12; also *Far Eastern Review,* XVI, p. 106 (February, 1920).
[23] *Millard's Review,* XI, Dec. 6, 1919, p. 12.
[24] *North China Herald,* CXXXIII, Nov. 29, 1919, p. 551.

Chinese Government contended that in complying with the Mongolian appeal to restore the old order of things, it was moved by a desire to assist in establishing a general peace on an enduring basis. Reference was also made to the impossibility of continuing in force arrangements which had lapsed owing to the dissolution of the Russian Empire, and which were a constant invitation to unrest.[25]

The Russian Minister entered a prompt protest against this action of the Chinese Government. In a note communicated to the Foreign Office November 24th, he observed that "treaties between states may not be cancelled by the one-sided action of one of the contracting parties." Russia therefore maintained "her unquestionable right to determine her attitude in this question as soon as a Government of the whole of Russia" had been recognized. The Tsarist representative insisted also that all rights belonging to Russia and her citizens in Outer Mongolia remained unaffected by China's action.[26] The Chinese reply to Prince Koudacheff's note was dated December 10, 1919. It disclaimed all responsibility for any infraction of the Treaty of 1915 and insisted that the cancellation of Mongolia's autonomy had been done at the request of the Mongolians themselves. "With regard to the diverse advantages of Russian citizens and commerce in Outer Mongolia, the Chinese Government recognizes the necessity of their maintenance insofar as they do not conflict with Chinese sovereignty in Outer Mongolia and with the interests of Outer Mongolia."[27]

Shortly after the apparently satisfactory settlement of the Mongolian question, the Chinese Government took steps to reassert its authority in still another region which had fallen under the influence of Russia. In 1912, following the example set by the princes of Outer Mongolia, the Buriat Mongol tribes of the Barga district of western Heilungkiang province had ousted all Chinese officials and set up an autonomous govern-

[25] Statement, Chinese Minister of Foreign Affairs, Nov. 23, 1919, *Far Eastern Review*, XVI, Feb., 1920, pp. 106-7.
[26] *China Year Book*, 1921-22, p. 578.
[27] *Ibid.*, p. 578.

ment of their own. The Barga region (also known as Hulunbuir or Hailar) lay squarely astride the Chinese Eastern Railway, and the situation growing out of the autonomist movement
was consequently of interest not only to China but to Russia
as well.[28] In 1915 the Russian Government finally prevailed
upon the Government of China to accept an arrangement under
which Hulunbuir was to be set apart as a special district subject
directly to Peking; in this district Russia was to have preferential rights of an economic nature.[29]

The 1915 arrangement was short lived. As revolutionary
unrest spread eastward along the Trans-Siberian Railway, it
tended inevitably to infect the peoples of Hulunbuir. In January, 1920, General Chang Tso-lin, Inspector General of the
Three Eastern Provinces, transmitted to Peking a memorial containing what purported to be a request from the local chieftains
of Hulunbuir. These tribal leaders asked for "the abrogation
of Hulunbuir as a special territory, whereafter they will obey
the decision of the Central Government in all questions concerning their political administration." The request was also
made for the cancellation of the Sino-Russian convention of
1915 relating to the district.[30] In response to this petition
from the Barga Buriats, a presidential mandate was issued, on
January 28, 1920, announcing that "we shall condescend to
sanction their request in accordance with the popular desire." [31]
Against this action of the Chinese Government, the Russian
Minister entered a formal but ineffectual protest.[32]

The position of Prince Koudacheff in Peking at this time
was not an enviable one. Following the establishment of the
Soviet régime in Russia, he was forced to represent a government which no longer existed. China had recognized the Provisional Russian Government which was organized in March,
1917, but she declined to recognize the government which

[28] C. Walter Young, *The International Relations of Manchuria* (Chicago,
1929), p. 156, note.
[29] MacMurray, *op. cit.*, Vol. II, p. 1247.
[30] *North China Herald*, CXXXIV, Feb. 7, 1920, p. 344.
[31] *Ibid.*
[32] *China Year Book*, 1921-22, p. 627.

replaced it in November of that year.[33] Full recognition continued, however, to be accorded by the Chinese Government to
Russian diplomatic and consular authorities in China. This was
in spite of the fact that Koudacheff deliberately ignored two
telegrams from Petrograd, dated November 30 and December
17, 1917, in which Trotzky, as Commissar for Foreign Affairs,
summoned him either to support the policy of the Bolshevist
Government or to resign.[34] On January 23, 1918, he assured
the Chinese Government that no part of the Russian share of
the Boxer Indemnity payments which were still being deposited
in the Russo-Asiatic Bank, would be transmitted to the Bolshevist Government.[35] Until the Chinese Government finally
ceased making payments two and a half years later, these funds
were used to pay the salaries and expenses of Russian diplomatic and consular staffs in China.[36]

While many Russian interests in China, including the extraterritorial rights of Russian citizens, remained for the moment
unaffected by the political changes in the mother country, signs
were not wanting to indicate that the treaty structure on which
those interests depended was being steadily undermined. The
legation guard of thirty or forty men stationed in Peking and
the consular guard of ten men at Tientsin were withdrawn early
in 1918.[37] As already noted, the Russian Minister had felt
called upon to protest against the unilateral denunciation of the
Russo-Chinese treaties and conventions relating to Outer Mongolia and Hulunbuir, and to the control of the liquor traffic
along the Sungari River. Another formal protest was filed at
the Waichiao Pu against the application of the revised tariff
rates, fixed by the Shanghai Tariff Conference in 1918, to trade
across the Russo-Chinese land frontier.[38]

One influence of the utmost importance which helped to
undermine Prince Koudacheff's position was the intimation,

[33] *Ibid.*, p. 623.
[34] *China Year Book*, 1921-22, p. 624.
[35] *Ibid.*
[36] *Millard's Review*, XI, Feb. 28, 1920, p. 615.
[37] M. J. Pergament, *The Diplomatic Quarter in Peking*, p. 18.
[38] *China Year Book*, 1921-22, p. 624, 627.

repeatedly made known, that the new Russian Government of the Soviets was disposed to pursue a liberal policy in the Far East. The first attitude of the Soviet Government toward China had been one of suspicious hostility. In December, 1917, Leon Trotzky, then Soviet Commissar for Foreign Affairs, issued a vigorous protest against the Chinese military occupation of the railway zone at Harbin.[39] When it became evident, however, that the Chinese were not masters in their own house [40] the Russian authorities evinced a willingness to recognize China's exclusive political rights within the railway zone, while reserving Russia's economic and financial rights in the railway itself. In July, 1918, M. Chicherin, who had replaced Trotzky as Commissar for Foreign Affairs, announced that [41]

"We have notified China that we relinquish the conquests of the Tsarist government in Manchuria, and that we recognize Chinese rights in this territory, where the principal trade route runs, namely, the Eastern-Siberian Railroad. This railroad, which is the property of the Chinese and Russian people, has already devoured millions of the money of these peoples, and therefore of right belongs to these peoples and to nobody else. More than this, we are of the opinion that as the Russian people advanced funds to defray part of the expenses of this railroad, these should be repaid and China buy the railroad outright, without waiting for the terms embodied in this particular treaty violently imposed upon China."

The glaring injustice of certain decisions made by the Peace Conference at Paris furnished the background for the first definite proposal made to China by the Soviet Government. In 1919, hundreds of thousands of copies of a Russian manifesto, printed in Chinese, were circulated throughout China.[42] This pronouncement, signed by Karakhan, Deputy Commissar for Foreign Affairs, and bearing the date of July 25, 1919, was

[39] Alfred L. P. Dennis, *The Foreign Policies of Soviet Russia* (New York, 1924), pp. 282, 314.
[40] Apparently there was an informal exchange of views in April, 1918, at Chita, between representatives of China and Communist Russia. *Ibid.,* p. 314.
[41] Quoted by Paul S. Reinsch, "Bolshevism in Asia," *Asia,* XX, pp. 310-315, April, 1920.
[42] Dennis, *op. cit.,* p. 315.

addressed to "the Chinese people and the governments of North and South China." [48] China was informed that "the Russia of the Soviets and her Red Armies . . . are marching towards the East . . . not for the purposes of oppressing nor with the spirit of tyrannizing or conquest. . . . We are marching to free the people from the yoke of the military force of foreign money which is crushing the life of the people of the East, and principally the people of China. We are not only bringing help to our working classes but also to the Chinese people; and we want once more to remind them of that which we have continually told them, since the great revolution of October, 1917, and which the public press in the pay of the Americans, Europeans, and Japanese have perhaps suppressed. Ever since the government of workmen and peasants took the power into their hands in October, 1917, that government has in the name of the Russian people called upon the people of the whole world to establish an enduring peace. This peace must be based upon mutual renouncement of all seizure of other people's land, and of all forced contribution from any people." Taking full advantage of the resentment provoked in China by the decision of the Peace Conference with regard to Shantung, the Soviet Government declared that "all people, whether they are great or small, whether they have lived until now with a free life or whether they form against their own will a part of another country, shall be free in their inner life and no power shall interfere with them within this limit."

The Russian Government, continued the manifesto, had already "declared null and void all the secret treaties concluded with Japan, China, and the ex-Allies, the treaties which were

[48] The text here given is based upon the French version transmitted to Peking from Irkutsk in March, 1920, an English translation of which appears in the *China Year Book*, 1924, pp. 868-70. The French version, including the provision, apparently spurious, relating to the Chinese Eastern Railway, has been used in this instance because it was relied upon by the Chinese Government during subsequent negotiations with Joffe and Kara-khan. For a translation of the original Russian text, published in the Moscow *Izvestia* for August 20, 1919, see J. B. Condliffe (ed.) *Problems of the Pacific*, 1927, pp. 265-68. In this version, the paragraph relating to the Chinese Eastern Railway does not appear.

to enable the Russian government of the Tsar and his Allies to enslave the people of the East and principally the people of China. . . . The Soviet Government invites henceforth the Chinese government to enter into negotiations with the object of cancelling the treaty of 1896, the protocol of Peking of 1901 and all the agreements concluded with Japan from 1907 to 1916. . . . (Previous) negotiations on this subject lasted until March, 1918. But the Allies suddenly took the Government of Peking by the throat, filled the pockets of the Mandarins and the Chinese newspapers with money, and forced the Chinese Government to refuse to have any relations whatever with the government of workers and peasants of Russia. Without waiting for the restoration of the railway of Manchuria to the people of China, Japan and the Allies seized it for themselves, invaded Siberia and forced the Chinese soldiers to assist them in this unheard-of and criminal act of brigandage. . . ." Since the European nations and their American and Japanese allies had refused to permit the Chinese people to know the truth, Russia desired once more to announce that

1. ". . . the Soviet Government has given up all the conquests made by the government of [the] Tsars which took away from China Manchuria and other territories. The population of these territories shall decide for themselves to which country they would like to belong, as well as the form of government which they would like to adopt in their own countries."

2. "The Soviet Government returns to the Chinese people without demanding any kind of compensation, the Chinese Eastern Railway, as well as all the mining concessions, forestry, gold mines, and all the other things which were seized from them by the government of [the] Tsars, that of Kerensky, and the brigands, Horvat, Semenoff, Koltchak, the Russian ex-generals, merchants and capitalists." [44]

[44] During subsequent negotiations at Peking, both Joffe and Karakhan denied the existence of this clause relating to the Chinese Eastern Railway. *China Year Book*, 1924, p. 861. Karakhan to C. T. Wang, Nov. 30, 1923, *ibid.*, pp. 875-6. It is absent from the translation of the authentic Russian text given in *Problems of the Pacific*, 1927, pp. 265-8. How it came to be included in the Chinese official translation of the French text which reached Peking from Irkutsk is a mystery which has not so far, apparently, been explained.

3. "The Soviet Government gives up the indemnities payable by China for the insurrection of Boxers in 1900. The Soviet Government is obliged to repeat this assertion for the third time, for we are told that, in spite of our willingness to forego and give it up, this indemnity money is still held in the hands of the Allies for the payments of the salary and imaginary expenses of the former imperial minister at Peking and the former imperial consuls in China. The rights and powers of all those slaves of the Tsar have long been taken away from them. Nevertheless, they still continue to remain in their posts and cheat the Chinese people by the help of Japan and the Allies. The Chinese people should know this and kick these liars and thieves out of their country."

4. "The Soviet Government has abolished all the special privileges and all the factories owned by the Russian merchants in the Chinese territory; no Russian official, priest, or missionary should be allowed to interfere with Chinese affairs; and if they should commit any crime, they must be judged according to the local laws in local law courts. No authority or law court, whatever, should be allowed to exist in China except the authority and law court of the Chinese people."

5. "Besides these principal points, the Soviet Government, represented by its plenipotentiaries, is ready to negotiate with the Chinese people all the other questions and to settle once for all, all the cases of acts of violence and injustice which were committed towards China by the former government of Russia, acting together with Japan and the Allies."

The Russian note sounded the warning that "if the Chinese people, following the example of the Russian people, wish to become free and to avoid the fate reserved for them by the Allies at Versailles in their object of making China into a second Korea or another India, the Chinese people should understand that they have no other ally or brother in their struggle for liberty except the Russian peasants and workmen and their Red Army." And in conclusion, the formal proposal was made for the establishment of official relations between China and Russia.[45]

[45] The Karakhan manifesto represented one aspect of a determined campaign begun at this time by the Bolshevist leaders to enlist Oriental support in their struggle against the capitalist governments of the West. Already, on August 1, 1918, M. Chicherin had addressed a cordial letter to Dr. Sun Yat-sen, leader of the disgruntled autonomists at Canton. This

Not until March, 1920, following the decisive defeat of the
counter-revolutionary forces of Admiral Kolchak in western
Siberia, was a formal copy of the Karakhan note transmitted to
the Peking Government. On March 26, 1920, Mr.
Yanson, Representative for Foreign Affairs of the Council of Commis-
sars of the People of Siberia and the Far East, cabled the French
text from Irkutsk to the Waichiao Pu at Peking.⁴⁶ In official
circles, the note was taken to be a frank request for Chinese

letter hailed Dr. Sun as the persistent leader who had "continued to march
at the head of Chinese Democracy against the northern Chinese and foreign
imperialistic governments of oppression." At a time when the "Peking
government, which is the puppet of foreign bankers, is ready to join these
robbers"—the imperialistic governments—"the Russian laboring classes
appeal to their Chinese brothers and call them to a common struggle. For
our success is your success. Our defeat is your defeat. . . . Long live the
union of the Russian and Chinese proletariat!" Dennis, *op. cit.*, p. 315.
During 1919 and 1920 the newly constituted authorities in Russia were
busy establishing special training schools and oriental research institutes
on a lavish scale. The purpose of these institutions was not only to investigate conditions among Oriental peoples, but to train agitators capable of
carrying the communist gospel of unrest to the peoples of all Asiatic countries. Joseph Castagne, *Le Bolchevisme et l'Islam*, Paris, 1922, Vol. I,
pp. 46-73. At the Second Congress of the Communist Internationale, Comrade Lao Si-tao reported that the national revolutionary movement in
China was making great progress, partly in consequence of the denial of
China's just claims at Paris. In the forefront of the revolutionary agitation
were the students, who had formed an alliance with the industrial laborers.
In Shanghai a socialist party with strict Marxian tenets was rapidly gain-
ing in popularity. A weekly magazine published by the party had a wide
circulation. The industrial proletariat of China, although small, was violently revolutionary. The actual center of the revolutionary movement was
Shanghai, for there were gathered Sun Yat-sen and his associates of the
First Revolution, the central office of the Federation of Student Unions, the
national headquarters of the Laborers' Unions, and the Chinese Socialist
Party. "Stated briefly," said Comrade Lao, "the intellectuals of China, the
students, and the workers, represent promising material for revolutionary
agitation. . . . The support of the Chinese revolution is of significance
not merely for China, but for the revolutionary movement of the entire
world. . . ." *Der Zweite Kongress der Kommunist. Internationale, Proto-
koll der Verhandlungen vom 19. Juli in Petrograd und vom 23. Juli bis 7.
August, 1920, in Moscou. Bibliothek der Kommunistischen Internationale,*
Hamburg, 1921, Vol. 22, pp. 173-77. At a congress of Chinese workmen
in Moscow in June, 1920, M. Chicherin voiced the hope that the organization
of Chinese workers in Russia would serve as a link between the Russian
Soviet Republic and the future Chinese Soviet Republic. *Izvestia*, June 14,
1920, reported in *The New Russia*, II, July 22, 1920, p. 381. On the subject
of communist activity in China, see also Dennis, *op. cit.*, pp. 315-18;
Weigh, *op. cit.*, pp. 303-330.
⁴⁶ *China Year Book*, 1924, pp. 867-8.

recognition of the Soviet régime. Ostracized in Europe, Russia was seeking friends in the Orient. Since social revolutions in Europe had so far failed to materialize, national revolutions in Asia might serve, at least temporarily, as substitutes for them. Political and economic unrest among Oriental peoples, whatever its objective, would weaken the capitalist West by shutting it off from markets, sources of raw materials, and fields for profitable investment. Politically, Communist Russia desired China as an ally against imperialistic Japan, whose militarists continued to fish in the troubled waters of eastern Siberia.[47] The Soviet Government also desired to secure China's coöperation in suppressing the plots and intrigues of Anti-Bolshevist leaders, then using Chinese soil as a base from which to launch attacks upon that government.

Although the communist appeal to the national sentiments of the Chinese evoked a sympathetic response in many quarters, the first official reaction was one of skepticism. Doubt was even expressed as to the genuineness of the Karakhan note.[48] In other quarters it was pointed out that the promise to return "Manchuria and other regions" was of little value, since Manchuria had never ceased to be Chinese territory. The fear was also expressed that the principle of self-determination might, according to its communist interpretation, be used as a clever device by which Russia could recover in future what she now seemed willing to give away. The skeptics suggested, further,

[47] Cf. Leo Pasvolsky, *Russia in the Far East* (New York, 1922), pp. 85-87.

[48] The Peking Cabinet, according to one report, stated in a circular communication to the provincial authorities that "according to a telegram from Li Chai-ao, High Chinese Commissioner in Siberia, it has been learned by inquiry with the representatives of the Soviet Government that they had not issued such a note. It is therefore feared that the communication, is a forgery. . . . The Central Government is, however, paying special attention to the matter; and if the Russian Government truly represents the people and is willing to negotiate, we would certainly commence negotiations without hesitation." H. K. Tong, "Russian Soviet Would Befriend China," *Millard's Review*, XIII, June 5, 1920, pp. 24-26. The caution of the Chinese Government at this time is to be explained in considerable degree by the fact that it was still under the control of the pro-Japanese militarists of the Anfu clique. A distinct change in Peking's attitude toward Russia took place following the expulsion of the Anfu group in July, 1920.

that the Soviet Government merely proposed to abandon rights and concessions in China over which it no longer had any actual control.[49] In speculating as they did, the Chinese skeptics had the full support of the Russian and French diplomatic representatives in Peking. Prince Koudacheff protested to the Waichiao Pu against its acceptance of the Karakhan note on the ground that the Soviet Government was not competent to represent the whole of Russia. The French Minister supported the stand of his Russian colleague and advised the Chinese Government particularly against stopping payments of the Russian share of the Boxer Indemnity, which were urgently needed to meet the expenses of the Russian Legation and Consulates.[50]

Quite regardless of whether China was yet ready to recognize the Soviet Government, it was evident that something would have to be done to regulate trade across the long frontier between the two countries. In the spring of 1920, the Chinese local authorities in the province of Sinkiang felt compelled to enter into negotiations with the Communist Government of Tashkent, in Russian Turkestan, for the settlement of outstanding questions relating to commerce and the repatriation of Russian soldiers and refugees. On May 27, 1920, ten resolutions were adopted at a conference of Chinese and Russian delegates held in I Ning City, in Ili.[51] The two parties agreed that "with a view to benefiting the people on the borders of the two countries and to strengthening the relations between the two countries," an organization should be set up to facilitate negotiations regarding commercial and foreign affairs. Arrangements were made for the collection by China of duties on merchandise transported from Ili into Russia. The Fifth Resolution provided that "In case of disputes arising out of trade between the nationals of the two parties and in all civil and criminal cases, the matters will uniformly be decided and disposed of in accordance with the law of the country in which they reside."

[49] H. K. Tong, *op. cit.*
[50] *North China Herald*, CXXXV, Apr. 17, 1920, p. 123, Chinese press translation.
[51] Text, *Treaties and Agreements, 1919-1929*, pp. 23-25.

This was a formal abandonment of Russia's right to exercise extraterritorial jurisdiction within the province of Sinkiang. The two parties agreed upon arrangements for the return to Russia of refugees and defeated soldiers who had crossed the border into China. The Russian representatives declared that they lacked authority to settle the question of property and merchandise belonging to Chinese nationals in Russia, which had been repeatedly confiscated and detained. The announcement was made, however, that "the Tashkent Government has already established an investigation and reparation commission." The Russian delegation suggested that a Chinese Commissioner for Commercial and Foreign Affairs should "proceed to Russia to enter into direct negotiations; this would be a more effective arrangement."

In April, 1920, the interest of the Peking Government was aroused by the creation of a new state, the Far Eastern Republic, called into existence by a constituent convention meeting at Verkhne-Udinsk.[52] Set up to serve as an outpost of Soviet Russia against Japan, the Far Eastern Republic immediately sought recognition as a means of strengthening its position. Its hopes in this direction were encouraged by the sympathetic attitude of Li Yuan, the Chinese Resident Commissioner at Kiachta.[53]

In June, the Peking Government, feeling the need for reliable information concerning political conditions in Siberia, sent a commission of three foreign advisers to investigate. This commission, consisting of Mr. B. L. Simpson, M. Georges Padoux, and Dr. John C. Ferguson, had interviews not only with officials of the Far Eastern Republic, but with M. V. Vilensky, the Soviet representative accredited to that government. Vilensky informed the members of the commission that the friendly feeling on the part of the Siberians toward China was based on the fact that China, like Russia, was opposing Japan's ambitions, and because all Bolshevist leaders realized

[52] H. K. Norton, *The Far Eastern Republic* (London, 1923), pp. 136-8.
[53] *North China Herald*, CXXXVI, July 10, 1920, p. 83.

that the Russian Far East was largely dependent upon China for its food supplies.[54] The commission found that the reactionary party in Siberia was without any real strength. On the other hand, Siberia, far from being a political unit, was really divided into four areas. These were the region of Verkhne-Udinsk, which had a certain Bolshevist coloring, the region about Chita, still dominated by Ataman Semenov and the Japanese, the region of Blagovestchensk, where a number of Bolshevist elements were still intrenched, and the Maritime Province, in which a Republican Provisional Government had been organized in January, 1920. Three of these elements, however, could be grouped together to constitute the Far Eastern Republic.

In his capacity as head of the Republican Provisional Government at Vladivostok, M. Medvedev informed the members of the commission that the Far Eastern Republic, which he declared had succeeded to all Russian rights and privileges in the Far East, was willing to revise the old Sino-Russian treaties in a spirit of justice and reciprocity and without asking for consular jurisdiction. Nevertheless, prior to the election of a constituent assembly and the working out of satisfactory relations between the Far Eastern Republic and the Soviet Government, all treaties made by the former government would be merely provisional in character and would remain so until ratified by both the constituent assembly and by Moscow. To insure later ratification of such temporary agreements, the Provisional Government, in agreement with the local Soviet representative, proposed tri-partite negotiations between representatives of China and the Far Eastern Republic, with the Soviet delegate attending.[55] Meanwhile, the Chinese Government was asked to prevent Russian reactionaries from using Harbin and the headquarters of the Chinese Eastern Railway as a base for counter-revolutionary activity directed against the Provisional Government.

[54] The report of the commission is printed in *North China Herald,* CXXXVI, Aug. 21, 1920, pp. 478-480.
[55] Report of the Commission, *op. cit.*

The report of this commission of foreign advisers was in the hands of the Chinese Government when, toward the end of July, a mission from the Verkhne-Udinsk Government, headed by M. Ignatius Yourin, arrived at Kiachta. President Hsü, fearful of offending the French and Japanese representatives in Peking, instructed the Chinese local officials to refuse passports to the Russian delegates.[56] Immediately thereafter, however, the situation in Peking underwent a notable change. A brief civil war resulted in the defeat of the Anfu military clique which for years had controlled the capital, and its replacement by a new government whose patron saints were Generals Chang Tso-lin, Wu P'ei-fu, and Ts'ao K'un. Somewhat less amenable to Japanese influence than its predecessor had been, the new government decided to treat, at least unofficially, with the envoys from Verkhne-Udinsk. The Chinese Resident Commissioner at Kiachta was instructed to inform M. Yourin that the Chinese Government was willing to receive him as a commercial representative, but that it would decline to discuss matters of a politictal nature. The Russian delegate, having accepted these conditions, was given passports to proceed to Peking by way of Urga and Kalgan.[57] In deciding to receive the Russian mission, the Peking Government ignored the representations of the Russian Minister, Prince Koudacheff, and of the French Minister, M. Boppe. In addition, the government was in possession of a copy of the recent American note to Italy declaring that no useful purpose would be served by a recognition of the Soviet Government.[58]

On August 26, the Yourin mission left Kalgan, and a day or so later it was received unofficially in Peking by a representative of the Waichiao Pu. Conversations began almost immediately between M. Yourin and Mr. Chang Chu-sun, Councillor of the Ministry of Foreign Affairs. It was discovered at the

[56] *Millard's Review*, XIV, Sept. 4, 1920, pp. 4-6.
[57] *Ibid.*, XV, Jan. 1, 1921, pp. 237-9.
[8] Louis Fischer, *The Soviets in World Affairs: A History of the Relations between the Soviet Union and the Rest of the World* (2 vols., London and New York, 1930), Vol. I, p. 306.

outset that Yourin bore credentials from the Verkhne-Udinsk Government alone. He was immediately informed that the Waichiao Pu must decline to treat with him until similar credentials were presented from the other Siberian Governments, at Vladivostok and Blagovestchensk. These additional powers the Russian delegate undertook to procure as speedily as possible.[59] The Chinese authorities also demanded assurances that there would be no Bolshevist propaganda in any part of China.[60]

On September 16, the Waichiao Pu issued an official communiqué explaining the attitude of the government toward the mission from Verkhne-Udinsk and giving details of the conversations which had taken place with its official head.[61] China, according to this explanation, was merely following the policy of her recent allies in the war by considering the resumption of commercial relations with Russia. Moreover, in view of the prevailing chaos in Siberia and the inability of the Tsarist official representatives in China to carry out the functions for which they were responsible, some *modus vivendi* was urgently needed to regulate trade between the two nations and to protect Chinese citizens and their interests in Siberia.

While M. Yourin was endeavoring to secure credentials as the representative of all Siberia, the Peking Government ratified the commercial agreement which had been signed between representatives of General Yang Tseng-hsin, Military Governor of Sinkiang, and delegates representing the Russian local government of Tashkent.[62] This agreement was in harmony with the resolutions adopted in the I Ning City conference of the previous May. Bureaus of trade and foreign affairs were to be established by China in Russian territory, and by Russia in two trade centers of Sinkiang. Russian trade across the frontier was

[59] *Millard's Review*, XV, Jan. 1, 1921, pp. 237-9.
[60] Waichiao Pu statement, Sept. 16, 1920, *North China Herald*, CXXXVI, Sept. 25, 1920, p. 806.
[61] *Ibid.*
[62] *North China Herald*, CXXXVI, Sept. 25, 1920, p. 806; Pasvolsky, *op. cit.*, pp. 87-8.

to be subject to the general tax regulations of Sinkiang and to the Chinese Martime Customs tariff. Commercial disputes between citizens of the two countries, and all civil and commercial cases of whatever nature were to be tried in the courts of the locality concerned. In ratifying this agreement, the Peking Government took care to deny that it had any political significance or that it was in any way connected with the Yourin mission.[63] In Moscow, however, the agreement was published with a flourish on the eve of the arrival there of a party of Chinese officials, headed by General Chang Shih-lin, who were touring Russia in their capacity as private citizens.[64]

In spite of the fact that General Chang readily admitted that his visit was devoid of political significance, he was shown special attention by the officials of the Soviet Foreign Office. On October 2, he was honored with a note from M. Karakhan, Acting Commissar for Foreign Affairs. Inclosed with the note was a memorandum which the Chinese general was asked to transmit to his government.[65] The memorandum expressed regret that the Chinese Government had not yet seen fit to resume formal relations with Russia, and "the enemies of the Russian and Chinese peoples" were blamed for obstructing the

[63] Dennis, *op. cit.*, p. 319. Professor Dennis apparently reached the conclusion that the actual initiative which led to the Yourin mission to Peking was taken in Moscow. *Ibid.*, p. 318 .

[64] Various opinions have been expressed concerning the significance of this Chinese mission. Professor Dennis considered it to be a "scouting body." *The Foreign Policies of Soviet Russia*, p. 319. Mr. Pasvolsky asserted that General Chang, "one of the younger followers of Wu P'ei-fu, was charged with the task of negotiating with the Commissariat of Foreign Affairs." *Russia in the Far East*, p. 88. The Russian Foreign Office thought General Chang headed an official "Military and Diplomatic Mission" which, however, lacked plenipotentiary powers. *North China Herald*, CXXXVII, Oct. 23, 1920, p. 221. None of these views seems to have been correct. Reuter's Peking correspondent reported on October 20, 1920, that General Chang was one of the Anfu generals formerly attached to the Frontier Defense Force. At the outbreak of the Chihli-Anfu war in July, 1920, he was in Russia, presumably on an errand connected with the political schemes of his superior, General Hsü Shu-tseng. After the defeat of the Anfu clique, Chang requested permission to remain in Russia for the purpose of making a private investigation of conditions there. To this request the Peking Government made no reply. General Chang's visit to the Soviet capital, therefore, seems to have had no official significance. *Ibid.*

[65] Text, *China Year Book*, 1924, pp. 870-72.

establishment of friendly relations between them. Recalling the terms of its Declaration of July 25, 1919, the Soviet Government declared that it would unswervingly abide by the principles laid down in that Declaration. The questions on which the Soviet Government now proposed to negotiate with China were then dealt with under seven heads.

1. Russia declared "null and void all the treaties concluded with China by the former Governments of Russia," renounced "all seizure of Chinese territory and all Russian concessions in China," and restored to China "without any compensation and forever, all that had been predatorily seized from her" by the Tsar's Government.

2. The Governments of both Republics were to "take necessary measures for immediately establishing regular trade and economic relations." A special treaty on this subject was to be concluded on the basis of the most-favored-nation principle.

3. The Chinese Government was to pledge itself (a) "not to proffer any aid to Russian counter-revolutionary individuals, groups or organizations, nor to allow their activities in Chinese territory" and (b) "to disarm, intern and hand over to the Government of the Russian Socialist Federated Soviet Republic all the detachments and organizations to be found in Chinese territory at the time of the signing of this Treaty, which are fighting against the R. S. F. S. R. or States allied with her, and to give over to the Government of the R. S. F. S. R. all their arms, munitions and property."

4. Neither government was to claim the right to exercise extraterritorial jurisdiction over its citizens residing in the territory of the other.

5. The Chinese Government was to pledge itself (a) to sever relations with the diplomatic and consular officials of the former Tsarist Government and to expel all such from China; (b) to hand over to the Soviet Government "the buildings of the Embassy and consulates and other property and archives of the same, situated in Chinese territory and belonging to Russia."

6. The Soviet Government renounced all claim to the Russian portion of the Boxer Indemnity payments, "provided that under no circumstances shall the Government of the Chinese Republic pay any money to the former Russian consuls or to any other persons or Russian organizations putting up illegal claims thereto."

7. "Following immediately upon the signing of the present Treaty," the two Republics were to exchange diplomatic and con-

sular representatives. "The Russian and the Chinese Governments agree to sign a special treaty on the way of working the Chinese Eastern Railway with due regard to the needs of the Russian Socialist Federated Soviet Republic, and in the conclusion of the treaty there shall take part, besides China and Russia, also the Far Eastern Republic."

While General Chang was playing the rôle of unofficial Chinese ambassador to Russia,[66] informal negotiations were proceeding at Peking between M. Yourin and a representative of the Waichiao Pu. In November, Yourin informed the Chinese Government that he had received the authorizations necessary to act on behalf of all the governments of Siberia.[67] Thereupon, the Chinese Government evinced a willingness to resume conversations which had been dropped in September. In a note to the Waichiao Pu dated November 30, the head of the Chita mission [68] dealt with political issues in general terms,

[66] The communication handed by Karakhan to General Chang seems to have been duly transmitted to the Foreign Office at Peking, and also to have been formally acknowledged by the Chinese Government under date of November 23, 1920. The supposed reply ran in part as follows: "The contents of this communication have received the attention of the Chinese Government and particularly the principle of international equality and reciprocity. By virtue of the many thousands of miles of common frontier, the relations between China and Russia naturally should be of the closest nature. . . . The Chinese Government is therefore anxiously awaiting the earliest opportunity of opening direct negotiations with Russia along the lines indicated in the communication now under reply. The Chinese Government would, however, take this opportunity earnestly to invite the attention of the Russian authorities to the fact that since the Russian revolution, many thousands of Chinese citizens who are now residing in Russian territories have been subject to untold hardships and maltreatment of diverse character. . . . While awaiting the opportunity to open negotiations, the Chinese Government would call upon the authorities throughout Russia to accord due protection and proper treatment to Chinese citizens within their respective jurisdictions. The Chinese Government is confident that if the Chinese people in Russia were allowed to live and pursue their legitimate callings peacefully and unmolested, it would hasten the day when the old cordial relations may normally be resumed and the historical ties between the Chinese and Russian peoples again be placed on a formal and official basis." *North China Herald,* CXLIX, Dec. 1, 1923, p. 591.
[67] *Millard's Review,* XV, Jan. 1, 1921, pp. 237-9.
[68] In November, the Verkhne-Udinsk Government moved to Chita, which Siberian partisans had captured from Ataman Semenov following the latter's abandonment by the Japanese. Norton, *op. cit.,* pp. 146-7.

but pleaded forcefully for a commercial agreement between China and Siberia.⁶⁹ In order to secure commercial arrangements which would facilitate trade across the frontier, the Far Eastern Republic, declared M. Yourin, was willing to revise all treaties and agreements between China and Tsarist Russia and to eliminate all privileges which were not reciprocal, or which contained "the element of imperialistic aggressiveness alien to the principles of equal opportunities and equal rights, anything that may have any connection . . . with the outrages committed against China by the former imperialistic government, and, finally, anything that may be derogatory to the dignity of a nation and its sovereignty." The new agreement which was to define the mutual relations between the two countries would "be based entirely upon the principles of equal opportunities. . . ." Consuls and trade commissioners were to be exchanged. With reference to the Chinese Eastern Railway, the Siberian representative suggested that "the interests, rights, and obligations of the two sides should be fully guaranteed in accordance with the principle of mutual justice."

Proposals couched in such broad terms were not entirely satisfactory to the Waichiao Pu officials. China on her part had proposals to make which were of a more definite character. M. Yourin was informed that before entering into negotiations for a commercial agreement, the Chinese Government demanded assurances to the following effect: that Russian officials would abstain from spreading propaganda in Chinese territory which was not suited to the social institutions of China; that Chinese merchants in Siberia would be indemnified for their losses arising out of the revolutionary disturbances there; that Chinese residents in Siberia would be accorded facilities for trade and travel; and that Chinese grievances resulting from incidents along the Sinkiang frontier and in Zaibaikal would be settled on the basis of justice to those concerned. On December

⁶⁹ *Millard's Review*, XV, Jan. 1, 1921, pp. 237-9. One of Yourin's colleagues stated at this time that political questions were of far less immediate importance than the vital need of giving eastern Siberia access to supplies of food and clothing from China. *North China Herald*, CXXXVII, Dec. 11, 1920, p. 722.

13, M. Yourin accepted these conditions in a formal communication to the Waichiao Pu.[70] The Chinese Government, however, was not to be satisfied with mere promises. M. Yourin was presented with a bulky document containing details of the incidents complained of, statements of the damages or losses suffered by Chinese merchants, and proposals for the settlement of these claims.[71]

The Far Eastern Republic was unwilling or unable to pay the indemnities demanded by the Chinese Government, and in January negotiations between the two parties came temporarily to an end.[72] For several months thereafter, the situation remained unchanged. M. Boppe, the French Minister, exerted his influence to prevent the conclusion of any agreement between China and Siberia.[73] Russian emigrés constantly reminded the Manchurian dictator, Chang Tso-lin, of the dangers from Soviet propaganda within his domains. And Chang Tso-lin's influence was paramount in Peking.

Negotiations were finally resumed in the spring of 1921. In April these negotiations took definite form. An agreement was drafted which, announced M. Yourin, embodied "all questions of our mutual relations, particularly those respecting consular representation, navigation of the Sungari, the status of Russians in the Chinese Eastern Railway zone in connection with the abolition of extraterritoriality," and other matters.[74] On his way back to Chita for consultation with his government, the Soviet envoy, on May 27, expressed confidence that a trade agreement would soon be signed.[75] The cordial welcome accorded him on his return to Peking, July 25, appeared fully to warrant such confidence.[76]

[70] *Millards' Review*, XV, Jan. 1, 1921, pp. 237-9.   [71] *Ibid.*
[72] *North China Herald*, CXXXVIII, Jan. 22, 1921, p. 191.
[73] Yourin's statement to Dalta Press representative, May 25, 1921, *North China Herald*, June 4, 1921, CXXXIX, p. 652. For a month after its arrival in Peking, Boppe succeeded in preventing the Yourin mission from leasing a residence to be used as its headquarters.
[74] *Ibid.*   [75] *Ibid.*, p. 651.
[76] *Ibid.*, CXL, July 30, 1921, p. 312. In contrast with the official coolness attending his original arrival in Peking, Yourin was met at the station on this occasion by representatives of the President, the Cabinet, and the Waichiao Pu.

Ultimately several influences caused the Peking Government to revert to its earlier policy of caution, and to defeat the hopes of M. Yourin for a commercial agreement with China. In the first place, rumors began to circulate during the spring of 1921 that the Moscow Government and the Government of Dr. Sun Yat-sen at Canton were engaged in negotiating an agreement which provided for mutual recognition.[77] The rumors, if well founded, were of more than casual significance, for the Canton Parliament had, on April 7, elected Dr. Sun as "President of the Republic"; thereafter he claimed to be the legal chief executive of all China.[78] In the second place, Chinese fears regarding the possible spread of communist ideas in the country were revived by the arrest at Harbin, in April, of several Russians who were traveling to Peking under diplomatic passports. One member of the party, said to be a secretary to the Yourin mission, was returning from Chita to Peking with an indorsed draft of the trade agreement with China. One of his companions was accused of possessing apparatus which could be used to counterfeit Bank of China notes. The baggage of another member of the party was reported to contain large quantities of gold and Romanov notes, together with a supply of what the Chinese authorities considered to be Bolshevist literature suitable for popular distribution.[79]

A third influence inducing delay on the part of the Peking authorities was the overthrow by counter-revolutionary Kappelist troops of the government at Vladivostok which had affiliated with the Far Eastern Republic.[80] This unexpected development, coming in May just when prospects for the success of M. Yourin's mission seemed very bright, raised questions as to the

[77] *North China Herald*, CXXXIX, Apr. 2, 1921, p. 11. On March 28, the vernacular press in Shanghai reported that an agreement had already been concluded providing, among other things, that the Canton Government, in exchange for financial assistance from Moscow, should aid the Soviet Government in spreading Bolshevist ideas in China.
[78] *North China Herald*, CXXXIX, Apr. 16, 1921, p. 155.
[79] *North China Herald*, CXXXIX, May 14, 1921, p. 446.
[80] *North China Herald*, CXXXIX, June 18, 1921, p. 806. The success of the Kappelist *coup d'état* was made possible by the interference of the Japanese military authorities at Vladivostok. Norton, *op. cit.*, p. 253.

stability of the Far Eastern Republic. Finally, in June, Chinese apprehensions were aroused by information that Soviet troops had invaded Mongolia in pursuit of White Russian forces under the command of Baron Ungern von Sternberg.[81] Seeking a solution of the Mongolian problem, M. Yourin attempted to deal first with the Waichiao Pu officials in Peking, and then with General Chang Tso-lin at Mukden. In both cases his efforts ended in failure. The Peking authorities refused to proceed further with commercial negotiations, and the Siberian envoy then returned with his suite to Chita to take up his new duties as Minister for Foreign Affairs of the Far Eastern Republic.[82]

The failure of M. Yourin's mission was a grievous disappointment to him. From the point of view of China, however, that failure was rendered less serious by the fact that, in September, 1920, shortly after M. Yourin's arrival in Peking, the Chinese Government had terminated official relations with the Tsarist Minister, Prince Koudacheff. This step was entirely to the liking of the Siberian envoy. Nevertheless, he lost thereby a certain diplomatic advantage, for at the same time that the Chinese Government withdrew recognition from the Tsarist representative, it took over the control of all Russian interests in China. As a result, M. Yourin was deprived of an extremely important *quid pro quo* which he pretended to offer in return for a trading agreement between China and the Far Eastern Republic.

The anomalous position of Prince Koudacheff, as already indicated, had been apparent for some time. He claimed to represent Russia's official interests in China. On the other hand, evidences multiplied that he was quite unable to discharge his official responsibilities. Passports issued to Chinese citizens by the Russan Minister and Consuls were not honored in Russia. In some instances, Russian nationals in China, while continuing

[81] For an account of conditions in Outer Mongolia at this time, see Chap. VI.
[82] *North China Herald*, CXL, July 30, 1921, p. 312; Aug. 6, 1921, p. 386.

to insist on their extraterritorial rights, declined to acknowledge the authority or submit to the control of the local Russian Consuls.[83] Even more serious was the fact that Prince Koudacheff was not always able to command the obedience of the Russian Consuls themselves.[84]

On September 22, the Russian Legation in Peking was notified by the telegraph administration that, in consequence of instructions issued by the Waichiao Pu, no more messages in code would be transmitted for it.[85] The Minister for Foreign Affairs, Dr. W. W. Yen, explained to Prince Koudacheff that such telegrams might be connected with political activities which would create trouble for the local Chinese authorities. Dr. Yen suggested that the existing situation would be simplified if Prince Koudacheff voluntarily retired. This the Russian Minister declined to do. He declared that he could be relieved of his responsibility to the 300,000 Russian nationals in China only by recall or by action of the Chinese Government in withdrawing recognition from him.[86]

The next day, September 23, a presidential mandate appeared terminating official relations with the Russian Minister.[87] The mandate mentioned the fact that in consequence of civil war in Russia, there existed in that country "no united government,

[83] *Millard's Review*, XIV, Oct. 9, 1920, pp. 281-84.

[84] In August, 1920, Ataman Kalmikov, the leader of a guerrilla band operating against the Bolsheviks in Siberia, fled across the border into Manchuria, where he was interned by the Chinese authorities. Subsequently he managed to escape during a visit to the Russian consulate at Kirin, where he had been concealed contrary to the instructions of the Russian Minister in Peking. *China Year Book, 1921-22*, p. 625. This incident undoubtedly hastened the decision of the Chinese Government—behind which stood the Manchurian dictator, Chang Tso-lin—to assume jurisdiction over unruly Russian elements in China, and particularly in the Three Eastern Provinces.

[85] *North China Herald*, CXXXVI, Sept. 25, 1920, p. 802.

[86] *Ibid.*

[87] Text, *China Year Book*, 1921-22, p. 626. The foreign press in Peking promptly jumped to the conclusion that Yourin would replace Koudacheff as Russian Minister. The Chinese Government insisted, however, that the consideration shown the Yourin mission and the withdrawal of recognition from the Tsarist Minister were two matters which were wholly unrelated. *North China Herald*, CXXXVII, Oct. 16, 1920, p. 148. See also the statement issued in Washington by Dr. Wellington Koo, Chinese Minister to the United States, *New York Times*, Oct. 2, 1920.

expressing the will of the people. . . ." With regard to the
diplomatic and consular representatives of Russia in China,
"they have long ago lost their representative character and have
indeed no ground to continue discharging the responsible duties
devolving upon them." However, China "while now ceasing to
recognize the Russian Minister and Consuls, nevertheless pre-
serves with regard to Russian citizens, the same friendly feelings
as before." Efficient measures were to be taken to safeguard
"the persons and property of peaceful Russian citizens residing
in China," and the appropriate local authorities were instructed
to "devise adequate measures with regard to . . . Russian concessions, the leased territory of the Chinese Eastern Railway
and the Russian citizens residing everywhere in China." A copy
of this mandate was transmitted immediately to Prince Koudacheff.

The ex-Tsarist Minister on September 24 informed the
Waichiao Pu that all Russian Consuls in China were being
informed by telegram of the action of the Chinese Government.[88] He requested, however, that since Russian citizens in
China would henceforth be deprived of any official Russian protection, care should be taken "to have the order of the President
. . . thoroughly executed in regard to efficient measures towards the safeguarding of the persons and property of peaceful
Russian citizens." This safeguarding, he declared further, "must
be based on the exact application of the *status quo* of the Russo-
Chinese Treaties" because as the Chinese Government had been
warned on several occasions, "all infringements which have
been made in the last few years of the Russo-Chinese Treaties
can only become lawful when they shall have been agreed to
by a regular All-Russian Government recognized as such by
the Chinese Government." Seven specific instances of infringement by the Chinese Government of those treaties were then
listed.

Following the issuance of the presidential decree, Chinese
officials in the provinces were instructed from Peking to assume

[88] Koudacheff to Waichiao Pu, *China Year Book, 1921-22,* pp. 626-7.

charge of Russian local interests. At Tientsin, on September 25, the Commissioner for Foreign Affairs took over control of the Russian Concession and assumed charge of the archives in the municipal buildings.[89] In the case of the Concession at Hankow, a similar transfer was effected on September 28.[90] The Russian consular premises at Urga and Kirin were forcibly taken over by the Chinese authorities.[91] The consulate at Kobdo was placed under the care of the "mayor" of the local Russian community, and that at Canton, on the island of Shameen, was sealed by the British Consul. The remaining nineteen Russian consulates in China and Mongolia were formally given into the custody of the Chinese local authorities, and copies of the inventory lists and receipts communicated to the Diplomatic Body at Peking.[92]

With the closing of these consulates, Russian consular jurisdiction in China came actually, if not legally, to an end. It was not contended, however, that the treaty rights of Russians were thereby abrogated. The Chinese Government assumed only the right to act as trustee for Russian interests until such time as Russia was competent and able to reassert jurisdiction over her nationals and their interests in China.[93] It was officially announced that the Chinese Government proposed to follow Russian law so far as possible in criminal cases involving Russians, but to apply Chinese law in civil cases.[94] Early in October, the Vice Minister of Justice, Mr. Chang Yi-peng, was sent from Peking to northern Manchuria to supervise the closing of Russian courts there and to make the arrangements necessary for the handling of cases involving Russians.[95] The

[89] *North China Herald*, CXXXVII, Oct. 2, 1920, p. 12.
[90] *Ibid.*
[91] *China Year Book, 1921-22*, p. 627.
[92] *Ibid.*
[93] It should be recalled that a precedent for such action already existed in the case of German rights between March, 1917, when diplomatic relations with Germany were severed, and the following August, when war was declared.
[94] *North China Herald*, CXXXVII, Oct. 2, 1920, p. 12.
[95] *North China Herald*, CXXXVII, Oct. 9, 1920, p. 82. The system of Russian courts within the zone of the Chinese Eastern Railway had been

Peking Government declared that there would be the smallest possible interference with the administrations then existing in the Russian Concessions at Hankow and Tientsin, and that the municipal councils would continue to function as in the past. The promise was also made that the assumption of Chinese control in these areas meant merely that the powers and privileges formerly exercised by the local Russian Consuls would henceforth be exercised by the Chinese Commissioners for Foreign Affairs.[96]

Chinese trusteeship for Russian interests in China did not meet with the approval of the diplomats representing the Treaty Powers in Peking. The theory of Chinese trusteeship was entirely logical. But from a practical point of view, it was quite evident that, barring the reëstablishment in Russia of a government modeled after that of the Tsarist régime, the Chinese Government intended to withhold recognition from any Russian Government which insisted on the restoration of Russia's political rights in China. Another breach would thus be made in the edifice of foreign rights and interests in China, already weakened by the elimination of Germany and Austria-Hungary from the list of Treaty Powers.

The American State Department was apparently the first to take positive action designed to safeguard Russian interests in China. It was announced in Washington on October 2 that the American Government had invited an exchange of views among the powers relative to the recent action of the Chinese Government.[97] In Peking, at the same time, the diplomatic representa-

established in consequence of the Russian Imperial Ukase of July 20 (Aug. 2), 1901. They were provided for in no treaty between China and Russia, and the Chinese Government had never admitted their legality. See W. W. Willoughby, *Foreign Rights and Interests in China* (Baltimore, 1927), Vol. I, p. 158.

[96] *North China Herald,* CXXXVII, Oct. 2, 1920, p. 11.

[97] *New York Times,* Oct. 2, 1920. It was reported in Peking September 24 that the American Minister, Mr. Charles R. Crane, had received instructions to consult with the representatives of the other powers relative to the possibility of taking over the administration and court systems in the Russian Concessions and along the Chinese Eastern Railway pending the formation of a recognized government in Russia. *North China Herald,* CXXXVII, Oct. 2, 1920, p. 10.

tives of the powers were being importuned by Prince Koudacheff to see that Russian interests in China suffered no harm
at the hands of the Chinese.[98] In response to this plea, the
French and the Japanese Ministers advanced a proposal to place
those interests under the joint trusteeship of the powers.[99]

An exchange of views among the foreign diplomats in
Peking resulted finally in a note addressed to the Waichiao Pu
by the Doyen of the Diplomatic Body on October 11. The
Chinese Government was requested to give formal assurances
that the measures taken in compliance with the presidential
mandate of September 23 would "in no case constitute a permanent amendment of the legal status of Russians, recognized
by treaties, but must be considered purely provisional and subject to the agreement of the future officially recognized Russian
Government." The suggestion was then made that "the provisional *modus vivendi* for the administration of Russian interests . . . be elaborated by agreement between the Chinese
Government and the Diplomatic Body."[100]

The reply of the Chinese Minister of Foreign Affairs to this
note was dated October 22.[101] The members of the Diplomatic
Body were assured that "the arrangements made at present are
naturally of a temporary nature and will have to be reconsidered
as soon as a lawful Government, recognized by China, shall
have been constituted in Russia." Meanwhile, Russian citizens
residing in China would "continue to enjoy the rights secured
to them by treaties." With regard to the Russian Concessions,
"the Chinese Government will take over the management of
all administrative affairs within their limits, temporarily and
without introducing any changes," except such as might be necessary by way of improvement. Concerning extraterritorial
rights, Dr. Yen's flat statement that "Russian consular jurisdiction must, of course, cease" indicated not the slightest disposi-

[98] *China Year Book, 1921-22*, p. 628.
[99] *North China Herald*, CXXXVII, Oct. 9, 1920, pp. 115-16. Already
the branches of the Russo-Asiatic Bank in China had been brought under the
protection of the French flag. *Ibid.*, Oct. 2, 1920, p. 24.
[100] Text, *China Year Book, 1921-22*, pp. 628-29.
[101] Text, *Ibid.*, p. 629.

tion to negotiate with the powers regarding the matter. But "in the trying of cases in which foreigners are plaintiffs and Russians defendants, the Chinese courts may apply Russian laws, but only those which do not conflict with Chinese legal rights." It was possible, however, that specially qualified persons, versed in Russian law, might be "employed as advisers to the Chinese law courts." The Chinese Government, said Dr. Yen, was "exerting itself in every way to preserve the fundamental rights of Russian citizens"; consequently there was "no need to negotiate with the Diplomatic Body a provisional method for governing Russians."

Dr. Yen's veiled intimation that the Peking diplomats were presuming to interfere in a matter which was of no direct concern to their governments did not meet with unqualified acceptance in the Legation Quarter. The apprehensions of the foreign powers were strengthened by the appearance, on October 30, of a presidential mandate prescribing "Rules for the Administration of Russian Citizens residing in China." [102] These regulations provided that

1. Russian citizens in China should continue to enjoy rights to reside and trade in treaty ports or in other places where they had hitherto been allowed to reside. Their lives and property were to be protected, but they were "bound to obey Chinese laws and regulations," both those in force at the moment and those which might be promulgated in future. Russians engaged in missionary activity might continue to rent premises in the interior provided they observed the regulations governing such matters and secured the usual permission from the appropriate local authorities.

2. Russian residents in China who were suspected of carrying contraband might be subjected to examination by the local police authorities.

3. Russian citizens violating the laws and disturbing the public peace, or who were suspected of such violation, might "apart from legal consequences," be required to leave the country or to submit to official surveillance.

On the day following the appearance of these regulations, two more presidential mandates were issued providing for the

[102] Text, *China Year Book, 1921-22,* pp. 644-45.

organization of a system of Chinese courts in the zone of the
Chinese Eastern Railway.[103] A tribunal was to be set up at
Harbin with branches at other localities within the railway zone.
Appeals were to be taken to a special Court of Appeal at
Harbin and ultimately to the Supreme Court at Peking. Foreign
advisers and investigators might be attached to these local
courts. These advisers and investigators, with purely consulta-
tive functions, were to be chosen from among foreigners who
had had judicial experience under a foreign government or who
were barristers of recognized standing; the Presidents of the
Chinese Court of Appeal and of the Court of First Instance
at Harbin were to have supervision over them.

On November 18, the Doyen of the Diplomatic Body, acting
on behalf of his colleagues, transmitted a second note to the
Chinese Foreign Office.[104] In this communication, the foreign
representatives first expressed the opinion that the measures
already taken with regard to the rights of Russian citizens in
China directly contradicted the assurances given by the Chinese
Government regarding the protection of those rights. Particular
exception was taken to the President's mandates of October 31
providing for a system of courts within the zone of the Chinese
Eastern Railway. This mandate, declared the members of the
Diplomatic Body, would "have a tendency to abrogate the
extraterritorial rights of Russians in that territory by abolishing
the Russian law-courts and subjecting Russian citizens to the
jurisdiction of Chinese law-courts, in which the foreign advisers
. . . will have a very secondary position only." Complaint was
likewise made that the presidential mandates made no provision
for the application of Russian laws to Russians. It was pointed
out, also, that the Chinese authorities at Tientsin had assumed
control over the police of the Russian Concession, a control
which had formerly been vested in the municipal council. In
view of these and other considerations, the Diplomatic Body

[103] "Regulations for the Organization of the Judiciary in the Special
Manchurian Region," *China Year Book, 1921-22*, p. 638.
[104] *Ibid.*, pp. 629-31.

ventured to suggest that the Chinese Government modify its regulations concerning Russian rights in the following respects:

1. "To recognize that all the Russian Concessions must be served by their own police, depending upon the municipal councils, and to allow the municipal administrations of those Concessions to act on the basis of existing rules and regulations."

2. "To retain, as far as possible, the former Russian law-courts, both as institutions and as to staff; these law-courts to act henceforth in the name of China, but to apply Russian law. . . . These law-courts to deal with cases between Russians and, eventually, between Russians and foreigners. Disputes between Russians and Chinese may be examined either by mixed courts, to be composed locally of Chinese and Russian judges, in those cases where the plaintiff is of Russian nationality, or should he be Chinese, by the national court of the plaintiff or defendant. . . ."

3. "To institute in those Chinese centers with a considerable Russian population, posts of Russian advisers attached to the Chinese Commissioners for Foreign Affairs, these advisers to discharge administrative functions and to act as notaries public for Russian citizens. . . ." It would be useful in this connection "to create a special Bureau for Russian Affairs, to be composed of Russian advisers presided over by a high Chinese official, in the Chinese Ministry of Foreign Affairs."

To carry out these measures, the Diplomatic Body suggested that the Minister of Foreign Affairs convene a mixed conference composed of representatives of non-political Russian institutions in China, particularly those in the "leased territory" of the Chinese Eastern Railway. The representatives of the powers considered that "only a system on the general lines indicated above is capable of overcoming the difficulties which result from the Presidential Mandate of September 23 last, difficulties which are detrimental to the interests of the citizens of foreign powers which have signed treaties with China."

To this note, the Chinese Minister of Foreign Affairs replied at considerable length on November 29.[105] Denial was made that the measures thus far taken with regard to Russians contradicted in any way previous assurances given by the Chinese

[105] *China Year Book, 1921-22*, pp. 632-3.

Government. The withdrawal of recognition from the Russian Consuls had left the Chinese Government with no choice except to assume the functions formerly exercised by those officials. With regard to the Russian law-courts in the leased territory of the Chinese Eastern Railway, Dr. Yen observed that they were "based neither on the contract for the construction of this railway, nor on the treaty provisions relating to consular jurisdiction. They were established by the Russians in an arbitrary way, and the consent of the Chinese Government has never been obtained to them." The assertion that Chinese officials had infringed the administrative rights of the Russian Municipal Council at Tientsin was "probably the result of a misunderstanding": it did not take into consideration "the duty of officials to discharge the function with which they are entrusted. . . ."

With regard to the three specific suggestions for changes made by the Diplomatic Body, the Chinese Minister of Foreign Affairs declared:

1. "Orders have already been given that the Municipal Councils of the Concessions (should) continue to function as before on the basis of the regulations at present in force. With regard to the police, which is closely connected with the maintenance of local peace and order, the Chinese Government, in accordance with the spirit of the laws, must needs assume the corresponding duties. . . ."

2. Although the old Russian law-courts had never been recognized by China, the system of courts newly instituted in the Special Manchurian Region had, "for the convenience of Russians," been created on the old Russian model "both with regard to their organization and to the places where they are established." Moreover, "some of the former judges of the different grades of Russian courts have already been appointed advisers and investigators," and it was proposed to continue to appoint more of them.

3. "The former Russian notaries public have already been allowed to continue their functions."

The Diplomatic Body was reminded that the Ministry of Foreign Affairs had already established a commission for the study of Russian affairs, the head of which was Mr. Liu Ching-jen, formerly Minister to Russia. This commission was willing at all times to hear such opinions as might be expressed on behalf of Russian organizations in China. The representatives of the powers were asked to take account of the special difficulties occasioned by the presence in China of thousands of Russian refugees. In conclusion, Dr. Yen observed that

"Russians make raids into our frontier regions, molest Chinese citizens residing on Russian territory, confiscate the goods of Chinese merchants and, generally speaking, commit innumerable other deeds of the same kind. The Russians have thus long ago made manifest the impossibility of fulfilling the obligations resulting from the treaty stipulations. As for China, in consideration of the difficulties which have fallen to the lot of the Russians, and maintaining the most friendly feelings toward Russia, she has not only refrained from repudiating her obligations, but has on the contrary acted in a manner that has made her Government and people assume a new share of serious duties."

The diplomatic interference of the powers in a situation which actually concerned only China and Russia [106] yielded results which were partially satisfactory to the foreign representatives in Peking. On December 1, President Hsü Shih-ch'ang addressed a mandate to all local authorities, both civil and military, reminding them once again of their duty "to instruct the troops and police that they shall infallibly as before take effective measures for the protection of Russian citizens residing in China . . . so as to meet my desire to give protection and assistance to foreigners residing in China." [107] Moreover, the intolerable situation resulting from the sudden closing of the Russian courts in the Chinese Eastern Railway zone seemed likely to be relieved when, on December 2, the new system of Chinese courts for that region began to function. [108]

[106] Well-informed Chinese in Peking regarded this diplomatic meddling as an attempt to place additional restrictions on China's freedom of action. (*Millard's Review*, XV, Dec. 18, 1920, pp. 118-19.) This resentment was shared by at least one foreign writer—Mr. Roger S. Greene, in the *Peking Leader* for December 8. (*Ibid.*, p. 119.)

[107] Text, *China Year Book*, 1921-22, pp. 643-4.

[108] *China Year Book*, 1921-22, p. 638. It was estimated that the peremptory closing of the Russian courts in the railway zone left unsettled approximately 5,000 cases. The documents concerning these cases, which

Even these most recent measures of the Chinese Government did not completely allay the fears entertained by the Ministers representing the Treaty Powers. On December 14, the Diplomatic Body dispatched yet a third note to the Chinese Minister for Foreign Affairs.[109] While expressing satisfaction at the "benevolent assurances" contained in the Presidential Mandate of December 1, the representatives of the powers requested additional assurances on the following points:

1. "Will the Municipal police of the Russian Concessions remain under the orders of the Municipal Councils . . . and may it be taken for granted that the control of the Chinese authorities over the police will be enforced only through the medium of these Councils?"

2. "In what cases, by what procedure, and by what institutions, does the Chinese Government consider that Russian laws shall be applied? . . ."

3. "Russian notaries public exercise their functions only on the leased territory of the Chinese Eastern Railway. How will the question of notaries public be solved in other places in China?"

4. "What will be the sphere of competence of the Russian Advisers" which were to be employed by the Chinese Government? "Does the Chinese Government intend to engage Russian Advisers in the provinces of Chinese Turkestan, Mongolia, and Peking itself?"

The Chinese Government delayed answering these questions until February 28, 1921. The representatives of the powers were then assured that [110]

1. Since the Chinese authorities were responsible for the maintenance of order in the Russian Concessions, it was essential that these authorities should have the right to superintend the police. However, a Russian police officer had been appointed, with the approval of the municipal council, to act as assistant for the direction of all police matters in the "ex-Russian Concession" at Tientsin.

the Chinese authorities attempted at first to translate into their own language, covered about 180,000 sheets. *Ibid.,* p. 639.
[109] Text, *China Year Book, 1921-22,* pp. 634-5.
[110] Yen to the Doyen of the Diplomatic Body, *China Year Book, 1921-22,* pp. 635-6.

2. All cases involving questions of private international law were to be governed by Rules for the Application of Laws, promulgated in 1918. Russian and not Chinese laws were to be applied in cases where the question arose as to the applicability of Chinese or Russian law, as well as in cases "in which, according to the provisions of the Rules [of 1918] foreign law is to be applied." As regards the procedure to be followed and the organ which was to apply Russian law in such cases, this was to be "the Chinese Court in which the case is being tried . . . which should apply Russian law, while using the forensic procedure laid down in Chinese law."

3. The Commissioners for Foreign Affairs at Tientsin and Hankow "who exercise Consular functions in the stead of Consuls" had been empowered to act concurrently, with the assistance of Russian advisers, as notaries public.

4. "The functions and powers of the Russian advisers attached to the offices of the Commissioners for Foreign Affairs are to assist the Commissioners in the arrangement of matters in which Russians are concerned. In the opinion of the Chinese Government there is at present no need to engage Russian advisers for Sinkiang, Mongolia, or Peking."

While this diplomatic duel was in progress, the liquidation of Russian interests in China went steadily forward. Russian post offices, both in China proper and in Manchuria, were forced to close their doors.[111] Valuables belonging to the old Tsarist Government and to the former Kolchak Government, deposited with banks in China, were sequestrated. Property belonging to the Omsk Ministry of Supplies, which had been given into the custody of the Russian Consulate General at Harbin, was taken over first by a mixed Russo-Chinese commission appointed by the Chinese Government, and later by the Chinese local authorities.[112]

Throughout most of the country, Chinese officials, acting nominally in place of the former Russian Consuls, assumed

[111] *North China Herald*, CXXXVII, Oct. 9, 1920, p. 82; Nov. 20, 1920, p. 533; Dec. 4, 1920, p. 672. The Russian post office in Harbin continued to function until January 26, 1921, when an armed guard, acting under orders from the Chinese Taoyin of Kirin-Penkiang, compelled it to suspend operations. *North China Herald*, CXXXIX, Apr. 16, 1921, p. 192.
[112] *China Year Book, 1921-22*, pp. 627-8.

jurisdiction over Russian nationals. At Shanghai, however, a peculiar situation existed. There not only was the Russian Consulate located in the International Settlement, but most Russian citizens resided and did business within the limits of that foreign controlled area where Chinese jurisdiction was, to say the least, ineffective.[113] The Russian Consul General, despite the instructions sent him in September by Prince Koudacheff, continued to exercise his functions, both administrative and judicial.[114] Ultimately, however, a solution of this problem was reached as a result of negotiations between the Shanghai consular body, the local Chinese Commissioner for Foreign Affairs, and the Peking authorities. It was agreed that a Bureau for Russian Affairs should be set up in the former Russian Consulate, to be controlled by the Chinese Commissioner for Foreign Affairs, but administered by the former Russian Consul General acting as his deputy.[115] Only administrative matters were to be handled by this new Bureau. Judicial matters involving Russians were to be handled either by the appropriate Chinese court or by the Shanghai Mixed Court. The consular body had already, by its own action, agreed to appoint the Russian ex-Vice Consul to sit as the Senior Consul's assessor in Mixed Court cases involving Russian nationals.[116] In line with the precedent established at Shanghai, Russian officials formerly in the consular service were appointed as advisers to the Chinese Commissioners for Foreign Affairs at both Tientsin and Hankow.[117]

[113] The British editor of the North China Daily News stated that as regards measures for handling Russian interests within the Settlement, "every suggestion ultimately breaks down on the unalterable fact that the Chinese Bureau of Foreign Affairs has no legal existence in Shanghai, and that no Chinese official can exercise any authority within its boundaries." North China Herald, CXXXVII, Oct. 30, 1920, p. 291.
[114] North China Herald, CXXXVII, Oct. 30, 1920, p. 291.
[115] China Year Book, 1921-22, pp. 645-6
[116] Ibid., p. 645. A Russian tribunal was also created to decide civil cases between Russian or foreign plaintiffs and Russian defendants in which the parties, before trial, agreed to submit to the decision of such a tribunal. Its decision was to be enforced by the police of the International Settlement with the sanction of the Mixed Court. Ibid., p. 646.
[117] China Year Book, 1921-22, p. 646.

As regards Russia's interests in northern Manchuria, special problems were created by the action of the Chinese Government in withdrawing recognition from Prince Koudacheff. The first of these problems concerned administration within the railway zone. The second concerned the administration of the railway itself.

The problem of administration within the railway zone had three aspects. These were, first, judicial administration, second, municipal administration, and third, police administration.[118] As already indicated, special Chinese courts, organized in accordance with the Presidential Mandate of October 31, began to function on December 2 in place of the old Russian tribunals, some of which had suspended operations only after a show of armed force by the Chinese authorities.[119] From the first, the special Chinese courts were swamped with unsettled cases carried over from the Russian régime. Verdicts and sentences pronounced by the Russian courts remained unexecuted. Moreover, many of the Chinese judges and procurators lacked the special training necessary in the handling of disputes involving Russians, and the government delayed employing competent Russians to assist in such work.[120] Eventually, but not until March 2, 1921, the Chinese Government created a special Section for the Liquidation of the old Russian Legal Cases in the Special Manchurian Region.[121] In criminal cases, this Section, to which Russian assessors were subsequently attached,[122] was instructed to apply the provisions of the Provisional Criminal Code of China, except that where Russian criminal law provided for punishment in a minor degree, the punishment imposed by the Chinese court was to be correspondingly reduced. In civil cases, "the existing Chinese laws and regulations" as modified by the

[118] Cf. Weigh, *op. cit.*, p. 245.
[119] *Ibid.*, p. 246.
[120] For a trenchant criticism of the Chinese Government's failure to meet its responsibilities during this period of transition, see Rodney Gilbert, "Russians under Chinese Jurisdiction," *North China Herald*, CXXXIX, Apr. 16, 1921, pp. 264-66.
[121] *China Year Book, 1921-22*, p. 639.
[122] *North China Herald*, CXXXIX, Apr. 9, 1921, p. 84.

1918 Rules for the Application of Foreign Law,[128] were to be applied.

The municipal administrations at Harbin and elsewhere within the zone of the Chinese Eastern Railway came under Chinese control not long after the issuance of the President's mandate of September 23, 1920.[124] In February, 1921, the announcement was made that municipal administrations within the railway zone would henceforth be subject to the supervision of the Harbin Taoyin and his assistant.[125] The Taoyin was appointed sole head of the Harbin municipal council, and on February 15, the Chinese flag was hoisted over buildings belonging to the municipality.[126]

Chinese control over the police of the railway zone had been established in March, 1920. At that time the Chinese authorities disarmed all Russian police on lands belonging to the railway, and replaced them by new appointees. A few Russian officers and constables were retained in the newly organized gendarmerie, but for the most part their places were taken by Chinese. Not only the railway zone itself, but the municipalities located therein were henceforth policed by forces under Chinese control. As a consequence of this step, Russian administrative and judicial institutions within the railway area were obliged to depend on Chinese police to execute their decisions.[127]

The difficulty of policing the railway zone with Chinese officers was immensely increased by the presence there of numerous Japanese troops. Allied military intervention in

[128] Text, *China Year Book, 1921-22*, pp. 654-7.
[124] *Ibid.*, p. 650.
[125] *North China Herald*, CXLV, Dec. 30, 1922, p. 869.
[126] *Ibid.*, CXXXVIII, Feb. 19, 1921, p. 450. The Chinese authorities were entirely within their legal rights in assuming control over municipal bodies within the railway zone, for the Harbin Taoyin presumed merely to exercise the functions formerly vested in the Russian Consul General. The Chinese position had been strengthened by an agreement, signed in October, 1920, between representatives of the government and of the Russo-Asiatic Bank. This agreement provided for a substantial increase in Chinese powers of administration over the Chinese Eastern Railway, which had the actual right—according to the Russian view—to administer the railway zone.
[127] *China Year Book, 1921-22*, p. 648; Weigh, *op. cit.*, p. 250.

Siberia had begun in the summer of 1918. Partly in consequence of this intervention, the Japanese Government eventually dispatched 60,000 troops to northern Manchuria.[128] The presence of these troops along the Chinese Eastern Railway was justified, according to Japanese contentions, under the provisions of the Sino-Japanese military conventions of May and September, 1918.[129] Numerous clashes, however, took place between Japanese soldiers and those belonging to China.[130]

On January 9, 1919, the Allied Governments reached an agreement relative to joint supervision over the Siberian railway system, including the Chinese Eastern Railway.[131] Subsequently, in April, 1919, the Allied commanders at Vladivostok agreed to apportion the responsibility for the military protection of the Siberian railways.[132] Chinese troops were to guard the entire Chinese Eastern Railway from Nikolsk to Manchuli and from Harbin to Changchun. One thousand American troops, however, were to be sent to Harbin.[133] Even after this agreement had been reached, Japanese forces continued to occupy the railway zone, and it became more and more apparent that Japan was ambitious to succeed to Russian rights of control over the railway. Only the steady opposition offered by the Allied Technical Board, in actual control of railway operations, prevented these ambitious plans from bearing fruit. On April 14, 1920, the members of the Technical Board, except for the Japanese member, protested formally against the unwarranted and arbitrary conduct of the Japanese military authorities within the railway zone. The resolution, approved by the representatives of Great Britain, the United States, France, China, Russia, and

[128] Weigh, *op. cit.*, p. 228. Quarterly report of Mr. MacMurray, transmitted to the Secretary of State Nov. 29, 1918. *United States Foreign Relations*, 1918, pp. 125-6.
[129] Willoughby, *Foreign Rights and Interests in China*, Vol. I, p. 430.
[130] Millard, *Democracy and the Eastern Question*, pp. 316 ff.
[131] MacMurray, *op. cit.*, Vol. I, p. 82.
[132] MacMurray, *op. cit.*, Vol. I, pp. 83-4.
[133] Actually, only 75 American troops were sent to Harbin. Before their arrival, General Horvath turned all barracks over to the Japanese, and it was necessary for even this small American force to find shelter in the Red Cross headquarters. E. T. Williams, *A Short History of China* (New York and London, 1928), p. 539.

Czecho-Slovakia, was transmitted to their respective governments.[134] Following this protest, a commission of foreign advisers to the Chinese Government was sent to investigate conditions along the railway. The findings of this commission, which received widespread publicity throughout China, were distinctly unfavorable to continued Japanese occupation of the railway zone.[135]

One consequence of Allied intervention in Siberia was that the management of the Chinese Eastern Railway itself came for a time under the control of representatives of the Allied Governments. The agreement of January 9, 1919, already mentioned, provided for the creation of two boards which were to supervise all railways within the zone of Allied military operations in Siberia.[136] The first of these boards, entrusted with powers of general supervision over the railways, was to consist of representatives from each of the Allied Powers maintaining troops in eastern Siberia, including Russia. The actual management of the railways was placed in charge of a second board, composed of technical experts named by the Allied Governments. An Allied Military Transport Board was also set up to coördinate the work of moving troops under the direction of the proper military authorities.

Inter-Allied administration of the Chinese Eastern Railway, however, no matter how efficient, did not harmonize with Chinese aspirations. The Chinese Government felt that only China and Russia could claim a legal interest in the railway. Moreover, it was feared that international control over the Chinese Eastern Railway might be merely a prelude to international

[134] Text, *Millard's Review*, XII, May 1, 1920, pp. 442-6.
[135] *North China Herald*, CXXXVIII, Jan. 15, 1921, p. 124. It is quite probable that the Chinese Government's willingness to negotiate with M. Yourin in September, 1920, rose out of its desire for aid in resisting Japanese encroachments in northern Manchuria. The Sino-Japanese military conventions of 1918, under the provisions of which Japan claimed the right to station troops in northern Manchuria, were terminated by mutual agreement on January 28, 1921. It is significant that with the subsequent withdrawal of Japanese troops from the Chinese Eastern Railway zone, the Peking Government showed more and more of a disposition not to be hurried into a treaty with the Far Eastern Republic.
[136] MacMurray, *op. cit.*, Vol. I, p. 82.

control over all the railways of China.[137] The ultimate objective of the Chinese Government was exclusive control by China
over the Chinese Eastern Railway. It was admitted, however,
that since "Russian business men" had a fractional capital interest in the line, the Chinese Government would have to protect
Russian interests in the railway and postpone its ultimate
redemption.[138]

In order to avert permanent international control of the
railway, the Chinese Government, on October 2, 1920, concluded an agreement with the Russo-Asiatic Bank which was
supplementary to the original railway contract of 1896.[139] The
Chinese Government announced its intention "to resume provisionally, pending such arrangement concerning the railway
as the Government may reach with the Russian Government that
may be recognized by China, the supreme control exercised
over the said railway by virtue of the contract and of the regulations in force, and to resume the advantages and particular
interests conferred upon China by the operating contract" of
1896 and the original statutes of the railway company. The
Chinese Government was given the right to name, in addition
to the President, "four members of Chinese nationality upon the
Board of Management," who were not required to be shareholders of the company. The five Russian members of the
board of management were to be named by the shareholders
of the company. Decisions of this board were not to be effective
unless approved by seven of its members. Of the five members
of the Committee of Audit (Comité de Revision) two, including the President, were to be of Chinese nationality. It was
agreed also that "the posts of the railway" should be shared
"in an equitable manner between Chinese and Russians."

[137] See the official statement of the Chinese Government issued following the signature of the agreement with the Russo-Asiatic Bank, *Far
Eastern Review*, XVI, p. 605. (November, 1920.)
[138] *Ibid.*
[139] Text, *Treaties and Agreements, 1919-1929*, pp. 29-31. See also
Manchuria, Treaties and Agreements, Pamphlet No. 44, Carnegie Endowment for International Peace, Division of International Law (Washington,
1921), pp. 210 ff.

Article VI of the agreement provided, finally, that "the rights and the obligations of the Company will henceforth be in every respect of a commercial character; every political activity and every political attribute will be absolutely forbidden to it. To this end, the Chinese Government reserves the right to prescribe restrictive measures of any character and at any time." [140]

However far this agreement fell short of meeting China's ultimate desires with regard to the Chinese Eastern Railway, it seemed likely, for a time at least, to mark the end of Russia's political influence in northern Manchuria.

[140] For the presidential mandate announcing this agreement, see *Far Eastern Review*, XVI, p. 605. (November, 1920.) For the views of Dr. C. C. Wang, Associate Director of the Chinese Eastern Railway, concerning the manner in which the new agreement was expected to work, see Hollington K. Tong, "Chinese Eastern Railway under New Management," *Millard's Review*, XV, Dec. 25, 1920, pp. 176-8.

CHAPTER VI

THE RECOGNITION OF SOVIET RUSSIA

THE failure of the Far Eastern Republic to secure a trading convention with China in 1921 had provoked keen disappointment in Moscow no less than in Chita. During March, 1921, the Soviet Government had managed to conclude such a convention with Great Britain, and in May this was followed by a similar agreement with Germany.[1] Since, according to socialist theory, political relationships must necessarily be shaped by economic facts, it could be assumed that this reëstablishment of commercial relations would be followed sooner or later by political recognition of Soviet Russia. Similar reasoning was applied by the Bolshevik leaders to the situation in the Far East. The Peking Government had remained indifferent in the face of ostensibly friendly overtures from Moscow. It had also rebuffed the efforts of M. Yourin to secure an agreement for the regulation of trade across the Siberian frontier. There was a possibility, however, that an emissary commissioned directly by the Soviet Government might succeed where the Chita envoy had failed. With this hope in mind, a Soviet mission, late in 1921, set out from Moscow on its way to China.

The attitude of the Peking Government toward Soviet Russia at this time was influenced by a disquieting series of events in Outer Mongolia. Following the abrogation of Mongolian autonomy in November, 1919, the Chinese commander, General Hsü Shu-tseng, had instituted measures designed to bring the entire region under his military control. His harsh rule extended even to outlying districts, and the tribesmen suffered grievously under abuses committed by undisciplined Chinese

[1] Louis Fischer, *The Soviets in World Affairs,* Vol. II, p. 467.

161

troops. Profane hands were even laid on the Hutukhtu him-
self.[2] In July, 1920, however, following the downfall of the
Anfu clique in Peking, General Hsü was dismissed from office.[3]
Hopes were expressed that this step presaged the adoption by
the Chinese Government of a more liberal policy toward the
Mongols. These hopes were not realized. Finally, in despera-
tion, the Mongol princes turned for assistance to the White
Russian adventurer, Baron Ungern von Sternberg. In late October, Ungern led a force of two thousand Mongols, Buriats,
Russian reactionaries, and Japanese, in an unsuccessful attack
upon the Chinese garrison at Urga.[4] Not discouraged by his
defeat, Ungern returned with a larger force in February, 1921,
when he succeeded in capturing the city. The Chinese commander was killed and his troops scattered.[5] Immediately thereafter the Hutukhtu, who had escaped from his Chinese guards
prior to the capture of the city, declared the independence of
Inner as well as Outer Mongolia, and proclaimed himself
Emperor.[6]

The Mongols, including the Hutukhtu, desired merely the
right to rule themselves without Chinese interference. Baron
Ungern, however, hoped to use Mongolia as a base from which
to attack the Bolsheviks of Siberia. Ultimately he dreamed of
establishing a Pan-Mongolian Empire on the foundations laid
by his remote ancestor, Ghengiz Khan.[7] Unwilling to be involved in any such scheme, the Hutukhtu turned again to
Peking. The Mongol revolt, declared the Buddhist prelate in
a note to President Hsü Shih-ch'ang, had been directed solely
against the military régime instituted by General Hsü Shu-tseng.
What Mongolia chiefly desired was autonomy; the friendly
assistance of the Chinese would be welcomed to the extent that

[2] *North China Herald*, CXXXVI, Sept. 11, 1920, p. 665. *Ibid.*, Aug.
14, 1920, p. 416.
[3] *Ibid.*, July 10, 1920, p. 80.
[4] *Ibid.*, CXXXVII, Oct. 30, 1920, p. 301. *Ibid.*, Nov. 20, 1920, p. 518.
Ibid,, Nov. 27, 1920, p. 587
[5] *Ibid.*, CXXXVIII, Feb. 19, 1921, p. 442. *Ibid.*, Mar. 26, 1921, p. 793.
[6] *Millard's Review*, XVI, Mar. 5, 1921, pp. 10-12.
[7] On this point see Fischer, *op. cit.*, II, pp. 534-7.

it aided toward the reëstablishment of peace and normal conditions in the country.[8] This overture was well received by the Chinese Government and the Mongolian ruler was invited to send to Peking a representative invested with plenipotentiary powers.[9] The resulting negotiations ended in a deadlock. Thereupon the Peking Government abandoned its conciliatory attitude and commissioned Marshal Chang Tso-lin with full power to deal drastically with the Mongolian insurgents and their anti-Bolshevik allies.[10]

At this point, the Soviet Government interfered. Russian troops, coöperating with the forces of the Far Eastern Republic, entered Outer Mongolia in pursuit of Baron Ungern. In a note dated June 15, M. Chicherin, Commissar for Foreign Affairs at Moscow, notified the Peking Government that Soviet troops had been compelled to cross the frontier into Mongolia, but that as soon as the Ungern forces had been crushed, they would be withdrawn.[11] Replying to this note, the Chinese Foreign Office notified M. Chicherin that Marshal Chang Tso-lin had been given full power to deal with the Ungern forces, and that the troops at his disposal were sufficient for this purpose.[12] In spite of this polite intimation that China was competent to manage her own affairs, Russian troops continued their operations against the reactionary forces in Mongolia. Baron Ungern barely escaped capture when Urga was taken by the invading army on July 5. Subsequently he fell into the hands of the Soviet military authorities and was executed.[13]

---

[8] *North China Herald*, CXXXIX, Apr. 23, 1921, p. 234.
[9] *Ibid. Millard's Review*, XVI, Apr. 30, 1921, pp. 445-6.
[10] Presidential Mandate, May 30, 1921, *North China Herald*, June 4, 1921, p. 650.
[11] *North China Herald*, CXL, July 9, 1921, p. 87. When Ungern's capture of Urga was imminent, M. Yourin, the envoy of the Far Eastern Republic at Peking, notified the Chinese authorities that his government was prepared to dispatch disciplined troops to Outer Mongolia for the purpose of suppressing the reactionary Russian forces there. These troops, he promised, would coöperate with the Chinese armies and would be promptly withdrawn as soon as prevailing disorders had ceased. The Chinese Government declined the offer. *Millard's Review*, XVI, Mar. 5, 1921, p. 10.
[12] *North China Herald*, CXL, July 9, 1921, p. 92.
[13] Fischer, *op. cit.*, II, p. 537. *North China Herald*, CXL, Sept. 24, 1921, Supplement, p. 467.

The end of the Soviet campaign against Baron Ungern left Russian and Siberian troops to the number of 6,500 on Mongolian soil. Thousands of Russian Whites were said still to be operating in the region. The presence of the Red forces eliminated the possibility of further danger from that quarter, and also removed the menace of a Chinese invasion. Five days after the capture of Urga, the Young Mongol leaders set up a People's Revolutionary Government.[14] Early in August, this new government appealed to the Soviet Government not to withdraw its troops "until the complete removal of the menace from the common enemy"—the reactionaries under Ungern.[15] To this appeal Commissar Chicherin replied on August 10 that "the appearance of the Soviet troops on the territory of autonomous Mongolia has for its sole aim the destruction of the common enemy, thus removing the danger which threatens the Soviet territory, and safeguarding the free development and self-determination of autonomous Mongolia. . . . Having firmly decided to withdraw its troops from the territory of autonomous Mongolia . . . just as soon as the menace to the free development of the Mongolian people and to the security of the Russian Republic and of the Far Eastern Republic shall have been removed, the Russian Government, in complete harmony with the People's Revolutionary Government of Mongolia, notes that this moment has not yet arrived."[16] In a second note dated September 10, the Mongolian Minister for Foreign Affairs asked for Russian assistance in the restoration of peaceful relations between Mongolia and China. Commissar Chicherin replied on September 14 that "more than once has the Russian Government approached the Government of China, both directly and through representatives of the Far Eastern Republic who were in communication with the latter, with

[14] Chicherin afterward admitted that the People's Revolutionary Mongolian army which supported this government was created in Russian territory. Dennis, *op. cit.*, p. 322.
[15] Translation from Moscow *Izvestia*, Aug. 10, 1921, text in Pasvolsky, *op. cit.*, pp. 176-7.
[16] Translation from Moscow *Izvestia*, Aug. 12, 1921, text in Pasvolsky, *op. cit.*, pp. 177-9.

offers to begin negotiations on this question. In the near future the Russian Government expects to enter into permanent relations with the Government of China by means of a trade delegation which is being sent to Peking." [17] The head of this delegation, said the Soviet Commissar, would be instructed to use his good offices in bringing about negotiations between China and Mongolia regarding matters which were of interest to both, and thereby "remove the possibility of a conflict" between the peoples and governments of the two countries.[18]

The Soviet mission to which M. Chicherin had referred in his note to the Mongolian Government arrived in Peking December 12, 1921. It was headed by Mr. Alexander K. Paikes.[19] The Soviet envoy announced that the attitude of his government toward China was "unquestionably friendly and peaceful." Chinese apprehensions with regard to Russian military activity in Mongolia were said to be due to "misunder-

---

[17] Translation from Moscow *Izvestia*, Sept. 17, 1921, text in Pasvolsky, *op. cit.*, pp. 180-81.

[18] Foreign business men returning from Outer Mongolia at this time reported that extraterritorial rights were not recognized by the Mongolian Government. Foreigners, however, were permitted to travel in any part of the country provided they carried passports from the Ministry of Foreign Affairs at Urga. *North China Herald*, CXLI, Oct. 22, 1921, p. 224.

[19] *North China Herald*, CXLI, Dec. 17, 1921, p. 751. There is some doubt as to whether Paikes carried credentials from the Chita or the Moscow Government or both. Whatever the appearance, the reality was that he represented the policy of the Soviet Government. It is possible that Paikes' errand in the Far East at this time was not unconnected with the Washington Conference. On arriving at Harbin, the Soviet envoy warned China that this conference had been called by the powers "for the purpose of attempting in a peaceful way to arrange with as little cost as possible the division among themselves of the globe and the enslavement of the weaker nations. China should not expect for herself any good results from the Conference. Even if some privileges and resolutions in favor of China were adopted, they will . . . remain on paper and will never be realized." *Ibid.*, Dec. 24, 1921, p. 824. Originally the Soviet Government had intended to invite representatives of Asiatic states to an international gathering which would rival the conference at Washington. Subsequently abandoning this plan, the Moscow Government left the matter to be dealt with by the Communist Internationale. Under the auspices of the latter, a Congress of Peoples of the Far East met at the Soviet capital in January, 1922. Here the Washington Conference was attacked for its failure to protect "the working masses and enslaved colonial peoples" from the menace of "an armed capitalistic peace." The Four Power Pacific Treaty was denounced as a "Quadruple Alliance of bloodsuckers." Dennis, *op. cit.*, p. 307.

standing." [20] The Soviet Government entertained no aggressive designs with regard to any Chinese territory. Troops of the Far Eastern Republic had already been withdrawn from Mongolia and only Red forces remained temporarily to prevent a renewal of White Guardist activity. Even these forces would be withdrawn after an agreement had been reached with the Chinese Government for the maintenance of order in that region. With regard to the Chinese Eastern Railway, said Paikes, Russia was fully prepared to recognize China's sovereignty in the railway zone. The Soviet Government desired only that the railway itself remain in Chinese hands, and that both Russia and the Far Eastern Republic be given an economic outlet to the Pacific Ocean. [21]

The attitude of sweet reasonableness reflected in these public utterances of the Russian representative created a distinctly favorable atmosphere in Peking. Four days after his arrival in the Chinese capital, Paikes presented his credentials to Dr. Yen, Minister of Foreign Affairs. [22] After a delay of several weeks, the government authorized representatives of the Ministry of Communications and the Waichiao Pu to begin unofficial conversations with him relative to the Chinese Eastern Railway and also to the question of restoring official relations between the two countries. [23]

Despite rumors to the contrary, Paikes at first denied the existence of any treaty between Soviet Russia and Mongolia. Subsequently, however, the text of such a treaty, concluded at Moscow, November 5, 1921, appeared in the newspapers. [24] By this agreement, the two governments accorded each other *de jure* recognition, and agreed to exchange plenipotentiary representatives and consuls. Both parties bound themselves to

[20] *North China Herald*, CXLI, Dec. 24, 1921, p. 824.
[21] *Ibid.*, Dec. 31, 1921, p. 887. *Weekly Review of the Far East*, XIX, Dec. 31, 1921, pp. 186, 190-91.
[22] *Weekly Review of the Far East*, XIX, Dec. 31, 1921, p. 208.
[23] *North China Herald*, CXLII, Jan. 21, 1922, p. 150.
[24] Dennis, *op. cit.*, p. 323. For the text of the treaty, see *Treaties and Agreements, 1919-1929*, pp. 53-6.

suppress the activity on their respective territories of "organizations, groups, or individuals, having as their purpose to struggle against the other party or to overthrow its government or the governments of States allied with it." Measures were likewise to be taken to prevent arms from reaching such persons or groups. A boundary commission, formed in accordance with a special agreement to be concluded as soon as possible, was to delimit the frontier between Mongolia and the Soviet Republic. Subject to certain safeguards, each party renounced the right to exercise extraterritorial jurisdiction over citizens of the other party residing in its territory. The agreement contained a general most-favored-nation clause which was specifically applied to the payment of customs duties, which each country was to fix for itself, and to rights to own and lease land and buildings. The Soviet Government, "wishing to assist the wise measures of the People's Government of Mongolia in the matter of the organization . . . of a postal and telegraphic exchange," agreed to turn over "without compensation, as the full property of the Mongolian people, the buildings of telegraphic offices with the telegraphic equipment therein which belong to the Russian Republic and are located within the boundaries of Mongolia" (Article 10). Article 11 provided, however, that "taking into consideration the full importance of regulating the questions of postal and telegraphic communications between Russia and Mongolia, as well as the transmission of transit telegraphic correspondence through Mongolia, in order to strengthen the mutual cultural and economic relations which unite the peoples of both countries, the parties agree that a special agreement on this subject shall be concluded in the shortest possible time." None of the thirteen articles of the agreement touched upon the rights or interests of China in Mongolia.

The publication of this agreement provoked keen resentment in Peking. Faced with the published text, Mr. Paikes was now ready to admit what it was no longer possible to deny. On

May 1, 1922, therefore, he received a sharp note from the Waichiao Pu.[25] Reminding the Soviet envoy of repeated declarations by his government "that all previous treaties made between the Russian Government and China shall be null and void, that the Soviet Government renounces all encroachments on Chinese territory and all concessions within China, and that the Soviet Government will unconditionally and forever return what has been forcibly seized from China by the former Imperial Russian Government and the Bourgeoisie," the Chinese Foreign Office complained that now the Soviet Government had "suddenly gone back on its own words and secretly and without any right concluded a treaty with Mongolia. Such action on the part of the Soviet Government is similar to the policy the former Imperial Russian Government assumed toward China." The note observed, further, that "Mongolia is a part of Chinese territory and as such has long been recognized by all countries. In secretly concluding a treaty with Mongolia, the Soviet Government has not only broken faith with its previous declarations, but also violates all principles of justice. The Chinese Government finds it difficult to tolerate such action, and therefore we solemnly lodge a protest with you to the effect that any treaty secretly concluded between the Soviet Government and Mongolia will not be recognized by the Chinese Government."

Even this protest of the Chinese Government failed to halt the diplomatic rapprochement between Russia and Mongolia. On May 31, 1922, a second Russo-Mongolian agreement was signed at Urga.[26] It provided for the restoration to the Soviet Republic of "all buildings and property on the territory of Outer Mongolia, which previously belonged to the former Russian Government and which are now under the supervision of the consulates of the latter," and also of "buildings and property of former Russian public local governments which are located in the City of Urga and in other places." At the

[25] Text, Dennis, *op. cit.*, pp. 323-4.
[26] Text, *Treaties and Agreements, 1919-1929*, pp. 102-103.

same time, questions concerning the property and buildings of firms and institutions nationalized in Russia were "postponed for a more detailed familiarization with such property by both parties." The Mongolian Government was accorded the right to confiscate all property belonging to persons "who fled upon the occupation of Mongolia by forces of the People's Government" as well as the property of all persons "who participated in actions of common enemies of the Russian Socialist Federated Soviet Republic and Mongolia." These provisions were to come into effect, however, only in the event that similar measures were applied "with respect to citizens of other countries." [27]

Chinese resentment against the policy revealed in these Russo-Mongolian agreements convinced the authorities at Moscow that nothing short of heroic measures would serve now to bridge the widening gap between the two countries. In any case, the time was ripe for a shift in the direction of Soviet diplomacy, for the international conferences held at Genoa in April and at The Hague in June of 1922 had ended in failure. Rebuffed in Europe, Russia once more turned her face toward the East. In July a new Soviet mission was sent to China, at the head of which was Mr. Adolph A. Joffe, a diplomat of the first importance who had recently been one of the chief Russian delegates to the Genoa Conference.

With the members of his suite, Mr. Joffe arrived in Peking,

[27] In June, 1922, the Mongolian Government notified foreign land-owners in Urga that they must surrender their title deeds in exchange for thirty-year leases which were subject to revision at the end of five-year intervals. It was reported that ninety per cent of such foreign property was held by Chinese, the remainder being in the hands of Russians and Americans. *North China Herald*, CXLIII, June 3, 1922, p. 660. *Weekly Review of the Far East*. XXI, June 10, 1922, p. 43. In September, Prince Chi Chen-shen, who claimed to represent Outer Mongolia, complained to the Chinese Government that the Mongol tribes were completely under the yoke of the Reds who were collecting illegal taxes and generally oppressing the people. The government was asked to bring these matters to the attention of the Soviet envoy in Peking. About this time, the Chinese Government decided to establish a commission for the rehabilitation of Mongolia; ominously the commission was placed under the chairmanship of the Minister of War. *North China Herald*, CXLIV, Sept. 30, 1922, p. 939. *Ibid.*, CXLV, Oct. 14, 1922, p. 76.

August 12, 1922.[28] He was received with enthusiasm by educational leaders headed by Chancellor Ts'ai Yuan-p'ei of Peking National University, Dr. Hu Shih, and other similar scholars of national reputation. At a dinner given to a group of these admirers shortly after his arrival, the Soviet envoy gladdened the hearts of his guests by heaping ridicule upon the foreign journalists in China. Chancellor Ts'ai, responding in kind, linked friendship for Russia with the elimination of foreign rights and special privileges in China.[29]

Mr. Joffe's reception in official circles was somewhat less cordial than that accorded him by the scholars. His mission was at best a difficult one. Of first importance was the need of reëstablishing diplomatic relations between the Peking and the Moscow Governments. At the same time, Russian influence in Mongolia must not be sacrificed. The third problem concerned Russia's economic and financial interests in the Chinese Eastern Railway, which the Peking Government was not too anxious to recognize. When, on September 2, the Soviet envoy proposed that formal negotiations be opened on the basis of the Karakhan declarations of 1919 and 1920, the Minister of Foreign Affairs, Dr. Wellington Koo, immediately raised the question of the Russian occupation of Outer Mongolia and demanded that this Chinese territory be evacuated as a condition precedent to the beginning of formal negotiations.[30] But before this knotty problem could be settled, or even discussed, Mr. Joffe suddenly left Peking for Changchun, where a conference opened September 6 between representatives of the Japanese and the Far Eastern Republican Governments.

The abrupt departure of the Soviet representative was disconcerting but the knowledge that such a conference was to be held on Chinese territory without formal notice to the Chinese authorities gave rise to still graver apprehensions. Nor were these apprehensions stilled when an official observer representing the Chinese Government was excluded from the sessions

[28] *Ibid.*, CXLIV, Aug. 19, 1922, p. 512.
[29] *North China Herald*, CXLIV, Sept. 9, 1922, pp. 716-17.
[30] *China Year Book*, 1924, p. 859. Dennis, *op. cit.*, p. 325.

of the conference. Chinese fears were reflected in separate
notes despatched to the Tokyo and Chita Governments announcing that China must refuse to recognize any decisions of
the conference adversely affecting her sovereignty.[31]

Fundamental disagreements between the Russian and the
Japanese representatives brought the Changchun conference to
an end on September 25, and a week later Mr. Joffe returned
to Peking. In the exchange of views which followed, Dr. Koo
again raised the issue of Mongolia. Aside from the continued
presence there of Russian troops, Chinese merchants were complaining of unjust and arbitrary treatment.[32] Referring to the
presence of Soviet troops in Mongolia, the Russian envoy protested that it was inadmissible thus to pick out any separate
question from "the whole complexus of questions to be discussed at the Conference." With regard to the complaints of
the Chinese merchants, he declared, further, that the local Mongolian authorities and not the Russian military command were
responsible for all measures of internal administration.[33]

The Russian envoy attempted to turn the point of Dr. Koo's
attack by charging that the Chinese authorities had been lax
in dealing with White Guardists who used Chinese soil as a
base for subversive intrigues directed against the Soviet Government. Particularly was this true in northern Manchuria,
where Chinese officials even assisted "the White bandits in their
urge to deal a blow at the Russian people." [34] Following this
remonstrance, the Peking Government on October 27 issued
an order directing local authorities to disarm all bands of White

[31] *China Year Book, 1924*, p. 859. *North China Herald*, CXLV, Oct.
7, 1922, p. 11.
[32] *China Year Book, 1924*, pp. 859-60.
[33] *Ibid.* Joffe's excellent press bureau began to inquire at this time why
protests were made regarding the presence of Russian troops in distant Urga
while other governments were permitted to maintain legation guards in
Peking itself. Dennis, *op. cit.*, pp. 324-5.
[34] Joffe to the Waichiao Pu, Oct. 14, 1922, *China Year Book, 1924*, p.
860. *Weekly Review*, XXIII, Jan. 27, 1923, p. 340. Bolshevik forces occupied Vladivostok October 25, 1922, following the Japanese evacuation of
the city. In consequence, great numbers of reactionary Russians who had
enjoyed the protection of Japan, fled across the border into Manchuria.
North China Herald, CXLV, Nov. 4, 1922, p. 292.

Russians who sought shelter in Chinese territory. Even this measure, however, did not completely mollify Mr. Joffe. He insisted that a representative of the Soviet Government be allowed to participate in the work of disarming and evacuating these White forces.[35] This flank attack did not divert Dr. Koo from his main objective. He continued to insist that Soviet troops be withdrawn from Outer Mongolia prior to the opening of any Sino-Russian conference. With regard to Joffe's protest relative to conditions in northern Manchuria, the Chinese Foreign Minister declared that the Chinese Government favored neither the Red nor the White parties. Its policy was to refrain from interfering with the internal affairs or quarrels of other nations. All defeated White Guards entering Chinese territory had been disarmed and either interned or deported, and local authorities had been ordered to take strict measures to prevent their being supplied with arms.[36]

Mr. Joffe next attempted to create a diversion by alleging that the Chinese Eastern Railway was being grossly mismanaged. In a memorandum to the Waichiao Pu under date of November 3, 1922,[37] he charged that the general manager of the railway, Mr. Boris Ostroumoff, was "guilty of most corrupt practices, and may, if he and his more intimate colleagues are left any longer in charge, compromise the finances of the railway so deeply as to bring about a catastrophe."[38] The powers represented at the Washington Conference, continued the note,

[35] *China Year Book, 1924,* p. 860.
[36] *North China Herald,* CXLV, Nov. 18, 1922, p. 431. The situation at this time was complicated by the refusal of the Manchurian dictator, Marshal Chang Tso-lin, to recognize the authority of the Peking Government. Following his defeat at the hands of General Wu P'ei-fu in the spring of 1922, Marshal Chang retired to his capital at Mukden and announced that henceforth he would tolerate no interference by the central government in the domestic affairs of the Three Eastern Provinces under his control. It followed that whatever pledges the Waichiao Pu might make to Joffe regarding the suppression of White Guardist activities in northern Manchuria could be given effect only if Marshal Chang saw fit to enforce them.
[37] Text, *North China Herald,* CXLV, Nov. 18, 1922, p. 426.
[38] Ostroumoff, a White Russian, was appointed to his post in 1920 by the Russo-Asiatic Bank. *China Year Book, 1924,* p. 860.

had no legal interest in the railway, in spite of their resolution on the subject. Moreover, the French-protected Russo-Asiatic Bank not only lacked any legal title to the railway, but it had actually usurped Russia's right, "thereby acting in a way to hamper the establishment of friendly relations between the Russian and the Chinese people." Only the Russian Government now had a right to interfere, since more than any other government it was concerned with the future of this railway, "which was built with the Russian people's funds and is Russian property until Russia of her own free will decides to confer elsewhere her right of ownership." The Soviet Government desired an immediate change in the railway management, together with the arrest of Ostroumoff and his trial in a competent court; a Chinese commission, assisted by a staff of competent accountants, should immediately be sent to Harbin to institute a searching inquiry into the affairs of the railway; finally, Mr. Joffe demanded the establishment "provisionally— pending the settlement of the entire question . . . at the forthcoming Russo-Chinese Conference—of a new management, in agreement with Russia. . . ." The Soviet envoy pointed out in conclusion that the action of the Chinese Government at this juncture would have an important bearing on the policy which the Soviet Government would pursue regarding the Chinese Eastern Railway, and might, indeed, "prove the decisive factor."

The Chinese Foreign Minister promptly reminded the Soviet representative of the bearing which the Karakhan declarations of 1919 and 1920 seemed to have on the question at issue. In a note delivered to the Waichiao Pu on November 6, Mr. Joffe explained the interpretation which his government placed on these two declarations. The Russian Government still regarded them as the basis of its present policy. It was quite wrong to infer, however, that by these declarations Russia had renounced all of her interests in China. The Soviet Government merely renounced the "predatory and violent policy of the Tsar's Government and promised to renounce those rights which had accrued to Russia from this policy. But, firstly, until all these questions shall have been settled on (the basis of) a free accord between Russia and China, Russia's rights in China will not have lost their strength, and, secondly, these Declarations do not at all annul Russia's legal and just interests in China." [39] In particular, declared Joffe, "even if Russia vests in the Chinese people her title to the Chinese Eastern Railway, this will not annul Russia's interests in this line, which is a portion of the great Siberian Railway, and unites one part of the Russian territory with another." In conclusion, China was warned that the declarations of 1919 and 1920 could not be regarded as being valid forever, and that "unless the Chinese Government discontinues its ignoring of Russian interests, Russia will, perhaps, after all, be obliged to consider herself free from these promises which she had voluntarily given." [40]

Replying to this note on November 11, Dr. Koo stated that the question of reforming the administration of the Chinese Eastern Railway had occupied the attention of the Chinese Government for two years. However, the present charges of mismanagement would be investigated and if discovered to be well founded, steps would be taken to punish the offenders. Mr. Joffe's proposal for a joint provisional administration of the railway was rejected. The Chinese Government, said Dr. Koo, considered that a satisfactory solution of existing difficulties lay in a recognition of China's complete and exclusive control over the railway. He therefore requested the Soviet Government to declare once more its intention of returning to China, without compensation, all rights and interests in the railway. [41]

Dr. Koo's memorandum to the Soviet representative had

[39] *North China Herald*, CXLV, Nov. 18, 1922, p. 421. *Weekly Review*, XXIII, Jan. 27, 1923, p. 340.

[40] *China Year Book, 1924*, pp. 860-61. Russia's claims to the railway rested in general on the fact that by decree of the Bolshevik Government, all railways had been nationalized in 1918, at which time the Russo-Asiatic Bank, the legal owner of the Chinese Eastern Railway, was also nationalized. Consequently the railway shares held by that bank became state property. Dennis, *op. cit.*, pp. 325-6. Soviet military authorities contended at this time that if their government surrendered the railway entirely, Vladivostok and the Maritime Province would become untenable. Fischer, *op. cit.*, II, p. 795.

[41] *North China Herald*, CXLV, Nov. 18, 1922, p. 426.

quoted the following passage from the Karakhan declaration of 1919: "It is the intention of the Workers' and Peasants' Government to restore to China, without any compensation, all rights and interests referring to the Chinese Eastern Railway." Replying to this memorandum, Joffe denied that the authentic text of the 1919 declaration contained any such clause. That declaration merely laid down the fundamental program of the Soviet Government without concrete propositions or detailed conditions. It was true that the declaration of September 26, 1920, had declared "void of force all the treaties concluded with China by the former Government, renounced all seizures of Chinese territory and all Russian concessions in China, and restored to China, without compensation and forever, all that had been predatorily seized from her by the Tsar's Government and the Russian Bourgeoisie." But, argued the Soviet envoy, Article III of that note also required the Chinese Government to pledge itself not to aid Russian counter-revolutionary individuals, groups, or organizations, or to tolerate their activities in Chinese territory. He pointed out, further, that the note of 1920 proposed that the Russian and Chinese Governments conclude a special treaty relative to the operation of the Chinese Eastern Railway, "with regard to the needs of the Russian Socialist Federated Soviet Republic." Finally, Mr. Joffe denied that there was any truth in the rumors, about which the Chinese Foreign Minister had inquired, that Russian troops were being concentrated on the Manchurian border preparatory to a military occupation of the railway zone.[42]

Early in December, Mr. Joffe began to display distinct signs of irritation over the dilatory tactics of the Chinese Foreign Office. He demanded peremptorily that the Chinese authorities in northern Manchuria cease lending aid to Russian monarchists in that region. In spite of Soviet protests, he declared, "the Chinese Eastern Railway is freely controlled by the criminal White Guards."[43] The situation was not improved by a

[42] *China Year Book, 1924*, p. 861.
[43] Memorandum of December 20 to the Waichiao Pu, *Weekly Review*, XXIII, Jan. 27, 1923, p. 340.

176 *China's Foreign Relations*

series of border incidents which gave rise to complaints on the
part of the Chinese Government. When Dr. Koo protested
against the action of the Soviet authorities in seizing the
wharves, terminals, and other properties of the Chinese Eastern
Railway in Vladivostok, Joffe retorted sharply that for five years
China had arbitrarily been disposing of Chinese Eastern Railway and Russian property generally, and that the railway had
been allowed to become an instrument of military intervention
and a stronghold for the White Guards. He reminded the
Chinese Foreign Minister that Russia had invested nearly
800,000,000 gold roubles in this railway.[44]

Dr. Koo had intimated that compensation would be asked
from Moscow for the aid which had been rendered to destitute
White refugees in China. In a final note dated January 9,
1923, Mr. Joffe heaped ridicule upon the Chinese pretense of
neutrality between Reds and Whites, and announced that no
demand for compensation could possibly be entertained. The
Chinese Government was reminded that it had participated,
with other foreign governments, in armed intervention in
Siberia. The Soviet Government was entitled to hope that "the
Chinese Government will alter its hostile position *vis-a-vis*
itself, that it will finally make its choice between Reds and
Whites, while desisting from its unacceptable policy of being
'neutral' between both, and that it will at last cease its propaganda inimical to Russia." The very fact that China had permitted White refugees to enter her territory was cited as evidence of the Chinese Government's "downright and irrecon-
cilable hostility" toward its Soviet neighbor.[45]

A week after delivering himself of this parting blast, Mr.
Joffe left unceremoniously for the south. His health had not
been good, and he felt the need of a vacation in a more moderate climate than Peking was able to offer. The state of his
health, however, did not prevent him from having a number

[44] *China Year Book, 1924*, p. 862. *China Review*, IV, p. 21, Jan. 1923.
It should be recalled that much of this money had been borrowed from
French capitalists and that the debt had been repudiated.
[45] *Weekly Review*, XXIII, Jan. 27, 1923, pp. 340-41.

of conversations with Dr. Sun Yat-sen in Shanghai, where the Kuomintang leader had taken refuge following a political overturn at Canton. The result of this exchange of views was a formal statement, issued January 26, 1923, and signed jointly by Dr. Sun and Mr. Joffe.[46] Both signatories agreed that China was not ready for the introduction of either communism or the soviet system. In response to a request made by Dr. Sun, Mr. Joffe reaffirmed the principles laid down in the Karakhan note of September 26, 1920, and declared that "the Russian Government is ready and willing to enter into negotiations with China on the basis of the renunciation by Russia of all the treaties and exactions which the Tsardom imposed on China, including the treaty or treaties and agreements relating to the Chinese Eastern Railway." Pending the satisfactory settlement of the railway question at a competent Russo-Chinese conference, Dr. Sun agreed that the administration of the Chinese Eastern Railway should temporarily be reorganized without prejudice to the rights and interests of either party. With regard to the Mongolian question, Mr. Joffe declared that "it is not and has never been the intention or purpose of the present Russian Government to pursue an Imperialistic policy in Outer Mongolia or to cause it to secede from China." Dr. Sun, therefore, did not view an immediate evacuation of Russian troops from that region "as either imperative or in the real interest of China, the more so on account of the inability of the present Government at Peking to prevent such an evacuation being followed by a recrudescence of intrigues and hostile activities by White Guardists against Russia and the creation of a graver situation than that which now exists."

Following this gratifying exchange of views with Dr. Sun, Mr. Joffe, having accepted a cordial invitation extended by Viscount Goto, Mayor of Tokyo, took ship for Japan. His abrupt departure from China, coupled with the knowledge that even an innocent vacation in Japan might develop political significance, gave rise to certain misgivings on the part of govern-

[46] Text, *China Year Book, 1924*, p. 863.

ment leaders in Peking. Despite their apparent unwillingness to enter into formal negotiations on the subject, Waichiao Pu officials were becoming increasingly aware of the need for some understanding with Russia relative to the Chinese Eastern Railway. Particularly was this true since the Far Eastern Republic had, on November 15, 1922, been formally incorporated into the Soviet Union.[47] Reports reached Peking that Soviet troops were being concentrated along the Manchurian frontier and that Soviet military commanders were planning to seize the railway by main force.[48] There were fears also lest Mr. Joffe's friendly conversations with Viscount Goto might result in an agreement prejudicial to China's rights in the railway.[49]

When it became evident that China was genuinely desirous of resuming negotiations, the Soviet Government proposed that a Chinese representative be sent to Moscow for the purpose. After some hesitation, the Peking Government rejected this suggestion.[50] Instead, it was decided to wait until Mr. Joffe's health permitted his return to Peking. In anticipation of the

[47] Fischer, *op. cit.*, I, p. 373; II, p. 541.
[48] *China Review*, IV, p. 21, Jan., 1923. *North China Herald*, CXLVI, Jan. 27, 1923, pp. 217, 224, 225; *Ibid.*, Feb. 10, 1923, pp. 395-6. Reuter's correspondent at Chita reported on December 7 that the people of Siberia regarded the Chinese Eastern Railway as their own property. The commander of the Red army which had occupied Vladivostok declared in a public address at Chita that "the time has now come when we must actively assist our brothers laboring in the zone of the Chinese Eastern Railway." *North China Herald*, CXLV, Dec. 23, 1922, p. 786. However, on January 27, 1923, Joffe assured a correspondent of a Shanghai newspaper that the railway would not be seized by a Red army. *North China Herald*, CXLVI, Feb. 3, 1923, p. 310.
[49] These fears were reflected in a telegram despatched to Joffe by Wang Wen-pu, a member of the Chinese Parliament. Wang asked the Soviet envoy if there was any truth in rumors to the effect that Russia planned to transfer the Harbin-Changchun section of the Chinese Eastern Railway to Japan and that a separate Russo-Japanese agreement would be concluded providing for the navigation of the Sungari and the Amur Rivers. Joffe replied that he was visiting Japan for his health and was conducting no negotiations, *China Year Book, 1924*, p. 864.
[50] *China Year Book, 1924*, p. 864. In February Premier Chang Shaotseng decided apparently to accede to the proposal. Parliament, however, on being informed of the action which the government proposed to take, insisted that whatever negotiations were carried on would have to be conducted in Peking, and that the question of recognizing the Soviet Government must not be considered until after all outstanding questions between China and Russia had been settled. *North China Herald*, CXLVI, Feb. 17, 1923, p. 428.

resumption of negotiations, Dr. C. T. Wang was appointed, on March 26, as *Tupan* of Sino-Russian affairs, with power to negotiate on China's behalf in the forthcoming Sino-Russian conference.[51]

The expected return of Mr. Joffe to Peking continued to be delayed, not only by the state of his health, but by the promising character of certain intimate conversations into which he had entered with Viscount Goto. Rather than miss the opportunity presented by China's anxiety to resume negotiations, the Soviet Government finally decided to send to Peking Mr. L. M. Karakhan, the author of the famous declarations of 1919 and 1920. China stood at the moment in particular need of a friend. The steady disintegration of authority at Peking, combined with an alarming increase in lawlessness in the provinces, caused foreigners long resident in the country to recall the Boxer days of 1900. Prevailing disorders appeared to reach a climax when, early on the morning of May 6, 1923, bandits wrecked an express train bound from Pukow to Tientsin. Of the thirty-five foreigners on the train, one was murdered in cold blood and twenty-six more, including several women, were taken captive.[52] The patience of the foreign powers was exhausted. Immediate demands were made that the Peking Government take energetic steps to effect the release of the foreign captives. This was not finally accomplished until five weeks later. In consequence of this outrage, the powers addressed to the Chinese Government a note which demanded among other things, that the railways be protected thereafter by a force of Chinese guards specially recruited for the purpose and officered by foreigners. The fact that the note was signed by representatives of fifteen powers appeared to indicate that the foreign governments were determined once more to join forces for the suppression of disorder in China.[53]

[51] *North China Herald*, CXLVI, Mar. 31, 1923, p. 853.
[52] *China Year Book, 1924*, p. 818.
[53] For the texts of the notes exchanged between the Diplomatic Body and the Waichiao Pu on this subject, see *China Year Book, 1924*, pp. 819-829.

Convinced that this new attitude of the powers presaged foreign intervention, the Chinese turned to greet Mr. Karakhan with open arms. On his arrival in Harbin, August 14, 1923, he was given an official welcome and honored with an elaborate banquet.[54] The Soviet envoy broke his journey to Peking long enough to pay his respects to Marshal Chang Tso-lin at Mukden.[55] Shortly thereafter, he addressed a cordial letter to Dr. Sun Yat-sen. It was already known that Marshal Feng Yuhsiang was sympathetically disposed toward Soviet Russia. Having fortified himself by these friendly overtures to each of the principal Chinese leaders, Mr. Karakhan felt prepared to open negotiations with the central government.

On his arrival in Peking on September 2, the new Russian envoy was greeted not only by officials of the Waichiao Pu but by great crowds of enthusiastic students.[56] He had come to China with two objects in view. The first of these was to negotiate an "equal" treaty, and the second to fight imperialism.[57] It was with the latter objective that he busied himself at the outset. In a public statement issued four days after his arrival, he charged that the foreign powers desired to see China remain a "sick man," without a strong army, divided, weak, entangled in internal difficulties, and incapable of resisting foreign aggression. Only the Soviet Republics and the Russian people wanted to see China "strong, powerful, possessing a strong army, and capable of defending the interests and sovereignty of its people." Referring to the note presented by the

[54] *North China Herald*, CXLVIII, Aug. 18, 1923, p. 457. *Ibid.*, Sept. 1, 1923, pp. 597-9. The day before this banquet, the Russian monarchist newspaper at Harbin, the *Russky Golas* warned the Chinese authorities against being deceived by the honeyed words of the Bolsheviks. The editor was promptly arrested and fined for "insulting the representative of a friendly power."

[55] Mr. Fischer has stated that after several brief interviews, Chang and Karakhan reached an agreement concerning the general principles which should govern a settlement of the Chinese Eastern Railway question, and the Marshal pledged himself to execute the treaty embodying these principles once it had been signed. Fischer, *op. cit.*, Vol. II, p. 542.

[56] *North China Herald*, CXLVIII, Sept. 8, 1923, p. 659.

[57] Karakhan made this confession to Mr. Fischer some time later. Fischer, *op. cit.*, Vol. II, p. 542.

powers on August 10 in connection with the Lincheng bandit outrage, Mr. Karakhan said, "I greet the unanimous resistance which was offered by all China, without distinction of groups or parties, to [these] totally unheard-of demands." [58] On another occasion, at a luncheon given in his honor by Dr. C. T. Wang, he declared that nothing pleased him more during his recent stay in Harbin than the fact that he saw there "a Chinese administration, Chinese laws, and the realization of Chinese sovereignty." [59]

On September 7, the Soviet envoy, paying his first official call at the Waichiao Pu, informed the Chinese Minister for Foreign Affairs that his government would insist upon formal recognition prior to the commencement of negotiations. [60] Subsequently, following the inauguration of President Ts'ao K'un on October 10, he requested permission to present his credentials directly to the President himself. The Waichiao Pu officials were apprehensive concerning the probable consequences of this step, which would bring automatically into force all of the old Sino-Russian treaties. Instead, the government proposed the settlement of all outstanding differences between the two countries, after which it would be prepared to recognize Soviet Russia. Meanwhile Mr. Li Chia-ao would be appointed as China's "Diplomatic Representative" at Moscow. Karakhan replied that his government could not accept Mr. Li in any such capacity and reiterated his demand for formal recognition prior to the opening of formal negotiations. [61]

China's refusal to meet the wishes of the Soviet Government in the matter of recognition did not prevent a subsequent exchange of views between Mr. Karakhan and Dr. C. T. Wang, *Tupan* of Sino-Russian affairs. The subjects discussed ranged from the question of recognition to that of the Chinese Eastern Railway. After some weeks, Dr. Wang asked that a date be

[58] *China Year Book, 1924,* p. 866.
[59] *Ibid.*
[60] *Ibid.*
[61] *China Weekly Review,* XXVI, Oct. 13, 1923, pp. 250, 258. *China Year Book, 1924,* p. 867.

182   *China's Foreign Relations*

set for the opening of formal negotiations.[62] The Soviet envoy declined to name such a date until formal recognition had been accorded to his government. His views were set forth in a note dated November 30.[63] "The point of view of the Soviet Government," he said, "is that the establishment of normal relations must precede the beginning of the Conference. On this my Government insists, as a preliminary evidence of sincerity and friendliness on the part of the Chinese Government." The Soviet Government had the right to demand such a proof of sincerity and friendliness, for it had not forgotten that "the Chinese Government participated in the intervention in internal Russian affairs against the Soviet Government; that it supported the White Guardist organizations and institutions with sums derived from the Boxer Indemnity; that the territories of Mongolia and Manchuria were places of arms for onslaughts on Soviet Russia, and that, finally, the Whites are still being patronized and their hostile activities are allowed against Soviet Russia and her citizens." Since, said Mr. Karakhan, it was well known that the policy of China with regard to the Soviet Union was "coördinated with the policy of the Imperialistic Great Powers," it was necessary for the Soviet Government to be satisfied that China was now "pursuing her own Russian policy, disregarding in this matter the opinions of the Great Powers." After all, the difference between the Chinese and the Russian points of view on this question concerned only a matter of procedure. "You proposed to solve all the questions immediately by way of a preliminary agreement, making this a payment for the recognition of the Soviet Republics by China. I, on the other hand, demand that normal relations between both countries be reëstablished without any special pay for it."

In the negotiations which would follow China's recognition of the Soviet Government, Mr. Karakhan promised that the principles enunciated in the declarations of 1919 and 1920 would be fully adhered to and that not a single question would

[62] Wang to Karakhan, Nov. 21, 1923, *China Year Book, 1924,* p. 876.
[63] Karakhan to Wang, *China Year Book, 1924,* pp. 873-6.

be settled "without full regard for the legal interests and rights of the Chinese people." He felt compelled, however, to correct one of Dr. Wang's statements with reference to the Chinese Eastern Railway. "Never and nowhere," declared the Soviet envoy, "could I have said that all the rights on the Chinese Eastern Railway belong to China." Russia had property rights in the railway as a commercial enterprise. Nevertheless, continued Karakhan, "I am willing to discuss at the Conference any proposition of yours, including the proposition that all the rights (in) the line should pass over to China, on conditions to be discussed and decided at the Conference." He confirmed what had been promised four years before, "that the sovereignty of China in the territory of the railway is fully recognized by us, and that we shall not insist on any one of those privileges which the Tsarist Government had, and which the other foreign Powers still have today, in the Railway Zone." Authentic texts of the declarations of 1919 and 1920 were inclosed with this note of the Soviet representative. Neither included the supposed pledge of the Soviet Government to return the Chinese Eastern Railway unconditionally and without compensation.[64]

In his reply to this note, Dr. Wang expressed appreciation of Karakhan's declared intention to settle outstanding questions on the basis of the declarations of 1919 and 1920.[65] He noted certain discrepancies, however, between the French text of the 1919 declaration as received by the Peking Government, and the text now submitted to the Soviet envoy. "It is true," he admitted, "that the text received by my Government was in the form of a telegram, but the same was signed and certified as a true copy by Mr. Yanson, Delegate Plenipotentiary for Foreign Affairs of the Council of Commissaries of the People of Siberia

[64] This pledge appears in the official Chinese translation of Karakhan's "open letter" of July 26, 1919, which was transmitted to the Peking Government in March, 1920, by Yanson, the Soviet representative at Irkutsk. Karakhan later informed a foreign press correspondent that no official knowledge of Yanson's action had ever reached him at Moscow. Consequently, he considered that the text of the declaration which appeared in the Soviet *Journal* must be regarded as the only authentic one. Lawrence Impey, in *China Weekly Review*, XXVII, Jan. 12, 1924, p. 233.

[65] Wang to Karakhan, Jan. 9, 1924, *China Year Book, 1924*, pp. 877-8.

and the Far East. Accordingly, the text received by my Government should be regarded as authoritative." With regard to the matter of recognition, Dr. Wang reiterated the view that outstanding questions must be solved prior to the resumption of normal diplomatic relations. "In your opinion," he informed the Russian envoy, "the Union of Soviet Russia has by its declarations of 1919 and 1920 shown its complete friendliness to China. In the opinion, however, of the Chinese people, this friendliness still leaves something to be desired, since the troops of your Government are still stationed in Chinese territory, namely, in Outer Mongolia." [66] In conclusion, Dr. Wang again asked that a date be set for the formal opening of a conference.

An exchange of views relative to the Russian share of the Boxer Indemnity revealed the fact that Mr. Karakhan did not regard the declarations of 1919 and 1920 as having abrogated the treaties concluded by the Tsarist Government with China. On November 15 the Soviet emissary sent to the Waichiao Pu a note in which he referred to reports that the government in-

[66] Shortly after his arrival in Peking, Karakhan expressed the opinion that the interests of Mongolia would best be protected if it remained under Chinese sovereignty, though with a certain amount of autonomy. "Russia," he said, "not only will place no obstacles in the way of such a settlement, but will do all it can to accelerate a mutual understanding between these two peoples. . . . Russia has no desire to annex Mongolia because there is nothing there that Russia needs. Annexation also is contrary to the frequently enunciated Russian desire to help small peoples to obtain self-determination. Russia is ready to withdraw the last of the Russian troops from Mongolia when China is able to guarantee no more White Guard attacks from this territory." *China Review*, V, p. 111, Oct., 1923. A foreign merchant returning from Urga at this time reported that the Red Guard of two hundred men which remained in the city was obviously being kept there only for moral effect, the government being actually in the hands of the Young Mongols themselves. *North China Herald*, CXLIX, Nov. 24, 1923, p. 526. On January 3, 1924, the Mongolian Prime Minister received the credentials of Comrade Alexei Vasilieff as Minister of the Union of Socialist Soviet Republics. The new Minister, while making it clear that Soviet Russia was not yet willing to recognize the independence of Mongolia, said that after all the difference between independence and autonomy was more imaginary than real. *North China Herald*, CL, Mar. 15, 1924, p. 402. *China Year Book, 1924*, p. 582. Subsequently the Urga Government attempted to open negotiations with the Chinese Government through a special representative sent to Peking for the purpose. Fischer, *op. cit.*, Vol. II, p. 544.

tended to use the Russian share of the indemnity funds for the payment of its diplomatic and consular officials abroad. He proposed instead that these funds be devoted exclusively to educational purposes, in accordance with a request made to him by the heads of eight of the principal educational institutions in Peking.[67] The Waichiao Pu replied that the government, having taken cognizance of the 1919 declaration renouncing the Russian share of the indemnity, had already assigned the funds in question to a purpose of its own choosing.[68] In a second note under date of December 13, 1923, Mr. Karakhan insisted that while the declarations of 1919 and 1920 did contain a renunciation of the Boxer Indemnity, the Chinese Government would acquire rights thereunder only by the conclusion of a formal treaty embodying the principles set forth in those declarations. It was therefore necessary to "protest most emphatically" against the action of the Chinese Government in disposing of these funds "without the knowledge and consent" of the Soviet Government, prior to the conclusion of a formal treaty on the subject.[69] The Soviet envoy demanded, therefore, "that the Chinese Government stop forthwith disposing illegally of the Russian share of the Boxer Indemnity," and repeated his suggestion that the money be used for educational purposes.

Informal conversations between Dr. Wang and Mr. Karakhan were resumed in February, 1924. Both sides were now ready to make concessions. The Russian representative consented to sign a preliminary agreement which, while providing for immediate recognition of the Soviet Government by China, would set forth in detail the guiding principles of a treaty which was to be negotiated later. The preliminary draft of the agreement embodying this compromise was signed March 14, 1924.[70] Article XV provided that it was to come into effect from the date of signature.

[67] *China Year Book, 1924*, p. 872-3.   [68] *Ibid.*, p. 873.
[69] Karakhan to Waichiao Pu, *China Review*, VI, pp. 62-3, Feb., 1924.
[70] Text, *China Year Book, 1924*, pp. 880-83.

No sooner was the agreement signed than opposition to it developed in the Chinese cabinet. Members of the cabinet voiced their fears concerning the possible effect of such an agreement on the country's relations with various foreign powers. Article IX contained the provision "that the future of the Chinese Eastern Railway shall be determined by the Union of Socialist Soviet Republics and the Republic of China, to the exclusion of any third parties or party." And the French Minister had, on March 12, warned the government that French interests in the Russo-Asiatic Bank must not be jeopardized by any agreement between Russia and China, and demanded that the French Legation be notified before any actual settlement of the Chinese Eastern Railway question.[71] The American and the Japanese Governments were likewise known to look with disfavor on any diplomatic rapprochement between Peking and Moscow. Members of the government pointed out also that by accepting the agreement, China would be bound to accord immediate recognition to the Soviet Government; at the same time the old Sino-Russian treaties would actually be cancelled only after the conclusion of a formal treaty some time in the future.[72] The cabinet therefore decided to notify Mr. Karakhan that in proceeding to sign such an agreement, Dr. Wang had exceeded his authority.

On being notified of the cabinet's decision the Soviet envoy on March 16 transmitted to Dr. Wang what amounted to a virtual ultimatum. He was willing, he said, to wait three days for confirmation by the Chinese Government of the agreement concluded on March 14. Thereafter he would not consider himself bound by the terms of that agreement. At the same time, the Soviet Government would hold the Government of China responsible not only "for the breaking off of the negotiations and the breaking up of the agreement," but for "all the ensuing consequences" as well.[73] The Chinese delegate replied

[71] *China Weekly Review*, XXVIII, Mar. 22, 1924, p. 126.
[72] *North China Herald*, CL, Mar. 22, 1924, p. 434.
[73] *China Year Book, 1924*, p. 879.

that his government had no desire to break off negotiations.[74] On March 19, however, Mr. Karakhan addressed to Dr. Wang a second note[75] in which, after accusing the Chinese Government of bad faith, he charged that its action in disavowing "the signature of its official delegate" had been taken at the behest of the Great Powers, particularly France. The Chinese Government, he declared, had no reason to be dissatisfied with the agreement of March 14, provided comparison were made between its terms and those of treaties existing between China and Third Powers. The Sino-Russian agreement provided for the abandonment of consular jurisdiction, special rights and privileges in connection with Concessions, and the Boxer Indemnity. In vain did China strive, first at Versailles and then at Washington, to free herself from such humiliating fetters as these. "China got a promise at Washington that a commission would be created to discuss the question of extraterritorial rights; however, until today this commission has not been created yet, for France is against it. And yet in the agreement signed, these rights are entirely relinquished." In conclusion, the Soviet delegate announced the receipt of instructions from his government to the effect that (a) the negotiations with "the official delegate of the Chinese Government" must be considered as ended; (b) that any attempt to resume the discussion of agreements already arrived at and signed would be resolutely rejected; (c) that upon the expira-

[74] The country's reaction against the Government's refusal to approve the agreement of March 14 was already producing a change of heart in Peking. It was reported that Marshal Chang Tso-lin, greatly perturbed over the rupture of negotiations, had sent a personal agent to Peking to investigate the cause. Marshal Wu P'ei-fu bitterly upbraided the Peking officials for the unexpected turn of events. Chinese students who had hoped to benefit by the release of the Russian portion of the Boxer Indemnity were very much wrought up against the clique headed by Wellington Koo, which was charged with responsibility for the government's action. Minister Alfred Sze cabled from Washington that the government would never again have so favorable an opportunity to recognize the Soviet Government on terms favorable to China. *China Weekly Review*, XXVIII, Apr. 5, 1924, p. 210.
[75] *China Review*, VI, May, 1924, pp. 134-5. *China Year Book, 1924*, pp. 879-80.

tion of the time limit set in Mr. Karakhan's note of March 16, the Soviet Government would not consider itself bound by the agreement of March 14, and would reserve "its full right of freely establishing the conditions of future treaties with China." Furthermore, after the expiration of that time limit, the Chinese Government would have no opportunity to resume negotiations until after it had, unconditionally and without preliminary agreement, "established normal official relations with the Government of the Union of Soviet Socialist Republics." China was warned also against "committing an irretrievable mistake" which would not be without a bearing on the future relations between the Soviet Union and the Republic of China.

The Chinese authorities were disconcerted but not entirely disheartened by the uncompromising tone of the Russian note. Mr. Karakhan was informed that future negotiations would be carried on directly by the Waichiao Pu.[76] The Soviet delegate declined to negotiate. The Chinese Government, he said, had the choice of accepting or rejecting *in toto* the agreement previously signed by its accredited representative; if fresh negotiations were desired, they must be preceded by China's unconditional recognition of the Soviet Government.[77] Dr Koo then invited Karakhan to have a personal talk with him at the Foreign Office. Declining this invitation on the score of illness, the Russian representative nevertheless sent his secretary to act for him.[78] Following this conversation, the Chinese Foreign Minister in a note dated April 1,[79] announced the willingness of his government to approve the agreement of March 14 provided certain specific changes were made in it.[80] In case the

[76] Koo to Karakhan, Mar. 22, 1924, summary in *North China Herald*, CL, Mar. 29, 1924, p. 474.
[77] Karakhan to Koo, Mar. 25, 1924, Text, *China Review*, VI, pp. 136-8, May, 1924.
[78] Two meetings were held, on March 28 and March 29. *North China Herald*, CLI, Apr. 5, 1924, p. 2.
[79] Text, *China Year Book, 1924*, pp. 885-6.
[80] Dr. Koo pointed out that while the Chinese Government, under Article IV of the agreement, declared null and void all treaties and agreements between China and any third party affecting the sovereign rights of the U. S. S. R., the obligation of the Soviet Government concerning the same principle was limited only to those treaties and agreements concluded between

proposed changes could not be made in the text of the agreement, Dr. Koo suggested that they be effected by a supplementary exchange of notes.

Mr. Karakhan betrayed no outward signs of a willingness to accept these conciliatory overtures. But he remained in Peking, ostensibly for the purpose of discussing with the Japanese Minister, Mr. Yoshizawa, the terms of a possible agreement between their respective countries.[81] For all the world knew, the Sino-Russian negotiations were at an end. Nevertheless, such negotiations were proceeding in secret. The utmost secrecy was necessary, for despite outward professions to the contrary, Dr. Koo frankly informed the Russian delegate that his government still feared the diplomatic intervention of the Great Powers.[82]

Tsarist Russia and any third party. No mention was made of treaties and agreements concluded by the Russian Government since the revolution and third parties affecting the sovereign rights and interests of China. China desired also that Russia's pledge to withdraw the Red troops from Outer Mongolia should be made more definite, and that a provision be added making it clear that the Soviet Government had no intention of violating China's territorial sovereignty. Finally, the transfer of properties in China held by the Russian Orthodox Church should be postponed pending an investigation into the nature, number, and location of such properties.
    [81] *China Weekly Review,* XXVIII, Apr. 19, 1924, p. 274.
    [82] Fischer, *op. cit.,* Vol. II, p. 546. The French Minister on March 29 again called the attention of the Chinese Government to the fact that the Russo-Asiatic Bank, under the protection of France, had interests in the Chinese Eastern Railway which must not be compromised by any separate agreement between China and Russia. In another note of April 2, the French Minister claimed also that his government must be consulted concerning any disposition which might be made of the Russian Concession at Hankow. *North China Herald,* CLI, Apr. 12, 1924, p. 42. The Waichiao Pu, in a note dated April 9, denied the right of either the French Government or the Russo-Asiatic Bank to interfere in a settlement of the Chinese Eastern Railway question. *North China Herald,* CLI, Apr. 12, 1924, p. 42. *China Review,* VI, p. 153, May, 1924. The American Legation, also, on May 3, reminded the Chinese Government of the resolution adopted at the Washington Conference in which the powers reserved the right to insist on China's responsibility for the performance or non-performance of obligations toward foreign stockholders, bondholders, and creditors of the Chinese Eastern Railway which the powers deemed to result from the contract under which the railway had been built. The French Legation sent a similar reminder on May 7. *North China Herald,* CLI, May 17, 1924, p. 242. It seems apparent that neither the French Government nor French financiers had any vested proprietary rights in the Chinese Eastern Railway nor any claims in the original Russo-Chinese Bank other than such as might be recoverable directly from the Russian Government. C. Walter Young, *The International Relations of Manchuria,* pp. 171-2, p. 11, note. The rights

Not until May 31 did the foreign diplomats in Peking learn from a communiqué issued by the Waichiao Pu that an agreement had been signed that morning by Dr. Koo and Mr. Karakhan.[83]

The settlement reached on May 31 included an Agreement on General Principles, an Agreement for the Provisional Management of the Chinese Eastern Railway, seven Declarations, and an exchange of notes.[84] The first article of the Agreement on General Principles provided for the immediate recognition by China of the Soviet Government and for the transfer to that government of the legation and consular buildings formerly belonging to the Tsarist Government. By Article II, the two parties, agreed to hold, within one month, a conference which would have power to conclude and carry out detailed arrangements relative to all questions in accordance with the principles set forth in subsequent articles of the agreement. The governments of the contracting parties agreed (Article III) to annul at the conference all conventions, treaties, agreements, protocols, contracts, etc., "concluded between the Government of China and the Tsarist Government, and to replace them with new treaties, agreements, etc., on the basis of equality, reciprocity and justice, as well as the spirit of the Declarations of the Soviet Government of the years 1919 and 1920." The Soviet Government (Article IV) declared null and void all treaties and agreements concluded between the former Tsarist Government and any third parties affecting the sovereign rights or interests of China; both governments declared that in future neither would conclude treaties or agreements tending to prejudice the sovereign rights of the other.[85]

Article V of the agreement dealt with Outer Mongolia, which

claimed by the American Government rested on a foundation which was even more flimsy. See *New Republic*, XXXIX, July 30, 1924, pp. 260-61.
[83] *China Year Book, 1924*, pp. 887-8.
[84] Texts, *Treaties and Agreements, 1919-1929*, pp. 133-44.
[85] Supplementing this provision was the announcement of the Chinese Government contained in the fourth of the accompanying declarations to the effect that it did not recognize as valid any treaty or agreement concluded between Russia since the Tsarist régime and any third party or parties affecting the sovereign rights and interests of China.

the Soviet Government consented to recognize as "an integral part of the Republic of China" and to respect China's sovereignty therein. The forthcoming conference was to fix a time limit for the withdrawal of Russian troops from the region and also adopt measures designed to safeguard the frontiers; the Soviet Government promised that thereafter the troops in question would be withdrawn. The contracting parties pledged themselves (Article VI) "not to permit, within their respective territories, the existence and/or activities of any organizations or groups" whose aim it was "to struggle by acts of violence" against the government of the other party.[86] Each agreed, furthermore, "not to engage in propaganda directed against the political and social systems" of the other. It was agreed that the forthcoming conference should provide for a redemarcation of the national boundaries of the two parties; it was also to settle, "on the basis of equality and reciprocity," all questions relating to the navigation of rivers, lakes, and other bodies of water common to their respective frontiers. (Articles VII and VIII.)

The principles which were to be applied by the conference in settling the Chinese Eastern Railway question were set forth in Article IX of the agreement. The railway was declared to be a purely commercial enterprise, with direct control over its own business operations. All other matters affecting the rights of the national and local governments of China were to be administered by the Chinese authorities. The Soviet Government consented to the redemption by China, "with Chinese capital," of the railway together with all appurtenant properties. Thereafter all shares and bonds of the railway were to be transferred to China, and the Soviet Government was to assume responsibility for the claims of all shareholders, bondholders, and creditors incurred prior to the revolution of March, 1917. It was agreed

[86] In a note supplementing this article of the agreement, Dr. Koo promised that the Chinese Government would "discontinue the services of all the subjects of the former Russian Empire now employed in the Chinese army and police force, as they constitute by their presence or activities a menace to the safety of the Union of Soviet Socialist Republics." *Treaties and Agreements, 1919-1929*, pp. 139-40.

that the future of the railway was to be determined by the Republic of China and the Union of Soviet Socialist Republics "to the exclusion of any third Party or Parties." Until the questions relating to the Chinese Eastern Railway were settled at the forthcoming conference, the rights of the two governments arising out of the original railway contract of 1896, as modified by the present agreement and the supplementary agreement for the provisional management of the railway, were to continue unchanged.

The remaining articles of the agreement dealt with a variety of subjects. The Soviet Government renounced special rights and privileges relating to all Concessions in any part of China (Article X) together with its share of the Boxer Indemnity (Article XI). However, by an accompanying declaration (IV) the Chinese Government promised it would not transfer any of these concession rights to any third power or to any foreign organization. It was agreed, furthermore (Declaration V), that the Russian share of the Boxer Indemnity should, "after the satisfaction of all prior obligations secured thereon, be entirely appropriated to create a fund for the promotion of education among the Chinese people." A joint commission was to be set up to administer this fund. Article XII of the agreement announced the relinquishment of Russian rights of extraterritoriality and consular jurisdiction.[87] The next article contained the stipulation that simultaneously with the conclusion of a commercial treaty at the forthcoming conference, the delegates of the two governments were to draw up a customs tariff "in accordance with the principles of equality and reciprocity." The conference was to deal also (Article XIV) with "claims for the compensation of losses." Article XV provided, finally, that

[87] The sixth declaration provided, however, that at the forthcoming conference, the two governments would establish equitable provisions "for the regulation of the situation created for the citizens of the Government of the Union of Soviet Socialist Republics by the relinquishment of the rights of extraterritoriality and consular jurisdiction . . ." it being understood that such citizens of the Soviet Union were to be "entirely amenable to Chinese jurisdiction."

the agreement should take effect from the date of signature.

An Agreement for the Provisional Management of the Chinese Eastern Railway was signed at the same time as the Agreement on General Principles.[88] It contained provisions for the joint administration of the railway as a commercial enterprise until such time as this question had been finally settled at the conference.

The news that the government had finally agreed to a settlement of the Russian question was received by the Chinese people with surprising unanimity.[89] Various members of Parliament sent to Mr. Karakhan a message of congratulation in which they declared that the agreement represented a "victory over international imperialism."[90] Commenting on the favorable terms of the agreement, Dr. Koo stated in the course of a public address that "up till now it was not the Chinese Government that drew up the treaties with other Powers; they were forced on China from the outside. But it is quite different in the present case." [91]

By contrast with the enthusiasm among the Chinese, word that the agreements had been signed was received by foreign diplomats in Peking with surprise and even some measure of consternation.[92] The resident representative of the Russo-Asiatic Bank immediately addressed a note to the Waichiao Pu in which he protested that the settlement had been made without the knowledge of shareholders and bondholders of the Chinese Eastern Railway.[93] The Japanese Legation also notified both Karakhan and the Chinese Government that Japan's "acquired privileges and interests" in the same railway must not be compromised.[94] In answer to the Japanese note, Dr. Koo denied that the Agreement of May 31 had compromised the legitimate

[88] Text, *Treaties and Agreements, 1919-1929*, pp. 141-44.
[89] *North China Herald*, CLI, June 14, 1924, p. 402.
[90] Fischer, *op. cit.*, Vol. II, p. 549.
[91] *Ibid.*, p. 550.
[92] *North China Herald*, CLI, June 7, 1924, p. 361.
[93] *Ibid.*, p. 362.
[94] *Ibid.*, June 14, 1924, p. 402.

claims of Japan and the other powers with regard to the Chinese Eastern Railway, and promised that those claims would receive due consideration at the coming conference.[95]

The Sino-Russian conference which was supposed to open not later than one month after the signing of the Peking agreements was delayed for a number of reasons. At Shanghai the Russian consulate was located in the International Settlement, and diplomatic negotiations were necessary before it could be transferred to the control of the Soviet authorities.[96] Likewise at Canton, the old Russian consular buildings were located in the British Concession at Shameen. When the Soviet authorities requested the transfer of this property, they learned that it had been forfeited to the British municipality for failure to pay back rates and taxes.[97] Protracted negotiations were necessary also before Mr. Karakhan, by now appointed as the first Russian Ambassador to China, was able to secure possession of the Russian Legation buildings located in the Legation Quarter at Peking.[98]

The most important influence tending to delay the Sino-Russian conference, however, was the attitude of the Manchurian dictator, Chang Tso-lin, who for two years had declined to recognize the authority of the Peking Government. Shortly after the publication of the Koo-Karakhan agreement, Marshal Chang let it be known that he would decline to permit any

[95] *Ibid.*, June 21, 1924, p. 454. Notes of similar import were transmitted at the same time to the Governments of France and the United States.
[96] *North China Herald*, CLII, July 12, 1924, p. 42. The transfer at Shanghai was finally effected July 24.
[97] *Ibid.*, July 26, 1924, p. 126. The situation at Canton was further complicated by the refusal of the government there to recognize as valid the Peking agreement of May 31. The Kuomintang authorities announced, however, that while they were unable formally to receive the credentials of the Soviet Consul-General who was coming to Canton, they would accord him unofficial recognition as had been done in the case of the German Consul. *North China Herald*, CLII, Aug. 23, 1924, p. 293.
[98] Before agreeing to the transfer of the Russian Legation, the representatives of the remaining eight Protocol Powers secured from Karakhan a statement to the effect that his government still regarded itself as a cosignatory of the Boxer Protocol. *North China Herald*, CLII, Aug. 23, 1924, p. 281. *Ibid.*, Sept. 13, 1924, p. 410. *Ibid.*, Sept. 20, 1924, p. 454.

change to be made in the management of the Chinese Eastern Railway until separate arrangements regarding the matter had been concluded between himself and a representative of the Soviet Government.[99] Aside from demanding a voice in the disposition of the Chinese Eastern Railway, which lay entirely within his dominions, the Mukden dictator took exception to that provision of the May 31 agreement which called for the suppression of White Guardist activities in China. The measures taken to enforce this provision in Manchuria, he insisted, would be harmful to the interests of his government.[100] Chang demanded also that some arrangement be made for the redemption by the Soviet Government of the millions of paper roubles which had been accepted in good faith and were still held by the merchants of Manchuria.[101]

In July, a Soviet agent began separate negotiations at Mukden with representatives of Marshal Chang. The discussions were not confined to the question of the Chinese Eastern Railway. They dealt as well with boundaries and with rights of navigation on the Sungari, Amur, and Ussuri Rivers.[102] When Marshal Chang showed a disposition to demand greater concessions than the Soviet representatives were willing to grant, Mr. Karakhan threatened to inaugurate the formal Sino-Russian

[99] *North China Herald,* CLI, June 14, 1924, p. 402. See also the resolution adopted by the provincial assembly and other public bodies in Fengtien. *North China Herald,* CLI, June 21, 1924, p. 442. Mr. Fischer has expressed the view that Chang Tso-lin's opposition to the agreement of May 31 resulted in part from pressure exerted at Mukden by the representatives of France, Great Britain, and Japan. *Op. cit.,* Vol. II, p. 547.

[100] Statement made at Shanghai by Chang's representative, Yang Ta-shin, *North China Herald,* CLII, Aug. 2, 1924, p. 162.

[101] *China Weekly Review,* XXIX, July 5, 1924, p. 168. *North China Herald,* CLII, Aug. 9, 1924, p. 202.

[102] *China Weekly Review,* XXIX, Aug. 2, 1924, p. 315. The Peking Government was fully aware of these negotiations. In a press interview given July 19, Dr. Koo stated that while, in her dealings with foreign powers, China was ordinarily represented by the central government, there were nevertheless occasions when local authorities, acting under instructions from the Waichiao Pu, were authorized to carry on negotiations affecting local interests. The Chinese Foreign Minister did not say whether such instructions had been issued to the Mukden Government. He did confess, however, that he had not been apprised by Mr. Karakhan that negotiations were proceeding at Mukden. *North China Herald,* CLII, July 26, 1924, p. 121.

negotiations at Peking without waiting for a preliminary agreement with the Mukden Government.[103] Internal developments in China, however, made such a step unnecessary. Toward the end of the summer civil war, beginning near Shanghai, played into the hands of the Soviet representatives. Late in August, the tuchun of Kiangsu, General Ch'i Hsieh-yuan, with the nominal support of the Peking Government, declared war on General Lu Yung-hsiang who, as tuchun of Chêkiang, had long considered himself independent of Peking. After some hesitation, Chang Tso-lin announced his support of General Lu and prepared to wage war on the Chihli faction then in control of the central government.[104] Thereafter military necessity compelled him to make his peace with Soviet Russia, and on September 20, a formal agreement was signed between "the Autonomous Government of the Three Eastern Provinces of the Republic of China and the Government of the Union of Soviet Socialist Republics."

The Mukden Agreement[105] followed textually many of the appropriate clauses of the Peking agreements of May 31, and included substantially the same provisions for joint administration of the Chinese Eastern Railway as a commercial enterprise. The Peking agreements had provided that the Chinese members of the board of directors, as well as various high officials of the railway, should be appointed by "the Government of the Republic of China." The document signed at Mukden substituted for this phrase "the Republic of China," thereby indicating that where appointments of this sort were made, they would be made by Chang Tso-lin himself. The Mukden agreement also contained a new clause modifying the original contract of 1896 for the construction and operation of the railway. The contract had limited the concession period to eighty years, after which the line together with all of its appurtenances should pass free of charge to the Chinese Government. This period was now shortened to sixty years, with the proviso

[103] *Ibid.*, Aug. 16, 1924, p. 242.
[104] *China Year Book, 1925*, pp. 831-36.
[105] *Treaties and Agreements, 1919-1929*, pp. 148-52.

that the two contracting parties might subsequently take up the question of reducing the concession period still further.

Article II of the Mukden agreement, relating to propaganda, was a repetition of the mutual pledges which Dr. Koo and Mr. Karakhan had previously agreed upon at Peking. The third Article, however, dealt at some length with the question of passenger and freight traffic on the Lower Amur and on the Sungari up to Harbin. Specific arrangements regarding this matter were to be worked out within two months by a commission which was to be constituted for the purpose. Commissions were also to be organized to demarcate the boundaries and to draw up a commercial treaty and a customs tariff. The agreement contained no reference to the redemption of paper notes held by the people of Manchuria.

Administrative changes in the Chinese Eastern Railway followed shortly after the signature of the Mukden agreement. Marshal Chang and the Soviet Government each appointed five members of the new board of directors and a military subordinate of the Mukden dictator was named president of the railway. The new administration promptly discharged all White Russian officials and replaced them with new appointees acceptable to the Soviet Government.[106]

When it became known that the Soviet Government had concluded a separate agreement with Chang Tso-lin, the Chinese Foreign Minister addressed an emphatic protest to the Soviet Embassy, calling attention to the fact that Marshal Chang was then in open rebellion against the central government.[107] A second protest, telegraphed directly to Moscow on October 2, declared that it was contrary to international practice for a friendly power to enter into an agreement with a "local official" without the consent of the government concerned.[108]

The Soviet Government, however, could afford to ignore

[106] *North China Herald*, CLII, Oct. 11, 1924, p. 57. Acting on orders from Mukden, the Harbin police immediately arrested the retiring general manager, Mr. Ostroumoff, together with three other men who had occupied high executive positions in the railway administration.

[107] Note of September 25, 1924, *ibid.*, Oct. 4, 1924, p. 2.

[108] *Ibid.*, Oct. 11, 1924, p. 57.

these protests. On October 23, the Peking Government was overturned by a military *coup d'état* engineered by General Feng Yu-hsiang. President Ts'ao K'un, after being forced to resign, was placed under arrest and various members of his cabinet, including the Foreign Minister, Dr. Koo, sought refuge in the foreign settlements at Tientsin. A Provisional Government was organized, at the head of which was Marshal Tuan Ch'i-jui, who assumed the title of Chief Executive. The quondam rebel, Chang Tso-lin, promptly announced his support of the new government.

Early in 1925 the Provisional Government notified the Soviet Ambassador of its desire to inaugurate the conference which had been so long delayed. Apparently both governments were now anxious to reach a final agreement regulating their mutual relations. Mr. Karakhan on March 6 informed the Waichiao Pu that the last of the Red troops had been withdrawn from Mongolia.[109] On its part, the Peking Government, now enjoying the momentary confidence of Chang Tso-lin, issued a mandate on March 13 recognizing the validity of the Mukden agreement of the previous September.[110] Preliminary negotiations began at Mukden toward the end of March.[111] Subsequently these

[109] *China Year Book, 1925,* p. 428. Following the receipt or this information, the Peking Government on March 28 advised the government at Urga of its intention to reassert Chinese claims with regard to Outer Mongolia. In a spirited reply to this note, the Urga Government declared, in effect, that it would resist any attempt to cancel the autonomy which it then enjoyed. Instead of meddling in the affairs of her neighbors, China was advised to cease her internal strife, free herself from foreign control, and concentrate on domestic reform. Only in case the Peking Government declared itself in favor of racial self-determination would the Mongolian Government consent to negotiate regarding relations between the two countries. *North China Herald,* CLVII, Oct. 3, 1925, p. 13. The Russian attitude toward Outer Mongolia was set forth in a speech delivered at Tiflis about March, 1925, by M. Chicherin, Commissar for Foreign Affairs at Moscow. The Soviet Government, declared Chicherin, recognized Mongolia as a part of the whole Republic of China, "enjoying, however, autonomy so far-reaching as to preclude Chinese interference with the internal affairs and established independent relations of Mongolia." *China Year Book, 1925,* p. 428.
[110] *North China Herald,* CLIV, Mar. 21, 1925, p. 466.
[111] *Ibid.,* Mar. 28, 1925, p. 510. *Ibid.,* CLV, Apr. 4, 1925, p. 8.

conversations were transferred to Peking, Chang Tso-lin having agreed to appoint Mr. Cheng Chien as his personal representative to act with Dr. C. T. Wang during the course of the negotiations.[112]

At the last moment, the Soviet Ambassador interposed new objections which once more delayed the opening of the conference. He denounced the employment of White Guards in the military service of Chang Tso-lin and his subordinates, and demanded not only that further enlistments of these former Russian troops should cease, but that such troops as had already been enlisted should immediately be disbanded.[113] A second cause of friction arose out of the joint Sino-Russian management of the Chinese Eastern Railway. On April 9, General Manager Ivanoff of the railway issued an order directing the dismissal of all workmen and employees who had not, by June 1, adopted either Chinese or Soviet citizenship.[114] This order was countermanded by General Pao Kuei-ch'ing, President of the Railway, who insisted that in issuing it the general manager had acted without consulting the board of directors and had therefore exceeded his authority.[115] General Pao's action drew strongly worded protests from both Ambassador Karakhan and the Soviet Consul-General at Harbin.[116] The Soviet authorities described the action of the Chinese President of the Railway as illegal, without force, and an act of overt assistance to irresponsible criminal and monarchist elements which were still to be found in the employ of the railway. The ire of the Soviet Ambassador was also aroused by alleged attempts on the part of the Chinese authorities to take over

[112] *China Year Book, 1926-7*, p. 1098. *North China Herald*, CLV, Apr. 18, 1925, p. 89.
[113] Notes to Waichiao Pu, April 11 and May 22, 1925, *North China Herald*, CLV, Apr. 18, 1925, p. 85. *Ibid.*, May 30, 1925, p. 366. It was the Chinese contention that the enlistment of these troops constituted no infraction of the Peking agreement since they had all become naturalized Chinese citizens.
[114] *North China Herald*, CLV, May 30, 1925, p. 362.   [115] *Ibid.*
[116] *Ibid.*, pp. 362. *China Weekly Review*, XXXII, May 30, 1925, p. 374.

lands properly belonging to the Chinese Eastern Railway.[117]
Mr. Karakhan objected also to the construction, with Japanese
capital, of the Taonan-Tsitsihar Railway, a feeder for the South
Manchuria Railway, which when completed would compete
with the Chinese Eastern Railway in tapping the rich resources
of northern Manchuria.[118]

It was the Chinese contention that such problems as these
should be taken up in the course of the Sino-Soviet conference.
The Russian Ambassador, however, insisted that they were
questions which must be settled satisfactorily before the opening of the conference.[119] The deadlock thus created was not
broken until the shrill and passionate outcry against foreign
privileges in the country, prompted by sanguinary encounters
between Chinese and foreigners in the Yangtse Valley and at
Canton during the summer of 1925, had completely altered the
situation. Here was a heaven-sent opportunity to demonstrate
to the Chinese the contrast between the ostensibly friendly policy of the Soviet Government and the aggressive designs of the
unregenerate imperialists. And the intense reaction of the
Chinese against the misdeeds of the foreign powers suggested
that the time had arrived to realize the Soviet dream of linking
China with Russia in a common struggle against Western capitalism and imperialism. Forgetting past grievances,[120] therefore, Mr. Karakhan proposed to the Peking Government the

[117] *China Weekly Review,* XXXII, May 30, 1925, pp. 374-5. This dispute dated back to August, 1923, when the Chinese Chief Administrator of
the railway zone, acting on instructions from Marshal Chang Tso-lin, seized
control of the Land Department of the Railway. *North China Herald,*
CXLVIII, Aug. 18, 1923, p. 450.

[118] *North China Herald,* CLV, May 30, 1925, p. 362. For details
of the Sino-Japanese agreement of September 3, 1924, providing for the
construction of the Taonan-Tsitsihar Railway, see Young, *op. cit.,* pp. 209-
212. On the question of the strategic importance of this railway to Japan,
see Malcolm W. Davis, "Railway Strategy in Manchuria," *Foreign Affairs,*
IV, pp. 499-502. April, 1926.

[119] *North China Herald,* CLV, May 30, 1925, p. 362.

[120] With regard to Ivanoff's order directing the dismissal of certain
employees of the Chinese Eastern Railway, both sides had agreed before
June 1 to leave the matter to be settled by the Soviet Consul-General and the
Chinese Commissioner of Foreign Affairs at Harbin. *North China Herald,*
CLV, June 20, 1925, p. 466.

immediate opening of the long delayed conference. Prompt
action was necessary, since the Soviet representative was leaving
within a few days for Moscow. Dr. C. T. Wang, hastily summoned from Shanghai, prevailed upon him to delay his departure one day in order to be present at the formal opening of
the conference on August 26.[121]

The real work of the conference, left in the hands of six
committees, did not begin in earnest until after Mr. Karakhan's
return from Moscow on December 1. Six problems were dealt
with: the negotiation of a commercial treaty, reparation for
losses, the Chinese Eastern Railway, the redemarcation of
boundaries, navigation, and juridical questions.[122] The attempt
to negotiate a commercial treaty ended in failure. The Soviet
Government was anxious that the size of its consular staff
should not be limited, and also that its consular agents should
be permitted, where necessary, to act as official trade representatives.[123] The Chinese Government, on the other hand, was
apprehensive lest an inordinately large consular staff be utilized
for propaganda purposes. Another obstacle in the way of a
satisfactory commercial agreement was the failure to agree concerning questions of land ownership and mixed residence in the
interior of China. The Soviet negotiators took the stand that
since their nationals were not clothed with extraterritorial rights,
they should be permitted to live anywhere in the country and
also to own land wherever they might be. The Chinese representatives contended, however, that mixed residence in the

[121] *North China Herald*, CLVI, Aug. 29, 1925, p. 242. *Ibid.*, Sept. 5,
1925, p. 285. In his address at the formal opening of the conference, Dr.
Wang referred to the fact that the delay had been "the source of much
suffering to our people. . . ." In his reply, Karakhan said that the Chinese
people had suffered still more from "the disgraceful policy of imperialism
and the no less disgraceful unequal treaties which still bind by chains the
living body of China." The delay in holding this conference could hardly
be the source of much suffering. "But quite another thing is the delay and
doubtful prospects of the Conference on unequal treaties, and I am not
surprised that the Chinese are carrying on with such energy a struggle
against the unequal treaties." *China Year Book, 1926-7*, pp. 1098-99. Obviously the reference was to the delay of the Treaty Powers in carrying out
the pledges which they had given at Washington.
[122] *China Year Book, 1926-7*, p. 1099.   [123] *Ibid.*, p. 1100.

interior of the country might easily become the fruitful cause of unnecessary complications, since the people were largely unaccustomed to having foreigners reside in their midst.[124]

The committee handling the question of Chinese losses suffered during the Russian Revolution considered first the question of rouble notes held by Chinese, and then the claims of merchants for property confiscated or damaged. It was asserted that notes having a face value of 1,257,722,000 roubles were held in China, and that these had been accepted in good faith in return for goods and services.[125] The attitude of the Soviet delegates was that these notes had been acquired by speculators, and that the holders thereof were entitled to no compensation whatever. On the other hand, the Russian representatives consented to examine documents showing the amount of Chinese goods and property which had either been purchased and not paid for, or requisitioned or confiscated during and after the revolution of 1917. These losses approximated 20,000,000 roubles.[126] In the end, however, the Russians alleged that the evidence contained in the documents was either inadequate or not entirely legal.[127] Nevertheless, Russia was willing to reimburse the merchants to the extent of $5,000,000.[128]

The committee on juridical questions succeeded in drafting a convention providing for the extradition of criminals, and in addition a treaty relating to judicial aid in civil and criminal cases involving Russians resident in China. Progress was also made with a draft treaty concerning the succession of property, and the legal status of Soviet nationals arising out of the abrogation of extraterritoriality likewise received consideration.[129] The work of the remaining committees was less successful. No progress was registered with regard either to the redemarcation of boundaries or the navigation of the Sungari, Amur, and other rivers. The attitude of the Mukden Government made impossible any agreement relating to the Chinese Eastern Railway.

[124] *Ibid.*   [125] *China Year Book*, 1926-7, pp. 1100-1101.
[126] *Ibid.*, p. 1101.   [127] *Ibid.*
[128] *China Weekly Review*, XXXVII, June 19, 1926, p. 75.
[129] *China Year Book*, 1926-7, pp. 1099-1100.

Abandoning his earlier policy of conciliation, Marshal Chang
Tso-lin notified the Soviet Ambassador in February that Manchuria was not a vassal of Peking, "nor are we a tribute
bearer." The Three Eastern Provinces constituted an autonomous part of the Chinese Republic and were entitled to equal
treatment with any other section of the country. Mr. Karakhan
was warned, therefore, that any agreement concerning the railway arrived at between the Peking Government and the Soviet
Government without the sanction of the Three Eastern Provinces would not only not be recognized, but would be regarded
as null and void. Moreover, the Three Eastern Provinces would
take up arms in case the Peking Government and the Soviet
Ambassador acted independently in negotiating an agreement
relating to the Chinese Eastern Railway.[130]

In June, the sessions of the conference were adjourned for a
period of two months.[131] The recess, taken ostensibly because
of the hot weather period, marked the final collapse of the
Peking negotiations. In March, 1926, Marshals Chang Tso-lin
and Wu P'ei-fu, forgetting their former enmity, had launched
a joint attack upon the pro-Russian forces of Marshal Feng

[130] *North China Herald*, CLVIII, Feb. 27, 1926, p. 375. For the declaration of independence adopted by various public bodies in Manchuria,
see *ibid.*, Feb. 6, 1926, p. 222. In January, 1926, Marshal Chang had succeeded, after great difficulty, in crushing the rebellion of one of his principal subordinates, General Kuo Sung-ling, who, because of his presumed
association with Marshal Feng Yu-hsiang, was suspected of having Soviet
backing. Marshal Chang's belief that some measure of Russian influence lay
behind Kuo's treachery was strengthened by the conduct of General Manager
Ivanoff of the Chinese Eastern Railway. When the situation at Mukden
was most critical, Ivanoff hindered the movement from northern Manchuria of troops loyal to Marshal Chang by insisting that transportation
charges be paid before troop trains were furnished. Subsequently, all traffic
on the line between Changchun and Harbin was suspended. Thereupon the
Chinese military authorities took it upon themselves to seize and operate
trains in violation of all schedules and signals. When Ivanoff tried to
prevent this, he was arrested by the Chinese authorities. *North China
Herald*, CLVIII, Jan. 23, 1926, pp. 139-40. Malcolm W. Davis, "Railway
Strategy in Manchuria," *Foreign Affairs*, IV, p. 501, April, 1926. The
Soviet General Manager was released only after Chang Tso-lin had received
a three-day ultimatum from M. Chicherin, Commissar for Foreign Affairs
at Moscow. For the texts of the Russian notes, see *China Year Book,
1926-7*, pp. 1102-5.
[131] *China Year Book, 1926-7*, p. 1099.

Yu-hsiang, then in control of the Peking Government. Toward the end of the month, the victories of the allies made it expedient for Dr. C. T. Wang, in charge of the Sino-Soviet negotiations, to seek safety within the foreign Concessions at Tientsin.[132] In April Peking fell into the hands of the allied troops, the leaders of which declared their intention of ridding north China of Bolshevist influence. Marshal Chang formally requested the recall of Mr. Karakhan and intimated furthermore that once his troops entered Peking he would not be responsible for the safety of the Soviet Ambassador.[133]

The Soviet Government, however, had its own reasons for discontinuing negotiations at Peking. Following the allied capture of the capital, there was a period of several months during which a central government was virtually non-existent. Little was to be gained, apparently, by negotiating with a government that had become only an empty pretense. Under the circumstances it was more advantageous to establish relations with regional militarists, such as Chang Tso-lin, in whose hands lay the actual authority in the country. The Soviet authorities, also, were watching with both interest and sympathy the rising power of the Kuomintang in southern China which gave promise of consolidating the country under a government which would look to Moscow for advice and support.

[132] *North China Herald*, CLVIII, Mar. 27, 1926, p. 557.
[133] *Ibid.*, CLIX, Apr. 17, 1926, p. 99. *Ibid.*, Apr. 24, 1926, pp. 146, 151. *Ibid.*, May 1, 1926, p. 194. Karakhan finally left Peking September 10, 1926. *Ibid.*, CLX, Sept. 18, 1926, p. 547.

CHAPTER VII

THE WASHINGTON CONFERENCE

THE Washington Conference had two objects. The first of these centered around the desire of the Great Powers to limit naval armaments. The second concerned the need for a practical effort to remove causes of international misunderstanding which, as long as they persisted, encouraged the growth of naval armaments. Many, if not most of these causes of misunderstanding, arose out of existing conditions in the Pacific area and the Far East. Recognition of this fact prompted the American Government, in agreement with the Governments of Great Britain, France, Italy, and Japan, to extend to the Chinese Government an invitation to participate in the work of the Conference.

The Peking Government heartily welcomed the opportunity to present China's accumulated grievances before representatives of the powers. The first news that such an opportunity would be afforded was received by the country at large with undisguised enthusiasm. In Peking the opinion was freely expressed that Japan was being summoned before an international tribunal to answer for the misdeeds of her militarists on the Asiatic mainland.[1] For a month, the Chinese press discussed the approaching Conference with lively interest and unvarying optimism. The conviction was widespread that the development of events since the Versailles Conference had revealed to statesmen everywhere the dangers of allowing the interests of weaker nations to be eclipsed by the selfish ambitions of the stronger powers. It seemed likely, therefore, that the powers were now in a mood not only to revise the Shantung settlement in the

[1] *North China Herald,* CXL, Sept. 10, 1921, pp. 795-6.

205

interest of justice to China, but to give sympathetic attention to numerous other grievances, such as the treaty tariff, extraterritoriality, and foreign concessions.

As the date for the opening of the Conference approached, however, this early enthusiasm decreased noticeably and even gave way to a feeling of morbid pessimism.[2] The reason for this marked change of attitude lay in the internal condition of the country. The treasury at Peking was empty, and the government lived from day to day on borrowed money. In October, it was estimated that the unsecured loans of the Peking Government had reached the staggering total of $376,000,000. In addition to this sum, Chinese banks held short time notes of the government amounting to $50,000,000.[3] During November, Peking depositors in the Bank of China and the Bank of Communications, whose financial stability depended in part on the condition of the public treasury, began hurriedly to withdraw their funds. A financial panic, which promised to effect not only Chinese but foreign banks, was averted only when Marshals Ts'ao K'un and Chang Tso-lin decided to rescue the central government by remitting several million dollars for its support.[4] The international credit of the Chinese Government suffered also through its failure to meet payments due November 1 on a loan of $5,500,000 made by the Continental and Commercial Bank of Chicago.[5] The desperate financial situation at Peking led to suggestions from certain quarters that the only cure for the financial ills of the country lay in an international receivership which would make possible a reorganization of Chinese finances under foreign supervision.[6]

[2] H. K. Tong in *Weekly Review of the Far East*, XVIII, Sept. 17, 1921, pp. 105-6.
[3] Rodney Gilbert in *North China Herald*, CXLI, Nov. 5, 1921, p. 358.
[4] *North China Herald*, CXLI, Nov. 26, 1921, pp. 558-60.
[5] This default led to a remonstrance by the American Department of State. *Weekly Review of the Far East*, XVIII, Nov. 5, 1921, pp. 439-40. *China Review*, I, p. 314. (November, 1921.) Subsequently the American representative of Dr. Sun Yat-sen, Mr. Ma Soo, notified Secretary Hughes that with a view to protecting the credit of the Chinese nation, the Canton Government was willing to assume responsibility for the refunding and ultimate payment of this loan. *China Review*, I, December, 1921, p. 346.
[6] *Weekly Review of the Far East*, XVIII, Nov. 5, 1921, pp. 439-40. *Ibid.*, Nov. 12, 1921, pp. 502-4.

The condition of the public treasury reflected itself in frequent changes in the membership of the cabinet. It was difficult if not impossible to find a minister of finance capable of satisfying demands for funds made by the provincial militarists. On September 17, Premier Chin Yun-p'eng tendered his resignation following a stormy cabinet meeting during which Dr. Yen, the Minister of Foreign Affairs, had resisted the Premier's demand that, in the interest of financial retrenchment, the size of the Chinese delegation to the Washington Conference should be reduced by half.[7] Following the resignation of the Premier, Dr. Yen made known his intention of retiring from office unless adequate provision were made for the support of a full Chinese delegation. In October, Premier Chin was induced to resume office after assurances from Marshals Ts'ao K'un and Chang Tso-lin that they would thereafter remit certain revenues for the support of the central government. Subsequent events, however, belied these assurances of the militarists. In November rumors circulated in Peking that the civil employees of the government, whose salaries were many months in arrears, intended to organize a strike to enforce payment of their just claims. In both Chinese and foreign circles it was freely predicted that the Peking Government was on the verge of utter and final collapse.[8]

Even more serious, if possible, than the financial chaos at Peking was the political disunity within the country. The government at Canton declined to recognize either the legality or the authority of the administration carried on at Peking. On May 7, 1921, Dr. Sun Yat-sen, having been elected by the rump parliament whose members had fled from Peking in 1917, formally assumed office as "President of the Republic of China." Dr. Sun immediately issued an appeal for international recognition.[9]

[7] *North China Herald*, CXL, Sept. 24, 1921, p. 917.

[8] *Weekly Review of the Far East*, XVIII, Nov. 19, 1921, pp. 541-2. See also article by Rodney Gilbert in *North China Herald*, CXLI, Oct. 22, 1921, pp. 255-8.

[9] Text, *China Review*, I, July, 1921, p. 13. The *China Review*, published in New York, was established to advance the interests of the Canton Government.

When it first became known that Far Eastern affairs would receive attention at the Washington Conference, frenzied attempts were made to smooth out the political differences which separated Canton from Peking. The Peking authorities were disposed to be conciliatory. Dr. C. C. Wu, the son of the Minister of Foreign Affairs at Canton, and one of the delegates who had represented China at the Paris Conference, was approached with the suggestion that he accept a place on the delegation representing the Peking Government. Dr. Wu, then Vice-President of the Board of Foreign Affairs at Canton, promptly declined to consider the suggestion. He replied that any such proposal must come to him through his government, whose approval would have to be forthcoming before he could accept.[10] His government, however, was not disposed to give serious consideration to the proposal. The Minister of Foreign Affairs, Dr. Wu Ting-fang, let it be known that Canton would insist on separate representation at Washington.[11]

Secretary Hughes was apprised of this decision through Mr. Ma Soo, the Cantonese representative in the United States.[12] Dr. Wu insisted that in view of the Peking Government's record with regard to Japan, no delegation representing that government could be expected to approach an international conference table with clean hands.[13] When the American Government, despite these intimations, still failed to see the necessity for a second Chinese delegation at the Conference, Dr. Sun Yat-sen announced that none of the decisions of the Conference relating to China would "be recognized as having any validity or force," so far as his government was concerned.[14]

[10] *Weekly Review of the Far East,* XVIII, Oct. 22, 1921, p. 350. *North China Herald,* CXL, Sept. 24, 1921, p. 919.
[11] *North China Herald,* CXL, Aug. 20, 1921, p. 533.
[12] Text of the note, *China Review,* I, August, 1921, p. 88.
[13] Wu Ting-fang to Ma Soo, *China Review,* I, September, 1921, p. 111.
[14] Letter signed by Sun Yat-sen and Wu Ting-fang, transmitted by Ma Soo to Secretary Hughes. *China Review,* I, October, 1921, p. 232. Dr. Sun rejected all suggestions that his government send an unofficial delegation to the Conference. His views in this connection were expressed in a letter to Dr. Chiang Mon-lin in which he said that "In our eyes there is only one legal government in China. It is out of the question that the

Not until the last moment did the Peking Government abandon its hope for a delegation representing the entire Chinese nation. On October 6 appeared a presidential mandate naming the four plenipotentiaries who were to have charge of China's interests at Washington. Dr. C. C. Wu, whose name had been included in the list in spite of his objections, immediately telegraphed to Peking declining to accept the appointment. The other chief delegates were Dr. Sao-Ke Alfred Sze, Minister to the United States, Dr. V. K. Wellington Koo, Minister to London, and Dr. Ch'ung-hui Wang, Chief Justice of the Supreme Court of China.[15] Assisting these chief delegates was a staff of one hundred and thirty-two persons.

The Chinese program at Washington embraced three objectives. Of first importance, in view of the distracted condition of the country, was the need of resisting any fresh impairment

delegates of the Canton Government should attend an international conference along with the delegates dispatched by the illegal Government at Peking. Should the Powers refuse to recognize the only legal Government at Canton, we will never dispatch our representatives to the Washington Conference. It follows, therefore, that no items relative to the Republic of China, which have been deliberated upon and decided at the Conference, will be binding upon our country." *North China Herald,* CXLI, Oct. 1, 1921, p. 11.

[15] It was originally intended that the Chinese delegation should be headed by the Peking Minister of Foreign Affairs, Dr. W. W. Yen. An official announcement to this effect was made public October 3. *North China Herald,* CXLI, Oct. 8, 1921, p. 83. Following the presidential mandate of October 6, it was announced that for the present Dr. Yen would be unable to proceed to Washington because of a number of unsettled diplomatic questions, particularly those relating to Russia and Portugal, which required responsible handling at Peking. *North China Herald,* CXLI, Oct. 15, 1921, p. 150. It seems likely, however, that Yen remained in Peking to protect the position of the Chinese spokesmen at Washington. During the Paris Conference, Japan had exerted pressure at Peking to secure modification of the attitude of the Chinese delegates in France. The possibility that these tactics might now be repeated arose out of the fact that certain members of the Peking Government were known to be amenable to Japanese influence. See Millard, *Conflict of Policies in Asia,* p. 258. Chinese fear of what might happen at Washington showed itself also in the decision of various non-political organizations in China to have their own unofficial observers in Washington. These "People's Delegates" were Dr. Z. T. David Yui and Dr. Mon-lin Chiang. Unembarrassed by official connections, it was expected that they would be able to offer sane advice to the official Chinese delegates and also render faithful and unbiased reports concerning the activities of these delegates. W. S. A. Pott in *Weekly Review of the Far East,* XVIII, Oct. 22, 1921, pp. 349-51.

of China's rights as a sovereign nation. Pessimists, some of whom possibly took their cue from Japanese propagandists,[16] were already predicting that the powers intended to use the Washington Conference for the purpose of subjecting China to some new type of international supervision and control. On the eve of the Conference, Dr. Yen expressed the conviction that international control of China could not become a reality. Not only would it fail to achieve its objects, but it would endanger the peace of the Far East. The Peking Minister of Foreign Affairs freely admitted the existence in the country of conditions which were far from satisfactory. He declared, however, that China was determined to prevent further restrictions on her territorial and political entity, and would risk wrecking the Conference in order to protect her rights in this regard.[17]

Having obtained from the powers pledges designed to safeguard China's future, the Chinese delegation hoped in the second place to secure the elimination of certain infringements on the nation's sovereignty which had no warrant in the treaties. The third objective centered around the desire to secure revision of existing treaties which placed obnoxious limitations on the nation's freedom of action.

Shortly after the original plenary session of the Conference, on November 12, it was decided to set up a Committee on Pacific and Far Eastern Questions, to consist of the heads of missions representing the Nine Powers.[18] At the first meeting of this committee, on November 16, Dr. Sze presented the claims of his government. China, he declared, was capable of solving existing domestic problems created by the change in her system of government, provided she had an unembarrassed opportunity to do so. This meant not only that she must be freed from the danger of foreign aggression, but that so far as circumstances would permit, "she be relieved from limita-

[16] R. L. Buell, *The Washington Conference,* New York, 1922, pp. 50-51.
[17] W. W. Yen, "The Washington Conference," *Weekly Review of the Far East,* XVIII, Nov. 12, 1921, pp. 494-6.
[18] *Conference on the Limitation of Armaments,* Washington, 1922, p. 66. This official record of the Conference proceedings will be referred to hereafter as *Proceedings.*

tions which now deprive her of autonomous administrative action and prevent her from securing adequate public revenues." [19] The Chinese delegate proposed therefore that the Conference adopt the following principles, whose application to specific problems concerning China could then be discussed: [20]

1. (a) "The Powers engage to respect and observe the territorial integrity and political and administrative independence of the Chinese Republic." (b) "China upon her part is prepared to give an undertaking not to alienate or lease any portion of her territory or littoral to any Power."

2. "China, being in full accord with the principle of the so-called open door or equal opportunity for the commerce and industry of all nations having treaty relations with China, is prepared to accept and apply it in all parts of the Chinese Republic without exception."

3. "With a view to strengthening mutual confidence and maintaining peace in the Pacific and Far East, the Powers agree not to conclude between themselves any treaty or agreement directly affecting China or the general peace in these regions without previously notifying China and giving her an opportunity to participate."

4. "All special rights, privileges, immunities or commitments, whatever their character or contractual basis, claimed by any of the Powers in or relating to China are to be declared, and all such or future claims not so made known are to be deemed null and void. The rights, privileges, immunities and commitments, now known or to be declared, are to be examined with a view to determining their scope and validity and, if valid, to harmonize them with one another and with the principles declared by this Conference."

5. "Immediately or as soon as circumstances will permit, existing limitations upon China's political, jurisdictional and administrative freedom of action are to be removed."

6. "Reasonable, definite terms of duration are to be attached to China's present commitments which are without time limits."

7. "In the interpretation of instruments granting special rights or privileges, the well established principle of construction that such grants shall be strictly construed in favor of the grantors, is to be observed."

8. "China's rights as a neutral are to be fully respected in future wars to which she is not a party."

[19] *Ibid.,* p. 866.   [20] *Ibid.,* pp. 866-8.

9. "Provision is to be made for the peaceful settlement of international disputes in the Pacific and the Far East."

10. "Provision is to be made for future Conferences to be held from time to time for the discussion of international questions relative to the Pacific and the Far East, as a basis for the determination of common policies of the Signatory Powers in relation thereto." [21]

In presenting this "Bill of Rights" for the consideration of the committee, the Chinese delegation indicated its disposition to proceed from the general to the particular. If the Conference first committed itself with regard to general principles, the Chinese could then point to specific instances in which those principles were being violated. General principles might even

[21] Mr. Ma Soo declared that the Ten Points submitted by the Peking delegation were distinctly disappointing. This, he said, was no time for "platitudes and inane generalities." *Weekly Review of the Far East,* XIX, Dec. 24, 1921, p. 147. The program of the Canton Government, a copy of which was submitted by the Cantonese representative on December 7 to the leaders of each of the delegations at Washington, was more concrete and somewhat more radical. Canton desired the withdrawal of international recognition from the Peking Government, non-interference by foreign powers in the political affairs of China, and the adoption of open diplomacy in dealings between China and the powers, and between the powers themselves with reference to China. In addition, the Canton Government desired to see the application of specific principles relating to China as follows:

1. Territorial integrity: (a) Settlement of the Shantung question by the cancellation of the Sino-Japanese treaty and notes of 1915, and recognition of the fact that China's declaration of war against Germany automatically terminated the Kiaochou leasehold. (b) Cancellation of the Sino-Japanese treaty and notes of 1915 relative to South Manchuria and Eastern Inner Mongolia; the railways in North and South Manchuria to be converted into Chinese state-owned properties. (c) Recognition by Great Britain of Chinese sovereignty in Tibet, which would be granted autonomy. (d) Relinquishment of all leased territories. (e) The restoration to China of all Settlements and Concessions; during an interim period, their administration to be vested in a council consisting of an equal number of Chinese and foreign members, with a Chinese chairman. (f) The withdrawal of foreign troops, whether their presence was warranted by the treaties or not.

2. Economic integrity: (a) Freedom from treaties imposing fiscal limitations of every sort. (b) Remission of the remainder of the Boxer Indemnity payments, and the use of such funds for educational and industrial purposes. (c) The elimination of spheres of interest or influence.

3. Administrative integrity: (a) The gradual abolition of consular jurisdiction by installments. (b) Japanese police agencies to be removed. (d) Telegraphic and wireless installations maintained in China by foreign governments and their nationals to be dismantled. Text in *China Review,* I, December, 1921, pp. 341-2.

The Washington Conference 213

be given a certain retroactive force.[22] Therein lay their danger. With one exception, therefore, the heads of the other delegations preferred to discuss concrete issues. The exception arose out of the American—and possibly the British—desire for a restatement in treaty form of the Hay Doctrine and the principles of the Open Door. At the third meeting of the committee, on November 21, Mr. Elihu Root proposed the adoption of a declaration in the form of four resolutions. In their final form, these resolutions bound the Powers, other than China,[23]

1. "To respect the sovereignty, the independence, and the territorial and administrative integrity of China;
2. "To provide the fullest and most unembarrassed opportunity to China to develop and maintain for herself an effective and stable government;
3. "To use their influence for the purpose of effectually establishing and maintaining the principle of equal opportunity for the commerce and industry of all nations throughout the territory of China;
4. "To refrain from taking advantage of conditions in China in order to seek special rights or privileges which would abridge the rights of subjects or citizens of friendly States, and from countenancing action inimical to the security of such States."

These resolutions were not intended to have retroactive force or to modify valid treaties and agreements then existing. According to Mr. Root, they merely restated and summed up views previously expressed by the powers, either during sessions of the present Conference, or in various exchanges of notes and declarations in the past.[24] With this interpretation generally

[22] Point I of the Chinese program, for instance, was designed to elicit from the powers formal recognition of the fact that Mongolia and Manchuria still lay within the territorial limits of China, despite the existence of certain agreements involving Japan which seemed to imply the contrary. Point II was then intended to secure application of the principles of the Open Door to those areas, in which Japanese influence tended to become not only paramount but exclusive. See the commentary prepared by ex-Secretary Robert Lansing and Dr. Paul Reinsch, high advisers to the Chinese delegation, *Far Eastern Review*, XVIII, January, 1922, p. 30.
[23] *Proceedings*, pp. 890, 900.   [24] *Ibid.*, p. 894.

accepted, the resolutions were adopted and subsequently embodied as Article I of the Nine Power Treaty relating to principles and policies to be followed in matters relating to China.[25] At the same time the powers took note of a separate declaration that "China upon her part is prepared to give an undertaking not to alienate or lease any portion of her territory or littoral to any Power." [26]

At the fourth meeting of the Far Eastern Committee, Dr. Sze asked for additional general consideration of China's Ten Points. Objection to this procedure was voiced by both Mr. Balfour and M. Sarraut.[27] Dr. Koo then announced that the Chinese delegation was prepared to submit for discussion a list of specific questions. There were two points, however, which he desired to emphasize: (1) "A stop must be put to further encroachments on the administrative and territorial integrity of China and a line must be drawn to safeguard the future; and (2) an earnest effort should be made to remove as many as possible of the existing limitations and infringements upon China's exercise of her sovereign rights." [28]

Before the next meeting of the committee, Secretary Hughes suggested to the Chinese delegates that instead of presenting a full list of matters concerning which they desired the Conference to take action, they submit these questions one at a time.[29] On November 23, therefore, Dr. Koo presented an elaborate argument in favor of the restoration to China of the right to fix her own tariff rates. China desired the powers to agree upon a definite period after which full tariff autonomy would be accorded. During this period of preparation, a maximum rate should be agreed upon, within which the Chinese Government would enjoy complete freedom to fix differential rates. For the

---

[25] *Ibid.,* p. 1621.   [26] *Ibid.,* p. 908.
[27] *Ibid.,* pp. 904, 910.   [28] *Ibid.,* p. 912.
[29] *Ibid.,* pp. 918-20. Prior to the Conference, Secretary Hughes, in conversations with Minister Sze at Washington, intimated that China should not ask too much lest the progress of the Conference be impeded; China should be content with a gradual redress of grievances. Telly H. Koo, "The Washington Conference," *Chinese Social and Political Science Review,* VII, April, 1923, p. 167.

purpose of affording immediate relief, Dr. Koo proposed that from January 1, 1922, the Chinese import tariff be increased to the twelve and one-half per cent rate mentioned in the commercial treaties of 1902 and 1903. Mr. Root called immediate attention to the fact that in the treaties to which reference had been made, the application of the twelve and one-half per cent tariff rate was linked with the abolition by China of all *likin* charges. A sub-committee was then organized to consider all aspects of the question. Under the leadership of Senator Underwood, this sub-committee spent six weary weeks composing differences and formulating recommendations. Its report, finally presented to the full committee on January 5, 1922, took the form of nine resolutions which, having been adopted unanimously, were incorporated in the Nine Power Treaty relating to the Chinese Customs Tariff. The treaty contained the following provisions: [30]

1. As soon as practicable, a Tariff Revision Commission should be convened at Shanghai for the purpose of raising the tariff rates on imports to an effective five per cent level, the work of this Commission to be completed within four months from the conclusion of the Conference, and the rates so fixed to become effective two months after publication without waiting for ratification.

2. A Special Conference representing China and the treaty powers should take immediate steps to prepare for the abolition of existing *likin* charges, with a view to levying the surtaxes provided for in the commercial treaties of 1902 and 1903. This Special Conference, which was to meet in China within three months after the effective date of the tariff treaty, was to authorize the levying of a surtax of not over five per cent *ad valorem* on luxuries and two and one-half per cent on other articles "as from such date, for such purposes, and subject to such conditions as it may determine."

3. Four years after the completion of the work of the Shanghai Tariff Commission, a further revision of the import tariff rates should be undertaken to insure that the specific rates should correspond to the five per cent *ad valorem* rates to which China was entitled under existing treaties. Thereafter the rates were to be similarly adjusted every seven years, "in lieu of the decennial revision authorized by existing treaties with China."

[30] *Proceedings*, pp. 1630-39.

4. Uniform rates of customs duties were to be levied on all frontiers of China, whether land or maritime. However, the Special Conference was authorized "to make equitable adjustments in those cases in which a customs privilege to be abolished was granted in return for some local economic advantage."

5. "Powers not signatory to the present Treaty whose Governments are at present recognized by the Signatory Powers, and whose present treaties with China provide for a tariff on imports and exports not to exceed 5 per centum *ad valorem,* shall be invited to adhere to the present Treaty.[31]

6. "The provisions of the present Treaty shall override all stipulations of treaties between China and the respective Contracting Powers which are inconsistent therewith, other than stipulations according most favored nation treatment."

In submitting the report of his committee, Senator Underwood read also a declaration by the Chinese delegate to the effect that "the Chinese Government have no intention to effect any change which may disturb the present administration of the Chinese Maritime Customs."[32] While voting with the other

[31] At the meeting of the Far Eastern committee on January 16, Baron de Cartier asked what powers would be entitled to representation in the Shanghai Tariff Commission and in the special conference which was to meet at a later date. Sir Robert Borden said he presumed that states which had formerly been a part of the Russian Empire, but which were now independent powers whose governments had been recognized, would be entitled to such representation. Senator Underwood observed that China's only binding obligation was in respect of those governments with which she had signed treaties. Other governments could not complain regarding taxes which might be collected at a Chinese customs house because they had no established right in regard to China's customs taxation. Dr. Koo stated emphatically that only such countries as had treaties with China relating to import duties were entitled to representation on the commission mentioned in the report of the sub-committee. *Proceedings,* pp. 1200-1204. The views expressed by Senator Underwood and Dr. Koo found confirmation in the resolution given above, which became Article VIII of the treaty relating to the Chinese customs tariff.

[32] In the 31st meeting of the Committee on Pacific and Far Eastern Questions, on February 3, Secretary Hughes asked whether this declaration should merely appear on the minutes of the Conference, or whether it should form an annex to the treaty on the customs tariff which would be signed by the Chinese representatives. Dr. Koo immediately protested that it would be sufficient to have the declaration appear in the minutes. "He felt certain that his colleagues around the table would not wish to make a treaty obligation . . . out of a matter which fell within the domestic policy of the Chinese Government." So far as he was aware, said Dr. Koo, there was no treaty or convention in which this policy had been stipulated. It occurred

members of the committee, Dr. Koo voiced his keen disappointment over the omission from the sub-committee's report of any reference to tariff autonomy. The Chinese Delegation, he said, felt bound to declare that "though this Committee does not see its way to consider China's claim for the restoration of her tariff autonomy, it is not their desire, in assenting to the Agreement now before you, to relinquish their claim; on the contrary, it is their intention to bring the question up again for consideration on all appropriate occasions in the future." [33]

The next concrete issue raised by the Chinese delegation was that of extraterritoriality. On November 25, Dr. Wang Ch'ung-hui presented arguments against the continued existence of consular jurisdiction, particularly in view of the fact that China had recently made much progress in the reform of her judicial system and in the codification of her laws. [34] The Chinese jurist asked, therefore, that the powers represented at the Conference agree to relinquish their extraterritorial rights in China at the end of a definite period. Meanwhile the powers should, at a date to be mutually agreed upon, designate representatives empowered to enter into negotiations with the Chinese Government for the adoption of a plan for the progressive modifica-

only in loan contracts made by the Chinese Government in 1896 and 1898 with two groups of foreign bankers. Mr. Balfour nevertheless insisted that the declaration be made an annex to the treaty. At this point Senator Underwood, who had vigorously supported Dr. Koo's stand, ventured to suggest that after the declaration had been reported by the chairman to the Plenary Session of the Conference, it would be just as strong and binding as if it were in the treaty. Mr. Balfour then said he would content himself with taking note of Senator Underwood's statement relative to the binding character of a declaration made under such conditions, and would interpose no further objections. Dr. Koo then recalled that in the sub-committee at the time the matter was under discussion, he had stated that "this declaration of intention not to disturb the present customs administration could not be reasonably construed to preclude the Chinese people from realizing their legitimate aspiration to make the Chinese Maritime Customs Service an institution more national in character." The Chinese delegate expressed confidence that "in suggesting to give to the declaration of the Chinese Delegation the solemnity of a public announcement at a Plenary Session of the Conference . . . Mr. Balfour had no desire to see the policy embodied in the declaration invested with the character of permanency." The British representative said that he had no such desire. *Proceedings*, pp. 1540-52.

[33] *Proceedings*, p. 1180.   [34] *Ibid.*, pp. 932-4.

tion and ultimate abolition of the existing system of consular jurisdiction, the carrying out of which would be distributed over the above-mentioned period.[35] Secretary Hughes suggested that whatever steps were taken should be preceded by an inquiry into existing conditions in China.[36] Mr. Balfour, expressing agreement with the American chief delegate, said it was his understanding that the difficulty lay, not so much in Chinese law itself, as in the administration of that law.[37] The work of formulating definite proposals was left to a sub-committee, of which Senator Lodge was made chairman. The sub-committee's report, submitted to the full committee on November 29, contained the following recommendations:[38]

1. The governments of the powers represented in the Conference, except China, should each appoint one member of a Commission having power to "inquire into the present practice of extraterritorial jurisdiction in China, and into the laws and the judicial system and the methods of judicial administration of China" with a view to reporting their findings of fact in regard to these matters, together with "their recommendations as to such means as they may find suitable to improve the existing conditions of the administration of justice in China, and to assist and further the efforts of the Chinese Government to effect such legislative and judicial reforms as would warrant the several powers in relinquishing, either progressively or otherwise, their respective rights of extraterritoriality."

2. The Commission would be constituted within three months after the adjournment of the Conference with instructions to submit its report and recommendations within one year after its first meeting.

3. Each of the powers represented on the Commission was to be deemed free to accept or to reject all or any portion of the Commission's recommendations, except that "in no case shall any of the said powers make its acceptance of all or any portion of such recommendations . . . dependent on the granting by China of any special concession, favor, benefit, or immunity, whether political or economic."

By a supplementary resolution, the Chinese Delegation, after

[35] *Ibid.,* pp. 934-6.　　　　　　　　[37] *Ibid.,* p. 938.
[36] *Ibid.,* p. 936.　　　　　　　　　　[38] *Ibid.,* p. 1010.

expressing its satisfaction "with the sympathetic disposition of the Powers," announced the intention of the Chinese Government "to appoint a representative who shall have the right to sit as a member of the said Commission, it being understood that China shall be free to accept or to reject any or all of the recommendations of the Commission. Furthermore, China is prepared to coöperate in the work of this Commission and to afford to it every possible facility for the successful accomplishment of its tasks." [39]

The resolutions of the sub-committee were adopted without amendment by the full committee,[40] this action being ratified subsequently by the Fourth Plenary Session of the Conference on December 10.[41]

The specific questions relating to China which had been dealt with thus far concerned foreign rights established by treaty. Matters which were next discussed related to infringements on China's sovereign rights which lacked treaty sanction. Of these the first concerned the existence in China of British, French, Japanese, and American post offices. At the sixth meeting of the Far Eastern Committee, on November 25, Dr. Sze asked that the powers concerned "agree at once to abolish all postal services now maintained by them in China." [42] The Chinese delegate explained that China now maintained an efficient postal system of her own, that the existence of foreign post offices interfered with and made difficult the development of this system, and that "the maintenance by foreign Governments of post offices in China is in direct violation of the latter's territorial and administrative integrity, and rests upon no treaty or other legal rights." [43] Secretary Hughes and Mr. Root indicated the general willingness of the American Government to accede to the request of the Chinese delegation.[44] Mr. Balfour and M. Viviani stated that the British and French Governments, respectively, were disposed to take similar action, provided the Chinese Government agreed not to disturb the existing admin-

[39] *Ibid.*
[40] *Ibid.*, p. 1012.
[41] *Ibid.*, p. 154.
[42] *Ibid.*, p. 940.
[43] *Ibid.*, p. 942.
[44] *Ibid.*, pp. 956-8.

220   *China's Foreign Relations*

istration of its postal system, at the head of which was a French Co-Director General.[45] The Japanese delegate, Mr. Hanihara, said that while Japan did not object to withdrawing her post offices under the guarantees suggested by the British and French delegates, it might be well to delay such withdrawal until after an investigation of actual conditions in China.[46] Dr. Sze asked how much delay was desired by the Japanese Government. The Japanese representative proposed that the question be referred for decision to the Ministers of the interested powers at Peking, they being in a position to know what was a reasonable and proper time limit.[47] This suggestion was opposed by Dr. Sze and did not meet with general support. It was then agreed that the matter should be considered by a sub-committee empowered to draft an appropriate resolution. Following the report of this sub-committee on November 28, the full committee adopted a declaration providing that the Four Powers having postal agencies in China agree to their abandonment subject to the conditions that (a) China maintain an efficient postal service, and that (b) an assurance be given by the Chinese Government that it contemplated no change in the existing postal system so far as the status of the foreign Co-Director General was concerned.[48]

Due to Japanese uncertainty, the date for the final withdrawal of the foreign post offices in question was not specified in the sub-committee's draft resolution. At the meeting of the full committee on December 12, however, Senator Lodge announced that the Japanese Government had agreed that the arrangement contemplated by the resolution should take effect not later than January 1, 1923. But the Japanese Government desired to place on record their desire "that a suitable number of experienced Japanese postal officers be engaged by China in the interest of the efficiency of the Chinese postal administration." [49]

On November 21, the powers had expressed their firm intention of respecting the sovereignty, independence, and territorial

[45] *Ibid.,* pp. 958-60.   [46] *Ibid.,* p. 962.   [47] *Ibid.,* p. 964.
[48] *Ibid.,* pp. 976-8.   [49] *Ibid.,* pp. 1128-30.

and administrative integrity of China, and of providing her
with the fullest and most unembarrassed opportunity to develop
and maintain for herself an effective and stable government.
Dr. Sze now determined to see how far the powers would go
in giving effect to these principles. On November 28, the Chinese delegate declared that "the maintenance upon Chinese
territory, without China's consent and against her protests, of
foreign troops, railway guards, police boxes, and electrical wire
and wireless communication installations" constituted a standing violation of the country's sovereignty and territorial and
administrative integrity.[50] He asked each of the powers represented in the Conference to declare that "without the consent
of the Government of China, expressly and specifically given
in each case, it will not station troops or railway guards or
establish and maintain police boxes, or erect or operate electrical
communication installations, upon the soil of China; and that
if there now exist upon the soil of China such troops or railway
guards or police boxes or electrical installations without China's
express consent, they will be at once withdrawn." [51] Mr. Hanihara asked for time in which to study the Chinese proposition,
and M. Viviani displayed irritation over the tendency of China's
delegates to present such important matters without giving preliminary notice of their intention to do so.[52] It was suggested
that better progress might be made if the Chinese delegates
presented the questions one at a time.

The next day, therefore, Dr. Sze submitted separate data
relating to the presence of foreign armed forces on Chinese
soil. Favorable action on China's request for the withdrawal
of these forces, he declared, would not affect the rights of the
several powers under the Protocol of 1901. The garrisons
which would be affected were almost entirely Japanese. Dr. Sze
charged flatly that Japanese troops then maintained in Shantung, at Hankow, in South Manchuria, and along the Chinese
Eastern Railway were there without China's formal consent.
Japan's so-called right to maintain armed forces along the South

[50] *Ibid.,* p. 980.   [51] *Ibid.,* p. 982.   [52] *Ibid.,* pp. 982-4.

Manchuria Railway rested upon Article III of the Treaty of Portsmouth between Japan and Russia. The Chinese delegate pointed out that China had never given her assent to this particular provision of the Portsmouth Treaty.[53] Mr. Hanihara, reading a prepared statement, admitted in effect that certain troops maintained by his government in China were there without treaty warrant. Troops along the South Manchuria Railway, however, were provided for by the Treaty of Peking of 1905. Their presence was necessary, furthermore, because of the prevalence of banditry in the areas adjacent to the railway.[54] Dr. Sze expressed pleasure at assurances given by the Japanese delegate that the Japanese troops then in China were not and had never been intended to serve any aggressive purpose, and that they would eventually be withdrawn; he added that he would be glad to learn later as to the time when they would be withdrawn.[55]

Dr. Sze returned to the attack at a subsequent meeting of the committee on December 2. "For the Powers (he said) to reach common accord as to principle so well set forth by Mr. Root in his first Resolution and then hesitate to apply it to the very cases which the Delegations here assembled are presumed . . . to have had in mind when the Resolution was agreed to, would leave the Conference in the position of enunciating a high principle of international relationship but unable or unwilling to maintain it in the face of the actual facts of particular cases." [56] The Chinese delegate declared bluntly that the presence of Japanese troops in Shantung, at Hankow, and along the South Manchuria and Chinese Eastern Railways constituted a standing violation of the principle, already assented to by the Conference, of respecting the territorial and administrative integrity of China. The steady extension of Japanese military and police control over Chinese territory was referred to, and

[53] *Ibid.*, pp. 988-90.
[54] *Ibid.*, pp. 1004-6. For an able discussion of Japan's legal "right" to maintain railway guards in South Manchuria under the Treaty of Peking of 1905, see C. Walter Young, *Japanese Jurisdiction in the South Manchuria Railway Areas*, Baltimore, 1931, pp. 261-284.
[55] *Proceedings*, p. 1008. [56] *Ibid.*, p. 1040.

the Conference was asked "to take appropriate measures to prevent further aggressions of this character and to relieve China of these impositions under which it is laboring to maintain its independence and integrity." [57]

Secretary Hughes, doubtless having in mind the use of American marines in the Caribbean area, admitted by implication that the troops of one power might be stationed on the territory of another for the general protection of life and property, regardless of treaty. He suggested, therefore, that the difference between the Chinese and the Japanese positions concerned questions of fact, namely, as to whether adequate protection for life and property existed which would warrant Japan in withdrawing from China her troops and police. M. Viviani proposed that the determination of the facts in question be left to the Commission on Extraterritoriality, which would be empowered to investigate the situation on the spot.[58] Chinese opposition prevented the adoption of this suggestion.[59] Instead, the committee, except for the Chinese delegate who did not vote, adopted the following resolution prepared by a sub-committee: [60]

"Whereas the Powers have from time to time stationed armed forces, including police and railway guards, in China to protect the lives and property of foreigners lawfully in China;

"And whereas it appears that certain of these armed forces are maintained in China without the authority of any treaty or agreement;

[57] *Ibid.*, p. 1048. Mr. Hanihara attempted somewhat lamely to refute this argument at the meeting of the committee on December 7. Reading from a prepared statement, the Japanese delegate said, "It does not necessarily follow that because a certain principle is accepted, it should be applied in all cases immediately and without qualification. In proceeding to its practical application we must not lose sight of particular facts and circumstances that surround each individual case. . . . I should state in all frankness that the stationing of our troops and police in some parts of China is solely due to our instinct for self-protection. . . . We should only be too glad to be relieved of that responsibility, if the efficient system of protection and control over our nationals resident in China were in operation." *Ibid.*, p. 1088. Reports were then submitted giving specific instances of disordered conditions in Manchuria and elsewhere in China. *Ibid.*, pp. 1090-98.

[58] *Ibid.*, pp. 1048-50.   [59] *Ibid.*, p. 1188.   [60] *Ibid.*, p. 1192.

"And whereas the Powers have declared their intention to withdraw their armed forces now on duty in China without the authority of any treaty or agreement, whenever China shall assure the protection of the lives and property of foreigners in China;

"And whereas China has declared her intention and capacity to assure the protection of the lives and property of foreigners in China:

"Now to the end that there may be clear understanding of the conditions upon which in each case the practical execution of those intentions must depend;

"It is resolved: That the Diplomatic Representatives in Peking of the Powers now in conference at Washington . . . will be instructed by their respective Governments, whenever China shall so request, to associate themselves with three representatives of the Chinese Government to conduct collectively a full and impartial inquiry into the issues raised by the foregoing declarations of intention made by the Powers and by China and shall thereafter prepare a full and comprehensive report setting out without reservation their findings of fact and their opinions with regard to the matter hereby referred for inquiry. . . ." [61]

Having effectively sidetracked China's request for the withdrawal of alien troops stationed within her borders, the Far Eastern Committee turned its attention to the problem of elec-

[61] The adoption of this resolution meant a decided set-back for the Chinese. It recognized the right of any power, in the absence of specific treaty provision therefor, to station armed forces in China for the general protection of life and property. It announced the intention of the powers to withdraw certain foreign troops from China, but indicated that the actual withdrawal would be postponed for an indefinite period. Chinese disappointment over the terms of the resolution was reflected in a declaration read during the Fifth Plenary Session of the Conference on February 1, 1922. With reference to the maintenance of armed forces by a nation or nations within the borders of other states which had not given their express consent thereto, the Chinese delegation declared that, according to accepted principles of international law, the sending or stationing of such forces could rightfully be only a temporary measure designed to meet emergencies threatening imminent danger to the lives and property of foreign nationals, and upon the passing of such emergency, the forces sent should be immediately withdrawn. It was likewise the understanding of the Chinese delegation that the obligation to make such withdrawal could not, as a general principle, be rightfully postponed until the government of the state where such forces were located had consented to an inquiry by representatives of other powers into its own domestic conditions relative to the maintenance of law and order, and a report had been made declaring that there was no necessity for the presence of such foreign armed forces. *Proceedings*, p. 216.

trical communications. On November 29 the Chinese delegation asked that action be taken which would "lead to the immediate abolition or surrender to the Chinese Government of all
electrical means of communication, including wireless stations,
now maintained on Chinese soil without the consent of the
Chinese Government." [62] The representatives of the powers
were reminded that China had developed a system of telegraph
stations fully adequate for the transmission of messages by
wire, and had also entered into contracts for the installation of
high-powered wireless apparatus which would put her into
communication with other countries. [63] Foreign electrical installations interfered with the continued development of the Chinese system by diverting business properly belonging to it, and
constituted also an indefensible infringement of China's territorial and administrative integrity. In the opinion of the Chinese delegates, these foreign installations could have no
significance except as they seemed to serve the "purely political
aims" of the powers concerned. Although China recognized no
legal obligation to do so, she was "willing to pay to the foreign
Governments owning them the fair value of such stations" as
might conveniently be incorporated into her own system of
electrical communications. [64] Dr. Sze recognized a distinction
between electrical installations established in the Legations at
Peking under the provisions of the Protocol of 1901, and others
which lacked justification with reference to any treaty or contract. Concerning the first of these, China would consent to
their continued operation provided, first, that they were used
only for official and not for commercial purposes, and, second,
that an agreement were reached regarding the wave length
which they might use. [65]

At a subsequent meeting of the Far Eastern Committee, the
representatives of the powers took the following action relative
to China's request: [66]

[62] *Proceedings,* p. 990.
[63] *Ibid.,* p. 992.
[64] *Ibid.,* p. 994.
[65] *Ibid.,* pp. 1020-22.
[66] *Ibid.,* p. 1078.

1. Radio stations in China, whether maintained under the provisions of the Protocol of 1901, or operated from the grounds of the foreign Legations in Peking, should confine their operations to the transmission of government messages, except during times of emergency when they might be used temporarily for the transmission of commercial messages.

2. Radio stations operated on Chinese soil by a foreign government or its citizens should limit the messages sent and received by the terms of the treaties or concessions providing for their establishment.

3. Foreign radio stations maintained on Chinese soil without the consent of the Chinese Government should be transferred to the Government of China upon full and fair compensation being paid, "as soon as the Chinese Ministry of Communications is prepared to operate the same effectively for the general public benefit."

4. Questions relating to radio stations in leased territories, in the South Manchuria Railway zone, and in the French Concession at Shanghai, were to be settled by negotiations between the Chinese Government and the foreign governments concerned.

5. Agreements which would prevent interference between the wave lengths used by Chinese and foreign radio stations were to be negotiated between the Chinese Ministry of Communications and the owners or managers of the foreign stations concerned.

Some weeks after the adoption of this resolution, the French delegate, M. Viviani, suggested the creation of an international committee, composed of representatives of China and of the interested powers, which should draw up practical recommendations for coöperation in the development of a system of radio communications in China.[67] Mr. Root thereupon proposed the organization of an international committee empowered to inquire into existing concessions, contracts, treaties, and loans, relative to electrical communications in China, and between China and other countries. The committee would have power also to confer with the Chinese Government relative to the adequacy of existing services and the need for additional services.[68] The proposal to establish an international committee with such broad powers aroused the apprehensions of the Chinese. Dr. Sze said that China would coöperate willingly with

[67] *Ibid.*, p. 1428.   [68] *Ibid.*, pp. 1430-32.

the other Powers in the adoption of common policies applicable to all governments and equally beneficial to all. He voiced the opinion that "so important an international question should be dealt with as a whole, and not by taking China as a single unit for international discussion. As this Conference has been called . . . for the purpose of assisting China by the removal of existing limitations on her sovereign rights, I am inclined to think that the public might have misapprehension should any such commission be appointed to deal with . . . such a subject, which is manifestly China's own and sole problem." [69] Dr. Sze's stand was warmly supported by Senator Underwood. The Conference accordingly contented itself with a declaration announcing that its previous action with regard to radio stations in China should not be taken as an expression of opinion concerning whether or not such stations were or were not authorized by the Chinese Government. Furthermore, agreements reached between the Chinese Government and the interested foreign governments relative to radio stations in the leased territories, the South Manchuria Railway area, and the French Concession at Shanghai, should conform with "the principle of the Open Door or equality of opportunity approved by the Conference." [70]

The Chinese delegate abstained from voting on this declaration which, said Dr. Sze, constituted a declaration by the eight powers. He then declared that the Chinese Government did not "recognize or concede the right of any foreign Power or of the nationals thereof to install or operate without its express consent, radio stations in Legation grounds, settlements, concessions, leased territories, railway areas or other similar areas." [71]

The discussion concerning the maintenance of foreign troops in China had given the Chinese an opportunity to deliver an oblique attack upon Japan's special interests in Manchuria. That attack had been beaten off. A second opportunity of the same sort arose during the consideration of leased territories. These leaseholds, declared Dr. Koo on December 3, had originally been

[69] *Ibid.*, p. 1438.   [70] *Ibid.*, pp. 1462-64.   [71] *Ibid.*, p. 1466.

granted by China for the sole purpose of preserving the balance
of power in the Far East. With the elimination of Germany
and the temporary eclipse of Russia, the need for maintaining
such a balance of power had ceased to exist. Consequently, "the
Chinese Delegation believed that the time had come for the
interested Powers to relinquish their control over the territories
leased to them." [72] Dr. Koo asked that pending the termination of such leases, the areas concerned should be demilitarized.
He stated, further, that the Chinese Government was prepared
to respect and safeguard the legitimate vested interests of the
different powers within the territories in question. [73]

M. Viviani then read a formal statement to the effect that
France was prepared "to join in the collective restitution of
territories leased to various Powers in China, it being understood that this principle being once admitted and all private
rights being safeguarded, the conditions and time limits of the
restitution shall be determined by agreement between the Chinese Government and each of the Governments concerned." [74]
For the Japanese Government, Mr. Hanihara stated that Japan
had already declared her willingness to restore to China the
leased territory of Kiaochou. With regard to the Kwantung
leased territory, however, "the Japanese Delegates desire to
make it clear that Japan has no intention at present to relinquish
the important rights she has lawfully acquired and at no small
sacrifice." [75] Mr. Balfour suggested that the Kowloon leasehold, held by Great Britain, was of peculiar importance because
of its strategic position with regard to the great port of Hongkong. The Kowloon Extension was held only for the purpose
of affording security to Hongkong and it was necessary, therefore, that it be dealt with in a different spirit from other leased
territories which had been acquired for totally different reasons.
On the other hand, "the British Government would be perfectly
ready to return Weihaiwei to China as a part of a general
arrangement intended to confirm the sovereignty of China and

[72] *Ibid.*, p. 1060.
[73] *Ibid.*, p. 1062.
[74] *Ibid.*, p. 1064.
[75] *Ibid.*, p. 1064.

to give effect to the principle of the Open Door. This surrender, however, could only be undertaken as part of some such general arrangement. . . ." [76]

Secretary Hughes observed that Japan had made reservations concerning Kwantung and Great Britain with regard to Kowloon, and asked if these reservations would prevent the carrying out of arrangements for the return of other leased areas.[77] Mr. Balfour said it was the policy of his government to make use of the surrender of Weihaiwei to assist in securing a settlement of the Shantung question, and that if such a settlement could be reached, the British Government would do their best to promote a general settlement by restoring Weihaiwei to the central government of China.[78] M. Viviani announced that in view of the special interests which, according to the statements of the other delegations, tended to complicate the restoration of certain leased territories, his government desired to examine the new situation thus created.[79] Subsequently, on February 2, M. Sarraut explained once more the policy of the French Government with regard to Kwangchow-wan. France was ready to relinquish its leasehold rights provided all other powers having leased territories should restore them to China *pari passu*. But even if this condition were not fulfilled, France was still willing to arrange directly with the Chinese Government the conditions under which, and the time when, the restitution of Kwangchow-wan should become effective.[80] The final British declaration was made by Mr. Balfour at the plenary session of the Conference on February 1. The British delegate stated that since Japan had already agreed to restore Kiaochou to the sovereignty of China, he was ready to announce "that Great Britain proposes to hand back Weihaiwei to the country within whose frontier it lies." [81]

One item on the Chinese agenda was the request that the powers abstain in future from concluding between themselves "any treaty or agreement directly affecting China or the general

[76] *Ibid.*, pp. 1066-68. [77] *Ibid.*, p. 1070. [78] *Ibid.*
[79] *Ibid.* [80] *Ibid.*, p. 1518. [81] *Ibid.*, p. 226.

peace in these regions without previously notifying China and giving to her an opportunity to participate." Dealing with this question on December 8, Dr. Koo said that such agreements fell roughly into two divisions, "the one being in the nature of mutual engagements to abstain from certain action in special parts of China, the other being engagements for mutual assistance in support of the general interests of all foreign powers in China, or of the special interests claimed by the parties to the agreement." [82] The first type of agreement, explained the Chinese delegate, tended to violate the principles of the Open Door by dividing China into distinct spheres of interest or influence. Sir Auckland Geddes suggested that a declaration embodying the substance of the Chinese proposal should be added as a supplement to the Root Resolutions adopted on November 21. [83] Mr. Hanihara voiced the opinion that if such a declaration were adopted, China should be made a party to it. [84] Secretary Hughes then proposed that the committee accept a resolution providing that the Nine Powers attending the Conference, including China, "declare that it is their intention not to enter into any treaty, agreement, arrangement, or understanding, either with one another, or, individually or collectively, with any Power or Powers, which would infringe or impair the principles which have been declared by the Resolution adopted November 21st by this Committee." In this form, the resolution became Article II of the Nine Power Treaty Relating to Principles and Policies. [85]

The Far Eastern committee then dealt more directly with the question of spheres of interest. Already, Mr. Balfour had announced that "so far as Great Britain was concerned, spheres of interest were things of the past," since on October 31, 1921, the Parliamentary Undersecretary of the British Foreign Office had declared before the House of Commons that the policy of spheres of influence in China had been "superseded by one of international coöperation. . . ." [86] On December 12, Dr.

[82] *Ibid.,* p. 1104.   [83] *Ibid.,* p. 1114.   [84] *Ibid.,* p. 1122.
[85] *Ibid.,* pp. 1124, 156.   [86] *Ibid.,* pp. 1108, 1118.

Wang Ch'ung-hui presented the Chinese views on the subject. Spheres of interest, he said, seriously hampered the economic development of China. Moreover, the system was contrary to the policy of equal opportunity for the commerce and industry of all nations. There was also a tendency to use economic claims for the purpose of advancing ulterior political aims which threatened the political integrity of China.[87] Consequently, the Chinese delegation asked "that the Powers represented in this Conference disavow all claims to a sphere or spheres of interest or of influence or any special interests within the territory of China." [88]

At this point, Mr. Root said it was his understanding that China now asked to be relieved from the effect of certain restrictions and stipulations which were collateral to grants made at various times by the Chinese Government. He suggested the desirability of specifying the particular restrictions from which China now asked to be relieved.[89] Dr. Wang said he would be prepared to furnish a list of these at the next meeting of the committee. On December 14, therefore, the Chinese delegate read the list of restrictive stipulations which his government desired to have abrogated. The first of these was the Sino-Japanese treaties and notes of May 25, 1915. Second came fourteen inter-power agreements having reference to China, including the Root-Takahira and the Lansing-Ishii Agreements. In the third group were various non-alienation agreements relating to Hainan, the Yangtse valley, the Tonking border, Fukien, and the coast of China.[90] Referring to the Sino-Japanese treaties and notes of 1915, Dr. Wang declared that they vitally affected "the very existence, independence, and integrity of China" and that "in the common interests of the Powers as well as of China, and in conformity with the principles relating to China already adopted by the Committee," they should be reconsidered and canceled.[91] Mr. Hanihara served immediate notice that if "there was a question of making the validity of the Treaty or

---

[87] *Ibid.,* p. 1144.   [88] *Ibid.,* p. 1146.   [89] *Ibid.,* p. 1146.
[90] *Ibid.,* pp. 1152-4.   [91] *Ibid.,* p. 1160.

Agreements of 1915, or the change or abrogation thereof, the subject of discussion at this Conference, he desired to announce that the Japanese Delegation could not agree to such a course. He believed this question was one to be taken up between Japan and China if it were to be taken up at all, and not at this Conference." [92] To avoid what threatened to develop into a dangerous impasse, the chairman, Secretary Hughes, hastily suggested that the meeting adjourn to permit an informal discussion of the questions raised by the Chinese delegate.

Chinese and American views relative to spheres of influence were substantially similar, and at the meeting of the Far Eastern Committee on January 18, Secretary Hughes presented the following resolution on "The Open Door in China": [93]

1. "With a view to applying more effectually the principles of the open door or equality of opportunity in China for the trade and industry of all nations, the Powers other than China represented at this Conference agree:

(a) Not to seek or to support their nationals in seeking any arrangement which might purport to establish in favor of their interests any general superiority of rights with respect to commercial or economic development in any designated region of China;

(b) Not to seek or to support their nationals in seeking any such monopoly or preference as would deprive other nationals of the right of undertaking any legitimate trade or industry in China, or of participating with the Chinese Government, or with any local authority, in any category of public enterprise, or which by reason of its scope, duration or geographical extent is calculated to frustrate the practical application of the principle of equal opportunity. . . ."

2. "The Chinese Government takes note of the above Agreement and declares its intention of being guided by the same principles in dealing with applications for economic rights and privileges from Governments and nationals of all foreign countries, whether parties to that Agreement or not."

3. "The Powers including China represented at this Conference agree in principle to the establishment in China of a Board of Reference to which any question arising on the above Agreement and Declaration may be referred for investigation and report."

[92] *Ibid.*   [93] *Ibid.,* pp. 1268-70.

The three resolutions, entirely innocuous because lacking any retroactive force, were accepted unanimously by the members of the Committee. The American Government, however, desired the adoption of a fourth resolution providing that "The Powers including China represented at this Conference agree that any provisions of an existing concession which appear inconsistent with those of another concession or with the principles of the above Agreement or Declaration may be submitted by the parties concerned to the Board of Reference when established for the purpose of endeavoring to arrive at a satisfactory adjustment on equitable terms." [94] Secretary Hughes was careful to explain that the reports of the board of reference would have no binding force. The nations would in no way part with their right to maintain what they conceived to be their interests, and the legitimate rights of their nationals would remain unimpaired. An opportunity would merely be provided for avoiding unnecessary disputes by affording an opportunity for general consideration, through an appropriate body, of the merits of a particular claim. [95] The Hughes proposal, obviously designed to pave the way for an examination of monopolistic privileges acquired in the past, alarmed both the French and the Japanese. M. Sarraut asked whether the decisions of the board would have any bearing on concessions already granted. [96] The American Secretary admitted that the proposed resolution might have a certain retroactive effect. [97] The French delegate immediately expressed opposition to this interpretation, and Baron Shidehara subsequently proposed an amendment to the resolution depriving it of any retroactive force. [98] It was not just, said the Japanese representative, that concessions already granted by China should be subjected to examination in the light of this new agreement. Dr. Sze favored the adoption of the resolution in its original form. [99] Faced, however, with the determined opposition of France and Japan, Secretary Hughes withdrew the objectionable proposal, with the understanding that any dele-

[94] *Ibid.,* p. 1226.　　[95] *Ibid.,* p. 1228.　　[96] *Ibid.,* p. 1232.
[97] *Ibid.,* p. 1236.　　[98] *Ibid.,* pp. 1240, 1250.　　[99] *Ibid.,* p. 1262.

gate might subsequently press for its separate consideration.[100] Dr. Sze reserved the right to exercise this privilege on another occasion.[101]

The three resolutions just adopted seemed to guarantee that future agreements with regard to China would not conflict with the principles of the Open Door. The adoption of the fourth resolution might have paved the way for a reconsideration of past agreements which, by conferring monopolistic privileges, violated those principles. French and Japanese fear of disturbing the *status quo* prevented the adoption of the Hughes resolution. Nothing daunted, however, the Chinese delegation determined to approach the same problem from a different angle by asking the Conference to determine the status of existing commitments concerning China. On January 19, Dr. Koo made three suggestions: (a) All powers which had any claim or claims on China should make them known; (b) in order to clear up the status of all existing commitments, the Far Eastern Committee should try to determine which of these were valid; (c) after the validity of existing commitments or claims had been determined, steps should be taken to harmonize them with each other and with the principles already adopted by the Committee.[102]

After discussing the Chinese proposals, the Committee, on January 21, adopted the following resolutions which, if they did not go the whole way toward realizing Chinese desires, at least simplified the situation among the powers themselves:[103]

1. "The several Powers other than China will at their earliest convenience file with the Secretariat General of the Conference . . . a list of all treaties, conventions, exchanges of notes, or other international agreements which they may have with China, or with any other Power or Powers in relation to China, which they deem to be still in force and upon which they may desire to rely. . . . Every treaty or other international agreement of the character described which may be concluded hereafter shall be notified by the Govern-

100 *Ibid.*, p. 1264.   102 *Ibid.*, pp. 1286-90.
101 *Ibid.*, p. 1268.   103 *Ibid.*, pp. 1364-66.

ments concerned within sixty days of its conclusion to the Powers who are signatories of or adherents to this Agreement."

2. "The several Powers other than China will file with the Secretariat General of the Conference, at the earliest convenience . . . a list, as nearly complete as may be possible, of all those contracts between their nationals, of the one part, and the Chinese Government or any of its administrative subdivisions or local authorities, of the other part, which involve any concession, franchise, option or preference with respect to railway construction, mining, forestry, navigation, river conservancy, harbor works, reclamation, electrical communications, or other public works or public services, or for the sale of arms or ammunition, or which involve a lien upon any of the public revenues or properties of the Chinese Government or of any of its administrative subdivisions. . . . Every contract of the public character described which may be concluded hereafter shall be notified by the Governments concerned within sixty days after the receipt of information of its conclusion to the Powers who are signatories of or adherents to this Agreement."

3. "The Chinese Government agrees to notify in the conditions laid down in this Agreement every treaty, agreement or contract of the character indicated herein which has been or may hereafter be concluded by that Government or by any local authority in China with any foreign Power or the nationals of any foreign Power whether party to this Agreement or not, so far as the information is in its possession."

4. "The Governments of Powers having treaty relations with China, which are not represented at the present Conference, shall be invited to adhere to this Agreement."

The Committee adopted at the same time a resolution providing that "the Signatory Powers will not support any agreements by their respective nationals with each other designed to create Spheres of Influence or to provide for the enjoyment of mutually exclusive opportunities in designated parts of Chinese territory." [104]

The Chinese delegation, still hoping for some action relative

[104] *Ibid.,* p. 1366. It is apparent that this resolution was designed merely to prevent the creation of new spheres of interest; it did not abolish old ones. Actually, as Professor Ichihashi has pointed out, "this much discussed question was allowed to rest without any solution." *The Washington Conference and After,* Stanford University, 1928, p. 259.

to old agreements, next asked that some machinery be created
to which questions concerning the validity of existing commitments could conveniently be referred, so that conflicts of this
nature might be fairly adjusted.[105] Dr. Koo asked in particular
that definite terms of duration be attached to China's existing
commitments which were without limit of time. The chairman
of the committee suggested that since these commitments existed
apparently between at least two parties, of which China was
one, the question was naturally one to be settled in the course
of negotiations between China and the power or powers directly
concerned.[106] Dr. Koo intimated that for the purpose of handling controversies of the type he had in mind, his government
desired to find a substitute for diplomatic action.[107] Obviously
anxious not to deal further with a question of peculiar delicacy,
Secretary Hughes then said that since China was a member of
the Permanent Court of International Justice, that body might
be utilized in the settlement of such disputes.[108] Thus China's
attempt to secure reconsideration of old agreements which crippled her freedom of action, and in some instances conflicted
also with the principles of the Open Door, ended in dismal
failure. The powers were disposed, as Baron Shidehara said on
one occasion, to look forward to the future with hope and confidence; but like genteel retired burglars, they had no thought
of relinquishing their hold on past gains. In particular, the
Japanese claims to exceptional interests in Manchuria remained
undisturbed.

In spite of the disturbing rumors which had circulated in
October, the only real attempt during the Conference to subject
China to additional international supervision occurred during
the consideration of the Chinese Eastern Railway question. The
general question of railways came to the fore on January 19
with the adoption of a resolution which, as Article V of the
Nine Power Treaty, took the following form: [109]

[105] *Proceedings*, p. 1386. [107] *Ibid.*, pp. 1390-92.
[106] *Ibid.*, p. 1388. [108] *Ibid.*, p. 1394.
[109] Text of the original resolution, *ibid.*, p. 1282.

"China agrees that, throughout the whole of the railways in China, she will not exercise or permit unfair discrimination of any kind. In particular there shall be no discrimination whatever, direct or indirect, in respect of charges or of facilities on the ground of the nationality of passengers or the countries from which or to which they are proceeding, or the origin or ownership of goods or the country from which or to which they are consigned, or the nation-ality or ownership of the ship or other means of conveying such pas-sengers or goods before or after their transport on the Chinese Railways."

"The Contracting Powers, other than China, assume a corre-sponding obligation in respect of any of the aforesaid railways over which they or their nationals are in a position to exercise any control in virtue of any concession, special agreement or other-wise."

At the time the above action was taken, the representatives of the Nine Powers also, in a separate resolution, recorded their hope "that to the utmost degree consistent with existent rights, the future development of railways in China shall be so con-ducted as to enable the Chinese Government to effect the uni-fication of railways into a railway system under Chinese control, with such foreign financial and technical assistance as may prove necessary in the interests of that system." [110] The representa-tives of the powers then considered the problem of the Chinese Eastern Railway. On January 23, the Far Eastern Committee discussed recommendations of a sub-committee of technical advisers dealing with this artery of international communica-tion. The Chinese Eastern Railway, declared the technical ad-visers, constituted an indispensable factor in the economic development of Siberia and North Manchuria and the nations represented in the Conference were interested in its preserva-tion, efficient operation, and maintenance as a free avenue of commerce, open to the citizens of all countries without favor or discrimination.[111] Except for the technical adviser representing China, the members of the sub-committee united in recommend-ing that: [112]

[110] *Ibid.*, p. 1286.   [111] *Ibid.*, p. 1376.   [112] *Ibid.*, p. 1378.

1. An international finance committee, consisting of one representative of each of the Conference Powers, should be set up at Harbin. This committee would replace the Interallied Committee then operating at Vladivostok, and the Technical Board at Harbin. It would exercise general financial control over the railway, and be entrusted with the exercise of the trusteeship which the Allied powers had assumed in 1919 "and which cannot be relinquished until the general recognition by the Powers of a Russian Government."

2. Railway operations should be left in the hands of the Chinese Eastern Railway Company.

3. An effective police force should be provided for the maintenance of order within the railway zone. This force should consist, if China so desired, of Chinese. As a temporary measure, however, it was essential that the police force be paid by and subject to the control of the international finance committee.

The Chinese delegation set its face resolutely against any proposal for international control of the railway. The Chinese technical adviser on the sub-committee of experts submitted a separate report in which he expressed his fundamental disagreement with the recommendations of the other members of the committee.[118] In the end, therefore, the members of the full committee had to content themselves with a resolution providing that "the preservation of the Chinese Eastern Railway for those in interest requires that better protection be given to the Railway and the persons engaged in its operation and use; a more careful selection of personnel to secure efficiency of service, and a more economical use of funds to prevent waste of the property." It was recommended that the subject be dealt with immediately through proper diplomatic channels.[114] In adopting this resolution, moreover, the powers other than China reserved "the right to insist hereafter upon the responsibility of China for performance or non-performance of the obligations toward the foreign stockholders, bondholders and creditors of the Chinese Eastern Railway Company, which the Powers deem to result from the contracts under which the railroad was built and the action of China thereunder and the obligations

[118] *Ibid.*, pp. 1378-80.   [114] *Ibid.*, p. 1502.

which they deemed to be in the nature of a trust resulting from the exercise of power by the Chinese Government over the possession and administration of the railroad." [115]

In coming to the Conference, the Chinese delegation had hoped fervently that an opportunity would be offered for a revision, by the powers, of the Versailles settlement relative to Shantung. China desired general international action for the purpose of effecting this revision. Japan, however, refused to abandon the view, upon which she had continued to insist since 1920, that the Shantung question should be settled by direct negotiations between the Chinese and the Japanese Governments alone. It was consequently impossible to bring the matter before the Conference as a whole. Late in November, however, Secretary Hughes and Mr. Balfour tendered their good offices to the two delegations concerned, in the hope of bringing about a private settlement of the vexing dispute. At the tenth meeting of the Far Eastern Committee, on November 30, Admiral Baron Kato announced that the Chinese delegates had consented to enter into "conversations" on the subject of Shantung. [116] Mr. Sze made it clear, however, that the Chinese delegation had not solicited or asked for the meeting of representatives of the two delegations, since the government and people of China had always hoped "to be able to present this very important question to the consideration of the Conference. . . ." It was only because the Chinese Government deeply appreciated the friendly sympathy and interest which Mr. Hughes and Mr. Balfour had manifested in offering their good offices that the Chinese delegation agreed to accept the kind offer, "of course in the hope that a fair and just settlement may be soon reached and reported to the Conference, and without qualifying its freedom to seek other methods of settlement in the unhappy event of inability to reach an agreement for a fair and just settlement." [117]

Negotiations between the delegates of the two powers opened December 1, and the discussions extended over the next two

[115] *Ibid.*, pp. 1502-4.   [116] *Ibid.*, p. 1034.   [117] *Ibid.*, p. 1036.

months. At each meeting, representatives of the British and American delegations were present for the purpose of interposing from time to time with helpful suggestions.[118] At its plenary session on February 1, 1922, the chairman, Mr. Hughes, announced to the Conference that the Japanese and Chinese representatives had finally reached an agreement relating to Shantung, the terms of which he reported.[119] The former German leased territory at Kiaochou was to be restored to China within six months after the treaty became effective. Japan was to be compensated only for public properties purchased or constructed by the Japanese, it being understood that public schools, shrines, and cemeteries were to be left in the hands of the local Japanese community. The Japanese garrison at Tsingtao was to be withdrawn within thirty days. Troops and guards along the Tsingtao-Tsinan Railway were likewise to be evacuated within six months. The railway itself with its branches, together with wharves, warehouses and similar properties, was to be transferred to China in return for a payment to Japan of 53,406,141 gold marks plus the amount which Japan had spent during her administration of the railway for permanent improvements and additions. The entire sum was to be paid in Chinese treasury notes, secured on the properties and revenues of the railway, and running for a period of fifteen years. China, however, had the option of redeeming these notes at the end of five years or at any time thereafter upon six months previous notice. Pending the redemption of the treasury notes, a Japanese traffic manager and a Japanese chief accountant were to be retained by China in the railway administration. Finally, China was of her own volition to open Kiaochou to foreign residence, industry, and trade.

The final settlement of the Shantung question did not cover the broader question of the Sino-Japanese treaty and notes of 1915 which, in view of its explosive character, had thus far been kept from the floor of the Conference. With regard to

[118] W. W. Willoughby, *China at the Conference*, Baltimore, 1922, p. 283.
[119] *Proceedings*, p. 200.

this matter, Baron Shidehara read a formal statement at the meeting of the Committee on Pacific and Far Eastern Questions on February 2.[120] The Japanese delegation, while appreciating the difficult position in which the Chinese representatives found themselves, did not feel at liberty to concur in the proposal that international engagements which China had entered into "as a free sovereign nation" should now be canceled by action of the Conference. It was presumed that the Chinese delegation had no intention of calling in question the legal validity of the compacts of 1915. Indeed, the insistence by China "on the cancellation of those instruments would in itself indicate that she shares the view that the compacts actually remain in force and will continue to be effective unless and until they are cancelled." Note was taken of the Chinese contention that the treaties and notes in question stood in opposition to principles adopted by the Conference with regard to China's sovereignty and independence. But it had "been held by the Conference on more than one occasion that concessions made by China *ex contractu,* in the exercise of her own sovereign rights, cannot be regarded as inconsistent with her sovereignty and independence." Instead of examining old grievances which one of the nations represented at the Conference might have against another, the Japanese delegation expressed the opinion that it would be "more in line with the high aim of the Conference to look forward to the future with hope and with confidence." Having in view, however, the changes which had taken place in the situation since the conclusion of the compacts of 1915, the Japanese delegation took the occasion to make the following declaration: [121]

1. "Japan is ready to throw open to the joint activity of the International Financial Consortium . . . the right of option granted exclusively in favor of Japanese capital, with regard, first, to loans for the construction of railways in South Manchuria and Eastern Inner Mongolia, and, second, to loans to be secured on taxes in that region. . . ."

2. "Japan has no intention of insisting on her preferential right

[120] *Ibid.,* p. 1508.   [121] *Ibid.,* pp. 1510-12.

under the Sino-Japanese arrangements in question concerning the engagement by China of Japanese advisers or instructors on political, financial, military or police matters in South Manchuria."

3. "Japan is further ready to withdraw the reservation which she made, in proceeding to the signature of the Sino-Japanese Treaties and Notes of 1915, to the effect that Group V of the original proposals of the Japanese Government would be postponed for future negotiations."

The Japanese statement recalled, finally, that "all matters relating to Shantung contained in those Treaties and Notes have now been definitely adjusted and disposed of."

At the next meeting of the committee, on February 3, Dr. Wang Ch'ung-hui read a formal statement in answer to that presented by Baron Shidehara.[122] While appreciating Japan's action in renouncing certain exclusive privileges obtained in 1915, the Chinese delegate expressed his deep regret that the Japanese Government had not been "led to renounce the other claims predicated upon the Treaties and Notes of 1915." The Japanese delegation had expressed the opinion that the abrogation of those agreements would constitute "an exceedingly dangerous precedent . . . with far-reaching consequences upon the stability of the existing international relations in Asia, in Europe, and everywhere." It was the Chinese contention, however, that a still more dangerous precedent would be established "with consequences upon the stability of international relations which cannot be estimated, if, without rebuke or protest from other Powers, one nation can obtain from a friendly, but, in a military sense, weaker neighbor, and under circumstances such as attended the negotiation and signing of the Treaties of 1915, valuable concessions which were not in satisfaction of pending controversies and for which no *quid pro quo* was offered. . . . No apprehension need be entertained that the abrogation of the agreements of 1915 will serve as a precedent for the annulment of other agreements, since it is confidently hoped that the future will furnish no such similar occurrence." For the following

[122] *Ibid.*, pp. 1556-60.

reasons, therefore, the Chinese delegation asked that the Conference subject the 1915 Treaties and Notes to an "impartial examination with a view to their abrogation":

1. "In exchange for the concessions demanded of China, Japan offered no *quid pro quo*. The benefits derived from the agreements were wholly unilateral.

2. "The agreements, in important respects, are in violation of treaties between China and the other Powers.

3. "The agreements are inconsistent with the principles relating to China which have been adopted by the Conference.

4. "The agreements have engendered constant misunderstandings between China and Japan, and, if not abrogated, will necessarily tend, in the future, to disturb friendly relations between the two countries, and will thus constitute an obstacle in the way of realizing the purpose for the attainment of which this Conference was convened. . . ."

The Conference felt constrained to take no action of the sort desired by the Chinese delegation. Instead, it was agreed to spread on the minutes of the Conference the Japanese statement and the Chinese reply thereto, together with a statement in which Secretary Hughes declared the policy of the American Government relative to rights secured to Japan by the treaties and notes of 1915.[123] In addition, Dr. Koo announced formally that "the Chinese Delegation reserved their right to seek a solution on all future appropriate occasions, concerning those portions of the Treaties and Notes of 1915 which did not appear to have been expressly relinquished by the Japanese Government." [124]

The Conference ended its work on February 6, 1922. During the whole of its sessions, the Chinese delegation had occupied a position of peculiar difficulty. There was dissension within its own ranks, and on December 5, Mr. Phillip K. C. Tyau, Secretary-General of the delegation, resigned in protest against the failure of the Conference to give more definite and prompt consideration to China's problems.[125] The decision of China's

[123] *Ibid.*, p. 1564.   [124] *Ibid.*
[125] Dr. Tyau's example was followed by three other members of the Chinese delegation. *China Review*, I, December, 1921, pp. 387-8.

chief delegates to enter into direct negotiations with Japanese representatives relative to Shantung provoked demonstrations of protest not only in China, but among Chinese in the United States as well.[126] In consequence, the three Chinese chief delegates felt compelled on December 8 to telegraph their resignations to Peking. President Hsü Shih-ch'ang and his cabinet, after considering the matter, reached the unanimous conclusion that the resignations should not be accepted. A telegram to this effect was accordingly transmitted to the delegates at Washington on December 9.[127]

The Chinese delegates could not conceal the fact that they lacked authority to speak officially for the independent government at Canton which claimed to represent more than half of the people of China. Equally significant was the fact that the Peking Government of which they were the official representatives was known to be bankrupt, chaotic, and utterly disorganized. On December 17, the cabinet headed by Chin Yun-p'eng resigned following the sudden arrival in Peking of the Manchurian dictator, Marshal Chang Tso-lin.[128] After conferences between Chang Tso-lin and the tuchun of Chihli, Marshal Ts'ao K'un, a new cabinet headed by Mr. Liang Shih-yi was gazetted December 25. The Foreign Minister, Dr. Yen, although reluctant to take office under the new premier, was persuaded to do so until the negotiations at Washington had been concluded.[129] The new cabinet was unpopular from the very outset. Liang Shih-yi had been involved in Yuan Shih-k'ai's attempt to restore the monarchy, and was rumored also to be suspiciously friendly with various highly placed Japanese officials. Color was given to these rumors by the government's

[126] On December 8 this popular resentment flared up in a monster mass meeting and parade at Shanghai in which 20,000 were reported to have participated. *North China Herald*, CXLI, Dec. 10, 1921, p. 706. For the resolutions adopted at this mass meeting, see *ibid.*, Dec. 17, 1921, p. 751.
[127] *North China Herald*, CXLI, Supplement, Dec. 17, 1921, p. 605. In presenting their resignations, the Chinese delegates said "because of the present state of affairs in China, the standing of our country in international relations is anything but favorable, and those proposals which we have placed before the conference are not making progress as we desire." Mention was made also of "strong opposition from various quarters in China."
[128] *North China Herald*, CXLI, Dec. 24, 1921, p. 818.
[129] *Ibid.*, Dec. 31, 1921, p. 887.

action in granting amnesty to five Anfu leaders who, after
being driven from power in 1920, had found secure refuge in
the Japanese Legation in Peking.[130] More ominous was the
appointment to office of two men whose pro-Japanese intrigues
had provoked the student uprising of May, 1919.[131]

In January, General Wu P'ei-fu, the most powerful of the
Yangtse tuchuns, denounced the leaders of the newly formed
cabinet and threatened war unless they retired. General Wu
charged specifically that Premier Liang, without the knowledge
of his Minister for Foreign Affairs, had cabled to the Chinese
delegates at Washington, instructing them to arrange for the
transfer of the Shantung negotiations to Peking.[132] Although
Premier Liang immediately issued an official denial that there
was any truth in these charges, their ultimate effect was to
compel his retirement from office.[133] Thereafter, Dr. Yen
served for a time as Acting Premier. Without the steady support made possible by his presence in Peking, it is questionable
whether the Chinese representatives at Washington would have
been able to accomplish even as much as they did.

Of the three objectives which had formed the basis of the

[130] *Weekly Review of the Far East*, XIX, Jan. 7, 1922, p. 237.
[131] *North China Herald*, CXLII, Jan. 14, 1922, p. 79. One of these,
Ts'ao Ju-lin, was named to be High Industrial Commissioner, and the
other, Lu Tsung-yu, was appointed Mayor of Peking. Due to popular
opposition, neither of these appointees actually assumed office.
[132] *North China Herald*, CXLIII, Apr. 8, 1922, p. 83. *Weekly Review of the Far East*, XIX, Jan. 21, 1922, p. 319. Liang was charged also
with having instructed the government's representatives at Washington to
accept Japan's proposal for joint control of the Tsingtao-Tsinan Railway,
together with a Japanese loan for its purchase by China. *Ibid.*, Jan. 14,
1922, p. 288. In this connection, it is known that on December 27, 1921,
two days after the appointment of the new cabinet, the Japanese Minister
in Peking, Mr. Torikichi Obata, called on Dr. Yen at the Chinese
Foreign Office. The Sino-Japanese negotiations at Washington had then
reached a deadlock over the question of the Shantung Railway. Mr. Obata
suggested that the Chinese delegates might perhaps be acting in excess of
their official authority. He pointed out the inadvisability of China's going
to extremes during the course of the negotiations, and expressed the hope
that Dr. Yen would cable his representatives to adopt a more reasonable
attitude. Yen replied that the delegates had not exceeded their authority,
and that their stand was fully in accord with the government's attitude
regarding the railway. He voiced the hope that Japan would see the
advantage of meeting the terms offered by China. H. K. Tong, in *Weekly
Review of the Far East*, XIX, Jan. 7, 1922, pp. 231-2.
[133] *North China Herald*, CXLII, Jan. 28, 1922, p. 218.

Chinese program at Washington, only the first had been gained
in its entirety. Not only had the powers refrained from adding
to existing limitations on China's sovereignty, but they had
agreed most solemnly to shape their future actions toward China
in accordance with specified principles designed to enable the
Chinese to solve their domestic problems in their own way
without the danger of foreign interference. The second objective, that relating to the elimination of foreign encroachments
having no warrant in the treaties, had been attained only in
part. The powers had agreed to withdraw their post offices and
to place certain restrictions on the operation of foreign radio
stations in China. They had not agreed to withdraw their
troops. With regard to the third Chinese objective, concerning
the revision of existing treaties, relatively little had been accomplished. Some relief in the matter of tariff revision was promised together with an investigation concerning the exercise of
extraterritorial rights. In addition, the Shantung question had
been satisfactorily settled, and certain pledges had been given
with regard to Weihaiwei and Kwangchow-wan. For the rest,
the powers showed little inclination to modify the *status quo*
whether established by treaty or otherwise. The Treaty Relating
to Principles and Policies looked to the future rather than the
past.

On the whole, the results of the Washington Conference
were disappointing to the most ardent of China's well wishers.
It should be noted, however, that the Conference was not called
primarily for the purpose of redressing all of China's grievances. Its purpose was rather "to clear up the general political
situation in the Pacific and Far East so as to render less likely,
in the future, international controversies or possible wars." [184]
With this aim in mind, intelligent self-interest on the part of
the powers required that some time and effort be devoted to a
consideration of China's special problems. By and large, those
problems were handled with some sympathy and a measure of
understanding. Conditions within China offered a standing

[184] Willoughby, *op. cit.,* p. 334.

temptation to unite regarding some form of joint intervention. Despite this fact, the powers pledged themselves in the most formal and solemn manner "to respect the sovereignty, the independence, and the territorial and administrative integrity of China" and "to provide the fullest and most unembarrassed opportunity to China to develop and maintain for herself an effective and stable government." This pledge, together with that relating to the principle of the Open Door, seemed to furnish assurance that the future would be comparatively free from the type of international rivalry which had hindered China's political and economic development in the past, and had likewise produced friction and jealousy among the powers themselves. With regard to more specific benefits for which China had hoped in coming to the Conference, only a beginning had been made. Further progress would depend, first, on the ability of the Chinese to set their own house in order, and second, on the willingness of the powers to carry out in good faith the pledges which they had given at Washington.

CHAPTER VIII

LEISURELY FULFILLMENT

IF the material results of the Washington Conference, so far
as China was concerned, were somewhat more meager than had
been expected, the Chinese delegation had at least secured from
the powers solemn pledges to refrain from interfering while the
nation made an honest attempt to solve its own internal problems. In March, 1922, the Peking Government appealed to all
factions to unite in taking advantage of the opportunity thus
presented.[1] The Chinese delegates also, on their return from
Washington, stressed the need for united effort in bringing
about the political and economic reconstruction of the country.

Before the work of domestic reconstruction could proceed,
however, it seemed necessary first to cleanse the Augean stables
at Peking. While the Washington Conference was still in session, Marshal Wu P'ei-fu had demanded the dismissal of the
Premier, Liang Shih-yi, on the ground that he was guilty of
treasonable intrigue. Premier Liang, backed by the Manchurian
dictator, Chang Tso-lin, declined to retire. Late in April, therefore, Wu declared open war on Marshal Chang.[2] After two
weeks of fighting, Chang Tso-lin, utterly defeated, was compelled to withdraw to his capital at Mukden. He immediately
announced that in future he would decline to recognize the
authority of the central government.[3]

To compensate for the defection of Marshal Chang, the new

[1] North China Herald, CXLII, Mar. 18, 1922, p. 730.
[2] It is hardly necessary to remark at this point that the faction in
control of the Peking Government stood to benefit by the increased customs
duties which had been promised by the powers at Washington.
[3] North China Herald, CXLIII, May 20, 1922, p. 515.

248

government at Peking attempted to patch up its long standing quarrel with the Kuomintang faction in the south. Dr. Sun Yat-sen rejected these overtures. In June, however, a political overturn at Canton resulted in the elimination of Dr. Sun and the installation of a government headed by General Chen Chiung-ming. The new government promptly intimated its willingness to consider proposals for the reunification of the country.[4] The conciliatory attitude of the southern leaders had been influenced in part by changes that had taken place in Peking. In June, President Hsü Shih-ch'ang, the legality of whose election in 1918 had never been conceded by the southern faction, was induced to retire from office. His place was taken by Ex-President Li Yuan-hung. In August the Parliament which had been illegally dissolved in 1917 reassembled in Peking. The veteran Kuomintang statesman, T'ang Shao-yi, was invited to become Premier in a cabinet which would represent all factions in the country except those headed by Chang Tso-lin and Sun Yat-sen. T'ang declined, however, to re-enter active political life. A cabinet was then built around the younger men who had championed China's cause at Washington. Dr. Wang Ch'ung-hui took office as Premier, with Dr. Wellington Koo as his Minister for Foreign Affairs. Whatever political reconstruction was undertaken would at least be in the hands of those who realized its international importance.

The powers meanwhile were engaged in executing some of the pledges requiring concerted action, upon which they had agreed at Washington. The work of revising the Chinese tariff rates so that they would yield an effective five per cent was undertaken by a Commission which held its first session in Shanghai on March 31, 1922.[5] Some time was spent in deciding upon the valuation to be used as the basis for the new rates. The Chinese delegation proposed that the rates should

[4] *North China Herald,* CXLIV, July 8, 1922, p. 82.
[5] Concerning the work of this tariff commission, see Clarence S. K. Chow, "The Revision of the Chinese Treaty Tariff in 1922," *Chinese Social and Political Science Review,* VII, (1923) No. 1, p. 1. Also *China Year Book, 1925,* pp. 462-67.

be based upon the Shanghai market values for the six-month period from October, 1921 to March, 1922, and that in computing these values, goods imported from countries not entitled to representation on the Tariff Revision Commission should be left out of account. The Japanese delegation countered with the proposal that the values prevailing during the four-year period from 1917 to 1920 inclusive should form the basis of the new tariff. The delegates of the other powers, however, expressed their preference for the Chinese proposal, and ultimately the Japanese delegation also agreed to accept it, subject to slight modifications in regard to the system of index numbers which it was proposed to use. The commission then proceeded, through separate committees, to deal with the reclassification and revaluation of goods. This work was finally completed toward the end of the summer.

At the last general meeting of the commission, on September 25, the delegates resolved to recommend to their respective governments that the publication of the revised tariff be authorized as from October 1, 1922, and that the new rates become effective two months thereafter, i.e., on December 1, 1922. All of the governments concerned, except one, signified their approval of the new tariff within the appointed time. The exception was Italy. In November the Italian Legation in Peking notified the Waichiao Pu that Italy would withhold her assent to the revised rates until the Chinese Government had agreed to recognize the claims of the Lloyd Triestino Steamship Company to three former Austrian Lloyd ships which had been seized in Shanghai on China's declaration of war against the Central Empires in 1917 and subsequently condemned by a Chinese prize court.[6] Eventually the Italian Government was persuaded to separate the two questions, which bore no relation to each other, and to allow the revised tariff to come into force on January 17, 1923.[7]

[6] *North China Herald*, CXLV, Nov. 11, 1922, p. 369. *Ibid.*, Dec. 2, 1922, p. 570. *China Year Book*, 1925, p. 467.
[7] *North China Herald*, CXLVI, Jan. 6, 1923, p. 10. *Ibid.*, Jan. 20, 1923, p. 150. At this time rumors began to circulate that a number of the Treaty Power Ministers in Peking were seeking to induce the Chinese

The Washington resolution relative to foreign post offices in China was carried out according to schedule. The twelve offices operated by Great Britain suspended operations November 30, 1922.[8] After signing four postal conventions with China on December 8, the Japanese Government withdrew twenty-four of its post offices on December 10 and forty-two more on December 31.[9] By the end of the year, also, the thirteen French post offices in addition to the single office maintained by the American Government at Shanghai had all ceased doing business.[10]

The evacuation of Japanese troops from Siberia made possible the withdrawal of inter-Allied control of the Chinese Eastern Railway. The last of the Japanese forces sailed from Vladivostok on October 25, 1922. Several days later the American Government notified the Waichiao Pu that its representatives on the inter-Allied Committee at Vladivostok and on the Technical Board at Harbin had been instructed to act with their colleagues in bringing their activities to a close.[11] Following this notification, the Technical Board at Harbin ceased functioning on November 1.[12]

Government to set aside the proceeds of the increased tariff for the service of certain unsecured foreign loans. The Shanghai General Chamber of Commerce, acting with the Bankers' Association and the Money Exchange Union, thereupon sent a telegram to Peking declaring that "it is plain that all the foreign loans have had their own security as mentioned in the contracts, which should be carried out accordingly." *Weekly Review*, XXIII, Jan. 20, 1923, p. 322.

[8] *China Year Book, 1925*, p. 402.

[9] During the negotiations of these postal agreements, a question arose concerning Japanese rights in southern Manchuria. The Washington resolution provided for the withdrawal of all foreign postal establishments in China "except in leased territories or as otherwise specifically provided by treaty." Both governments agreed that this exemption applied to Kwantung and Port Arthur. The Chinese Government objected, however, to the Japanese contention that by the terms of the Treaty of Portsmouth, the same exemption extended to the South Manchuria Railway Zone. Eventually it was agreed that the *status quo* in the railway zone should be maintained pending a final settlement of the matter by further negotiations between the two governments. *North China Herald*, CXLV, Dec. 16, 1922, p. 716. For the texts of the Sino-Japanese agreements of December 8, 1922, see *League of Nations Treaty Series*, Vol. XX, pp. 224, 246, 278, 318.

[10] *China Year Book, 1925*, p. 402.

[11] Note of American Legation, October 31, 1922. *North China Herald*, CXLV, Nov. 4, 1922, p. 293.

[12] *Weekly Review*, XXIII, Jan. 20, 1923, p. 297.

Of the pledges given at Washington by individual powers, the first to be redeemed were those which concerned Japan. On March 28, 1922, representatives of the Chinese and Japanese Governments signed, at Peking, an agreement providing for the withdrawal of Japanese troops stationed along the Shantung Railway.[13] The Japanese wireless station at Tsinan was to be closed simultaneously with the withdrawal of Japan's military forces from the city. The last of these forces departed from Tsingtao on May 5.[14] There remained in Shantung only the Japanese garrison at Kiaochou, and this also was withdrawn in December, 1922, following the conclusion of an agreement covering arrangements for the restoration of the former German leasehold to China.[15] On December 5, similar arrangements were completed for the transfer to China of the Tsingtao-Tsinanfu Railway, in accordance with the treaty which had been signed at Washington on February 4.[16] The Japanese garrison which had been stationed at Hankow since the Revolution of 1911 was ordered home July 2, 1922. By the end of the year, also, the Japanese Government was preparing to dismantle its wireless station at Hankow.[17]

At the Washington Conference, the Chinese delegates had tried unsuccessfully to secure the complete abrogation of the Sino-Japanese treaties and notes of 1915. The Japanese Government consented, as an act of grace, to abandon certain of its rights arising out of these agreements. It declined, however, to modify the treaty provision by which the lease of Port Arthur and Dalny had been extended to ninety-nine years. The term mentioned in the original Sino-Russian agreement of March 27, 1898, had been for twenty-five years. The fact that this original term was due to expire on March 27, 1923, provided the Peking Government with an opportunity to reiterate

---

[13] Text, *Treaties and Agreements, 1919-1929,* pp. 100-101.
[14] Statement issued December 2, 1922, by Japanese Legation in Peking, *North China Herald,* CXLV, Dec. 9, 1922, p. 643.
[15] Sino-Japanese agreement of December 1, 1922, *Treaties and Agreements, 1919-1929,* pp. 114-126.
[16] *Treaties and Agreements, 1919-1929,* pp. 127-9.
[17] Japanese Legation statement, December 2, 1922, *op. cit.*

its views regarding the treaties of 1915. A note from the Waichiao Pu to the Japanese Legation on March 10, 1923, repeated all of the arguments against the validity of these agreements which had been used by the Chinese representatives first at Paris and then at Washington.[18] The agreements, according to the Chinese Government, had been condemned from the beginning by Chinese public opinion and had recently been declared null and void by a resolution of the Chinese Parliament. In view of the fact that the original lease of Port Arthur was now about to expire, China considered that the present was an opportune time to improve existing relations between the two countries by declaring formally that all of the agreements of 1915 should be considered as abrogated. The Japanese Government, therefore, was requested to name a date for the discussion of questions incidental to the retrocession of Port Arthur and Dairen, together with other questions consequent upon the abrogation of the treaties.

The Japanese Government, taking only four days to frame its reply to this note, expressed its "sense of surprise and regret" over the nature of the Chinese communication.[19] Japan considered that the treaties in question had been signed by accredited representatives of the two governments, and that they had been ratified by the respective heads of states. The present attempt of the Chinese Government to cancel these agreements by unilateral action would not only contribute nothing to the advancement of friendly relations between the two countries, but must be regarded as contrary to the accepted principles of international intercourse. The Government of Japan had recently given evidence of its good will by waiving certain rights secured to it by the treaties and notes of 1915. Those treaties and notes, therefore, contained nothing which was "susceptible of further modification." Consequently, the Japanese Govern-

[18] *North China Herald*, CXLVI, Mar. 17, 1923, p. 711. *Weekly Review*, XXIV, Mar. 24, 1923, p. 144. The substance of this note was communicated by the Waichiao Pu to each of the foreign legations in Peking.
[19] *North China Herald*, CXLVI, Mar. 17, 1923, p. 712. *Weekly Review*, XXIV, Mar. 24, 1923, p. 148.

ment saw no occasion for entertaining in any way the proposals of China "respecting the discussion of the questions incidental to the restoration of Port Arthur and Dairen consequent upon the abrogation of the said Treaties."

The Chinese Parliament promptly gave voice to its dissatisfaction at the nature of the Japanese reply.[20] At the same time, various commercial and other public bodies throughout the country expressed their resentment by attempting to revive the boycott against Japanese goods.[21] The government, however, having done all that seemed expedient at the moment, decided after some hesitation not to press the matter further.[22]

Meanwhile negotiations were proceeding for the return to China of the British leased territory at Weihaiwei. In accordance with the terms of Mr. Balfour's letter of February 3, 1922, to Mr. Alfred Sze,[23] an Anglo-Chinese commission was formed in September, 1922, to agree upon detailed arrangements for the retrocession of the territory. The commission met for the first time at Weihaiwei on October 2, 1922.[24] Although the negotiators made considerable progress during the ensuing months, a point was reached in December which made it necessary for the British representative, Mr. Bertram Giles, to ask his government for further instructions. A delay of three months ensued, but in March, 1923, negotiations began once more in Peking, to which city they had been transferred at the request of the Chinese Government.[25] Finally, on May 31, the

[20] North China Herald, CXLVI, Mar. 24, 1923, p. 782. The House of Representatives, by a large majority, urged the government not to abandon its stand.

[21] North China Herald, CXLVI, Mar. 24, 1923, pp. 782-3. Ibid., Mar. 31, 1923, p. 867. At Peking, Tientsin, and Shanghai, in addition to other places, this boycott was actually effective for a brief time.

[22] North China Herald, CXLVII, Apr. 7, 1923, p. 9. If the members of the government actually cherished any resentment over the character of Japan's reply, it was probably alleviated in part by the knowledge that Secretary Hughes and Mr. Hanihara, the Japanese Ambassador at Washington, had agreed, on April 14, to cancel the Lansing-Ishii agreement of 1917. Treaties and Agreements, 1919-1929, p. 130.

[23] British Foreign and State Papers, Vol. CXVI (1922) pp. 435-8.

[24] North China Herald, CXLV, Oct. 21, 1922, pp. 150-51.

[25] Ibid., CXLVI, Jan. 13, 1923, p. 74. Ibid., Mar. 31, 1923, p. 853.

two delegations completed a draft agreement which was referred to their respective governments for final approval.[26] Under the terms of the proposed agreement, the territory was to be kept as a separate administrative area under a Chinese official designated by the central government. For a ten-year period, which was subject to renewal at the option of the British Government, China was to loan to Great Britain, free of charge, certain designated properties on the island of Liukungtao for the use of the British navy as a summer resort. The municipality, which was to be maintained as an area for international trade and residence, was to be governed by the Chinese with the assistance of representatives elected by the foreign rate payers.

The British Minister in Peking was authorized by his Government to sign this agreement. The Peking Government, however, was not satisfied that the terms of the agreement sufficiently protected China's sovereign rights in the territory.[27] Consequently negotiations began once more which, after proceeding in leisurely fashion for six months, finally terminated in a deadlock.[28] In February, 1924, Chinese claims with regard to the leased territory were laid directly before Premier Ramsay MacDonald by Mr. Chu Chao-hsin, Chinese Chargé d'Affaires in London.[29] As a result of this conference, negotiations were again resumed at Peking. The chief bone of contention was that clause in the draft agreement which granted to the British Government the right to renew the free lease of lands and buildings desired in connection with the maintenance of a summer sanitarium for the British fleet at Weihaiwei.[30] On this point neither side was willing to make concessions, and after the political changes brought about by Feng Yu-hsiang's *coup d'état* at Peking in October, 1924, the Brit-

[26] Text, *China Year Book, 1924,* pp. 831-37.
[27] *China Year Book, 1924,* p. 830.
[28] *North China Herald,* CXLIX, Dec. 29, 1923, p. 871.
[29] *Ibid.,* CL, Feb. 23, 1924, p. 273.
[30] Statement before the House of Commons April 16, 1924, by Mr. Arthur Ponsonby, Under Secretary of State for Foreign Affairs. *Parliamentary Debates,* 5th series, Vol. 172, p. 1387.

256 China's Foreign Relations

ish Government decided to suspend negotiations indefinitely.[31]

One of the resolutions of the Washington Conference from which much had been expected was that relating to the operation of consular jurisdiction in China. By the terms of the resolution, which not being in the form of a treaty required no ratification by the Powers concerned, an international commission for the investigation of extraterritoriality was to be constituted within three months from the adjournment of the Conference, that is, before May 6, 1922. Certain preparations had to be made, however, before the commission could begin its work. The American Government, early in April, 1922, suggested to the Chinese Minister at Washington, Dr. Alfred Sze, the desirability of having translations made of all codes of Chinese law and procedure together with necessary statistical information relating to the administration of justice in China.[32] Dr. Sze, accordingly, on April 13, 1922, addressed to Secretary Hughes a note requesting that the first meetings of the commission be delayed until the fall of 1923 in order to enable the Chinese Government to make the necessary translations and compile the statistical information desired.[33] On May 29, 1922, the Department of State informed Dr. Sze that each of the Powers had given its assent to the desired postponement.

The following October, the Peking Government made financial provision for a Judicial Investigation Commission which was to tour the provinces and prepare for the investigation by the international commission of the country's judicial system.[34] By this time, however, the chronic instability of the Peking Government had begun to manifest itself once more. Parlia-

[31] North China Herald, CLII, Nov. 8, 1924, p. 229. See also statement before the House of Commons, August 3, 1925 of Mr. Ronald McNeill, Under Secretary of State for Foreign Affairs. Parliamentary Debates, 5th series, Vol. 187, p. 948.
[32] Statement of Dr. Sze, China Weekly Review, Supplement, June 19, 1926, pp. 65, 67. See also Weekly Review of the Far East, XXI, Aug. 19, 1922, p. 450.
[33] It should be noted that the war between Wu P'ei-fu and Chang Tso-lin, which is sometimes cited as the reason for Dr. Sze's request, did not begin until April 29, 1922.
[34] North China Herald, CXLV, Oct. 28, 1922, p. 210. Weekly Review, XXIII, Dec. 30, 1922, p. 167.

ment was doing its best to justify the opinions of those who regarded its activities as a public scandal and a national disgrace. The political situation was further complicated by the intrigues of certain followers of Marshal Ts'ao K'un who desired his election to the presidency. In November the cabinet, including such able progressives as Wang Ch'ung-hui and Wellington Koo, was forced out of office by the combined machinations of old-style mandarins and self-seeking militarists.[35] A new cabinet, headed by General Chang Shao-tseng, which took office in January, 1923, was able to accomplish little. After a brief survey of the situation, a visiting American congressman, Mr. L. C. Dyer, announced that he had not observed any convincing evidence of the existence of a judicial system which would warrant him in supporting in Washington any movement to abolish extraterritoriality, thereby entrusting the lives and interests of Americans in China to Chinese administration of justice.[36] Disturbed conditions throughout the country led the Chinese General Chamber of Commerce at Shanghai to address a circular letter to various public bodies stressing the fact that the continuance of prevailing disorders tended to give the foreign powers a chance to step in and exercise control.[37] The Ministry of Justice also warned the provinces that the unsettled state of affairs in the country was making it difficult to carry out necessary judicial reforms.[38]

In spite of these discouraging conditions, the Peking Government, in May, 1923, served formal notice on the other Powers that China was ready to have the extraterritorial com-

[35] *North China Herald,* CXLV, Dec. 2, 1922, pp. 569-70. *Weekly Review,* XXIII, Dec. 2, 1922, p. 36. *Ibid.,* Dec. 9, 1922, p. 41.

[36] Interview given out January 30, 1923, in Peking. *Far Eastern Review,* XIX, p. 77, Feb. 1923. Mr. Dyer noted that the country was in a condition of chaos, with civil war south of the Yangtse and armed camps dominating the north; foreign steamers navigating the Yangtse had been fired on by Chinese troops, and foreign business was being hampered by Chinese official and military interference; in many parts of China foreign lives were being endangered by uncontrolled soldiers and bandits; in Peking there was no real evidence of a broad, constructive endeavor to achieve in governmental affairs unity of purpose or to bind China together as a nation.

[37] *Weekly Review,* XXIII, Jan. 20, 1923, p. 289. See also Charles A. Dailey, "Banditry, Bankruptcy, or Boxers?" *Weekly Review,* XXIII, Jan. 20, 1923, pp. 291-4.

[38] *North China Herald,* CXLVI, Mar. 1923, p. 564.

mission meet in Peking on November 1 of that year.[39] Some of the Powers indicated their willingness to act on this suggestion. Other signatories of the Washington agreements, however, insisted that the situation in China did not warrant the Powers in considering the abolition of extraterritoriality. They proposed, therefore, that the work of the commission on extraterritoriality should be postponed indefinitely.[40] Aside from the fact that the Powers represented at the Washington Conference had given an unconditional promise to appoint such a commission, the march of events in China seemed to support the contention that an investigation at that moment could hardly be expected to yield beneficial results. On May 5 the Pukow-Tientsin express had been wrecked by bandits at Lincheng, and for five weeks a considerable number of foreigners were held captive in the mountains of southern Shantung while negotiations proceeded for the incorporation of the bandit group in the Chinese army. Early in June, intrigue on the part of the militarists again forced the resignation of the Peking cabinet, and a week later even the President, Li Yuan-hung, was compelled to retire from office.[41]

The forced resignation of President Li seemed to mark the disappearance of any organized authority in Peking. There was no chief executive, there was only a shadow cabinet whose members were charged with holding office without warrant, and only routine matters could be dealt with by the Ministry of Foreign Affairs, which was left in charge of the Vice-Minister, Mr. Shen Jui-lin.[42] Eventually, on July 23, Dr. Wellington Koo was prevailed upon to assume office as Minister for

[39] Sze statement, *op. cit.*
[40] *North China Herald*, CXLVII, May 26, 1923, pp. 504, 506. *Ibid.*, June 9, 1923, p. 650.
[41] *North China Herald*, CXLVII, June 9, 1923, p. 649. *Ibid.*, June 16, 1923, pp. 722, 724. *Ibid.*, June 23, 1923, pp. 794-6.
[42] *North China Herald* CXLVIII, July 14, 1923, p. 83. Dr. Sun Yat-sen, then in power at Canton, issued a manifesto on June 29 asking the Powers to withdraw international recognition from the Peking Government which, he declared, "is not in fact or in law a government, does not perform the primary functions or fulfil the elementary obligations of a government, and is not recognized by the Chinese people as a government." *North China Herald*, CXLVIII, July 7, 1923, p. 10.

Foreign Affairs.[43] When Marshal Ts'ao K'un, having been elected by Parliament, took office as President on October 10, 1923, a full cabinet began once more to function with some prospect that its authority would be respected in at least that portion of the country under the personal control of the new President. Under these circumstances, the American Government, prompted by the Chinese Minister at Washington, proposed that the international investigation of extraterritoriality in China should begin November 1, 1924. The French Government, however, was not yet ready to redeem the pledge which it had given at Washington, and as a consequence it seemed likely that the promised inquiry into China's judicial system would have to be postponed for an indefinite period.[44]

The refusal of the French Government to coöperate in giving effect to the agreements signed at Washington was due ostensibly to a dispute concerning the manner in which the remaining installments of the Boxer Indemnity should be paid. The indemnity payments to the Allied Powers had been suspended following China's entrance into the World War. In 1922, when these payments again fell due, the French Government proposed that the major portion of its share of the indemnity should be used in satisfying creditors of the Banque Industrielle de Chine, the sudden collapse of which in 1921 had seriously damaged French prestige in the Orient. What re-

[43] In addition to the Lincheng bandit outrage, concerning which the Powers were then preparing to make demands, the Waichiao Pu was compelled at this time to handle several other questions of momentary importance resulting from the extension of the anti-Japanese boycott movement up the Yangtse valley. The boycott movement, resulting from the refusal of the Tokyo Government to negotiate concerning the return of the Liaotung peninsula, led early in June to violent clashes between Chinese pickets and Japanese marines, first at Changsha, and then at Wanhsien. In the former encounter, two Chinese were killed when the marines fired into the mob, and in consequence Japanese residents were compelled to withdraw from the city. *North China Herald,* CXLVII, June 16, 1923, pp. 728-9. *Ibid.,* June 23, 1923, pp. 803, 804. The Japanese Legation in Peking placed the blame on the Chinese authorities for their failure to suppress the "unlawful" boycott movement. *North China Herald,* CXLVIII, July 7, 1923, p. 18.

[44] Statement of Dr. Sze, *op. cit.* In March, 1924, the Chinese Chargé in London, Mr. Chu Chao-hsin, received a notification to this effect from the British Government. *North China Herald,* CL, Mar. 8, 1924, p. 353.

260   China's Foreign Relations

mained thereafter was to be applied to the development of
Franco-Chinese educational and charitable institutions.[45] The
Chinese Government accepted this proposal.[46] Several months
later, however, a controversy arose concerning the actual amount
of money which China was bound to pay for the purposes
agreed upon. The Peking Government desired to make payment in francs in accordance with an agreement of 1905 by
which indemnity installments were to be paid in the currencies
of the creditor nations, thereby guaranteeing those creditors
against loss in exchange. Now that the franc had greatly depre-
ciated, due to economic conditions resulting from the World
War, the French Government insisted that China pay in "gold"
francs at the pre-war rate of exchange.[47] When the Peking
Government, due to parliamentary opposition, declined to meet
French wishes, the French Minister promptly enlisted the support of the diplomatic representatives of the other remaining
protocol signatories. Thereafter, on February 24, 1923, the
eight Ministers addressed to the Waichiao Pu a joint note de-

[45] De Fleuriau, French Minister at Peking, to W. W. Yen, Chinese
Minister for Foreign Affairs, July 9, 1922. *Treaties and Agreements, 1919-
1929*, pp. 103-4. French text in *China Year Book, 1924*, p. 837.
[46] Yen to de Fleuriau, July 27, 1922, *Treaties and Agreements, 1919-
1929*, p. 104. French text, *China Year Book, 1924*, p. 840.
[47] The Protocol of 1901 required China to pay an indemnity totaling
450,000,000 Haikwan taels, which was to "constitute a gold debt." The
value of the Haikwan tael in terms of "the gold currency" of each country
was specified, that for France being one tael as equal to 3.75 francs. The
Protocol provided, further, that the total amount of the indemnity "in gold"
should bear interest at four per cent per annum, and that principal and
interest should "be payable in gold or at the rates of exchange corresponding
to the dates at which the different payments fall due." (Final Protocol,
September 7, 1901, Article VI, MacMurray, *op. cit.*, Vol. I, pp. 280-81.)
By a supplementary arrangement agreed upon in 1905, the Chinese Government recognized that the total amount of the indemnity constituted "a debt
in gold, that is to say, for each Haikwan Tael due to each of the Powers,
China must pay in gold the amount which is shown in Article VI of the
Final Protocol as the equivalent of one Tael." In making payments on this
basis, it was agreed that China should fix "the value of the Haikwan Protocol Tael in relation to the money of each country either in silver, according
to the price of silver on the London market, or in gold bills, or in telegraphic
transfers, at the choice of each Power. (The Diplomatic Representatives of
the Protocol Powers to Prince Ch'ing, July 2, 1905. MacMurray, *op. cit.*
Vol. I, p. 319.) The French Government was one of those which elected
to receive its installments of the indemnity by telegraphic transfer.

claring that their Governments were unanimously of the opinion
that "the Protocol of 1901, as well as the arrangement of
July 2, 1905, provides in a manner absolutely clear and indis-
putable that the indemnity of 1900 must be paid in gold, i.e.,
for each Haikwan tael due to each of the Powers, China must
pay the sum in gold which is shown in Article VI as the equivalent of one tael." [48] Several months later, the government at
Paris informed the Chinese Minister, Mr. Ch'en Lu, that until
China consented to pay the French share of the Boxer Indemnity in gold francs, France would decline to ratify the Washington treaty providing for increases in the Chinese tariff rates.[49]

After assuming office as Minister for Foreign Affairs in the
summer of 1923, Dr. Wellington Koo drew up a lengthy reply
to the joint note of the Protocol Ministers.[50] It was his contention that the phrase "in gold," used in the agreements of
1901 and 1905, referred only to the respective gold currencies
of the signatory powers in contrast with the silver Haikwan
tael in terms of which the indemnity of 1901 was expressed.
By "gold" was meant not "gold metal" but simply "gold currency." In support of his argument, Dr. Koo called attention
to the fact that while the Protocol declared the indemnity to be
"a gold debt," it fixed the equivalent of the Haikwan tael in
gold "not as a certain quantity of the gold metal, but in the
currencies of the Signatory Powers issued on the basis of their
respective gold standards." Since Belgium, France, and Italy,
had each asked in 1905 that their shares of the indemnity be
paid by telegraphic transfer in their respective currencies, China
was now entitled to make such payments on the basis of current
rates of exchange.

The eight Ministers, in a second collective note of February
11, 1924,[51] flatly rejected the Chinese contention that the word

[48] Signed by the representatives of the Netherlands, Belgium, the
United States, France, Great Britain, Italy, Spain, and Japan. *China Year
Book, 1924*, pp. 841-5.
[49] *North China Herald*, CXLVII, May 12, 1923, p. 362.
[50] Note of December 27, 1923, *China Year Book, 1924*, pp. 842-5.
[51] *China Year Book, 1924*, pp. 845-9.

"gold" in the agreements of 1901 and 1905 did not refer to gold metal but only to the gold currencies, whether theoretical or actual, of the Protocol Powers. They insisted once more that the debt was an actual gold debt and that for each Haikwan tael owed to Belgium or Spain or France or Italy, China was bound to pay 3.75 francs in gold, or 3.75 times 0.290322 grammes of fine gold. Dr. Koo was reminded that the arrangements for telegraphic transfer made in 1905 referred "solely to the manner of execution of the obligations subscribed to by the Chinese Government in 1901." The character and total amount of the debt owed by virtue of an obligation could not be presumed to depend "upon the means adopted for the settlement of this debt." In conclusion the eight Ministers stated that they required "only the complete and unmodified execution of the conventions drawn up in 1901 between China and the Signatory Powers with regard to the indemnity of 1901." This complete execution was necessary "in order to cause to be respected the right of each one of the interested Powers to receive the proportion of a total indemnity determined among themselves, whose service and guarantees have been placed under their common control."

In addition to withholding ratification of the Washington treaty relating to the Chinese tariff and refusing to participate in the work of the extraterritoriality commission, the French Government adopted other means of forcing a favorable settlement of the gold franc dispute. On one occasion the French Minister prevented the Banque de l'Indo Chine from releasing to the Peking Government certain surplus funds belonging to the sale gabelle.[52] A deaf ear was turned to China's request for the opening of negotiations concerning the retrocession of the French leased territory at Kwangchow Wan.[53] In March, 1924, the Peking Government addressed to the Powers a note which, after expressing the hope that the technical difficulty resulting

[52] *North China Herald,* CXLIX, Nov. 3, 1923, p. 298.
[53] *Ibid.,* CXLV, Oct. 7, 1922, p. 17. *Ibid.,* Oct. 28, 1922, p. 208. *Ibid.,* Dec. 30, 1922, p. 843.

from the non-ratification of the Washington treaties would soon be removed, suggested that time would be saved if a preparatory conference were held to do the committee work of the formal tariff conference which would follow.[54] Again France declined to coöperate until the gold franc dispute had been settled.[55]

In October, 1924, the Peking Government was overturned by a *coup d'état* executed by Marshal Feng Yu-hsiang. Having secured military control of the capital, Marshal Feng placed President Ts'ao K'un in confinement pending trial for bribery, ordered the arrest of various members of parliament who had participated in the corrupt presidential election of 1923, and drove the youthful Manchu Emperor from his place of retirement in the Forbidden City. Thereafter a provisional government came into existence at the head of which was the ex-Premier, Tuan Ch'i-jui, who now assumed the title of Chief Executive.[56] On December 9 the Ministers in Peking representing the Protocol Powers consented to accord the new government *de facto* recognition with the understanding that it would "respect and duly fulfil all Treaties, Conventions, and other engagements entered into by the former Manchu and Republican Governments, and all rights, privileges and immu-

[54] *New York Times*, Mar. 18, 1924, p. 8.
[55] *China Review*, VI, p. 128, April, 1924. *North China Herald*, CLI, June 14, 1924, p. 402. The virtual bankruptcy of the Peking Government was clearly revealed in a report submitted about this time by Dr. W. W. Yen as chairman of the Commission for the Readjustment of Finance. The government was incurring an estimated deficit of $121,000,000 per year. One of Dr. Yen's recommendations was that immediate steps be taken to expedite the holding of the Special Customs Tariff Conference and to secure permission to levy the surtaxes provided for in the Washington Treaty. It was estimated that these surtaxes would produce additional revenue to the amount of $25,000,000 annually. *North China Herald*, April 26, 1924, p. 122. *China Year Book, 1924*, p. 736. In May Dr. Yen stated in the course of a press interview that if China's creditors and friends expected her to fulfil obligations which the central government was called upon to discharge, they must see to it that no unnecessary embarrassment was imposed on the government. The holding of the Special Customs Conference and the granting of the Washington surtaxes would be merely the fulfilment of a promise which in fairness and justice should have been carried out long before. *North China Herald*, CLI, May 17, 1924, p. 201.
[56] See *China Year Book, 1925*, pp. 840-48.

nities enjoyed by foreigners in China by virtue of such international engagements, which according to international usage,
can only be modified by the mutual consent of the contracting
parties." The Protocol Ministers intimated, further, that their
governments were willing and anxious to proceed as soon as
practicable with the carrying out of the measures contemplated
by the Washington treaties and resolutions.[57] In reply to this
note, the Waichiao Pu, referring to the Washington treaties and
resolutions, stated that [58]

"These measures, which were purposely restricted to those which
were immediately practicable, were unconditionally agreed upon
to be forthwith carried out. The Chinese Government regrets the
delay which has unexpectedly occurred and hopes that, with the
assurance of friendly assistance now given by the Governments concerned, these measures can soon be put into execution, in accordance
with the intentions and agreements of the Washington Conference. It
wishes to add, furthermore, that in view of the desire of the Chinese
Government to consolidate the friendship between China and the
friendly Powers on a permanent and sound basis, it hopes that the
Powers concerned will also at an early date give sympathetic consideration to the other well known aspirations of the Chinese people, submitted in recent years to different international conferences
by the Chinese Government, so that their relations may be further
improved to their mutual benefit."

Despite the fact that the French Minister had signed the
joint note of December 9, the government at Paris continued
to insist on a satisfactory settlement of the gold franc dispute
as a condition precedent to its ratification of the Washington
treaties. But in February, 1925, negotiations began at Peking
which promised to yield results.[59] The Chinese Minister for

[57] *Chinese Social and Political Science Review*, IX, No. 1, (Jan. 1925),
p. 174. In Peking this note was regarded as an effort on the part of the
Powers to halt the advance of Bolshevism in China, and to prevent the
government from succumbing to Soviet propaganda by repudiating its
treaties and other international obligations. *North China Herald*, CLIII,
Dec. 13, 1924, p. 435.
[58] Note of December 23, 1924, *Chinese Social and Political Science
Review*, IX, No. 1 (Jan. 1925), pp. 175-6.
[59] *North China Herald*, CLIV, Feb. 28, 1925, p. 334. On February 23,
the Kuomintang issued a manifesto protesting against any acceptance of

Foreign Affairs reminded the French Minister that there was no apparent connection between the gold franc issue and the ratification of the Washington tariff treaty.[60] In a note dated April 9, the French Minister then notified the Waichiao Pu that his government was prepared to ratify the Washington treaty as speedily as this could be accomplished.[61] Three days later the gold franc dispute was finally settled by an exchange of notes between the French representative and the Chinese Minister for Foreign Affairs.[62] China met the demand of France as regards gold payments, which were to be made, however, in gold dollars rather than francs. In return for this concession, France agreed that the indemnity payments should be resumed as from December 1, 1924, instead of December 1, 1922.[63] The Banque Industrielle de Chine was to be rehabilitated with the indemnity funds, any surplus being reserved for mutually beneficial educational and philanthropic purposes.[64]

French contentions with regard to the indemnity payments, and denying that the Peking Government had power to negotiate a settlement in any case. The attitude of the Kuomintang had widespread popular support. *North China Herald*, CLIII, Dec. 27, 1924, p. 526.

[60] Note of April 8, 1925, *Chinese Social and Political Science Review*, IX, No. 4, Oct. 1925, p. 838.

[61] *Ibid.*, pp. 839-40.

[62] Texts, *China Year Book, 1925*, pp. 1297-1300. *Chinese Social and Political Science Review*, IX, No. 3, July, 1925, pp. 557-562.

[63] The indemnity funds which had been accumulated during this two-year period, amounting to approximately $12,000,000, were immediately released to the Chinese Government. *North China Herald*, CLV, April 4, 1925, p. 2.

[64] Following the precedent established in the case of France, the Chinese Government agreed also to pay in American gold dollars the remaining installments of the Indemnity due to Belgium and Italy. A certain portion of both the Belgian and the Italian shares, however, was to be devoted to educational and philanthropic work for the benefit of China. For the agreement of October 1, 1925, with Italy, see *Treaties and Agreements, 1919-1929*, pp. 160-64. The substance of the Belgian agreement is given in *China Year Book, 1928*, p. 634.

The British Government, in December, 1922, notified China that it had decided to devote its remaining shares of the Boxer Indemnity to purposes mutually beneficial to both countries. This decision was ratified by Parliament on June 30, 1925. *Treaties and Agreements, 1919-1929*, p. 155. Subsequently a Statutory Committee was set up, on which there were three Chinese members, for the purpose of recommending the uses to which these funds should be put. For a résumé of the Committee's report, see *China Year Book, 1928*, pp. 631-4.

The Japanese Government, in March, 1923, decided to use a small por-

Following the settlement of the gold franc dispute, the French Government, in July, proceeded to ratify the Nine-Power Treaty relating to Principles and Policies concerning China, and the Nine-Power Treaty relating to the Chinese Customs Tariff. The treaties thus came finally into force on August 5, 1925.[65] The Powers were now ready to give effect to the pledges regarding China upon which they had agreed at Washington three and one-half years before.

Meanwhile the attitude of the Chinese toward the modest program adopted at Washington had undergone a radical change in consequence of a series of incidents which revealed, as if in a sudden flash of lightning, not only the privileged position enjoyed by foreigners in the country, but the keen resentment of the Chinese people against that privileged position. On May 30, 1925, student agitators entered the International Settlement at Shanghai to protest publicly against the treatment which had been meted out to Chinese laborers employed in Japanese mills. A mob which speedily collected about the student demonstrators soon got out of hand. A small detachment of Sikh and Chinese constables defending the Louza Police Station were finally ordered by the Inspector in charge—who was of British nationality—to open fire on the crowd. The result was that four Chinese were instantly killed and five more mortally wounded.[66] Chinese resentment against what was

tion of its share of the indemnity for education, scientific, philanthropic, and cultural purposes beneficial to both countries. *China Year Book, 1928,* p. 635.

On June 14, 1924, the American Secretary of State, Mr. Hughes, notified the Chinese Minister in Washington that, in accordance with an act of Congress, dated May 21, 1924, further installments of the American share of the indemnity would be remitted for use in connection with educational and other cultural activities in China. *Treaties and Agreements, 1919-1929,* pp. 132, 147, 156.

The Government of the Netherlands announced its intention of using its remaining shares of the Indemnity to conduct a scientific survey of the Yellow River—long known as "China's Sorrow"—and to draw up a scheme for the permanent improvement of that river. *China Year Book, 1928,* pp. 634-5.

[65] *China Year Book,* 1926, p. 1107.

[66] See the Shanghai Municipal Police reports for May and June, 1925, *North China Herald,* CLVI, Aug. 1, 1925, p. 95 and August 8, 1925, pp. 133-5. Details of the 1925 disorders are given also in *China Year Book, 1926,* pp. 919 ff.

regarded as an inexcusable massacre of unarmed students manifested itself immediately in the form of a general strike and
boycott of foreign goods in which students, laborers, and merchants joined forces. Economic paralysis descended on Shanghai
which lasted throughout the better part of the summer.

News concerning what had happened at Shanghai spread
over the country like wildfire. Anti-foreign riots broke out at
Chinkiang, Hankow, Kiukiang, and even as far west as Chungking, at the head of the Yangtse gorges. In some of these riots
lives were lost and much property destroyed. It was at Canton,
however, that the most serious encounter between Chinese and
foreigners took place. There, on the afternoon of June 23,
thousands of students, workmen, citizens, and soldiers paraded
on the Shakee bund opposite the island of Shameen, on which
were located the French and British Concessions. A Frenchman
was killed by a shot fired into the concessions from the direction of the bund. Thereupon firing became general on both
sides, the French marines using machine guns. Several foreign
casualties resulted, but the killed and wounded among the Chinese numbered approximately one hundred and twenty.[67] As a
result, within a few days Hongkong was in the grip of a general strike, and at Canton a boycott of British goods began
which lasted into the next year.

The immediate consequence of these sanguinary encounters
was that all China flamed with bitter resentment against the
treaty-privileged foreigners. British, French, American, and
Japanese merchants declared with practically one voice that
force had been used only in defense of their lives and legitimate
interests. To the Chinese, however, what was vastly more significant was the fact that foreigners had shot down Chinese
citizens on Chinese soil. No longer content with the program
which the Powers had adopted at Washington, patriotic Chinese
everywhere now demanded a general revision of the unequal
treaties.[68] The more radical elements insisted on the immediate
return of all foreign concessions, the withdrawal of foreign

[67] *China Year Book, 1926*, pp. 965 ff.
[68] See *North China Herald*, CLVI, July 18, 1925, pp. 17, 32.

troops from the country, and the summary abrogation of extraterritorial rights. Even the conservatives raised voices in support
of tariff autonomy.[69]

By its immediate and emphatic protest to the Powers regarding the incident of May 30 at Shanghai, the Peking Government had earned for itself an unaccustomed popularity throughout practically the entire country.[70] Following up this advantage, the Foreign Office, on June 24, addressed to the Washing-

[69] In this connection, an illuminating statement was issued in August by
the Diplomatic Commission, an advisory body to the Peking Government,
which included in its membership such responsible Chinese leaders as Dr.
C. T. Wang and Admiral Ts'ai T'ingkan. The statement ran in part as follows: "Both at the Versailles Peace Conference and at the Washington
Conference, China asked for revision of these (unequal) treaties. She did
not get anything at the former, and what was promised her at the latter conference in the matter of tariff revision and abolition of extraterritoriality
[sic] has not been fulfilled in the last three years.

"The knowledge of international affairs is growing among the people,
and they cannot long tolerate the existence of the numerous foreign concessions within China, which like the colonies of the great Powers, are administered entirely by the foreigners. The extraterritorial privilege enjoyed
by the foreigners, and the freedom of fixing the tariff rates denied to the
Chinese are the two greatest grievances of the nation. . . .

"The first article of the Nine-Power Treaty concluded at the Washington Conference engages the signatory powers to respect the sovereignty, independence, and administrative integrity of China. The second section of the
same article engages the signatory powers to provide the fullest and most
unembarrassed opportunity to China to develop and maintain for herself an
effective and stable government. It is easy to see that the existence of the
unequal treaties is diametrically opposed to the spirit of this very first
article of the Washington agreement. No power can pretend to respect
the administrative and territorial sovereignty of China if she insists upon
the maintenance of her concessions, settlements, consular jurisdiction, and
the fixed rate of tariff. . . ." *China Weekly Review*, XXXIII, Aug. 8,
1925, p. 183.

More radical in tone was the statement of Hsu Ch'ien, prominent in
Kuomintang circles and former Minister of Justice in the Canton Government. Arguing against Chinese participation in the tariff conference which
had been promised at Washington, Dr. Hsu declared "if we want the
revision of the customs tariff at all, we must first demand the fundamental
revision of the unequal treaties, and in case this is accomplished, the
restoration of our tariff autonomy is a necessary incident. . . . The present
and future increase which China may probably get at the (tariff) conference can only serve the purpose of securing foreign obligations. Is this not
similar to 'taking a cup of poison in order to quench one's thirst?'" *China
Weekly Review*, XXXIII, Aug. 8, 1925, p. 183.

[70] For the Chinese note of June 3 protesting against the shooting at
Shanghai and subsequent correspondence, see *China Year Book, 1926*, pp.
930 ff.

ton Treaty Powers a note concerning the general revision of treaties.[71] The note referred to the growing feeling, shared by Chinese and foreigners alike, that "there should be a readjustment of China's treaty relations with foreign Powers to bring them more in line with the generally accepted conceptions of international justice and equity and more in conformity with existing conditions in China." The treaties in question had been imposed without regard for the principles which should permanently regulate the normal intercourse between friendly states and they had long since outlived whatever usefulness was originally claimed for them. The Chinese Government was convinced that so long as the inequalities and extraordinary privileges provided for by the treaties continued to exist, "there would always remain causes of disaffection which are apt to produce friction and disturb the cordial relations and good understanding between China and the foreign Powers. . . ." The Powers were reminded of the promise which they had made, following China's entrance into the World War, to assist her in effecting an improvement in her international status. Neither at Versailles nor at Washington had actual steps been taken to carry out this promise. Indeed, China's international status was even inferior to that of nations which had been defeated in the World War, for in none of these were to be found "extraterritorial courts, foreign concessions, leased territories, and an externally imposed conventional tariff." In conclusion the hope was expressed that the foreign powers would consent to a readjustment of China's treaty relations "on an equitable basis in satisfaction of the legitimate national aspirations of the Chinese people. . . ."

The Chinese note seemed to imply that the program adopted at Washington should be scrapped, and that the Powers should now consider the question of a fundamental modification of their formal relations with China. The reply of the Powers, transmitted to the Chinese Government on September 4, 1925, indicated in effect that they were not yet ready to abandon the

[71] Text, *Treaties and Agreements. 1919-1929*, pp. 153-4.

Washington program.[72] Two of the important questions raised by the Chinese Government's note were those relating to the conventional tariff and extraterritorial rights. In the opinion of the Powers, the most feasible method of dealing with these questions was by a "constant and scrupulous observance of the obligations undertaken" at the Washington Conference. To that end, the Powers were now prepared to appoint representatives to the tariff conference and also to the commission on extraterritoriality. Any fundamental revision of existing treaties must be delayed until the Chinese authorities had demonstrated "their willingness and ability to fulfil their obligations and to assume the protection of foreign rights and interests now safeguarded by the exceptional provisions of those treaties." However, either at the tariff conference, or at a subsequent time, the Powers would be ready to consider and discuss "any reasonable proposal" that might be made by the Chinese Government for a revision of the treaties on the subject of the tariff.[73]

Meanwhile the Chinese Government, having been informed officially by the American Minister that ratifications of the 1922

[72] Text of the American note, *Treaties and Agreements, 1919-1929*, pp. 157-60.

[73] On September 11, 1925, the Chinese delegate to the League of Nations, Mr. Chu Chao-hsin, addressed the Assembly on the subject of treaty revision. He reminded his hearers that under Article XIX of the Covenant, China was entitled to ask for a modification of treaties which had become obsolete. Three days later the Chinese delegate asked the Assembly to adopt the following resolution:

"The Assembly

"Having heard with keen interest the Chinese delegation's suggestion regarding the applicability of Article XIX of the Covenant to the existing situation in China,

"Having learned with satisfaction that a Conference of the Interested States is soon to take place in China to consider the questions involved,

"Expresses the hope that a satisfactory solution may be found at an early date." League of Nations *Official Journal*, Special Supplement, No. 33, pp. 43-5, 79.

The Polish delegate, however, informed Mr. Chu privately that he would be compelled to oppose specific mention of Article XIX since Germany might thereby be encouraged, by invoking the provisions of the same article, to ask for a revision of the Treaty of Versailles. *Far Eastern Review*, XXII, p. 202, May, 1926. As a consequence, the resolution, as adopted by the Assembly on September 22, referred merely to "the spirit of the Covenant," specific mention of Article XIX being omitted. League of Nations *Official Journal, op. cit.*, p. 102.

treaties had finally been deposited at Washington, issued to
the Powers an invitation to participate in a special tariff conference which was to meet in Peking on October 26, 1925.[74]
The invitation included the announcement that since the Chinese delegates to the Washington Conference had expressly
reserved the right to raise the question of tariff autonomy on
all appropriate occasions in the future, the Chinese Government
would not only ask for consideration of that question at the
forthcoming conference, but would expect that some arrangement be made "to remove the tariff restrictions hitherto imposed upon China."

The Governments of the Powers concerned promptly appointed their delegates, and the Tariff Conference began its
sessions on October 26. After a formal address of welcome
by the provisional Chief Executive, Marshal Tuan Ch'i-jui,[75]
the presiding officer, Mr. Shen Jui-lin, called upon Dr. C. T.
Wang to announce the Chinese program for the settlement of
the tariff question. With only a few preliminary remarks, Dr.
Wang then, on behalf of his government, laid before the conference the following proposals: [76]

"1. The participating Powers formally declare to the Government
of the Republic of China their respect for its tariff autonomy and
agree to the removal of all the tariff restrictions contained in existing treaties.
"2. The Government of the Republic of China agrees to the
abolition of *likin* simultaneously with the enforcement of the Chinese National Tariff Law, which shall take effect not later than the

[74] *China Year Book, 1926*, p. 1108. In addition to the eight powers,
not including China, whose representatives had attended the Washington
Conference, a similar invitation was extended to Denmark, Sweden, Norway, and Spain, each of which had signified its adherence to the Nine-
Power tariff treaty.
[75] Instead of dealing exclusively in polite generalities, Marshal Tuan
expressed frankly the aspirations of China with regard to the conference.
Referring to the Nine-Power Treaty by which the Powers had agreed to
respect the sovereignty, independence, and territorial and administrative
integrity of China, he said "Our people attach great importance to this
declaration, and I see an opportunity here for its realization. We wish,
therefore, to avail ourselves of this occasion to renew our claim for tariff
autonomy." *China Year Book, 1926*, pp. 1112-13.
[76] *Ibid.*, pp. 1114-15.

1st day of January in the 18th year of the Republic of China (1929).

"3. Previous to the enforcement of the Chinese National Tariff Law, an interim surtax of 5 per cent on ordinary goods, 30 per cent on A grade luxuries (namely, wine and tobacco) and 20 per cent on B grade luxuries shall be levied in addition to the present customs tariff of 5 per cent *ad valorem.*

"4. The collection of the above-mentioned interim surtaxes shall begin three months from the date of signature of the agreement.

"5. The decisions relative to the above four articles shall be carried into effect from the date of signature of the agreement." [77]

The Chinese proposals were received by the foreign delegates with sympathy coupled with a degree of apprehension. Dr. Wang had dealt with tariff autonomy and *likin* abolition as related but essentially separate matters. At subsequent meetings of the commission, it became evident that some of the foreign delegations, particularly those representing Japan, the United States, and Italy, were determined to insist upon the effective abolition of the *likin* system as a condition precedent to the grant of full tariff autonomy.[78] The Chinese delegation strenuously resisted all proposals to bracket the two. China was prepared to take independent action with regard to *likin* reform, and was willing to promise that this reform would be completely carried out prior to the enforcement of a national statutory tariff.[79] On the other hand, the powers must agree

[77] A warning of what the foreign delegates might expect was contained in a statement issued by Dr. Wang about two weeks before the opening of the conference. "The first item on the agenda of the forthcoming tariff conference," he said, "is Chinese tariff autonomy. . . . Under every phase of international law, China is entitled to control her own customs revenue, organization, and disposition of the net proceeds of the customs. Customs control is an essential part of her sovereignty, and the Powers have pledged themselves at Washington to respect that sovereignty. Continued foreign control is a violation of that pledge. If the Powers will not in an amicable manner consent to Chinese control of the customs, then we will be obliged to decline to recognize their control and take it over ourselves, despite their objections. This would not mean that China would refuse to recognize obligations for which certain proceeds of the customs revenue are pledged. . . . China will pay every cent she owes, but she will do so herself, not under what so looks like foreign compulsion." *China Weekly Review,* XXXIV, Oct. 17, 1925, p. 180.
[78] *China Year Book, 1926,* pp. 1119, 1125-6, 1127-8, 1135-6.
[79] For the specific proposals in this regard made by the Chinese delegation, see *Ibid.,* pp. 1122-25.

to recognize unconditionally China's right to tariff autonomy at the end of three years. When it became apparent that the Chinese delegation was prepared to break off negotiations rather than make concessions in this regard,[80] the conference finally, on November 19, agreed to adopt the following resolution which was subsequently to be incorporated in a treaty:[81]

"The Contracting Powers other than China hereby recognize China's right to enjoy tariff autonomy; agree to remove the tariff restrictions which are contained in existing treaties between themselves respectively and China; and consent to the going into effect of the Chinese National Tariff Law on January 1st, 1929.

"The Government of the Republic of China declares that *likin* shall be abolished simultaneously with the enforcement of the Chinese National Tariff Law; and further declares that abolition of *likin* shall be effectively carried out by the First Day of the First Month of the Eighteenth Year of the Republic of China (January 1st, 1929)."

Having agreed upon the grant of tariff autonomy at the end of a three-year period, the conference next considered the interim measures which should be authorized during that period. In its original proposals, the Chinese delegation had suggested the immediate imposition of an interim surtax of 5 per cent on ordinary goods, and a special surtax of 20 per cent on all luxuries with the exception of tobacco and intoxicants which were to pay a surtax of 30 per cent in addition to the conventional rates then in force. At the first session of the conference, Dr. Eki Hioki, for the Japanese delegation, had countered with the proposal that as an intermediate step leading to ultimate tariff autonomy, "a statutory tariff on a fair and reasonable basis be established for general application, subject to the provisions of a special conventional tariff on certain specified articles to be agreed upon separately between

<hr/>

[80] *North China Herald*, CLVII, Nov. 7, 1925, p. 234. *Ibid.*, Nov. 21, 1925, p. 326.
[81] *China Year Book, 1926*, p. 1136. The resolution had been framed by a sub-committee consisting of Dr. Wang, Mr. W. J. Oudendijk (the Netherlands), Mr. Silas Strawn (the United States), Sir Ronald Macleay (Great Britain), and Dr. Eki Hioki (Japan).

China and each of the Powers directly interested." In case this plan did not meet with general approval, Dr. Hioki proposed as an alternative that "a graduated tariff, so devised as to be acceptable to the Powers concerned, be established at an average rate of not more than 12½ per cent *ad valorem,* and generally in a manner consistent with the provisions of Article 2 of the Washington Treaty." [82] The American counter proposals were submitted by Mr. J. V. A. MacMurray to a subsequent session of the conference. Mr. MacMurray proposed that without waiting for the conclusion of a new tariff treaty, the Powers authorize the collection of the surtaxes upon which they had agreed at Washington, the 2½ per cent levy on ordinary goods to take effect February 1, 1926, and the 5 per cent levy on luxuries to be effective not later than July 1 following. [83] The American delegation proposed, further, that the conference draft a treaty which, after conceding China's right to tariff autonomy, would authorize the Chinese Government, during the interim period, to impose "a new and uniformly enforced schedule of duties at rates from 5 per cent (the present rate) to 12½ per cent on imports, and from 5 per cent (the present rate) to 7½ per cent on exports." [84]

Neither China or Japan looked with favor upon the American proposals. The Chinese delegation made it clear that if China were to refund her unsecured debts, compensate the provinces for the abolition of *likin* revenues, and meet the ordinary expenses of civil administration, she must be assured of far greater revenues from customs duties than any which the powers had thus far proposed to grant. [85] Japan was willing to authorize the immediate collection of the Washington surtaxes, as proposed by Mr. MacMurray. Further than that, however, the Japanese delegation desired either a special tariff convention between China and Japan providing special treatment for

[82] *China Year Book,* 1926, p. 1119.   [83] *Ibid.,* p. 1125.   [84] *Ibid.*
[85] Memorandum laid before the Committee on Tariff Autonomy on November 6 by Dr. W. W. Yen and Admiral Ts'ai T'ing-kan, *Ibid.,* pp. 1130-33.

Japanese imports, or a graduated tariff so adjusted as not to injure Japanese trade. Dr. Hioki objected particularly to the American plan for a uniform tariff at rates specified conditionally in the MacKay treaty of 1902 with Great Britain. A uniform tariff at the rate provided for in that treaty would be not only "unreasonable and unscientific," but would work to the detriment of trade between China and foreign countries. Japan also questioned the wisdom of increasing the duty on exports, as proposed by the American delegation.[86]

While negotiations regarding these matters proceeded, the Chinese delegation, on its own initiative, made two declarations of some importance. The first of these was to the effect that if China were to reform her fiscal system on lasting foundations, foreigners resident in the country, who had claimed general immunity from Chinese taxation on one pretext or another, must be compelled to "discharge, equally with the Chinese, their fiscal obligations towards the Chinese Government, in conformity with the provisions of the fiscal laws promulgated by China."[87] The other declaration announced the intention of the Chinese Government to relinquish, within three months after the close of the Conference, "the right to levy the existing Export Duty on native goods not destined for exportation to foreign countries and Coast Trade Duty, provided in the treaties, as an initial step towards the ultimate abolition of *likin*." Thereafter no export duty would be levied on native goods shipped from one Chinese port to another.[88]

In December, the sessions of the conference were momentarily suspended. The foreign delegates desired an opportunity to consult among themselves and with their governments. More than this, however, the suspension was due to the increasing violence of civil wars which had begun in October even before the delegates first met. When the conference opened, the

[86] Statement of Dr. Hioki, October 30, 1925, *China Year Book, 1926,* pp. 1126-7.
[87] *Ibid.,* pp. 1139-40.
[88] *China Year Book, 1926,* p. 1140.

Peking Government was largely controlled by the Fengtien party of Chang Tso-lin, with Feng Yu-hsiang and his Kuominchun playing the rôle of silent partner. As soon as it became evident that the revenues of the central government were likely to be increased, the war lords engaged in a scramble for a share of the proceeds. Wu P'ei-fu and Sun Ch'uan-fang both protested against negotiations between the Powers and the "illegal" government at Peking.[89] Sun Ch'uan-fang promptly expelled the Fengtien forces from Kiangsu and established his control over the five provinces of Fukien, Chekiang, Kiangsu, Kiangsi, and Anhwei. Wu P'ei-fu coöperated by launching an attack northward from his base in Honan. In November, Chang Tso-lin was faced with new dangers nearer home when one of his ablest lieutenants, General Kuo Sung-lin, took up arms against him. Finally, in December, Marshal Feng Yu-hsiang's Kuominchun joined the anti-Fengtien coalition. Despite diplomatic protests against the violation of the Boxer Protocol, communications between Peking and the sea were cut by the fighting armies. Not even the international military train to Tientsin was allowed to run, and for a period of ten days no mail reached the capital from the outside world.[90]

Completely defeated on all fronts, Marshal Chang again took refuge in his stronghold at Mukden. An immediate result of his defeat was reorganization of the government in Peking. Marshal Tuan remained as Chief Executive, but his powers were henceforth to be exercised by a cabinet in which Hsu Shih-ying was Premier and Dr. C. T. Wang, Minister for Foreign Affairs.[91] Within less than three weeks, inability to solve the acute financial problems which faced the government forced

[89] *North China Herald*, CLVII, Oct. 17, 1925, p. 95. *Ibid.*, Oct. 24, 1925, p. 140. *Ibid.*, Oct. 31, 1925, p. 181. T'ang Shao-yi and the Kuomintang leaders at Canton protested against holding any conference at all on the ground that China was entitled to assert her fiscal independence without consulting the Powers. *Ibid.*, CLVII, Oct. 10, 1925, p. 58. *Ibid.*, Nov. 14, 1925, p. 278.

[90] *North China Herald*, CLVII, Dec. 19, 1925, p. 506. *Ibid.*, Dec. 26, 1925, p. 550. *Ibid.*, CLVIII, Jan. 2, 1926, p. 8. *China Year Book 1926*, pp. 1025-29.

[91] *North China Herald*, CLVIII, Jan. 2, 1926, p. 4.

the resignation of the new Minister of Finance, Dr. Ch'en Chin-t'ao.[92]

At the very outbreak of civil war, three of the leading members of the Chinese delegation to the tariff conference had fled to the foreign concessions at Tientsin or to Mukden.[93] Following the Kuominchun capture of Tientsin, political uncertainty at Peking made it impossible to resume formal sessions of the conference. Nevertheless, an informal committee began meeting in January at the Dutch Legation. The British, American, French, Japanese, Italian, Dutch, and the Belgian delegates attended in addition to Dr. Yen, who represented the Chinese Government. Dr. Yen insisted that at least $100,000,000 must be realized from customs surtaxes in order to meet the financial requirements of the government. Of this amount 30 per cent would be devoted to the abolition of *likin* and another 30 per cent to securing foreign and domestic debts. Adminstrative expenditures would require 10 per cent, and the remaining 30 per cent would be used for constructive purposes.[94] After considering in detail the statistical information presented by the Chinese delegate, the other members of the committee, except for the Japanese, finally agreed in principle to authorize surtaxes which, according to estimates, would yield approximately $90,000,000. Even Japan, in her anxiety to have some provision made for repayment of the Nishihara loans of 1918 and 1919, was willing to agree to the collection of interim surtaxes yielding $70,000,000 annually.[95] The committee then proceeded to work out a tentative schedule of duties, the rates ranging from 10 per cent on ordinary goods to 32½ per cent

[92] *Ibid.,* Jan. 23, 1926, p. 134. In this connection, the following news dispatch from Peking dated February 9, 1926, deserves to be quoted: "More than a thousand yamen officials besieged the Cabinet office this morning (on the eve of the Chinese new year) demanding back pay. Consequently the ministers failed to show up for today's regular Cabinet meeting, which will either be postponed or be held secretly at the Premier's residence." *Ibid.,* Feb. 13, 1926, p. 271.
[93] *Ibid.,* CLVII, Nov. 21, 1925, p. 323.
[94] *North China Herald,* CLVIII, Feb. 13, 1926, p. 269.
[95] Statement of Dr. Wang, Feb. 5, 1926, *North China Herald,* CLVIII, Feb. 13, 1926, p. 269.

on tobacco and intoxicants.[96] When it became apparent that prolonged negotiations would be necessary to induce all of the delegations to accept the proposed schedule of duties, Dr. Wang, reversing his previous stand, proposed that the Powers authorize the immediate collection of the Washington surtaxes as a means of meeting the pressing needs of the government.[97]

At this point civil war again forced the suspension of negotiations. Beginning in March, Wu P'ei-fu and Chang Tso-lin, until now bitter enemies, joined forces in an effort to oust the Kuominchun from control of the capital. Once more Peking was cut off from the sea while the contending armies struggled for the possession of Tientsin. Bombs dropped from aeroplanes disturbed the diplomatic serenity of the capital.[98] By mid-April the Kuominchun forces had been compelled to withdraw from Peking northwestward toward Kalgan, and the city was occupied once more by Fengtien armies. Thereafter, for a period of several months, China lacked even the semblance of a central government. The chief Chinese delegate to the tariff conference, Dr. Wang, had fled to Tientsin on the outbreak of hostilities in March.[99] The Chief Executive, Tuan Ch'i-jui, first took refuge in the Legation Quarter, and then announced his retirement from office. The cabinet resigned en bloc.[100] The attempt of Dr. Yen to organize a regency cabinet ended after a few weeks in utter failure, for the victorious militarists had not yet been able to agree among themselves regarding a distribution of the spoils of office.

The political stalemate gave rise to rumors that the foreign delegates were preparing to desert the Tariff Conference entirely. Of the Chinese delegates, only two, Dr. Yen and Admiral Ts'ai, remained in Peking. Both the British and the

[96] *North China Herald,* CLVIII, Feb. 13, 1926, p. 269.
[97] Press statement, Feb. 26, 1926, *North China Herald,* CLVIII, Mar. 6, 1926, p. 415.
[98] *North China Herald,* CLIX, Apr. 10, 1926, pp. 50-51.
[99] *North China Herald,* CLVIII, Mar. 27, 1926, p. 557.
[100] *Ibid.,* CLIX, Apr. 17, 1926, p. 98. *Ibid.,* Apr. 24, 1926, p. 146.

American Governments, however, were loath to abandon negotiations until effect had at least been given to the promises which the Powers had made at Washington.[101]

On June 22, Dr. Yen finally abandoned his single-handed effort to perform the work of a cabinet. The brief meeting six days later of Chang Tso-lin and Wu P'ei-fu indicated that the victorious military commanders were less interested in forming a government than in continuing the campaign against the Kuominchun. As the summer heat of the capital increased, the foreign delegates became more and more convinced that patience had ceased to be a necessary virtue. On July 3, therefore, the following brief communiqué was issued from the Dutch Legation: [102]

"The delegates of the foreign Powers to the Chinese Customs Tariff Conference met at the Netherlands Legation this morning. They expressed a unanimous desire to proceed with the work of the Conference at the earliest possible moment, when the delegates of the Chinese Government are in a position to resume discussion with the foreign delegates of the problems before the Conference."

At first sight, this pronouncement merely called upon the Chinese to set up a government with which the foreign delegates could continue negotiations. Marshal Wu P'ei-fu imme-

[101] See the British note to the American Government dated May 28, 1926, *Chinese Social and Political Science Review,* XI, No. 2, April, 1927, Public Document Supplement, p. 105. Mr. Strawn said publicly in June that he did not intend to leave China until he had either accomplished the task for which his government had sent him to Peking, or had exhausted every possibility of doing so. *China Weekly Review,* XXXVII, July 17, 1926, p. 152. One reason for foreign reluctance to abandon the conference was undoubtedly the fear that Soviet Russia would take advantage of the situation for propaganda purposes. On his return to Moscow in September, 1925, Karakhan declared to American newspaper correspondents that he did not believe the forthcoming tariff conference in Peking would actually do anything to meet the demands of the Chinese people. Any upward revision of the tariff, he said, would be practically negligible, since the proceeds would go almost wholly to pay the interest on China's existing and future indebtedness to the European powers. The failure to secure substantial benefits would reveal to the Chinese people the futility of expecting the Powers voluntarily to abdicate their special privileges. Walter Duranty in *New York Times,* Sept. 17, 1925, p. 6.

[102] *China Year Book, 1926,* pp. 1141-2.

diately announced that a new Chinese delegation would be appointed within two weeks.[103] This was done by mandate on July 14.[104] Shortly thereafter, the new head of the Chinese delegation, Admiral Ts'ai T'ing-kan, invited the foreign delegates to meet with him informally on July 24. At this meeting, when the question of resuming the work of the conference came up for discussion, all of the foreign delegates expressed sympathy with the Chinese desire, but pointed out that in view of the prevailing hot weather, it would be better to wait until fall, when the Chinese Government might of its own accord fix a date for the resumption of negotiations.[105]

Fall came, but the negotiations were not resumed. Both the Kuominchun and the government at Canton had warned the foreign powers against reopening the conference.[106] Political paralysis continued at Peking. And what was of more significance, Marshal Wu P'ei-fu had suddenly gone to Hankow to take personal charge of the campaign against the Nationalists whose victorious armies, by this time, had reached the Yangtse River.

The tariff conference failed partly because the Peking Government had ceased to be effective as a channel of communication between China and the foreign powers. It failed also because of disagreement among the Powers over the question of what imports should bear the burden of the proposed surtaxes to be levied during the interim period pending the establishment of tariff autonomy. Another point of disagreement

[103] *North China Herald*, CLX, July, 1926, p. 50. Marshal Wu, who feared that the announcement of the foreign delegates meant the final end of the tariff conference, declared that if negotiations were not resumed, he might be compelled to declare China's customs autonomy forthwith. He thus reversed the stand which, as an opponent of the Peking Government, he had taken during the previous November.
[104] *China Year Book, 1926*, p. 1142.
[105] *China Year Book, 1926*, p. 1142.
[106] The Kuominchun protest was addressed to the Diplomatic Corps on July 12 by Paul Pao, Commissioner of Foreign Affairs at Kalgan. *China Year Book, 1926*, pp. 1142-3. The Acting Minister for Foreign Affairs of the Canton Government, Mr. Eugene Ch'en, addressed protests both to the American Minister at Peking and to Senator Borah in Washington. *Ibid.*, pp. 1143-46.

arose out of the insistence on the part of at least one Power that a portion of the revenue from the surtaxes should be earmarked for the service of unsecured foreign loans.[107] From the foreign point of view, negotiations broke down because of the disappearance of any government with which to negotiate. From the Chinese point of view, however, the Treaty Powers stood condemned by the fact that, after four years, one of their most important promises made at Washington had not yet been redeemed.[108]

One consequence of the disturbance of 1925 in China had been the tariff conference. Another was the long promised investigation of extraterritoriality.[109] Originally scheduled to convene in Peking on December 18, the Commission on Extraterritoriality did not hold its first session until January 12, 1926, the arrival of certain foreign delegates having been delayed because of the interruption of railway service resulting from civil war in the metropolitan area. On the commission were represented thirteen nations, namely, the United States of America, Belgium, China, Denmark, France, Great Britain, Italy, Japan, the Netherlands, Norway, Portugal, Spain, and Sweden. The Chinese member was Dr. Wang Ch'ung-hui, the country's foremost jurist. Mr. Silas Strawn, representing the

[107] This is apparent from the note of the British Government to the American Government on May 28, 1926 and the British proposals to the Washington Treaty Powers on December 18, 1926. *China Year Book, 1928,* pp. 756-61.
[108] In November, 1926, twenty-one organizations of Shanghai adopted several resolutions which were communicated to the National United Chambers of Commerce of China. One of the resolutions was in substance as follows: Since the delegates of the powers concerned have unanimously agreed upon the enforcement of tariff autonomy as from 1929, and as they have attached their signatures to the "Tariff Protocol" to that effect, the Chinese Government is under no obligation whatever to reopen the Tariff Conference. In suspending the Tariff Conference without Chinese consent and without previous notice, the foreign delegates have not only caused us great losses, but have forfeited all claims to our respect. The Chinese Government should therefore stand for no formalities, but enforce tariff autonomy beginning in 1929. *North China Herald,* CLXI, Nov. 20, 1926, p. 341.
[109] In September, 1925, while the Powers were preparing for this investigation, the Peking Government took hasty steps to effect certain judicial and prison reforms in the provinces. *North China Herald,* CLVI, Sept. 12, 1925, p. 334; *Ibid.,* Sept. 19, 1925, p. 374. *Ibid.,* CLVII, Oct. 3, 1925, p. 9.

American Government, was elected chairman of the commission.

During January and February, the commission studied the codes of law in force in China, as well as additional codes, still awaiting formal promulgation, which had been drafted by the Law Codification Commission of the Chinese Government. It considered also the reports of various commissioners relative to the operation of consular courts maintained by their respective Governments in China. The views of the Chinese commissioner were submitted on March 23 in the form of a lengthy statement.[110] Dr. Wang reminded his colleagues that they had been directed to inquire into the entire "present practice of extraterritorial jurisdiction in China." He considered, therefore, that the commission should give its attention to each of the following matters:

1. Consular jurisdiction.
2. The trial of mixed cases between Chinese and foreigners having extraterritorial rights.
3. The trial of cases between foreigners having extraterritorial rights and (a) foreigners having no extraterritorial rights, (b) foreigners of countries having no treaty relations with China.
4. Mixed courts, notably those at Shanghai and Kulangsu.
5. The quasi-right of asylum in premises occupied by foreigners or on foreign ships.
6. The practice followed by certain foreign consuls of issuing nationality certificates to Chinese citizens.
7. The claim of foreigners to exemption from taxation.
8. Certain special areas, including foreign settlements, leased territories, the Legation Quarter at Peking, and the railway zones.

The Chinese jurist pointed out that the extraterritorial system had become encrusted with a number of practices which had no warrant in the treaties. In the trial of mixed cases between Chinese and foreigners having extraterritorial rights, certain Powers enjoyed the right to have a consul present to watch proceedings on behalf of the foreign plaintiff. These

[110] "Memorandum of the Chinese Commissioner on the Present Practice of Extra-territorial Jurisdiction in China," *British Parliamentary Papers, China* No. 1 (1927) Cmd. 2797, pp. 3-11.

consuls, however, sometimes insisted on sitting as co-judges with the Chinese magistrate hearing the case. Dr. Wang declared also that treaty stipulations did not warrant the presence of a foreign assessor at the trial of cases between foreign plaintiffs enjoying extraterritorial rights and foreign defendants lacking such rights. He said further that the control exercised by the local consular body over the Shanghai mixed court lacked treaty sanction. In concluding his statement, the Chinese commissioner asked that consideration be given to all of the principal limitations on the nation's sovereignty which entitled foreigners to exemption from local law.

After some discussion, the members of the commission decided to investigate the first four of the items listed by Dr. Wang. With regard to the remaining items, the opinion of the commission was not unanimous. Except for one or two of its members, the commission was disposed to give consideration to the right of asylum, nationality certificates, and foreign exemption from local taxation. A majority of the commissioners seemed, however, to regard the question of special areas as being beyond the proper scope of their inquiry.[111] Dr. Wang continued to insist on a consideration of the entire list of matters. He refuted the argument that some of them were political and diplomatic rather than judicial in character. Dealing with the seventh point in his original list, he declared that the right of taxation was an inherent right of every state and there was no treaty between China and any of the foreign powers which contained a specific provision exempting foreigners from taxation. Nor was the practice warranted with reference to the extraterritorial status of the foreigners concerned. He pointed out again that numerous practices had developed under cover of the extraterritorial system which were not warranted by treaty stipulations. It was a cardinal rule of treaty interpretation, he said, that "if there be doubt whether certain powers have or have not been conferred by the terri-

[111] Memorandum submitted to the Commission by Dr. Wang on April 28, *British Parliamentary Papers*, China No. 1 (1927) Cmd. 2797, pp. 11-15.

torial sovereign, the doubt must be resolved in his favor." This rule had frequently been disregarded by foreigners who insisted on setting up doubtful claims despite the protests of the Chinese Government.[112]

In May the commissioners were able to begin their investigations in the provinces. Visits had already been paid to the model prisons, the supreme court, and other courts of justice in Peking. Leaving the capital on May 10, various members of the commission visited a number of cities in the Yangtse valley, including Hankow, Wuchang, Kiukiang, Shanghai, and Hangchow. No attempt was made to study conditions in the south, the government at Canton having formally declined to receive the traveling committee on the ground that extraterritoriality should be abolished immediately without investigation.[113] From Shanghai, therefore, the members of the commission went to Tientsin, Mukden, and Harbin before returning finally to Peking. Their report, which was completed September 16, 1926, was signed by every member of the commission, including Dr. Wang.[114]

The report of the commission was in four parts. The first dealt with the present practice of extraterritoriality in China, the second with the laws and judicial system of China, and the third with the administration of justice in China. The commission noted with appreciation the efforts that had been made by China in recent years to evolve a judicial system and to draft laws intended to carry out the program suggested in the treaties of 1902 and 1903. These efforts had resulted in the formation of a system of modern courts with their procedure (civil and criminal) and of a body of substantive law. With the general principles of these, the commission expressed itself as being satisfied.[115] Specific criticisms were aimed, however, at

[112] *Ibid.*
[113] Department of State, *Report of the Commission on Extraterritoriality in China*, (Washington, 1926), p. 6. See also George E. Sokolsky in *North China Herald*, CLIX, Apr. 24, 1926, p. 182.
[114] While approving the recommendations contained in Part IV of the report, Dr. Wang withheld unqualified approval of certain statements contained in Parts I, II, and III. *Report*, p. 109.   [115] *Report*, p. 51.

the military courts, and at the continued use of magistrates' courts in which no distinction was observed between administrative and judicial functions.[116] The actual administration of justice likewise came in for a measure of criticism, particular exception being taken to military interference with judicial processes.[117] It was also pointed out that the lack of a controlling central government and the continuance of civil war made difficult the work of the courts.[118]

The specific recommendations of the commission, which appeared in Part IV of the report, were as follows:[119] "The administration of justice with respect to the civilian population in China must be entrusted to a judiciary which shall be effectively protected against any unwarranted interference by the executive or other branches of the Government, whether civil or military."

In addition to considering suggestions made in the body of the report relative to the laws and to the judicial, police, and prison systems, the Chinese Government was asked to complete and put into force the following laws: Civil code, commercial code, revised criminal code, banking law, bankruptcy law, patent law, land expropriation law, law concerning notaries public. ,

It was likewise recommended that the Chinese Government should (a) establish and maintain a uniform system for the regular enactment, promulgation, and rescission of laws; (b) extend the system of modern courts, modern prisons and modern detention-houses with a view to the elimination of the magistrates' courts and of the old-style prisons and detention-houses; (c) make adequate financial provision for the maintenance of courts, detention-houses and prisons and their personnel. Prior to the reasonable compliance with the foregoing recommendations but after the principal items thereof had been carried out, the Powers concerned, if so desired by the Chinese Government, might consider the abolition of extraterritoriality

[116] *Ibid.*, pp. 80-82.
[117] *Ibid.*, pp. 90-97.
[118] *Ibid.*, pp. 89-90.
[119] *Ibid.*, pp. 107-9.

according to such progressive scheme (whether geographical, partial, or otherwise) as might be agreed upon.

With regard to the existing system of consular courts, the commission recommended, finally, that the following modifications be made:

1. "The powers concerned should administer, so far as practicable, in their extraterritorial or consular courts, such laws and regulations of China as they may deem it proper to adopt."

2. "As a general rule mixed cases between nationals of the powers concerned as plaintiffs and persons under Chinese jurisdiction as defendants should be tried before the modern Chinese courts . . . without the presence of a foreign assessor to watch the proceedings. . . . With regard to the existing special mixed courts, their organization and procedure should, as far as the special conditions in the settlements and concessions warrant, be brought more into accord with the organization and procedure of the modern Chinese judicial system. . . ."

3. "The extraterritorial powers should correct certain abuses which have arisen through the extension of foreign protection to Chinese as well as to business and shipping interests the actual ownership of which is wholly or mainly Chinese. The extraterritorial powers which do not now require compulsory periodical registration of their nationals in China should make provision for such registration at definite intervals."

4. "Necessary arrangements should be made in regard to judicial assistance . . . between the Chinese authorities and the authorities of the extraterritorial powers and between the authorities of the extraterritorial powers themselves, e.g., (a) All agreements between foreigners and persons under Chinese jurisdiction which provide for the settlement of civil matters by arbitration should be recognized, and the awards made in pursuance thereof should be enforced, by the extraterritorial or consular courts in the case of persons under their jurisdiction and by the Chinese courts in the case of persons under their jurisdiction, except when in the opinion of the competent court, the decision is contrary to public order or good morals. (b) Satisfactory arrangements should be made between the Chinese Government and the powers concerned for the prompt execution of judgments, summonses and warrants of arrest or search, concerning persons under Chinese jurisdiction, duly issued by the Chinese courts and certified by the competent Chinese authorities and *vice versa.*"

5. "Pending the abolition of extraterritoriality, the nationals of the powers concerned should be required to pay such taxes as may be prescribed in laws and regulations duly promulgated by the competent authorities of the Chinese Government and recognized by the powers concerned as applicable to their nationals."

The commission's report did not go the whole way in recognizing China's right to judicial autonomy. It did acknowledge, however, that some of the conditions set forth in the treaties of 1902 and 1903 had been met. Furthermore, it outlined a scheme of reform which, when completed, would warrant the Powers in abandoning their extraterritorial rights, certain reforms being introduced meanwhile in the system of consular courts then in existence. The powers, however, even if they accepted the recommendations of the commission, still retained the right to determine if and when the suggested reforms in the Chinese judicial system had actually been carried into effect.

CHAPTER IX

THE RISE OF NATIONALISM

No development of recent years has been more significant than the rapid development among the Chinese people of a spirit of nationalism. Students, merchants, bankers, industrial workers, and peasants have one after another felt its influence. The spread of modern education in China, associated in large part with the work of mission schools, revealed to the student class the position of inferiority occupied by their country in the family of nations, and stimulated an ardent desire for an improvement of that position.[1] Less interested in ideas than in profits, the merchants of the treaty ports, many of whom had industrial connections, desired customs autonomy in order to secure protection for domestic manufactures. The financial classes resented the privileged position enjoyed by certain foreign banks in which not only customs receipts but salt revenues were regularly deposited. Workers in foreign-owned factories, although in many cases receiving wages in excess of any to which they had ever been accustomed, were restless under the steady discipline of the modern factory. And even the peasant, normally content to till his fields and raise up sons to worship at the ancestral altars, began to feel vaguely that the foreigner was somehow responsible for the manifold ills from which the country suffered. For the foreigner, guaranteed special rights under the treaties, seemed to be largely immune from the oppression under which the natives themselves were compelled to suffer.

Quite unwittingly, the Powers themselves had by their blun-

[1] Cf. H. F. MacNair, *China's New Nationalism and Other Essays,* Shanghai, 1925, pp. 1-11.

ders contributed not a little to the growth of nationalist feeling among the Chinese. First in this series of blunders was the World War itself, which in addition to revealing to the Chinese the lack of any real unity among the western powers, fatally undermined the prestige of the white man in the Far East. Propaganda concerning self-determination and the rights of weaker nations, employed by the warring powers primarily to enlist support among the racial minorities of Europe, spread inevitably to the Orient where such ideas served as rallying cries in the struggle against western imperialism. The second blunder, the failure of the victors at Paris to restore Shantung to its rightful owner, stung the Chinese to a fury of patriotic resentment which stirred even provinces in the remote interior of the country. Finally, the long delay in giving effect to the program which had been agreed upon at Washington convinced growing numbers of Chinese that they would have to adopt radical expedients if they were ever to better the country's international position. What began as a movement in favor of treaty revision developed, particularly after 1925, into a movement designed to secure the complete abrogation of the treaties.[2]

[2] A significant development of 1924 had been the spread of a "Rights Recovery Movement" originating among the teachers of eight government schools in Peking. In July, the teachers issued a declaration reading in part as follows:

"With her massive territory, her abundant products, her diligent and industrious people, and her history of ancient civilization, China can still make her way in the world of today with its civilization of materialism. Unfortunately, however, internal disorders have led to invasions by other powers and various kinds of administrative affairs are supervised by foreigners, and practically every movement of the people is watched by them. Thus the finances of the country get worse, and the people become weak. They are oppressed by the powers as if they were their servants.

"The people under such a condition, however, are striving for something better and in recent weeks equal agreements have been concluded with two friendly countries, Russia and Germany. This very conclusion displeased those countries of an imperialistic turn of mind toward weaker nations, and they tried every artifice to prevent the equal treaties from being made.

"We think that all former treaties should be cancelled and replaced with new ones giving equal treatment, thus allowing the people of China a chance to become an independent race in the world, enjoying an equal status with the white race." *China Weekly Review,* XXIX, Aug. 2, 1924, p. 291.

Commenting on this declaration, which received widespread publicity, the Peking *Ching Pao* stated editorially, "If the diplomats of the foreign

Russia had set the pace by repudiating her international obligations. More significant, however, was the example of Turkey which, although a small nation, had compelled the Powers to renounce their extraterritorial rights in addition to other rights to interfere in the domestic concerns of the country.

Although the nationalist cause had adherents in all parts of China, the chief center of the movement was at Canton, to which city the Kuomintang leaders had fled following the dissolution of Parliament in 1917. There Dr. Sun Yat-sen, in spite of many vicissitudes, was engaged not only in organizing a modern government, but in elaborating grandiose plans for the political and economic reconstruction of the entire country. Associated with him in this work after 1923 was a Russian adviser, Michael Borodin, who soon came to enjoy a position of great influence in Kuomintang councils.[3] Having lost hope

Powers are keen eyed enough to see into the heart of things, they will at once modify their China policy . . . by cancelling all unequal treaties forced on China. If they abandon their aggressive policy, the Chinese people are every ready to treat them with sincerity and cooperate with them. If on the other hand, they warn us and send more troops to the country, we should welcome such action, because it would stimulate the whole nation to join the movement (for the recovery of national rights.)" *China Weekly Review*, XXIX, Aug. 2, 1924, p. 292.

Even certain members of Parliament, busy as they were for the most part with less laudable enterprises, formed an organization to agitate for the cancellation of "imperialistic and one-sided treaties between China and foreign Powers." *China Weekly Review*, XXIX, Aug. 23, 1924, p. 410.

Early in 1925, Dr. Ma Soo, referring to the rapid growth of the Rights Recovery Movement, said the movement had been helped "by the disappearance of the extraterritorial rights of Russians and Germans and by the decisions of the Washington Conference which, though embodied in documents stiff with provisional safeguarding clauses, nevertheless sharpened both China's appetite for and expectation of treatment as a modern self-governing state." Dr. Ma said also that agitation in favor of self-determination in Turkey, India, and Egypt had reacted powerfully on the similar movement in China. *China Weekly Review*, XXXI, Jan. 10, 1925, p. 153.

[3] Borodin, whose arrival in Canton coincided with the arrival of Karakhan in Peking, came to China not merely to advise Sun Yat-sen, but also to stir up Chinese nationalist sentiment against the imperialists. Shortly after his arrival, he published in one of the Canton newspapers an article in which the following statements were made: "I believe that it is part of a very subtile . . . propaganda to make the world believe that China is so 'different,' so 'backward,' that it is sorely in need of the civilizing influence of the more 'forward' countries. It serves as a justification for what the foreigner does here, for extraterritoriality, foreign courts, concessions, the Customs being in foreign hands, and for foreigners assuming the rôle of

that either Europeans or Americans would aid him in the task of building a new China, Dr. Sun had decided to accept advice and material assistance from Soviet Russia.[4]

The popular program which gradually took form in Dr. Sun's mind was set forth in a series of lectures which he delivered before groups of his followers at Canton during the early months of 1924.[5] In these lectures, which after publication soon became the Bible of Chinese nationalism, Dr. Sun insisted that three principles of reconstruction must be adopted and applied before China could regain her ancient greatness or even survive as an independent nation. The first of these was the Principle of Nationalism, the second the Principle of Democracy, and the third, the Principle of the People's Livelihood. To apply the first principle meant to overthrow imperialism and to achieve racial and national equality with the other nations of the world. By applying the second principle, militarism and mandarinism would be destroyed, and the people would have an opportunity to develop a system of constitutional government. In accordance with the third principle, a far-reaching program of social betterment must be carried out, designed to improve the economic well-being of the masses of people. Subsequently, Dr. Sun outlined the three periods into which the

protectors of the integrity of China and of its sovereignty. It allows foreign publications on Chinese soil maliciously to vilify and slander patriotic public men. It gives the innumerable servants of foreign interests here the opportunity of treating the laboring people of China as if they belonged to an inferior race, looking upon them with contempt." *North China Herald*, CXLIX, Nov. 17, 1923, p. 449. For an illuminating treatment of Borodin's activities at Canton, together with an estimate of his influence on the new Kuomintang program and on the revolutionary movement generally, see Fischer, *The Soviets in World Affairs*, Vol. II, pp. 636-677. Borodin insisted particularly that the Chinese revolution needed a popular basis, and therefore a program that would appeal to the workers and peasants. Prior to this, Dr. Sun had made his appeal primarily to the intelligentsia and the merchants. In addition to advice from Borodin, Dr. Sun received letters from Chicherin, Soviet Commissar for Foreign Affairs, and from Karakhan, then negotiating with the Peking Government, both of whom urged the adoption of a revolutionary program which would appeal to the Chinese masses. *Ibid.*, Vol. II, pp. 635-6.

[4] See John McCook Roots, "Chinese Head and Chinese Heart," *Asia*, XXVII, February, 1927, pp. 91-97.

[5] *San Min Chu I*, or *The Three Principles of the People*, edited by L. T. Chen and translated into English by Frank W. Price, Shanghai, 1927.

process of reconstruction was to be divided.[6] Of these the first was the period of military operations, during which the reactionary militarists then holding the country in their grip would be overthrown. Following this was to come the period of political tutelage, marked by the rule of an intelligent and purposeful minority while the people were being trained to an appreciation of their political responsibilities. Finally would dawn the period of constitutional government when the people would rule themselves by means of regularly elected officials.

Dr. Sun did not live to see the fulfilment of his dreams for a united China freed from the shackles of militarism and imperialism. Late in 1924 he started for Peking to participate in the work of the rehabilitation conference, the call for which had been issued by the provisional Chief Executive, Tuan Ch'i-jui.[7] When he arrived in the capital, early in January, 1925, he was already in the last stages of a fatal illness, and on March

[6] "Fundamentals of National Reconstruction," Arthur N. Holcombe, *The Chinese Revolution, A Phase in the Regeneration of a World Power,* Cambridge, 1930, Appendix B. For a fairly comprehensive treatment of Dr. Sun's political ideas, see *Ibid.,* Chapter V.

[7] On his way to Peking, Dr. Sun stopped several days in Shanghai. Prior to his arrival, rumors were afloat that the foreign authorities planned to deny him access to his home in the French Concession on the ground that his presence there would endanger the peace of the foreign settlements. Learning of these rumors, which seem actually to have been without foundation, Dr. Sun issued a strongly worded statement in which he declared that if the foreign authorities dared to obstruct his presence in Shanghai, he would "take some drastic steps to deal with them." "Be it remembered," he said, "that we, the Chinese people are not to be trifled with so long as we dwell in our own territories. Indeed the time has come when all foreign settlements in our country should be abrogated. Should the retrocession by the Powers concerned of their concessions in China be delayed any longer, I am afraid that some unhappy incident will happen, for every Chinese patriotic citizen has come to fully realize that China has already been infringed upon by some of the Powers long enough—so long that she can no longer tolerate such state of affairs." *China Weekly Review,* XXX, Nov. 22, 1924, pp. 377-8. Although the Kuomintang leader declined to receive representatives of the foreign newspapers published in Shanghai, he did make a statement to the local correspondent of the *Japan Chronicle.* For the immediate present, he said, his campaign would be confined to two things: the abolition of extraterritoriality and the restoration of China's customs autonomy. He was particularly bitter in his criticism of the extraterritoriality system. The foreigner in China acted like a king and insisted on being treated like one. For thirteen years, declared Dr. Sun, foreigners had been engaged in stirring up trouble in the country. Once foreigners were placed under Chinese law, this interference in China's domestic affairs could be prevented, and it might even have a salutary effect if one or two for-

12 he died. On the day before his death, he signed a will adjuring his followers not to abandon the revolutionary cause to which he had devoted forty years of his life. The work of national reconstruction must be carried to completion, and in particular "the abolition of unequal treaties should be carried into effect with the least possible delay." [8]

The revolutionary movement to which Sun Yat-sen had devoted the best years of his life was enormously strengthened by the outburst of popular feeling consequent on the clashes between Chinese and foreigners during the summer of 1925. Particularly was this true at Canton where radical labor leaders, following the Shakee massacre of June 23, organized an anti-British strike and boycott. The foreign colony on the island of Shameen was isolated, British goods could not be sold in Canton or elsewhere in Kwangtung, and the economic life of Hongkong was virtually paralyzed.[9] This situation continued without substantial change for fifteen months, despite two attempts to terminate the boycott by means of negotiations between the Hongkong and the Canton governments. In September, 1926, however, the authorities at Canton finally decided to adjust their differences with Hongkong in order to concentrate their attention on the campaign against the northern militarists. The Acting Minister for Foreign Affairs, Mr. Eugene Chen (Ch'en Yu-jen), notified the British Consul-General that arrangements had been made to end the boycott by October 10, subject to the levy of extra taxes on the import and export of luxuries for expenses in connection with the liquidation of the boycott movement.[10]

eigners were shot for encouraging civil commotions. *Japan Weekly Chronicle,* Dec. 11, 1924, pp. 790-91.

[8] Text, *San Min Chu I,* p. viii. This Will, consisting of only two brief paragraphs, is read regularly at all formal gatherings of Kuomintang members.

[9] See *China Year Book, 1926,* pp. 965-78.

[10] *China Year Book, 1928,* p. 976. *North China Herald,* CLXI, Oct. 2, 1926, p. 9. In the House of Commons on November 10, 1926, the British Secretary of State for Foreign Affairs, Sir Austen Chamberlain, declined to admit openly that the calling off of the Canton boycott against Hongkong had resulted from an understanding between the two governments. *Parliamentary Debates,* 5th series, Vol. 199, p. 1054. It seems more than likely, however, that before agreeing to terminate the boycott, the Canton authorities

On October 6, 1926, Mr. Chen formally notified the foreign powers having trading interests in Kwangtung that beginning October 11, the government intended to levy "a temporary internal tax on the consumption or production of such articles as are subject of trade between the Liang-Kwang Provinces (Kwangtung and Kwangsi) and other Provinces in China and foreign countries." The rate of taxation was to be "equivalent to half of the usual maritime or native Customs tariff, as the case may be, on general articles and to a full tariff on articles of luxury. . . ." [11] A month later, the Portuguese Consul-General at Canton, acting on instructions from the Senior Minister of the interested powers represented at Peking, notified the Canton Foreign Office that "In view of the levying by the Canton authorities of certain taxes on foreign trade, the diplomatic representatives at Peking of the Powers concerned declare that they cannot recognize the legality of this measure, which is in direct violation of treaties." [12] Mr. Chen promptly returned this note with the announcement that "My Government does not recognize the existence of the 'Senior Minister of the interested Powers at Peking (who lack juridical sanction) nor are the status and relations of the same powers *vis-a-vis* of my Government regulated on a basis which can properly entitle them to raise the question of a 'direct violation of treaties.' " He added that his government would be prepared to discuss not only this but other matters as soon as the powers came to appreciate the fact that real authority in the country had been transferred from Peking to Canton. [13]

received unofficial assurances that the British Government would not oppose the collection of the Washington surtaxes on imports.

[11] *China Year Book, 1928,* p. 1230.

[12] Note of November 5, 1926. *China Year Book, 1928,* p. 1231. A similar protest was transmitted at the same time to General Chang Chung-chang, military governor of Shantung, whose tax gatherers at Tsingtao had begun in August to levy special duties on imported tobacco and intoxicants. *North China Herald,* CLXI, Nov. 6, 1926, p. 244. General Chang replied that the new taxes were only temporary and would be abolished once the tariff conference met again to put the new tariff into effect. *North China Herald,* CLXI, Nov. 13, 1926, p. 295.

[13] Note of November 8, 1926 to the Portuguese Consul-General, *China Year Book, 1928,* p. 1231.

The uncompromising tone of Mr. Chen's note reflected the change in the spirit of the Southern Government brought about by the victorious progress northward of the nationalist armies commanded by General Chiang Kai-shek. Inspired with a revolutionary zeal which their enemies lacked, the nationalist forces were sweeping everything before them. In July the province of Hunan was overrun. Early in September, the Yangtse cities of Hanyang and Hankow were occupied. With the surrender of Wuchang a month later, the southerners had a base in central China from which to direct operations first against Shanghai and then against Peking. In December, the nationalist capital was transferred from Canton to the Wu-Han cities.

The rapid spread of nationalist authority created a situation with which, sooner or later, the foreign powers would have to deal. The Nationalists were committed not merely to the extermination of the northern militarists, but also to the cancellation of the unequal treaties. Moderate Kuomintang leaders were careful to explain that the movement was anti-imperialist, but not anti-foreign. What they desired was only that China should be accorded recognition as an equal in the family of nations.[14] Subsequent developments suggested, however, that these moderate views were not shared by all sections of the party. General Chiang Kai-shek declared that the people of China would never be satisfied with a mere revision of the treaties; what they demanded was the immediate and unconditional cancellation of the treaties. Foreigners must realize that the nationalist movement was not evolutionary but revolutionary. It would not end

[14] See the Declaration issued September 13, 1926, by the Central Executive Committee of the Kuomintang, text, *North China Herald*, CLX, Sept. 25, 1926, p. 584. Part III of the Declaration, dealing with foreign policy, read in part as follows: "Towards foreigners and foreign governments, there have never been feelings of animosity. Where any country seeks to act towards us in a spirit of imperialism, we are bound to combat its policy. When any country treats China on a footing of equality, we must exhibit towards it the most cordial friendship, to the mutual benefit materially and culturally of both countries. Hence among the powers having relations with China, there is no exclusiveness as to who are to be counted our friends; the measure of friendship is equality of treatment and the test is the conclusion of new treaties on a basis of reciprocal respect for each other's sovereignty."

until extraterritoriality had been summarily abolished and the foreign concessions returned.[15] The uneasiness aroused among foreigners by General Chiang's statement was not dispelled by later events at Hankow. The consolidation of nationalist power there was followed by an intensive anti-foreign agitation directed particularly against the British. A growing restlessness among the working classes culminated in a general strike which began November 27. Enormous and wildly enthusiastic mass meetings were held to greet the Nationalist officials who arrived early in December, accompanied by their Russian advisers. At these meetings, Kuomintang leaders denounced the unequal treaties and called for an intensification of the anti-British boycott.[16]

Great Britain, singled out by the nationalists for special attack, was the first power to acknowledge publicly that changed conditions in China required a change of attitude on the part of the powers toward China. British views were set forth in a memorandum communicated on December 18, 1926, to each of the governments which had participated in the Washington Conference.[17] The memorandum called attention to the gradual disappearance of political authority at Peking which, coupled with the development of a powerful nationalist government in the south, had created a situation entirely different from that existing at the time of the Washington Conference. Reference was made to the unsatisfactory results of the Tariff Conference and to the difficulty of carrying out the recommendations of the Extraterritoriality Commission so long as China lacked a government capable of entering into engagements on behalf of the entire country. The British Government now proposed that the Powers consent to the immediate collection of the Washington surtaxes, thereby legalizing what was already being

[15] *North China Herald,* CLXI, Nov. 27, 1926, p. 387. *China Weekly Review,* XXXIX, Dec. 4, 1926, p. 3.
[16] *China Year Book, 1928,* pp. 737, 1353-4. For an excellent treatment of this entire period, see H. Owen Chapman, *The Chinese Revolution, 1926-27,* London, 1928.
[17] *Treaties and Agreements, 1919-1929,* pp. 186-92.

done at Canton and Tsingtao. The surtaxes should be collected by the Customs Administration, but the funds derived therefrom were not to be used for the consolidation of unsecured obligations, nor were they necessarily to be deposited in foreign banks. By suggesting that the appropriate local authorities be left free to determine the place of deposit and the use of the surtaxes, the British memorandum, in effect, advocated the recognition of regional governments, the Powers not being called upon to choose between political factions.

With regard to the nationalist attack upon the treaties, the British Government proposed that the Powers issue a joint declaration announcing "their readiness to negotiate on treaty revision and all other outstanding questions as soon as the Chinese themselves have constituted a Government with authority to negotiate; and stating their intention pending the establishment of such a Government to pursue a constructive policy in harmony with the spirit of the Washington Conference but developed and adapted to meet the altered circumstances of the present time." In this joint declaration, the Powers "should make it clear that in their constructive policy they desire to go as far as possible towards meeting the legitimate aspirations of the Chinese nation." Specifically, they should declare their willingness to recognize China's right to tariff autonomy "as soon as she herself has settled and promulgated a new national tariff." At the same time China should be called upon to maintain that respect for the sanctity of treaties which was the primary obligation of all civilized states. Meanwhile the Powers should, for the time being at least, refrain from making ineffectual protests concerning minor matters. The British Government was convinced that "protest should be reserved for cases where there is an attempt at wholesale repudiation of treaty obligations or an attack upon the legitimate and vital interests of foreigners in China, and in these cases the protests should be made effective by the united action of the Powers." Finally, the joint declaration should show that it was the policy of the Powers to endeavor to maintain harmonious relations with China without waiting for or insisting on the prior establishment of a strong central government.[18]

Before the Powers could give adequate consideration to these proposals, a fresh series of events required the British Government to indicate how far it would go in condoning "minor" infractions of its agreements with China. Early in January, 1927, crowds of coolies led by agitators began to menace the British Concession at Hankow. Fearing to precipitate a clash similar to those which had taken place during 1925, the British authorities, having received assurances that the Chinese local officials would be responsible for the maintenance of peace and order, decided to withdraw their naval forces to warships lying at anchor in the river. Despite Chinese assurances, the entire Concession was overrun on January 4 by a disorderly mob bent on destruction. The situation became so serious that on January 5 the British Consul-General ordered the immediate evacuation of all women and children.[19] Three days later mob violence and widespread looting forced foreign residents to abandon the British Concession at Kiukiang.[20] Following the withdrawal of the British, Chinese officials took over provi-

[18] Instead of appeasing the wrath of the Nationalists, the British memorandum actually provoked new resentment. The Acting Minister for Foreign Affairs at Hankow, Mr. Chen, pointed out that the adoption of the proposal regarding the surtaxes would actually promote new civil wars, since every treaty port would thereafter become the bone of contention among rival militarists struggling for possession of the surtax revenues. Moreover, if the surtaxes were collected, two-thirds of the proceeds would go to the enemies of the Nationalists, since they continued to control most of the seaboard cities. These views were set forth in a telegram addressed by Mr. Chen on December 31 to the American Secretary of State. *North China Herald,* CLXII, Jan. 8, 1927, p. 3.

As a matter of fact, all factions in China took advantage of the British proposals to impose the Washington surtaxes without waiting for the approval of the Powers. The Hankow government began to collect them January 1, 1927. *North China Herald,* CLXII, Jan. 8, 1927, p. 3. Sun Chuanfang at Shanghai followed suit on January 20, 1927. *Ibid.,* Jan. 22, 1927, p. 114. In the north, the surtaxes became effective on February 1, 1927. *Ibid.,* Jan. 15, 1927, p. 55. The British Government advised its nationals to pay these surtaxes. The Japanese Government repeatedly protested against their collection. Other treaty powers apparently adopted no definite attitude, but did not interfere with the payment by their nationals. *China Year Book, 1928,* p. 1065.

[19] *China Year Book, 1928,* pp. 737-8.

[20] *North China Herald,* CLXII, Jan. 15, 1927, pp. 47, 53-4.

sionally the administration of the concessions at both Hankow and Kiukiang.

The growing seriousness of the situation in the Yangtse valley caused the Japanese and American Governments, following the example of the British, to define their attitude toward revolutionary China. Addressing the Japanese Diet January 18, 1927, the Minister for Foreign Affairs, Baron Shidehara, announced that his government had no objection to the levying of the Washington surtaxes but must have reasonable assurances that the additional revenue would not be used for purposes of civil war. During the prevailing civil commotion, Japan intended [21]

To respect China's sovereignty and territorial integrity and scrupulously to avoid interference in her domestic strife.

To promote solidarity and economic rapprochement between the two nations.

To assist the Chinese to attain the realization of their just aspirations.

To exercise patience and toleration with regard to the existing situation and simultaneously to use all reasonable means of protecting Japan's legitimate rights and interests.

The attitude of the American Government was set forth in an official statement issued January 27, 1927, by the Secretary of State, Mr. Frank B. Kellogg.[22] "The United States," said Mr. Kellogg, was "prepared to enter into negotiations with any Government of China or delegates who can represent or speak for China not only for the putting into force of the surtaxes of the Washington treaty but entirely releasing tariff control and restoring complete tariff autonomy to China." The United States, however, would expect most favored nation treatment and also that China should afford protection to American citizens, property, and rights. In addition, the United States was prepared to put into force at once such recommendations of the Commission on Extraterritoriality as could be en-

[21] *Japan Weekly Chronicle*, Jan. 27, 1927, pp. 81-2.
[22] *Congressional Record*, Vol. 68, pp. 4387-8. *Treaties and Agreements, 1919-1929*, pp. 193-7.

forced without waiting for a treaty, and to negotiate the release of extraterritorial rights as soon as China was "prepared to provide protection by law and through her courts to American citizens, their rights, and property." With regard to both tariff autonomy and extraterritoriality, the American Government was ready to negotiate either jointly with the other powers, or alone.[23]

The British, Japanese, and American Governments had indicated their willingness to make certain concessions in favor of Chinese nationalism. Meanwhile Mr. Chen had also declared the policy of his government in a statement issued at Hankow on January 22.[24] The question, said Mr. Chen, "is not what Great Britain and the other Powers may wish to grant China to meet 'the legitimate aspirations of the Chinese Nation' but what Nationalist China may justly grant Great Britain and the other Powers. . . ." The dominant aim of Chinese Nationalism was the recovery of China's full independence and the creation of a modern state having a government competent to "rule, administer, and tax China as the common possession of the Chinese people. . . ." In dealing with specific foreign issues involved in the recovery of China's full independence, the new government would "not disregard considerations of right and justice due to foreign nationals." But in this connection it was necessary to emphasize the fact that effective protection of foreign life and property in China no longer rested on "foreign bayonets or foreign gunboats" because the "arm" of Chinese Nationalism—the economic weapon or boycott—was "more puissant than any engine of warfare that the for-

[23] For several weeks Congress had been taking an active interest in the Chinese situation, and on the day following the appearance of Secretary Kellogg's statement, Representative Stephen G. Porter, Chairman of the House Committee on Foreign Affairs, reported a concurrent resolution requesting the President to enter into negotiations "with duly accredited agents of the Republic of China" for the relinquishment of American rights with regard to extraterritoriality and tariff control. *House Report* No. 1891, 69th Congress, 2nd session. The Porter Resolution was passed by the House of Representatives on February 21 by a vote of 262 to 43. The session closed before it could come to a vote in the Senate.

[24] Text, *China Year Book, 1928*, pp. 762-4.

eigner can devise." Mr. Chen then said that "the liberation of China from the yoke of foreign imperialism need not necessarily involve any armed conflict between Chinese Nationalism and the foreign Powers. For this reason, the Nationalist Government would prefer to have all questions outstanding between Nationalist China and the foreign Powers settled by negotiation and agreement. . . . In order to prove that this is no idle statement of policy the Nationalist Government hereby declares its readiness to negotiate separately with any of the Powers for a settlement of Treaty and other cognate questions on a basis of economic equality and mutual respect for each other's political and territorial sovereignty."

Meanwhile negotiations over the question of the British Concessions at Hankow and Kiukiang had begun at Hankow between Mr. Chen and Mr. Owen O'Malley who had come from Peking as the representative of the British Minister. The course of the negotiations was marked by moderation on both sides. The British representative made no attempt to insist on the restoration of the two Concessions. Moreover, on January 27, he communicated to Mr. Chen a new British memorandum suggesting lines along which other differences between Great Britain and China might be settled. This memorandum, the text of which was transmitted to the Peking Government at the same time by the British Minister, contained seven proposals.[25] The British Government was prepared to recognize modern Chinese law courts as competent courts for cases brought by British plaintiffs, and to waive the right of attendance of a British representative at the hearing of such cases. It was ready also to apply as far as practicable in the British courts in China the modern Chinese Civil Commercial Codes in addition to certain duly enacted subordinate legislation. Moreover, as soon as a revised Chinese Penal Code had been promulgated and was applied in Chinese courts, Great Britain stood ready to consider its application in British courts in China. In addition, the British Government was prepared to make

[25] *Treaties and Agreements, 1919-1929*, pp. 197-8.

302   *China's Foreign Relations*

British subjects liable for the payment of "such regular and legal Chinese taxation not involving discrimination against British subjects or British goods," as was in fact imposed on and paid by Chinese citizens. The government was prepared "to discuss and enter into arrangements according to particular circumstances at each port concerned for the modification of Municipal Administration of British Concessions, so as to bring them into line with the administrations of Special Chinese Administrations set up in former Concessions, or for their amalgamation with former Concessions now under Chinese control, or the transfer of police control of Concession areas to the Chinese authorities." Finally, Great Britain was ready to accept the principle that "British missionaries should no longer claim the right to purchase land in the interior, that Chinese converts should look to Chinese Law and not to Treaties for protection, and that missionary educational and medical institutions will conform to Chinese laws and regulations applying to similar Chinese institutions."

Although he regarded the new British proposals as falling far short of satisfying Nationalist desires, Mr. Chen intimated his willingness to consider them as a basis for discussion. He made it clear, however, that his government would decline to recognize the validity of agreements concluded by the British Government with Chinese local authorities regarding Concessions, no matter where located.[26] Of more immediate importance, meanwhile, were the negotiations with regard to the Concessions at Hankow and Kiukiang. The necessary documents were all ready for final signature when a new complication developed. To prevent a recurrence of what had taken place at Hankow and Kiukiang, the British Government had ordered armed reinforcements to Shanghai for the protection of the International Settlement. As a consequence, on January 30, Mr. Chen informed Mr. O'Malley that the concentration of British forces at Shanghai suggested intimidation and

[26] Chen to O'Malley, January 29, 1927, text, *North China Herald,* CLXII, Feb. 12, 1927, p. 217.

that under the circumstances it would be impossible for him to sign the agreements which had been drawn up.[27]

The deadlock at Hankow was broken by a compromise. Addressing the House of Commons on February 10, the British Secretary for Foreign Affairs, Sir Austen Chamberlain, announced that if the Hankow agreements were signed, only such troops as were already on their way would be landed at Shanghai. Other troops from the Mediterranean and from England would be concentrated at Hongkong and would not proceed to Shanghai unless they were required by the emergence of some fresh danger.[28] On being informed of this arrangement, Mr. Chen consented to resume negotiations.[29] On February 19 an agreement was signed by which Great Britain agreed to dissolve the Hankow municipality on March 15, after which the administration of the Concession area would be formally handed over to a new Chinese municipality. Regulations which were drafted for the government of the new municipality were to "remain in force until such time as arrangements have been negotiated for the amalgamation of the five Hankow Concessions and former Concessions into one unified municipal district." [30] These regulations [31] provided for a Director, appointed by the Nationalist Minister for Foreign Affairs, who was to be chief executive officer of the new Administrative District; an annual meeting of property holders and rate payers with power to adopt the annual budget, levy rates and taxes, and authorize loans; and a council of seven members, the chairman to be the Director of the District, and the other members,

[27] *China Year Book, 1928*, pp. 738-9. The Peking Government also protested formally against the sending of these troops to China. Waichiao Pu note to British Legation, January 31, 1927, text, *North China Herald*, CLXII, Feb. 5, 1927, p. 180.
[28] *Parliamentary Debates*, 5th series, Vol. 202, pp. 326-7.
[29] *North China Herald*, CLXII, Feb. 27, 1927, p. 305.
[30] *British Parliamentary Papers*, China No. III (1927) Cmd. 2869. *Treaties and Agreements, 1919-1929*, p. 203. The German Concession at Hankow had reverted to Chinese control in 1917 and the Russian Concession in 1920. Following the conclusion of the Chen-O'Malley agreement, there remained only the Japanese and the French Concessions.
[31] *Treaties and Agreements, 1919-1929*, pp. 205-213.

three Chinese and three British, to be elected at the annual meeting of the rate payers.

Negotiations relating to the Concession at Kiukiang were concluded March 2.[32] The British Government agreed to cancel the British Municipal Regulations and to hand over unconditionally the administration of the Concession area to the Nationalist Government as from March 15. In settlement of losses suffered by British subjects during the looting of the Concession, Mr. Chen handed to Mr. O'Malley a check for $40,000. In concluding these agreements, the Nationalist Minister for Foreign Affairs took the occasion to declare that changes in the status of other foreign Concessions would be effected only by negotiation and that the policy of the Nationalist Government was not "to use force or to countenance the use of force" in effecting such changes.[33]

The policy of patient conciliation which the powers, particularly Great Britain, had adopted toward the Nationalist Government underwent a sudden change as a result of a serious outbreak of anti-foreignism at Nanking. Following the Southern capture of the city on March 24, systematic and apparently premeditated assaults began against all foreigners. American, British, French, Italian, and Japanese nationals were murdered or wounded, among the wounded being the British Consul. Many others, who escaped actual injury, were subjected to shameful indignities. The American, British, and Japanese consulates were violated and other foreign houses and institutions were looted and in some cases burned. The murderous attacks upon the foreigners ceased only after British and Amer-

---

[32] *Ibid.*, pp. 213-15.

[33] Declaration of February 19, 1927, *Ibid.*, p. 205. Despite the assurances offered by Mr. Chen, the British Concession at Chinkiang was occupied by Nationalist troops late in March. Foreign residents of the area either fled to Shanghai or accommodated themselves as best they could on hulks and launches anchored in the river. *China Year Book, 1928*, pp. 751, 928 note. On April 3, also, a mob attempted to seize possession of the Japanese Concession at Hankow. The Japanese landed marines, used machine guns, dispersed the intruders, and continued to hold the Concession area. *North China Herald*, CLXIII, Apr. 9, 1927, pp. 53, 55-6. *China Year Book, 1928*, pp. 1045, 1229.

ican warships in the river had begun to drop shells on the city.[34]

On April 11, the United States, Great Britain, Japan, France, and Italy united in making the following demands on the government at Hankow in connection with the Nanking outrages: [35]

1. "Adequate punishment of the commanders of the troops responsible for the murders, personal injuries and indignities and material damage done, as also of all persons found to be implicated."

2. "Apology in writing by the Commander-in-Chief of the Nationalist army including an express written undertaking to refrain from all forms of violence and agitation against foreign lives and property."

3. "Complete reparation for personal injuries and material damage done."

The note concluded with the statement that "unless the Nationalist authorities demonstrate to the satisfaction of the interested governments their intention to comply with these terms, the said governments will find themselves compelled to take such measures as they consider appropriate."

The Five Powers had acted jointly in presenting their demands. The Nationalist Government, however, determined if possible to deal with each power separately. Consequently, on April 14, Mr. Chen addressed individual replies to each of the governments concerned. In his note to the British Government [36] he stated that his Government was prepared to make good all damage done to the British consulate at Nanking and also to compensate British nationals for their losses except in cases where it could be definitely proved that the damage done had "been caused by the British-American bombardment . . .

[34] *British Parliamentary Papers*, China No. 4 (1927) Cmd. 2953, pp. 3-27. *China Year Book, 1928*, pp. 723-29. The city as a whole was not shelled. Many of the foreigners had taken refuge in buildings belonging to the Standard Oil Company located on what was known as Socony Hill in a thinly settled portion of the city. The warships merely laid down a protective barrage of shrapnel around this area.
[35] *Treaties and Agreements, 1919-1929*, p. 216.
[36] *Ibid.*, pp. 216-18.

or by Northern rebels and *agents provocateurs.*" Mr. Chen intimated that defeated northern soldiers might have been responsible for the attacks. The question of punishment for the Nationalist commanders, therefore, should await the findings of either the government inquiry then in progress, "or of an international commission of inquiry to be immediately instituted by the Nationalist Government and His Britannic Majesty's Government." In case the international commission of inquiry were agreed upon, Mr. Chen suggested that it investigate also the bombardment of Nanking by British naval forces, and in addition "the other outrages committed successively by British-controlled armed forces at Shanghai on 30th May, by British armed marines and volunteers off the Shameen on 23rd June, 1925, and by British naval forces at Wanhsien last year." [37]

The Nationalist Government, continued Mr. Chen, naturally could not countenance the use, in any form, of violence and agitation against foreign lives and property. Consequently the proper military authorities would not only be instructed to give a written undertaking of the sort desired, but to see that effective measures were taken to afford proper protection to foreign lives and property. In conclusion, the Nationalist Minister for Foreign Affairs pointed out that the unequal treaties constituted the chief danger to foreign lives and property; this danger would persist as long as effective government was rendered difficult "by foreign insistence on conditions which are at once a humiliation and a menace to a nation that has known greatness and is today conscious of renewed strength."

Mr. Chen's note to the American Government was substantially similar to that addressed to the Government of Great Britain.[38] Toward Japan he was noticeably more conciliatory,

[37] The Wanhsien incident took place in August, 1926. British naval forces had been sent from Hankow to effect the release of two British merchant ships on which a number of British marine officers were being held prisoner by forces under the command of General Yang Sen. Chinese troops in possession of the ships offered resistance and a pitched battle ensued in the course of which the British gun-boats shelled the city. *China Year Book, 1928*, pp. 666-672.
[38] *Treaties and Agreements, 1919-1929*, pp. 219-20.

particularly since Japanese naval forces had refrained from participating in the bombardment of Nanking.[39] Each of the five governments considered the Nationalist replies the reverse of satisfactory. Great Britain, France, and Italy desired the adoption of measures calculated to enforce compliance with their demands, and Japan showed an inclination to follow the lead of the Three Powers.[40] The American Government, however, declined to associate itself with measures of coercion.[41] The powers decided, therefore, to abandon their plans for some form of joint action. Their decision was influenced in part by a desire not to embarrass the Nationalist Government which Chiang Kai-shek had just set up at Nanking as a rival to the one at Hankow. The new Nanking Government courted favor among the foreign powers, and in addition among the more conservative Chinese, by taking prompt steps to suppress the communists who, it was thought, had been responsible for the atrocities at Nanking. The powers gave the new movement their moral support by ceasing to have further dealings with the radicals at Hankow.[42]

[39] *Ibid.*, pp. 221-23.

[40] *North China Herald*, CLXIII, Apr. 30, 1927, p. 187. Baron Shidehara had uniformly followed a policy of conciliation in dealing with China. In April, 1927, however, the cabinet in which he served as Minister for Foreign Affairs was replaced by a new cabinet headed by General Baron Tanaka, who in addition to being Premier, took over control of the foreign office. Tanaka was committed to a "forward policy" with regard to China.

[41] It was stated officially at the White House on May 3 that President Coolidge was unable to see where the United States would gain by acting with the other powers in the immediate presentation of a second note—which would have taken the form of an ultimatum—to the Nationalist Government. *United States Daily*, May 4, 1927, p. 1.

[42] Statement of Sir Austen Chamberlain before the British House of Commons, May 9, 1927. *Parliamentary Debates*, 5th Series, Vol. 206, pp. 19-23.

The British diplomatic representative at Hankow, Mr. B. C. Newton, was recalled May 17. In explaining to Mr. Chen the reasons for his departure, he referred caustically to the inability of the Hankow Government either to maintain order or to observe its promises. That government had even shirked the responsibility of accepting the moderate terms presented for the settlement of the Nanking outrage. Mr. Newton declared, therefore, that his retention as representative of His Majesty's Minister "at the seat of a régime so totally incapable of discharging the responsibilities of a civilized government" was both useless and undesirable, and in accordance with instructions, he was leaving Hankow forthwith. *British Parliamentary Papers*, China No. 4 (1927) Cmd. 2953, pp. 30-31. In his rejoinder, Mr.

The Nationalists of the South had shown that they were prepared to break windows in order to compel action by the powers with regard to treaty revision. Less disposed to use violence, but no less determined in their opposition to the treaties were the authorities in the North. The policy of the Peking Government was to effect treaty revision by utilizing the normal processes of diplomacy. And the results of that policy, even if unsatisfactory from the standpoint of the extreme Nationalists, were nevertheless far from being insignificant. During the years from 1925 to 1928, the Peking Government negotiated new treaties with two of the smaller European powers, reasserted Chinese control over the administration of the Customs, and used for the first time a diplomatic formula which was later to pave the way for a general revision of treaties between China and the other powers.

The first of the new agreements was the Treaty of Commerce with Austria, signed at Vienna on October 19, 1925.[43] It provided for the usual exchange of diplomatic and consular representatives. The citizens of each contracting party were declared to be amenable in criminal and civil cases to the jurisdiction of the country where they resided. Otherwise they were to enjoy most favored nation treatment with regard to trade, travel, and residence in interior districts. It was agreed, however, (Article IV) that law-suits and other judicial cases concerning Austrian citizens in China were to be brought before the modern tribunals "with the right of appeal and in accordance with the new laws, regular proceedings being employed thereat." Provision was also made for the assistance, during the period of litigation, of lawyers and interpreters of Austrian or other na-

Chen accused the British of gross hypocrisy. On the one hand they had professed sympathy for Nationalist ideals, and on the other they had been guilty of political sabotage and military intervention. The disorder of which the British Government complained had been caused primarily by Nationalist resentment against the concentration of British armed forces at Shanghai and not by communist influence. Mr. Chen continued to insist that "the Nationalist Government at Wu-Han are the sole depository of state power in Nationalist China." *North China Herald*, CLXIII, May 21, 1927, p. 321.

[43] League of Nations *Treaty Series*, Vol. 55, p. 9. *Treaties and Agreements, 1919-1929*, p. 165.

tionality, provided they had been "duly recognized by the Court." Each party recognized the right of the other to determine, by appropriate municipal legislation, all matters relating to customs duties. However, on goods which were the produce or the manufacture of one of the contracting parties or of any other country, and which were imported or exported by citizens of the contracting parties, no higher duties were to be collected than those paid by nationals. Of some significance was Article V which read as follows: "The Government of each of the two Contracting Parties shall accord to workmen, citizens of the other, who may come to its territory, the same treatment as to workmen, citizens of any other nation, and grant them in accordance with the laws and regulations of the country the same protection as to national workmen." With regard to matters not specifically dealt with, the two parties agreed to apply "the principles of equality and reciprocity" which formed the basis of the present treaty.

The second treaty was that with Finland.[44] Signed at Helsingfors on October 29, 1926, it provided for the exchange of diplomatic and consular representatives. The nationals of each contracting party residing in the territory of the other were to be subject to the jurisdiction of local tribunals with regard both to their persons and property. They were to have the right, while conforming to local law, to travel, to reside, and to engage in commerce or industry in all places where the nationals of another nation enjoyed such rights, and were required to pay customs duties, taxes, or contributions decreed by law. A declaration appended to the treaty provided, however, that litigation involving Finnish citizens in China should be brought before the newly organized tribunals, with a guaranteed right of appeal. Furthermore, Finnish advocates and interpreters, officially accredited to such tribunals, might act as counsel during the proceedings.[45]

[44] League of Nations *Treaty Series*, Vol. 67, p. 345. *Treaties and Agreements, 1919-1929*, pp. 185-6.
[45] League of Nations *Treaty Series*, Vol. 67, p. 357. *Treaties and Agreements, 1919-1929*, p. 186.

The attitude of the northern authorities toward the tariff question was determined in very considerable degree by their urgent need for funds with which to finance their war against the South. The rapid advance of the Nationalist armies during 1926 had compelled the northern militarists to pool their resources. A coalition was formed, therefore, at the head of which was Chang Tso-lin. In December, 1926, Marshal Chang appeared personally in Peking to take over control of the government. Almost immediately, he announced his intention of enforcing collection of the Washington surtaxes in all territory under his control.[46] The new rates were to become effective from February 1, 1927, a mandate to this effect being issued in January.[47] The British Inspector-General of Customs, Sir Francis Aglen, was approached with the proposal that he assume responsibility for the collection of the additional surtaxes. Aglen immediately let it be known that he could supervise the collection of only such taxes as were permitted by the treaties. Thereupon he was summarily dismissed from office and another British subject, Mr. A. H. F. Edwardes, appointed to the headship of the Customs Administration. In taking this action, however, the Chinese Government was careful to announce that all foreign loans and indemnities and all domestic loans secured on the customs receipts remained unimpaired.[48]

The mandate ordering the dismissal of Sir Francis Aglen had been issued without the knowledge of the diplomatic corps. The British Minister, Sir Miles Lampson, immediately protested to Marshal Chang Tso-lin, to the Minister for Foreign Affairs, Dr. Koo, and to Mr. Lo Wen-kan, the newly appointed head of the Revenue Bureau.[49] On February 7, also, the Peking representatives of the Treaty Powers sent a formal communica-

[46] *North China Herald*, CLXI, Dec. 31, 1926, p. 615.
[47] *Ibid.*, CLXII, Jan. 15, 1927, p. 55.
[48] *Ibid.*, Feb. 5, 1927, p. 183. The Minister of Finance insisted that the Inspector General was an official of the government and should therefore "carry out Government orders in accordance with the Civil Service regulations governing the conduct of business." Statement issued February 1, 1927, text, *China Year Book, 1928*, p. 1077.
[49] *North China Herald*, CLXII, Feb. 12, 1927, p. 224.

tion to the Waichiao Pu remonstrating against the government's action. The protests of the foreign powers were without effect. The newly appointed Inspector General of Customs took office on February 11, and Sir Francis Aglen returned to England, it being understood that he would continue to receive his salary for a period of one year.[50]

A year after this episode, Marshal Chang Tso-lin, who meanwhile had assumed the title of Tayuanshuai or Generalissimo,[51] took steps to prepare for tariff autonomy which the powers had promised, albeit only in the form of a preliminary resolution, should become effective January 1, 1929. On March 5, 1928, a mandate was issued appointing a Customs Tariff Autonomy Commission. The members of the commission were reminded of the resolution which had been adopted by the powers at the 1925 conference, and ordered to devise measures for the restoration of tariff autonomy within one year.[52] The wording of the mandate left little doubt of the government's intention to proceed with the enforcement of a statutory tariff without waiting for the prior abolition of the *likin* system.[53]

In addition to negotiating treaties with Austria and Finland, and reasserting Chinese authority over the Customs Administration,[54] the Peking Government also adopted a new and sig-

[50] *Ibid.*, Aglen continued also to enjoy his title during this period, his successor, Mr. Edwardes, being merely Acting Inspector General.

[51] The title really carried with it supreme control over the navy as well as the army and in addition the power to appoint the Premier and through him the entire cabinet. Chang thus became an actual dictator. *North China Herald*, CLXIII, June 25, 1927, pp. 537-8.

[52] *North China Herald*, CLXVI, Mar. 10, 1928, p. 379. The Nanking Government on March 14, appointed a similar committee, but with somewhat greater authority. *Ibid.*, Mar. 17, 1928, p. 421.

[53] Opposition to this procedure was voiced immediately by the Japanese Minister, Mr. Kenkichi Yoshizawa. *North China Herald*, CLXVI, Mar. 10, 1928, p. 379. *Ibid.*, Mar. 17, 1928, p. 421.

[54] To this period belongs also the liquidation of the affairs of the Russo-Asiatic Bank in China. Following the Russian Revolution, the head office of this institution had been transferred from Petrograd to Paris, and the French Government consequently extended a measure of protection to its branches operating in China. In September, 1926, the bank was forced by financial reverses to go into voluntary liquidation. It was known that the assets of the bank in China probably exceeded its liabilities. To forestall prior action by the French Government, the Peking Government immediately

nificant policy with regard to the renewal of existing treaties. Each of these treaties, with few exceptions, provided that at the end of specified intervals, usually ten years, one party or both might demand a revision of certain clauses. Taking advantage of this provision, and also invoking the principle of *rebus sic stantibus,* the Chinese Government now insisted on its right to revise the entire treaty, or in case such radical revision were not agreed to by the other party, to terminate the agreement by unilateral action. Chinese experience first at Versailles, then at Washington, and finally during the Peking Tariff Conference, had revealed the difficulty of negotiating with the Treaty Powers as a unit. The new policy promised the advantage of permitting diplomatic pressure to be applied to the powers one at a time.

The first country to feel the effects of the new policy was Belgium. Article 46 of the Sino-Belgian treaty of November 2, 1865, read as follows: [55]

"If the Government of His Majesty the King of the Belgians should hereafter consider it necessary to introduce changes in any clauses of the present Treaty, he shall have full liberty in this respect to open negotiations after an interval of ten years has elapsed from the day of the exchange of ratifications, but it is necessary that six months before the expiration of the ten years he should officially inform the Government of His Majesty the Emperor of China of his intention to introduce changes, and of what they shall consist. In default of this official notice, the Treaty shall remain in force without changes for a new term of ten years and so on from ten years to ten years."

On April 16, 1926,[56] the Belgian Minister, M. le Maire de

appointed its own liquidators with power to wind up the affairs of all branches of the bank located in China. *North China Herald,* CLXI, Oct. 2, 1926, p. 8. *Ibid.,* Oct. 9, 1926, p. 54. For the Regulations issued by the Peking Government in this connection, see *Chinese Social and Political Science Review,* XI (1927), Public Document Supplement, pp. 85, 87.

[55] For the French and Chinese texts, see Maritime Customs, *Treaties, Conventions, etc., between China and Foreign States,* Shanghai, 1917, Vol. II, p. 21. English translation in *Chinese Social and Political Science Review,* XI (1927), Public Document Supplement, p. 60.

[56] It should be recalled that this date marked the final stage of the campaign of Chang Tso-lin and Wu Pei-fu against the Kuominchun. The

Warzee d'Hermalle, received from the Waichiao Pu a note announcing that the Chinese Government desired a revision of the treaty of 1865.[57] The Chinese note recalled that sixty years had elapsed since the conclusion of the treaty. During this long period, "so many momentous political, social and commercial changes" had taken place in both countries that considering all circumstances, it was "not only desirable but also essential to the mutual interest of both parties concerned, to have the said Treaty revised and replaced by a new one to be mutually agreed upon." The Belgian Government was reminded that in its reply to the Chinese note of June 24, 1925, it had expressed its readiness to consider China's proposal for the modification of existing treaties. Article 46 of the Treaty of 1865 provided for revision at the end of ten-year intervals. Accordingly, in pursuance of the provisions of that article, the Chinese Government had the honor to inform the Belgian Government that it was the intention of the Chinese Government to have the aforesaid treaty revised "and that, therefore, upon the expiration of the present decennial period on October 27 of this year all the provisions thereof, as well as the Tariff Schedule of Imports and Exports, and the Commercial Regulations appended thereto, will thereupon be terminated, and that a new agreement will have to take the place of the old ones." The Chinese Government meanwhile, said the note in conclusion, stood ready to open negotiations for the conclusion of a new treaty which should be based on principles of equality and reciprocity.

In his reply to this note, the Belgian Minister pointed out that under the terms of Article 46, his government alone had

defeated Kuominchun forces completed their evacuation of Peking on April 15 and 16. The Chief Executive, Tuan Chi-jui, had taken refuge in the Legation Quarter. The Premier, General Chia Teh-yao, resigned April 17, and the other members of the cabinet followed suit two days later. Meanwhile a self-styled Committee of Safety composed of Wang Shih-chen and several other retired officials had undertaken to preserve order in the capital. *North China Herald*, CLIX, Apr. 24, 1926, pp. 145-6.

   [57] Text, *China Year Book, 1928*, pp. 770-71. This note as well as subsequent correspondence is printed also in *Chinese Social and Political Science Review*, Vol. XI (1927), Public Document Supplement, pp. 9 ff.

the right to call for a revision of such clauses of the treaty as stood in need of modification.[58] Nevertheless, Belgium was not disposed to insist on her exclusive rights in this regard. As soon as the political situation in China permitted it, and after the work of the Customs Conference and the Commission on Extraterritoriality had been completed, the Belgian Government would not refuse, in agreement with the Chinese Government, to discuss "a modification of the clauses of the Treaty of 1865."

The Peking Government declined to consider limited revision, and on May 22 its diplomatic representative at Brussels was instructed to inform the Belgian Ministry of Foreign Affairs that whatever might be the result of the Tariff Conference and the Commission on Extraterritoriality, the Treaty of 1865 would still cease to be applicable on October 27, and that a new treaty would have to be negotiated to take its place.[59] A few weeks later the Belgian Minister in Peking was informed that in case the proposed negotiations were not concluded before the expiration of the old treaty, the Chinese Government would examine the possibility of finding a provisional *modus vivendi* which, while safeguarding the legitimate interests of Belgium, would in no way impair the inherent rights of China.[60]

In his next note, M. de Warzee announced that since a difference of opinion existed with regard to the legal meaning of Article 46, the Belgian Government contending that it alone had the right to take the initiative in revising the treaty, the matter would be submitted to the Permanent Court of International Justice at The Hague. The Chinese Government was reminded that both China and Belgium had already accepted the obligatory competence of the Court for disputes of this nature. Before taking this step, however, the Belgian Government desired to know the basis of the proposed *modus vivendi*

[58] Le Maire de Warzee to Waichiao Pu, April 27, 1926, *China Year Book, 1928*, p. 771.
[59] Telegram, Waichiao Pu to Wang King-ky, *China Year Book, 1928*, p. 771.
[60] Tsai Ting-kan to Le Maire de Warzee, July 24, 1926, *China Year Book, 1928*, p. 772.

which the Chinese Government had suggested.[61] The Chinese Government then proposed that the period of negotiations for a new treaty should be extended six months from October 27, 1926, and that during this period the following provisional arrangements should be in force: [62]

1. The diplomatic and consular relations between the two countries to continue without interruption.
2. The principle of tariff autonomy for each country to be recognized. For the time being, however, Belgian imports into China would be required to pay only such tariff charges as were generally applied to other foreign imports.
3. The principle of territorial jurisdiction for each country to be recognized. Temporarily, however, Belgian consular officers would be permitted to continue their exercise of extraterritorial functions "with the understanding that Belgium agrees to the formal renunciation of its consular jurisdiction in China in the new treaty to be concluded."
4. The question of the Belgian Concession at Tientsin to be reserved for settlement at the time of the negotiation and conclusion of the new treaty.
5. All questions not specifically covered by the above provisions to be dealt with and adjusted on the principles of "territorial sovereignty, equality, and reciprocity" which were to be accepted as the basis for the new treaty.

While unable to accept the terms of this provisional arrangement, the Belgian Government nevertheless intimated its willingness to enter into a *modus vivendi* on the following lines: [63]

1. Most favored nation treatment to be applied as regards Belgian commerce in China, the status in China of Belgian nationals, and navigation.
2. "Reserving the right of more thorough examination, His Majesty's Government would be disposed to accept the recommendations of the Commission of Extraterritoriality, consular jurisdiction being maintained so long as the two Governments shall continue to benefit therefrom."

[61] Le Maire de Warzee to Waichiao Pu, August 4, 1926, *China Year Book, 1928,* p. 773.
[62] Waichiao Pu to Le Maire de Warzee, September 2, 1926, *ibid.,* pp. 773-4.
[63] Le Maire de Warzee to Waichiao Pu, October 23, 1926, *China Year Book, 1928,* pp. 775-6.

3. "The modus vivendi to remain in force until the conclusion of the new Treaty based on equality and respect for territorial sovereignty, as soon as the circumstances in China permit of it and as soon as the conclusions reached in the work of the Customs Conference are known."

The Belgian Government meanwhile would not exercise its right of recourse to the Permanent Court of International Justice unless it were confronted by the Chinese Government with a *fait accompli*.

The concessions which both sides were willing to make regarding the proposed interim arrangements did not serve to bring them together on common ground. Dr. Wellington Koo, who had become Minister for Foreign Affairs in August, insisted that the interim arrangements should continue in force for only a limited period after which, if a new treaty had not been concluded, the Chinese Government reserved the right to terminate not merely the existing treaty but the interim arrangements as well.[64] The Belgian Government, on the other hand, fearing to be left thus without either treaty or *modus vivendi* felt compelled to reject this proposition. October 27, when according to the Chinese contention the existing treaty was due to expire, passed without an agreement having been reached. On November 5, M. de Warzee, replying to a virtual ultimatum which had been delivered to him the day before, informed Dr. Koo that the negotiations were at an end, and that the Belgian Government intended to ask the Permanent Court of International Justice for an interpretation of Article 46 of the treaty

[64] The policy of the Peking Government did not lack for support in the provinces. As early as September 20, 1926, the Chinese General Chamber of Commerce at Shanghai had addressed a circular telegram to the chief officials in the country, both north and south. It read in part as follows: "It is self evident that unfair treaties with foreign powers have been the chief cause of our industrial and commercial depression of recent years. Were the Belgian treaty to stand without fair revision on expiration, it would be a serious infringement of China's sovereignty, to say nothing of its direct hindrance to our industrial and commercial development." *North China Herald*, CLX, Sept. 25, 1926, p. 586. In November, the Shanghai Chamber sent a second telegram to Peking strongly supporting the government's stand. A similar telegram from Marshal Sun Chuan-fang was sent at the same time. *North China Herald*, CLXI, Nov. 6, 1926, p. 243.

of 1865. M. de Warzee asked whether the Chinese Government would coöperate in fixing the terms of the *compromis* necessary for this purpose.[65] The counter-move of the Chinese Government took the form of a presidential mandate, issued November 6, announcing the abrogation of the Belgian treaty and ordering the Ministry of Foreign Affairs to begin negotiations for a new agreement on the basis of equality and mutual respect for territorial sovereignty. The local authorities were directed meanwhile to extend full and due protection to the Belgian Legation, consulates, nationals, products, and ships in China, in accordance with the rules of international law and usage.[66] Dr. Koo lost no time in transmitting to M. de Warzee

[65] Aide-Memoire, *China Year Book, 1928,* pp. 779-80.
[66] *Ibid.,* p. 782. At the same time the government issued a long statement explaining its reasons for terminating the treaty. The statement ran in part as follows:
"Ever since the establishment of the Republic, the Chinese Government have cherished the unswerving desire to place China in the family of nations on a footing of equality with the other States and enable her to contribute her part to the achievement of the ideals of humanity. This guiding principle has been steadfastly observed because it represents the fervent aspirations of the entire Chinese nation. Its realization, however, cannot be consummated so long as there is in the relations between China and the other Powers a lack of equality and mutual respect for territorial sovereignty. The 'unequal treaties' which were exacted from China nearly a century ago have established between Chinese and foreigners discriminations that are now sources of endless discontent and friction with foreign Powers. Such a state of affairs is not as it should be, since the intercourse between nations, as between individuals, finds its rational *motif* in the exchange of mutual benefits which will endure and lead to lasting friendship. In an age which has witnessed the coming into existence of the League of Nations and the birth of the 'spirit of Locarno,' there does not seem to be any valid reason to justify international relations which are not founded on equality and mutuality. . . .
"No nation mindful of its destiny and conscious of its self-respect can be fettered forever by treaties which shackle its free and natural development and which are repugnant to the best traditions of international intercourse. Fruitful sources of misunderstanding and conflict, they are in their very nature bound to come to an end sooner or later. To endeavor to preserve them in the face of radically changed conditions and against the progress of modern international thought and life is to forget history and its teachings. It is to remove the injustice and danger of such treaties that Article 19 of the Covenant of the League of Nations expressly provides for the possibility of their revision from time to time.
"The general right of revision being admitted, the right of both parties to a treaty to terminate it by notice, where it contains a definite clause for revision at stated intervals, is all the more to be recognized. It would be

a copy of this mandate together with an offer to begin immediate negotiations for the conclusion of a new treaty.[67] In a note, dated November 16, Dr. Koo explained at length why it was impossible for his government to coöperate in submitting the matter in dispute to the Permanent Court of International Justice.[68] He insisted that the fundamental point at issue between the two governments was not "the technical interpretation of Article 46," but rather "the application of the principle of equality of treatment in the relations between China and Belgium." Such a question, being definitely political in character, could not possibly be allowed to come before a judicial tribunal. The action of the Chinese Government in terminating the Belgian Treaty harmonized with the spirit of Article 19 of the Covenant of the League of Nations, which clearly recognized the fundamental principle of *rebus sic stantibus* governing treaties which had become inapplicable. Consequently, if an appeal were to be taken to an international tribunal at all, the Chinese Government preferred that it be to the Assembly of the League by virtue of Article 11 of the Covenant.[69]

Meanwhile, in accordance with the mandate of November 6, the Peking Government was preparing to assume jurisdiction over Belgians and their interests in China. The Ministry of Home Affairs was instructed to make arrangements to take over administrative control of the Belgian Concession at Tientsin.[70] Revised regulations were promulgated on November 25

neither fair nor equitable to claim that such right appertains to only one of the two parties. If, as contended by the Belgian Government, Article 46 of the Treaty of 1865 is to be construed as giving solely to the Belgian Government the right to revise the Treaty, then such a provision would in itself constitute one of the unilateral and unjust privileges against which the Chinese Government protests and which is manifestly incompatible with the spirit of a treaty based on equality and mutuality which Belgium expressed herself as being ready to conclude. . . ." *China Year Book, 1928,* pp. 766-69.
   [67] Note of November 6, 1926, *China Year Book, 1928,* pp. 781-2.
   [68] Koo to Le Maire de Warzee, *China Year Book, 1928,* pp. 784-5.
   [69] Various Chinese groups threatened to organize a nation-wide boycott of Belgian goods unless Belgium refrained from taking her case to The Hague. *North China Herald,* CLXI, Nov. 20, 1926, p. 341. *China Weekly Review,* XXXVIII, Nov. 20, 1926, p. 336.
   [70] *North China Herald,* CLXI, Nov. 27, 1926, p. 390.

governing the trial of non-extraterritorial nationals in civil and criminal cases.[71] Commissioners of Foreign Affairs in all of the provinces were directed to apply these and other similar regulations in cases involving Belgians.[72] An attempt was made at the same time to prevent the Belgian assessor from occupying the bench in the Mixed Court at Shanghai.[73] In line with the government's policy, also, a Treaty Investigation Commission was created. The Commission, of which Dr. Koo was chairman and W. W. Yen and Wang Ch'ung-hui vice-chairmen, was directed to prepare for the revision of all treaties which were soon due to expire.[74]

Since the Chinese Government had rejected the Belgian proposal for a judicial settlement of the dispute, the Belgian Government proceeded alone to bring its case before the Court of International Justice, its application being filed with the Registrar of the Court on November 25, 1926.[75] The Court was asked to give judgment to the effect that the Chinese Government was not entitled to denounce unilaterally the treaty of 1865, and to indicate, pending judgment, any provisional measures to be taken for the preservation of the rights which might subsequently be recognized as belonging to Belgium or her nationals.[76] On January 8, 1927, the President of the Court made an order continuing in force provisionally, pending the final decision of the case, certain provisions of the treaty of 1865 relating particularly to Belgian property and shipping rights, the extraterritorial rights of Belgian nationals in China, and the protection of Belgian missionaries in the interior of the country.[77]

Early in January, however, an exchange of views between Dr. Koo and the Belgian Minister at Peking disclosed the fact that both governments preferred to settle their differences

[71] Text, *Chinese Social and Political Science Review*, XI (1927), Public Document Supplement, p. 61.
[72] *North China Herald*, CLXI, Nov. 27, 1926, p. 390.
[73] *Ibid.*, Nov. 20, 1926, p. 341.
[74] *Ibid.*, Nov. 13, 1926, p. 290.
[75] *Chinese Social and Political Science Review*, XII (1928), Public Document Supplement, pp. 23-5.
[76] *Ibid.*   [77] *Ibid.*, pp. 25-7.

through diplomatic channels. As a result of these conversations, the Belgian Government decided to resume negotiations for a new treaty and at the same time to suspend the action which had been brought before the Court of International Justice.[78] Dr. Koo, on his part, no longer insisted that the proposed negotiations be concluded within six months; he merely expressed the hope that the new treaty would "be completed within a period of time as brief as possible." [79] Formal negotiations were opened, therefore, on January 17, 1927. M. de Warzee announced at the outset that his government was prepared to return to China the Belgian Concession at Tientsin, reserving only property rights.[80] Dr. Koo, expressing the thanks of the Chinese Government for this friendly gesture, suggested that a commission of experts be appointed at an early date to arrange for the transfer of the Concession.[81] Pending the conclusion of the new treaty, the Chinese Government promised to grant adequate protection to Belgian nationals, including missionaries, and to their property and vessels in accordance with the rules of international law; to apply only the conventional tariff rates then in force to merchandise imported into China from Belgium or exported from China to Belgium; and to guarantee that civil and criminal suits involving Belgians would be heard by the modern courts only, with the right of appeal and the right to have the assistance of advocates and interpreters of Belgian or other nationality, duly approved by the courts.[82]

[78] Le Maire de Warzee to Waichiao Pu, January 13, 1927, *China Year Book, 1928*, p. 785. In a communication addressed to The Hague Court on January 17, the Belgian Government asked, in effect, that the proceedings be suspended during the course of negotiations which were going forward in Peking. A second request, dated February 3, asked that the Court Order of January 8 be revoked. The Court, taking note of these communications, granted both requests on February 15. *Chinese Social and Political Science Review*, XII (1928), Public Document Supplement, pp. 28-31.

[79] Koo to Le Maire de Warzee, January 14, 1927, *China Year Book, 1928*, pp. 785-6.

[80] *North China Herald*, CLXII, Jan. 22, 1927, p. 99.

[81] *Ibid*. The *China Year Book, 1926*, p. 605, gave the population of the Belgian Concession at Tientsin as 2000 Chinese and no foreigners.

[82] *Chinese Social and Political Science Review*, XII (1928), Public Document Supplement, pp. 28-9.

Regulations to this effect were promulgated by the Peking Government on April 1, 1927.[83]

The negotiations with Belgium constituted the first real test of the new policy of the Peking Government with regard to treaty revision. Belgium was a small country which could not be expected to offer effective resistance. Within a short time, however, the same policy was applied also to treaties with France, Japan, and Spain. On March 4, 1926, the French Minister in Peking had been notified that the Chinese Government did not intend to renew the commercial conventions of 1886, 1887, and 1895 regulating trade between Tonkin and the neighboring provinces of China.[84] The Chinese Minister in Paris was instructed at the same time to inform the French Foreign Office that on August 7, 1926, when the treaties were due to expire, the Chinese Government would terminate arrangements which had been made for reduced tariff rates on goods crossing the frontier between China and Tonkin.[85]

Early in August the French Minister proposed that the drafting of a new commercial agreement be deferred for a year to allow consideration to be given to the conclusions of the Peking Tariff Conference.[86] The Acting Minister for Foreign Affairs, Admiral Ts'ai T'ing-kan, rejected this suggestion and on August 6 notified the Commissioners of Foreign Affairs in all provinces that the conventions of 1886, 1887, and 1895 had become null

[83] *China Year Book, 1928,* p. 786.
[84] *North China Herald,* CLX, Aug. 14, 1926, p. 290. For the French and Chinese texts of these treaties, see Maritime Customs *Treaties,* etc., *op. cit.,* Vol. I, pp. 913, 925, 937. Article XVIII of the Convention of April 25, 1886, provided that "The present stipulations may be, according to the terms of Article 8 of the Treaty of June 9, 1885, revised ten years after the exchange of ratifications." The article referred to read as follows: "The commercial provisions of the present Treaty and the regulations supplementary thereto may be revised at the end of ten-year intervals, beginning from the date on which ratifications of the present Treaty are exchanged. But in case neither of the High Contracting Parties, six months before the end of such a period, indicates its desire to proceed with a revision, the commercial provisions shall remain in force for a new period of ten years and so on from ten-year period to ten-year period." *Ibid.,* Vol. I, p. 905.
[85] *North China Herald,* CLX, Aug. 14, 1926, p. 290.
[86] *China Weekly Review,* XXXVII, Aug. 14, 1926, p. 283.

and void.[87] In a note of September 2 addressed to the Chinese Legation in Paris, the French Minister for Foreign Affairs protested that the treaties of 1885 and 1886 did not authorize the Chinese Government to denounce the three commercial agreements, but only to ask for their revision. In the opinion of the French Government, the conventions in question would remain fully in force until the desired revision had been effected by mutual agreement.[88] Nevertheless, France was willing to enter into negotiations under certain conditions, the details of which were communicated by the French Minister to the Waichiao Pu on November 5. The Chinese Government having accepted these conditions, the chief among them being that the conventions of 1886, 1887, and 1895 were to remain in force pending the conclusion of a new agreement, negotiations began toward the end of the year which continued until the Nationalist capture of Peking.[89]

The ten-year period following which the Japanese Commercial Treaty of July 21, 1896, might be revised, was due to expire October 20, 1926. On that day, therefore, the Chinese Government notified the Japanese Minister in Peking of its desire, in accordance with Article 26 of that treaty, to have fundamental changes made not only in the Treaty of Commerce and Navigation of 1896, but also in the Protocol of October 19, 1896, the Supplementary Treaty of October 9, 1903, and the Annexes thereto.[90] The Chinese note recalled that thirty years

[87] *North China Herald*, CLX, Aug. 7, 1926, p. 242. The Treaty of Tientsin, dated June 9, 1885, remained in full force. The three conventions which the Peking Government attempted to terminate were merely supplementary to this treaty.
[88] Cosmé, French Chargé d'Affaires in Peking to C. T. Wang, September 10, 1928, *China Year Book, 1929-30*, pp. 830-31.
[89] *Ibid.*
[90] Koo to Yoshizawa, *China Year Book, 1928*, pp. 786-7. The wording of Article 26 of the Treaty of 1896 seemed to afford a peculiar advantage to Japan. The Article read as follows: "It is agreed that either of the High Contracting Parties may demand a revision of the Tariffs and of the Commercial Articles of this Treaty at the end of ten years from the date of the exchange of the ratifications; but if no such demand be made on either side *and no such revision be effected*, within six months after the end of the first ten years, then the Treaty and Tariffs, in their present form, shall remain in force for ten years more, reckoned from the end of the preceding ten years,

had elapsed since the conclusion of the Treaty of 1896. During
this long period there had been many economic, commercial,
and social changes in both countries. Consequently, to continue
to regulate the relations between two countries on the basis
of "such an antiquated treaty" would obviously be unsuitable
and give rise to many difficulties. Therefore the Chinese Government desired not to continue the aforesaid treaties in their
existing form, but wished to have steps taken immediately "to
effect their fundamental revision" with a view to promoting the
common interests of the two countries. The Chinese Government hoped the necessary revision could be effected within the
six-month period as provided in Article 26 of the treaty. If,
however, on the expiration of that period no new treaty had
been completed, the Chinese Government would be "confronted
with the necessity of determining and declaring its attitude
vis-a-vis the existing Treaties." All rights in this regard were
therefore reserved.

In spite of China's implied threat to denounce the treaty of
1896 in case a new agreement were not completed within six
months, the Japanese reply was distinctly moderate in tone.[91]
The Japanese Government was happy to enter into negotiations
for a revision of the treaty. However, the note of the Waichiao
Pu gave rise to the presumption that what was now contemplated was a fundamental revision not only of the "tariffs and
the commercial articles" of the treaty, but also of "the entire
Treaties and Notes in question." No such comprehensive revision was contemplated or sanctioned in any of the existing
stipulations between Japan and China. Nevertheless, the Japanese Government had no intention of limiting the scope of the
forthcoming negotiations to the questions defined in Article
26 of the Treaty of 1896. Sympathetic consideration would be
given to the wishes of the Chinese Government for a more
extensive revision of treaty provisions and it was hoped that

and so it shall be at the end of each successive period of ten years." Mac-
Murray, *op. cit.*, Vol. I, p. 73.

[91] Memorandum, Japanese Legation to Waichiao Pu, November 10, 1926,
China Year Book, 1928, pp. 787-8.

the same sense of moderation would mark China's action. In conclusion, the Japanese memorandum recalled the passage in Dr. Koo's note reserving to the Chinese Government the right to declare its attitude with regard to the existing treaties in case a new agreement were not concluded within the specified period. The Japanese Government considered that this reservation did not seem "to be entirely in line with the spirit of mutual confidence and helpfulness" which alone could "ensure the success of the proposed negotiations." In any case, the Japanese Government felt it due in frankness to state that their acceptance of the proposal for a revision of treaties between China and Japan was not to be construed "as an acquiescence in any rights asserted in the Waichiao Pu's communication."

Negotiations for the conclusion of the new treaty began at Peking on January 21, 1927. The Chinese plenipotentiary was the Foreign Minister, Dr. Koo, while Japan was represented by her Minister, Mr. Kenkichi Yoshizawa. The tentative proposals advanced by Dr. Koo concerned only general principles, and did not deal specifically with the concessions, extraterritoriality, or tariff autonomy.[92] Several months were spent in discussing the scope of the most favored nation clause. The negotiations were still far from completion on April 20, 1927, when the Treaty of 1896 was due to expire. Instead of following the precedent established in the case of the Belgian agreement, however, the Chinese Government consented to continue the old treaty in force for a period of three months to permit further negotiation.[93] Subsequently it became necessary to extend the treaty for additional periods of three months, the last beginning April 20, 1928.[94]

[92] *North China Herald*, CLXII, Feb. 12, 1927, p. 224. *Ibid.*, CLXII, Mar. 19, 1927, p. 448.
[93] *North China Herald*, CLXIII, Apr. 30, 1927, p. 198.
[94] *Ibid.*, CLXVII, Apr. 28, 1928, p. 136. During the course of these negotiations, numerous rumors were afloat concerning demands which the Japanese Government was alleged to have made on Marshal Chang Tso-lin. The demands concerned contracts to Japanese for the construction of additional railways in Manchuria, Japanese rights to own land in the interior of Manchuria, and the establishment of an additional Japanese consulate close to the Korean border. *Japan Weekly Chronicle*, July 28, 1927, p. 87. See also *China Weekly Review*, XLII, Sept. 24, 1927, p. 88. These rumors gave rise

The desire of the Chinese Government to revise the Treaty of October 10, 1864, with Spain was communicated to the Spanish Minister in Peking on November 10, 1926.[95] The

to a considerable amount of anti-Japanese agitation, particularly among the Chinese of Manchuria. *China Weekly Review*, XLII, Sept. 17, 1927, p. 76. The Chinese were alarmed also by reports that American bankers were preparing to make a loan of $40,000,000 to the Japanese owned South Manchuria Railway Company. *China Weekly Review*, XLIII, Dec. 3, 1927, pp. 1-2, 5-6. *North China Herald*, CLXV, Dec. 10, 1927, p. 436. At the same time, a loan was to be made by the Japanese to Chang Tso-lin in return for preferential rights in Manchuria. The loan negotiations in Peking were apparently in the hands, not of the Waichiao Pu, but of Marshal Chang's chief of staff, General Yang Yu-ting. On November 29, however, General Yang stated to a group of foreign newspaper correspondents that the proposed American loan to the South Manchuria Railway Company would constitute a great provocation to the Chinese Government and people. Furthermore, said General Yang, the Chinese Government was opposed to the construction of certain railways in Manchuria desired by Japan and by the South Manchuria Railway Company. *China Weekly Review*, XLIII, Dec. 10, 1927, pp. 32-3. The next day the Japanese Minister, Mr. Yoshizawa, expressed pained surprise at General Yang's statements which, he said, were very detrimental to relations existing between Japan and China with regard to Manchuria. *Ibid.*

In this connection, the following item appearing in the English supplement of the *Osaka Mainichi* for Nov. 20, 1931, is illuminating but hardly conclusive:

"A secret agreement was concluded between Mr. Yamamoto, former Governor of the South Manchuria Railway Company, and the late Marshal Chang Tso-lin, at Peking in May, 1928, as regards the construction of railways in Manchuria and Mongolia. As a result, a contract to build the Kirin-Huining and Changchun-Talai Lines was given to Japan with the understanding that the construction be commenced before May, 1929. Due to the sudden death of Marshal Chang, however, nothing has come of this contract so far. It is also reported that provisional contracts were also concluded as regards the construction of three railways, the Kirin-Wuchang, the Taonan-Tsoling, and the Yenki-Hailin Lines at the time of the Peking negotiations, but nothing is known for certain as the documents . . . have not been published."

If actually concluded, these agreements were signed apparently at a time when the victorious Nationalist armies were almost at the very gates of Peking. And if secret, the agreements constitute an obvious violation of the resolution adopted at the Washington Conference on February 1, 1922, requiring publicity for any and all such contracts.

[95] Official statement of the Chinese Government, November 10, 1927, *China Year Book, 1928*, p. 1402. The revision article of this treaty was less definitely one sided than in the case of either the Belgian or the Japanese treaty. Following the model of the British Treaty in 1856, it provided (Article XXIII) that "Either of the two High Contracting Parties may at the end of ten years ask for a revision of the Tariff or the Commercial Articles of this Treaty, with the understanding that if such request be not made within six months, reckoned after the first ten years, the said tariff will continue to be in force for ten years longer, reckoned in addition to the preceding ten years, and so on every ten years." *Maritime Customs Treaties*, etc., *op. cit.*, Vol. II, p. 382.

Spanish Government expressed its willingness to proceed with a revision of the treaty, but insisted that such revision should be restricted in accordance with Article 23, to the tariff and the commercial articles only. Unwilling to agree to any limitation on the scope of the proposed negotiations, the Chinese Government held that the treaty in its entirety should be terminated and replaced by a new agreement. The negotiations which began on August 8, 1927, were deadlocked almost from the beginning. On November 10, therefore, the Generalissimo issued a mandate announcing the abrogation of the Spanish treaty and directing the Ministry for Foreign Affairs to conclude a new one on the basis of equality and mutual respect for territorial sovereignty. All local officials were ordered meanwhile to extend full protection, in accordance with the rules of international law and usage, to the Spanish Legation, consulates, and the persons and property of Spanish nationals in China.[95a]

The Spanish Minister, Don Justo Garrido y Cisneros, entered an immediate protest against the unilateral denunciation of the treaty.[96] In a second note, dated November 17, M. Garrido announced that his government considered China's action in terminating the treaty

[95a] *China Year Book, 1928*, p. 1402. The Nationalist Government at Nanking likewise on Nov. 24, 1927, informed the Spanish Minister that it considered the treaty of 1864 to be null and void. On December 2, 1927, the Nanking Government issued the following regulations which were to apply pending the negotiation of a new Sino-Spanish Treaty: Diplomatic and consular representatives of Spain to receive treatment accorded to such officials by the general rules of international law; persons and property of Spanish subjects in China to receive protection according to Chinese law; Spanish subjects in China to be amenable to Chinese law and subject to the jurisdiction of Chinese courts; civil and criminal actions involving Spanish subjects to be dealt with according to the procedure governing nationals of non-treaty countries; imports into China from Spain and exports from China to Spain to be subject to the customs tariff as applied to non-treaty countries and their nationals; Spanish subjects in China to be required to pay such taxes and dues as were paid by Chinese citizens; all matters not specifically covered by the foregoing regulations to be dealt with in accordance with the general rules of international law and Chinese law. *China Year Book, 1929-30*, pp. 854-5.

[96] Spanish Legation to Waichiao Pu, November 14, 1927, *China Year Book, 1928*, pp. 1403-4.

"as lacking in friendship towards Spain not only in view of the consideration shown to the Chinese Republic during the civil war, but also having regard to the conciliatory policy of Spain in agreeing that the new negotiations begun last August should be conducted in accordance with the principles desired by the Peking Government and having declared that Spain would renounce the Capitulations when the state of peace and order in China should permit, thus uniting her voice to that of the Nations which have important interests in this Republic." [97]

The Chinese Government was reminded that its Minister for Foreign Affairs, Mr. Wang Yin-tai [98] had promised that pending the signature of the new Sino-Spanish Treaty there would be granted to Spain the same advantages and favorable treatment that were accorded to other nations with which China was then negotiating treaties. In its reply to this protest, the Wai-chiao Pu denied that any such promise had been made and asserted also that the government's action had been inspired entirely by a conviction that the termination of the treaty "could only strengthen the bonds of friendship between the two countries and redound to the common interests of China and Spain." [99] The Spanish Minister declined thereafter to enter into any negotiations with the Peking Government for the conclusion of a new agreement. [100]

Its preoccupation with the question of treaty revision did not prevent the Peking Government from considering the British proposals of January 27, 1927. One of those proposals suggested the willingness of the British Government to effect certain modifications in the administration of its concessions in China. Dr. Koo immediately took up with the British Minister, Sir Miles Lampson, the question of the British Concession at

[97] Garrido to Waichiao Pu, *China Year Book, 1928,* p. 1404.
[98] In June, 1927, Mr. Wang replaced Wellington Koo as head of the Foreign Office.
[99] In addition to denouncing the treaties with Belgium, France, and Spain, the Peking Government also, in October, 1927, issued new regulations prescribing the conditions under which foreign merchants might reside and carry on trade in the interior of the country. These regulations were somewhat more strict than those previously in force. Summary, *China Weekly Review,* XLII, Oct. 29, 1927, p. 11.
[100] *North China Herald,* CLXVI, Jan. 14, 1928, p. 43.

Tientsin,[101] meanwhile reserving China's rights with regard to a more comprehensive revision of the treaties.[102] Subsequently a joint commission was created which drafted an agreement concerning the Tientsin concessions similar to that concluded by Mr. Chen and Mr. O'Malley with regard to the Concession at Hankow. After being initialed on April 22, 1927, this agreement was referred for approval to the Peking and the British Governments.[103]

In the spring of 1928, all negotiations between the powers and the Peking Government came to an end. The final campaign of the Nationalists against the northern coalition began in April. Chang Tso-lin was compelled to withdraw from the capital on June 3. Two days later the first of the Nationalist forces entered the city. One consequence of the successful conclusion of the northern campaign was that for the first time in a decade, all China except for Manchuria was nominally under the control of a single government. Another consequence, no less significant, was the decision of the Nationalist Government to establish the national capital not at Peking but at Nanking. Peking, meaning "Northern Capital," was renamed Peiping, or "Northern Peace." Aside from the fact that during his lifetime Dr. Sun Yat-sen had often expressed the wish to have the capital located at Nanking, there were weighty political reasons for the change. In many Chinese minds, Peking, intimately associated with the obnoxious treaty régime which the Nationalists were determined to abolish, still represented the worst features of the old diplomatic tradition. At Nanking, far removed from this reactionary atmosphere, a fresh start could be made. Moreover, the transfer would automatically render in-

[101] On January 12, 1927, two weeks before receiving the proposals of Great Britain, the Peking Government sent representatives to call at certain legations with the suggestion that the Foreign Concessions at Tientsin be restored to Chinese control. *North China Herald,* CLXII, Jan. 15, 1927, p. 53. This action was obviously inspired by the Nationalist seizure of the British Concessions at Hankow and Kiukiang.

[102] *North China Herald,* CLXII, Mar. 19, 1927, p. 448.

[103] *Ibid.,* CLXIII, Apr. 30, 1927, p. 196. *Ibid.,* CLXIII, June 11, 1927, p. 453, *Parliamentary Debates,* 5th Series, Vol. 205, p. 1264.

effectual the most humiliating provisions of the Boxer Protocol which permitted the foreign powers to maintain in the Chinese capital a fortified legation quarter garrisoned with foreign troops. Finally, the establishment of the capital at Nanking promised to facilitate individual negotiations between China and the powers. At Nanking there would be no diplomatic corps to offer collective resistance to requests for treaty modification. One by one the foreign diplomats would have to come to Nanking to negotiate, and their coming might even stimulate recollections of a certain famous journey to Canossa.[104]

[104] Cf. *China Weekly Review*, XLV, June 30, 1928, pp. 174-5.

Chapter X

TARIFF AUTONOMY

THE attack upon the foreigners at Nanking in March, 1927, had two results. The first of these, already noted, was a marked change in the attitude of the foreign powers toward the Nationalists. The second was an open split in the Kuomintang. For some time there had been friction and dissension within the party. General Chiang Kai-shek resented the steadily mounting influence of the communists led by Michael Borodin. The left wing elements within the Kuomintang, however, coöperating with the communists, accused General Chiang of cherishing Napoleonic ambitions. The Nanking Incident brought matters definitely to a head. General Chiang was convinced that the disorders had been deliberately planned by his enemies, first in order to prevent his triumphal entry into the old Ming capital, and second in order to embroil him with the foreign powers.

General Chiang's fear that the communists were bent on accomplishing his downfall was strengthened when, on April 7, 1927, the Hankow Government published a mandate abolishing the post of Generalissimo of the Nationalist armies, a position which he had held since the beginning of the anti-Northern campaign, and appointing him instead Commander-in-Chief of only the first Nationalist Army Group which was to attack from the Shanghai-Nanking area northward along the Tientsin-Pukow Railway toward Peking. The same mandate appointed Marshal Feng Yü-hsiang Commander-in-Chief of the Second Army Group which was to move northward along the Peking-Hankow line.[1] A second mandate, issued on April 9, announced that the seat of the Nationalist Government would be

[1] Chapman, *The Chinese Revolution, 1926-27*, p. 109.

removed forthwith from Hankow to Nanking. The obvious
purpose of this change was to insure that in directing military
operations from Shanghai, General Chiang would be under the
control of the civil authority of the government.[2]

Not content with these measures, the radicals at Hankow
sought to cause General Chang further embarrassment by stirring up trouble among the labor unions of Shanghai. Early in
April General Chiang struck back at his enemies by ordering
the arrest of all communists and labor agitators first at Shanghai
and then at Canton.[3] On April 15, also, he took further steps
to protect his position by establishing at Nanking a Nationalist
Government rivaling that at Hankow. The Hankow faction re-
taliated by dismissing Chiang from all official posts and expell-
ing him from the Kuomintang.[4] Thereafter for a period of
several months there were two governments in China, each
claiming to represent the Nationalist cause.

Dr. C. C. Wu, the son of Sun Yat-sen's old friend Wu Ting-
fang, consented to serve as Minister for Foreign Affairs in the
newly founded Nanking Government. On assuming office he
announced that the policy of his government would be to continue the fight against the unequal treaties and to secure for
China an equal status in the family of nations. The treaties in
question, he declared, seriously impeded the development of the
country and at the same time failed to accomplish their supposed object of protecting foreign interests and foreign trade.
The powers were invited, therefore, to begin immediate negotiations for the conclusion of new treaties, especially since the
Chinese people, "irrespective of geographical situation and
political creed," were all united in "demanding international
justice and fair play." Meanwhile the Nationalist Government
would do all in its power to protect foreign life and property,
for the objection of the Chinese was not to the foreigner

[2] *Ibid.,* p. 109.
[3] *North China Herald,* CLXIII, Apr. 9, 1927, pp. 51-2; *Ibid.,* Apr. 16,
1927, pp. 102-4. *China Year Book, 1928,* pp. 1004-9.
[4] Chapman, *op. cit.,* pp. 109-11. *North China Herald,* CLXIII, April 23,
1927, pp. 142-4.

individually, but only to the system under which the foreigner lived.[5]

The foreign powers, however, in view of the fact that the Nanking incident still awaited a satisfactory settlement, showed no inclination to begin negotiations. To pave the way for such a settlement, Dr. Wu in June ordered the immediate evacuation of foreign properties illegally occupied by Nationalist troops.[6] A second proclamation issued by the Nanking Government on July 7 announced that since it was not the policy of the government to create enmity between Chinese and foreigners, it was consequently undesirable that there should be actions tending "to strain the friendly relations existing now between the Nationalist Government and the Powers." All concerned were therefore warned "not to fire on foreign gunboats or merchant-men, not to interfere with or molest foreigners, and not to endanger the lives and properties of foreign residents." Orders were issued at the same time forbidding any interference with the work of missionaries.[7]

Aside from the failure of the new Nationalist Government to make amends for the loss of foreign lives and the destruction of foreign property at Nanking, another influence tending to delay the establishment of formal relations between the powers and that government was its attitude relative to the

[5] *North China Herald*, CLXIII, May 21, 1927, p. 317.
[6] *Ibid.*, June 18, 1927, p. 497.
[7] *Ibid.*, CLXIV, July 9, 1927, p. 48. This proclamation was issued after the Japanese Government, in anticipation of the Nationalist advance north-ward, had sent troops into Shantung for the protection of Japanese and their interests at Tsingtao and Tsinanfu. Both the Nanking and the Hankow Governments protested formally against the sending of these troops. *China Weekly Review*, XLI, June 4, 1927, pp. 4, 20. *Ibid.*, June 18, 1927, p. 54. At this time, also, the Peking Government protested that the landing of eighteen hundred American marines at Tientsin violated the stipulations of the Washington resolution relative to the stationing of foreign troops in China. *Ibid.*, June 25, 1927, p. 94. Japan's action in sending troops to Shantung provoked a revival of the anti-Japanese boycott in the Yangtse Valley and southern China. *Ibid.*, July 2, 1927, p. 110. July, however, saw the collapse of Nanking's offensive against Shantung, and in September the Japanese Government decided to withdraw its forces except for a small detachment which was to remain at Tsingtao. *Ibid.*, XLII, September 3, 1927, p. 22.

conventional tariff. On July 20, 1927, the Nanking Government published a formal declaration announcing that since the customs tariff contained in the unequal treaties was incompatible with the nation's sovereignty, customs autonomy would be proclaimed on September 1 "as an initial measure towards securing an equal status in the family of nations." [8] Three laws were promulgated at the same time which were likewise to become effective September 1. The first of these was the Provisional Law on National Import Tariff.[9] It provided that in addition to the existing five per cent duty on imports, there should be collected a further duty of seven and one-half per cent on ordinary goods, fifteen or twenty-five per cent on luxuries depending on classification, and fifty-seven and one-half per cent on alcoholic liquors and tobacco products. The second law, applying to the six provinces of Kiangsu, Anhwei, Chêkiang, Fukien, Kwangtung, and Kwangsi, ordered the entire abolition of *likin* and other internal transit charges, together with the duties on coastwise trade and on goods shipped from one Chinese port to another.[10] The third law provided for excise duties on all articles manufactured in China, the rates in each case corresponding to the increased import duty on similar articles admitted into the country.[11]

The Nanking authorities had expected that the promised abandonment of the *likin* system would serve to enlist foreign support behind the new tariff law. The state of affairs at Nanking, however, made it seem extremely unlikely that this re-

[8] Text, *China Year Book, 1928,* pp. 1067-69.
[9] Text, *ibid.,* pp. 1069, 1070-72.
[10] Text, *ibid.,* pp. 1069-70.
[11] Regulations, *ibid.,* pp. 1066-67. In its frantic search for additional sources of revenue, the Nanking Government also, on July 11, announced an increase of fifty per cent in existing customs tonnage dues, which had hitherto been collected by the Customs administration. The foreign powers protested, and in August most of the consulates in Shanghai received authority from their governments to accept tonnage dues at the old rates, the money so collected being held in trust for the Chinese Government until such time as the order of July 11 had been rescinded or new treaties on the subject signed. Ships were permitted to clear on consular clearances. *China Year Book, 1928,* p. 710. See also *North China Herald,* CLXIV, August 6, 1927, p. 224; *ibid.,* August 20, 1927, p. 315.

form would actually be carried out. The government was shaken by the resignation on August 12, of the Commander-in-Chief, Chiang Kai-shek. The retirement at the same time of a small but influential group of elder statesmen who had been associated with General Chiang weakened the government still further.[12] A week after these defections, the very existence of the Nanking Government was menaced by military reverses in northern Kiangsu. A northern army commanded by Sun Chuan-fang first captured Pukow and then, on August 17, commenced a bombardment of Hsiakuan, the port of Nanking.[13]

The likelihood that the Nanking Government would not long survive civilian defections and military reverses furnished the powers with a pretext for opposing the enforcement of the new tariff law. The Japanese Minister, Mr. Yoshizawa, paying a visit to Nanking on August 8, had already informed both General Chiang and Dr. Wu that the collection of the new duties would not be permitted.[14] The other powers also let it be known that they would resist the enforcement of the new law.[15] This combination of circumstances forced the Nanking Government to announce that while its decision with regard

[12] *North China Herald*, CLXIV, Aug. 20, 1927, p. 311.

[13] On September 1, the day on which the new tariff was to become effective, the Nationalists were engaged in a desperate struggle to prevent Sun Chuan-fang's armies from crossing the Yangtse. This attack was repulsed and within a week Marshal Sun's forces were retreating in the direction of the Shantung border.

[14] *China Weekly Review*, XLI, Aug. 13, 1927, p. 290. In Shanghai, Mr. Yoshizawa announced that if the Nanking Government attempted to enforce tariff autonomy on September 1, Japan would be compelled to take "some adequate counter measures."

[15] *North China Herald*, CLXIV, Sept. 3, 1927, p. 397. Test cases were brought by foreign importers in the British Supreme Court in Shanghai, the American Court for China, and the Japanese Consular Court. The British judge held that the shipper was bound to pay only the conventional five per cent duty with the addition of the Washington surtaxes. *North China Herald*, CLXIV, Sept. 3, 1927, p. 419. The American commissioner, standing on somewhat firmer ground, expressed the opinion that while the proposed sur-taxes probably violated existing treaties, the question involved was a political one which could only be handled by the executive branch of the government. Thus the case was dismissed for lack of jurisdiction. *Ibid.*, p. 420, *Ibid.*, CLXV, Oct. 1, 1927, p. 28. The Japanese Court ruled that the shipper was required to pay only the five per cent duty provided for in existing treaties, not the Washington surtaxes, and certainly not the proposed addi-tional surtaxes. *China Year Book, 1928*, p. 1075.

to the enforcement of tariff autonomy as from September 1 remained unchanged, internal conditions in the country made it necessary to suspend temporarily the enforcement of the three fiscal laws.[16]

Disunity within the ranks of the Nationalists had been responsible in part for the failure of the attempt to enforce tariff autonomy. Nationalist China could hardly presume to address the powers with a single voice as long as separate governments existed at Nanking and Hankow, each claiming to represent the tradition of Sun Yat-sen. Even more important was the fact that prevailing disunity within the party seemed likely to result in the total failure of the campaign against the northern militarists. In the summer of 1927, separate armies, directed from Nanking and Hankow, launched attacks against the Northerners. After advancing as far as Shuntung, General Chiang's forces were beaten back until a forced retreat to the Yangtse became necessary. Equally unsuccessful in their campaign were the armies directed from Hankow. The Nationalists had planned originally to capture Peking during 1927. By August it had become apparent that if this plan were ever to be carried out, the differences which separated Nanking from Hankow would have to be composed. At first both factions showed a disposition to settle such differences by force of arms. Later, however, wiser counsels prevailed, and negotiations began for the reunification of the party. The way was already paved for a peaceful settlement by the fact that Borodin, aware that his support was crumbling, had decided in July to return to Russia, his example being followed by other Russians who had served as advisers to Hankow officials. Chiang Kai-shek remained as the only obstacle in the way of a united party, and in August he resigned his military command and went into retirement.[17] Thus in September it was possible, in consequence of numerous party conferences, to organize at Nanking a new government which was more widely representative of Kuomintang sentiment

[16] Proclamation of September 1, 1927, signed by Dr. C. C. Wu, text, *China Year Book, 1928*, p. 1076.
[17] *North China Herald*, CLXIV, Aug. 20, 1927, p. 311.

than had been the case with either the old Nanking Government or the now defunct government at Hankow.[18]

The new Nationalist Government, although composed for the most part of moderates and conservatives, still demanded the outright cancellation of the unequal treaties.[19] That fact alone was sufficient to cause the powers to continue to hold aloof. Actually, however, the time was not yet ripe for diplomatic negotiations. The new government really existed only as a skeleton organization. More than that, there were still many wounds in the body of the Kuomintang which remained to be healed. Internal readjustment being the prime necessity, questions of foreign policy had perforce to be neglected for the time being.

Ultimately a series of developments paved the way for the establishment of relations between the Nanking Government and the Treaty Powers. The first of these was the severance of relations between Nationalist China and Soviet Russia. On December 11, 1927, a group of labor agitators, radically inclined peasants, and communists, suddenly seized control of the city of Canton. Within two days the uprising was suppressed by loyal Nationalist troops, but not without bloody reprisals and much destruction of property.[20] Believing that certain members of the staff attached to the Russian consulate at Canton had been

---

[18] *Ibid.*, Sept. 24, 1927, p. 513.

[19] See the declaration of policy issued September 24, 1927. Part II of the declaration announced that it was the intention of the government "to abrogate completely all unequal treaties, restoring to us thereby our national sovereignty and our rightful position in the family of nations. In the past 80 odd years our country has been held in bondage by successive impositions of unequal treaties dictated by the Imperialists. The terror of militarism, the corruption of the mandarinate, the bankruptcy of our national finance, the resulting poverty of our people, the loss of our sovereignty, and the injustice suffered by our nationals abroad may all be traced to the unequal treaties. It is for this reason that in his last will our late leader [Dr. Sun] specifically instructed us to effect the abolition of unequal treaties within the shortest possible period, as the chief purpose of the Nationalist Revolution is to secure freedom and equality for China. This Government, therefore, pledges itself to labor unceasingly for the complete abrogation of all unequal treaties, restoring to China her sovereign status." *North China Herald*, CLXV, Oct. 1, 1927, p. 1.

[20] *North China Herald*, CLXV, Dec. 17, 1927, pp. 473-4

directly involved in the insurrection, the Nanking Government resolved upon drastic action. A mandate dated December 14 ordered the withdrawal of recognition from Consuls of the Soviet Union stationed in territory under Nationalist control. The Consuls concerned, with their staffs, were given one week in which to leave the country. The expulsion order applied also to officials and employees of the Dalbank, the Russian Mercantile Fleet, and all Russian trading agencies.[21] At Canton, Hankow, and other places, Chinese communists were hunted down and ruthlessly exterminated. Having turned her back upon Soviet Russia, Nationalist China began to look to the capitalist countries of the West for inspiration and some degree of moral support.

A second influence hastening the rapprochement between Nanking and the powers was the reorganization of the government on foundations that promised to be lasting. General Chiang Kai-shek, who had chosen Japan as his place of exile, returned to China in November, 1927. A month later party conferences resulted in his reëlection as Commander-in-Chief of the Nationalist armies. In these conferences, efforts were made to conciliate all factions within the party, including the radical Left Wing. But the communist *coup d'état* at Canton revealed the danger of flirting with the radicals, and as a result the Left Wing leader, Mr. Wang Ching-wei was forced to seek refuge abroad. With the party thus purged of all questionable elements, a reconstituted government was set up in February, 1928, consisting of a full list of cabinet members and a government council standing at the head of the entire system.[22]

The Minister of Foreign Affairs in the new government,

[21] *Ibid.*, Dec. 17, 1927, p. 485. *China Weekly Review*, XLIII, Dec. 24, 1927, pp. 90-94. Dr. C. C. Wu in a conversation with foreign newspaper correspondents on December 18 indicated, however, that the action of the Nationalist Government was not to be interpreted as a "break in political and commercial relations" between China and Soviet Russia. China, he said, would be glad if some arrangement could be made whereby trade relations could be continued without the "evil influences" which had previously hampered friendly relations between the two countries.
[22] *China Year Book*, 1929-30, pp. 1172-3.

General Huang Fu,[23] addressed himself immediately to the work of reëstablishing relations with the powers. The keynote of his policy was moderation. Little was said now about abrogating unequal treaties and more about negotiating for their cancellation or revision. Pending the conclusion of new agreements, moreover, the government was prepared to maintain and develop friendly relations with the foreign powers with a view to removing all sources of difficulty and misunderstanding between Chinese and foreigners.[24] Quite as important as General Huang's conciliatory attitude was the statement of the Minister of Finance, Mr. T. V. Soong, that the foreign personnel of the Salt Inspectorate would be restored to their positions, and that the Ministry of Finance would assume responsibility for the payment of loans secured on the salt revenues.[25]

Late in February the American Minister, Mr. MacMurray, visited Shanghai ostensibly in the course of an inspection tour of the Yangtse Valley. He remained in the city long enough to have an informal conference on February 26 with General Huang. The conference revealed the fact that both governments were genuinely anxious for a settlement of the Nanking dispute. Several days later, Mr. MacMurray departed for Hankow, leaving the American Consul-General, Mr. Edwin S. Cunningham, to explore the possibilities of a settlement with a repre-

[23] Dr. C. C. Wu had resigned on December 28, pleading that internal dissensions made it impossible for him to continue in office. Mr. Sun Fo followed suit by resigning from the Ministry of Finance. They and their followers announced that they would go abroad for the time being. Before leaving Shanghai, in January, Dr. Wu stated that while his mission was unofficial, he intended with other members of his party to visit various capitals in the West for the purpose of conveying the greetings of the Nationalist Government and thereby laying foundations for the negotiation of commercial treaties based on principles of equality and reciprocity. It was also his intention to study political conditions in India, Asia Minor, Turkey, and Egypt. *North China Herald*, CLXVI, Jan. 28, 1928, p. 125. *China Weekly Review*, XLIII, Feb. 4, 1928, p. 242.
[24] See General Huang's press statements, *North China Herald*, CLXVI, Feb. 25, 1928, p. 291. *Ibid.*, Mar. 10, 1928, p. 377. In January Chiang Kai-shek had declared that "the abrogation of all unequal treaties shall, whenever possible, be achieved by peaceful negotiations, though in an uncompromising spirit." *China Weekly Review*, XLIII, Jan. 28, 1928, p. 222.
[25] *North China Herald*, CLXVI, Feb. 25, 1928, p. 289.

sentative of the Nanking Foreign Office.[26] Meanwhile negotiations were likewise proceeding between General Huang and the British Minister, Sir Miles Lampson, who had also come to Shanghai in the course of a periodical inspection trip.

During these negotiations, both the British and the American representatives asked that the foreigners who had suffered at Nanking be compensated for their losses, that an official apology be made, and that those responsible for the outrages be punished. As an earnest of its good faith, the Nanking Government on March 16 issued a mandate announcing that nineteen soldiers who had been implicated in the Nanking disorders had been executed in addition to thirty-two other "local desperados," and also that orders had been issued for the arrest of Lin Tsu-han, Director of the Political Department of the Army, who had been principally responsible for the incident. A second mandate published at the same time ordered full protection to be given to foreigners and their property.[27] General Huang asked, on the other hand, that the American and British Governments express regret for the naval bombardment of Nanking, and also that the two governments announce their intention of dealing immediately with the question of treaty revision. Sir Miles Lampson declined to admit the responsibility of his government for the naval bombardment, and it was on this rock that the British negotiations foundered.[28]

The American negotiations proceeded more smoothly and when Mr. MacMurray returned late in March from his trip up the Yangtse, he found that substantial agreement had been reached with regard to all points at issue. On March 30, therefore, the Nanking Incident, so far as the United States was concerned, was finally liquidated by means of three notes exchanged between General Huang Fu and the American Minis-

[26] *Ibid.,* CLXVII, Apr. 7, 1928, p. 2. *Ibid.,* CLXVI, Mar. 10, 1928, p. 377.
[27] Texts of the mandates, *North China Herald,* CLXVI, Mar. 24, 1928, p. 466.
[28] *North China Herald,* CLXVI, Mar. 31, 1928, p. 511.

ter.[29] The Nationalist Government expressed its "profound regret" at the indignities to the American flag and to official representatives of the American Government, the loss of property sustained by the American consulate, and the personal injuries and material damages done to American residents at Nanking. Although it had been found that the incident "was entirely instigated by the communists prior to the establishment of the Nationalist Government at Nanking," that government nevertheless accepted responsibility therefor. The troops of the particular division which took part in the unfortunate incident had been disbanded, and the Nationalist Government had in addition taken effective steps for the punishment of the soldiers and other persons implicated. The Nationalist Government undertook to make compensation for all personal injuries and material damages done to the American Consulate and to its officials and to American residents and their property at Nanking. For this purpose a Sino-American commission would be set up to verify the actual injuries and damages suffered by Americans.

In his second note, General Huang asked that the American Government express regret for the part which its naval vessels had played in the bombardment of Nanking. In his reply, Mr. MacMurray referred to the situation existing in the city at the time and then stated: "The American Government therefore feels that its naval vessels had no alternative to the action taken, however deeply it deplores that circumstances beyond its control should have necessitated the adoption of such measures for the protection of the lives of its citizens at Nanking." The third matter dealt with in the exchange of notes was that of treaty revision. Referring to General Huang's request in this connection, Mr. MacMurray announced that his government entertained the hope that the remedying of the conditions which necessitated the incorporation of exceptional provisions in the earlier treaties might from time to time "afford opportunities

[29] Texts, *Treaties and Agreements with and Concerning China, 1919-1929*, pp. 223-6.

for the revision, in due form and by mutual consent," of such treaty stipulations as might have become unnecessary or inappropriate. To this end, the American Government was hopeful that there would be developed "an administration so far representative of the Chinese people, and so far exercising real authority, as to be capable of assuring the actual fulfillment in good faith of any obligations such as China would of necessity have for its part to undertake incidentally to the desired readjustment of treaty relations."

The completion of the Nationalist campaign against the Northerners in June, 1928, enabled the Nanking authorities to take up in earnest the problem of treaty revision. Already on November 24, 1927, Dr. C. C. Wu, invoking the principle of altered circumstances which had first been enunciated by the Peking Government, had notified the Spanish Minister in Peking, Mr. Garrido, of the termination of the Spanish treaty of October 10, 1864.[30] On April 16, 1928, also, General Huang Fu had addressed to the Portuguese Minister, Mr. J. A. Bianchi, a similar notification with regard to the Portuguese treaty of December 1, 1887.[31]

Early in June, Dr. C. T. Wang replaced General Huang Fu in charge of the Waichiao Pu.[32] The task which lay before the new Minister for Foreign Affairs was outlined for him in a declaration issued by the Nationalist Government on June 16. The government announced that since the unification of China had finally been consummated, the time was now ripe "to negotiate—in accordance with diplomatic procedure—new treaties on the basis of complete equality and mutual respect for each other's sovereignty."[33] On July 1, Dr. Wang informed the Italian Minister in Peiping that the treaty of October 26, 1866

[30] *China Year Book, 1929-30*, p. 854.
[31] *Ibid.*, pp. 858-9.
[32] General Huang had been criticized for signing the agreement with Mr. MacMurray relative to the Nanking incident, and was blamed also for his failure to prevent the clash between Nationalist and Japanese troops at Tsinanfu early in May.
[33] Text, *Chinese Social and Political Science Review*, XII (1928), Public Document Supplement, pp. 47-8.

between China and Italy had expired on June 30, and would have to be replaced by a new instrument.[34] The treaty of July 13, 1863 between China and Denmark having also expired on June 30, a notification to that effect was transmitted likewise to the Peiping representative of the Danish Government.[35] On July 7, also, the Ministry of Foreign Affairs issued an official pronouncement to the effect that all unequal treaties between China and other countries which had already expired should *ipso facto* be abrogated and replaced by new treaties. Furthermore, the Nationalist Government would immediately take steps to terminate "in accordance with proper procedure," such unequal treaties as had not yet expired and to conclude new agreements in their place. Where old treaties had expired, interim regulations would be applied to the nationals of the countries concerned pending the conclusion of new treaties.[36]

The interim regulations were published at the same time as the declaration of the Ministry of Foreign Affairs with regard to the treaties. Applying only to foreign countries and the nationals thereof whose treaties with China had already expired, and with which new treaties had not yet been concluded, these regulations contained the following provisions:[37]

"All diplomatic officials and consular officials of foreign countries stationed in China shall be entitled to proper treatment accorded under international law.

"The persons and properties of foreigners in China shall receive due protection under Chinese Law.

"Foreigners in China shall be subject to the regulations of Chinese Law and the jurisdiction of Chinese Law Courts.

"Pending the enforcement of the National Tariff Schedule, the regular customs duties on commodities imported into China from foreign countries or by foreigners, and those exported from China to foreign countries, shall be collected in accordance with the existing tariff schedule.

"All taxes and duties which Chinese citizens are under obligation to pay shall be payable equally by foreigners in accordance with the law.

[34] Text, *China Year Book, 1929-30*, p. 864.
[35] *Ibid.*, p. 869.   [36] *Ibid.*, p. 824.   [37] *Ibid.*, pp. 824-5.

"Matters not provided for by the foregoing Regulations, shall be dealt with in accordance with International Law and Chinese Municipal Law.[38]

A copy of these regulations was transmitted on July 11 to the Peiping representatives of Belgium, Spain, Portugal, Italy, and Denmark. When, however, a copy was delivered also to the Japanese Minister, trouble developed. The Peking Government had refrained from abrogating the Japanese treaties of 1896 and 1903. Dr. Wang now resolved to attempt what his predecessors in office had feared to do. On July 19, he notified the Japanese Minister, Mr. Yoshizawa, that the Treaty of Commerce and Navigation of 1896 and the Supplementary Treaty of 1903 had expired in October, 1926; that the said treaties were out of harmony with existing conditions in the two countries; that the Chinese Government had repeatedly extended the time for negotiating a new treaty, the last extension expiring on July 20, 1928; that in accordance with the Nationalist Government's declaration of July 7, it was the intention of that

[38] In this connection should be mentioned also the following regulations promulgated about this time defining the rights of missionaries to lease land in the interior:

1. "All foreign missionaries who are permitted by treaty agreements between their respective countries and China to establish mission stations and to open hospitals and schools in the interior of China may, in the name of their mission, lease land and construct or rent buildings for the above-mentioned purposes.

2. "All foreign missionaries, when leasing land for construction or renting or purchasing buildings in the interior of China, shall in conjunction with the owner of such property, first report their transactions to the local authorities concerned and obtain permission therefor in order to render such transactions legally valid.

3. "Whenever the area of land to be leased or the number and size of buildings to be rented or constructed or purchased by any foreign mission in the interior of China exceeds the requirement of the mission, the local authorities concerned shall not be permitted to approve the transactions.

4. "Whenever the land leased, and the building rented or constructed or purchased by any foreign mission in the interior of China are discovered to have been utilized for profit or any commercial purposes, the local authorities concerned shall stop such enterprises or declare the contract of lease invalid.

5. "All foreign missions which occupied land and buildings in the interior of China previous to the promulgation of these provisional regulations shall report their transactions to the local authorities concerned. . . ." *China Weekly Review*, XLV, July 28, 1928, p. 290.

344 *China's Foreign Relations*

government to conclude a new treaty with Japan based on principles of equality and mutuality; and that pending the conclusion of such a treaty the provisional regulations of July 7, a copy of which was inclosed, would be applied.[39]

In his reply to this communication, Mr. Yoshizawa, under instructions from his government, declared flatly that the treaty of 1896 contained no stipulation providing for its abrogation "without special mutual consent or agreement between both Contracting Parties." What the treaty did expressly provide was that if the revision contemplated by Article 26 was not completed within six months, then the treaty and the tariffs were to remain in force for a further period of ten years. The Japanese Government, therefore, was unable to accept the view that the treaty had expired. Consequently any attempt by the Nationalist Government to enforce against Japanese subjects the "so-called 'Provisional Regulations'" of July 7 would be regarded not only as an infringement of the terms of the treaty "inadmissible in the light of both treaty interpretation and international usages, but also an outrageous act disregarding good faith between the nations" in which the Japanese Government would be unable to acquiesce. Japan was still willing to continue negotiations for the revision of the existing treaties, but would do so only on condition that the Nationalist Government withdrew its declaration relative to the enforcement against Japanese subjects of the regulations of July 7. On the other hand, should the Nationalist Government decline to modify its attitude, the Japanese Government would be "obliged to take such measures as they deem suitable for safeguarding their rights and interests assured by the Treaties." [40]

In a memorandum dated August 14, Dr. Wang attempted to combat the Japanese arguments. He pointed out that according to the Chinese construction of Article 26, the treaty of 1896 would continue in force only in case neither party demanded

[39] *China Year Book, 1929-30,* p. 835.
[40] Yoshizawa to Wang, July 31, 1928, *China Year Book, 1929-30,* pp. 835-7.

its revision within six months following each decennial period. He recalled that the Chinese Government had already reserved to itself the right to decide on and make public its attitude toward the treaty concerned in case the negotiations for a new agreement could not be brought to a successful conclusion within six months. Consequently the Nationalist Government could not endorse the Japanese claim that the existing treaties were still in force. Referring to the provisional regulations, Dr. Wang stated that by enforcing these the Nationalist Government desired merely to maintain its political and commercial relations with all the friendly powers after the abrogation of old treaties and pending the conclusion of new ones, and that it was far from its intention to discriminate against any country. In conclusion, he again requested the Japanese Government to appoint a plenipotentiary who would forthwith open negotiations with the Nationalist Government for the purpose of concluding a new treaty.[41]

The diplomatic exchange between Dr. Wang and Mr. Yoshizawa revealed a state of tension between China and Japan which was not due wholly to the Nanking Government's attitude with regard to treaty revision. No arrangements had yet been made to compensate Japanese nationals for their losses sustained at the time of the Nationalist occupation of Nanking. There had been disturbances at Hankow where marines defending the Japanese Concession had, in April, 1927, fired upon a mob led by agitators and again in September of the same year had used machine guns against a detachment of Chinese troops who insisted on passing through the concession. At Amoy, also, Chinese resentment had been aroused by the arbitrary action of Japanese consular police in arresting, in Chinese territory, a number of Koreans who were charged with sedition.[42] Far more serious than any of these encounters, however, was the clash between Chinese and Japanese troops which took place in Tsinanfu in May, 1928. The month before, at the beginning

[41] *China Year Book, 1929-30,* p. 837.
[42] *North China Herald,* CLXVI, Mar. 31, 1928, p. 515.

of the final drive of the Nationalists for the possession of Peking, General Chiang Kai-shek had issued a manifesto asking the powers to refrain from interfering during the course of military operations, and promising that every effort would be made meanwhile to protect foreign lives and property.[43] Despite this promise, the Japanese Government decided to send troops into Shantung for the protection of Japanese interests at both Tsingtao and Tsinanfu.[44] The Nationalist forces occupied Tsinanfu on April 30. Three days later serious fighting broke out between Nationalist troops and the Japanese which lasted several days. On May 7 the Japanese commander gave General Chiang twelve hours in which to withdraw his troops from the city and also from the Shantung Railway zone. Sniping continued, however, until May 9 when Japanese artillery commenced a bombardment of the walled city, where many of the Nationalists had taken refuge.[45]

Fear of provoking Japan into an open declaration of war led General Chiang to withdraw his forces from the Tsinan area and to retire from active direction of the northern campaign.[46] The Japanese retained possession of Tsinan, thus cutting railway communication between Nanking and the north. Tsingtao was neutralized, the Japanese commander warning Chinese troops not to enter a seven-mile zone surrounding the city.[47] Both the Peking and the Nanking Governments were formally notified that if the prevailing disorder threatened to spread to Manchuria, the Japanese Government might be constrained "to take appropriate and effective steps" for the preservation of peace and order in that region.[48] Finally, after the Nationalist

[43] *China Weekly Review*, XLIV, Apr. 14, 1928, p. 206.
[44] Memorandum of April 20, 1928, from the Japanese Legation to the Waichiao Pu, *China Year Book, 1929-30*, pp. 878-9. For the protests of the Peking Government against Japan's action, see *ibid.*, pp. 879, 880.
[45] For the official Japanese and Chinese accounts of these events, together with the Chinese appeal to the League of Nations and the Japanese answer thereto, see *China Year Book, 1929-30*, pp. 881-92.
[46] Peking was captured a month later by armies commanded by Yen Hsi-shan, operating from Shansi, Feng Yü-hsiang, who advanced up the Peking-Hankow Railway, and Pai Ch'ung-hsi, who proceeded northward after circling Tsinan.
[47] *North China Herald*, CLXVII, June 2, 1928. p. 357.
[48] *China Weekly Review*, XLIV, May 26, 1928, pp. 379-80.

capture of Peking, representatives of the Japanese Government advised the new ruler of Manchuria, General Chang Hsueh-liang,[49] against concluding any agreement with the Nationalists as long as the Nanking Government declined to observe its international obligations.[50] That government had already invoked the principle of altered circumstances to justify its termination of the Japanese treaty of 1896. If the same principle were to be applied to numerous Sino-Japanese agreements relative to Manchuria, it was evident that Japan's special position in that region would be seriously menaced.

Meanwhile the Nanking Government, ignoring the set-back to its program caused by Japanese hostility, was strengthening its international position in other directions. The American Government had led the way in settling the questions arising out of the Nanking Incident. It was the American Government also with which Nationalist China was able to negotiate its first treaty. In June 1928, the American Secretary of State, Mr. Kellogg, consented to discuss with the Chinese Minister to Washington, Dr. C. C. Wu, the question of tariff autonomy. These negotiations culminated in a treaty which was signed at Peking on July 25 by Mr. MacMurray and the Chinese Minister of Finance, Mr. T. V. Soong.[51] This agreement, consisting of only two articles, provided that

"All provisions which appear in treaties hitherto concluded and in force between the United States of America and China relating to rates of duty on imports and exports of merchandise, drawbacks, transit dues and tonnage dues in China shall be annulled and become inoperative, and the principle of complete national tariff auton-

[49] Chang Tso-lin was mortally wounded on June 4 when the special train on which he was returning from Peking to Mukden was bombed on the outskirts of the latter city. His eldest son, Chang Hsueh-liang, succeeded him as ruler of the Three Eastern Provinces.
[50] Reuter interview with Premier Tanaka, July 22, 1928, *North China Herald*, CLXVIII, July 28, 1928, p. 134. *Ibid.*, Aug. 11, 1928, p. 221. In August Baron Hayashi attended the funeral of Chang Tso-lin as the official representative of the Japanese Government. On his return to Tokyo he announced that Chang Hsueh-liang had decided to wait three months before making any compromise with the Nationalists. *North China Herald*, CLXVIII, Aug. 25, 1928, p. 309.
[51] U. S. Department of State, *Treaty Series*, No. 773. *Treaties and Agreements, 1919-1929*, pp. 230-31.

omy shall apply subject, however, to the condition that each of the High Contracting Parties shall enjoy in the territories of the other with respect to the above specified and any related matters treatment in no way discriminatory as compared with the treatment accorded to any other country.

"The nationals of neither of the High Contracting Parties shall be compelled under any pretext whatever to pay within the territories of the other Party any duties, internal charges or taxes upon their importations and exportations other or higher than those paid by nationals of the country or by nationals of any other country."

The treaty was to become effective January 1, 1929 provided the necessary ratifications had been exchanged by that date. Otherwise it was to become effective four months subsequent to such exchange of ratifications.[52]

Following the American example, the German Minister, Dr. Herbert von Borch, signed with Dr. Wang at Nanking on August 17, 1928, a Sino-German Treaty of Friendship and Commerce.[53] Article I provided that

"For the purpose of attaining absolute equality of treatment in customs matters and in supplementing the arrangements between Germany and China of the 20th of May, 1921, the two High Contracting Parties agree that in all customs and related matters either of the High Contracting Parties shall within the territories of the other party not be subject to any discriminatory treatment as compared with the treatment accorded to any other country."

Reciprocal most favored nation treatment was promised as regards duties, internal charges, and taxes on the importation or exportation of goods. That portion of the agreement of May 20, 1921 according to which German import goods were to pay duties in accordance with the general tariff regulations prior to the general application of the autonomous tariff regulations was specifically annulled. Finally the two parties agreed to enter as soon as possible into negotiations for the purpose of concluding a Treaty of Commerce and Navigation

[52] Ratifications were exchanged at Washington, February 20, 1929.
[53] *Treaties and Agreements, 1919-1929*, pp. 232-3.

"based on the principle of perfect parity and equality of treatment."[54]

Meanwhile Sino-British differences with regard to the Nanking incident of March 1927 had been settled on August 9 by an exchange of notes between Dr. Wang and Sir Miles Lampson.[55] As in the case of the American settlement concluded in March, the Nationalist Government promised compensation for losses suffered by British nationals at Nanking. While insisting that the action of its war vessel in firing on the city was "absolutely necessary for the protection of British lives and property," the British Government nevertheless deeply deplored the fact that the circumstances existing at the time were such as to render necessary the adoption of this measure. Finally, Great Britain agreed to give consideration to the question of treaty revision.[56]

The American and the German treaties had been negotiated with what was in effect still a revolutionary government. On October 4, 1928, however, the Kuomintang leaders determined to regularize their position by promulgating the Five-Power Constitution or Organic Law, the main outlines of which had been formulated by Dr. Sun Yat-sen.[57] Chiang Kai-shek became Chairman of the State Council, which was the supreme governing organ in the new system. Subordinate to the State Council were five *Yuan* under one of which, the Executive *Yuan*[58] was located the Ministry of Foreign Affairs. The new

[54] A minor diplomatic victory at this time resulted from Cuba's formal recognition of the Nationalist Government. *North China Herald,* CLXVIII, Aug. 18, 1928, p. 262. *Ibid.,* Aug. 25, 1928, p. 308. This action was apparently prompted by the desire to develop an Oriental market for Cuban sugar, it being announced that a commercial treaty would shortly be concluded between the two countries.
[55] Texts, *China Year Book, 1929-30,* pp. 895-7. The notes were signed on behalf of the British minister by Sir Sidney Barton, H. M. Consul-General at Shanghai.
[56] The French settlement with regard to the Nanking incident was dated October 1, 1928, and that with Italy October 8. For texts of the notes, see *China Year Book, 1929-30,* pp. 897-900.
[57] Text, *Treaties and Agreements, 1919-1929,* pp. 233-37. Since this time the Nanking Government has referred to itself as "National" rather than "Nationalist."
[58] The others were the Legislative *Yuan,* the Judicial *Yuan,* the Examination *Yuan,* and the Control *Yuan,* the latter having charge of auditing and

government had the allegiance, nominal at least, of every leader of any importance in the country, even the ruler of Manchuria, Chang Hsueh-liang, being included among the members of the State Council.[59]

The newly constituted National Government took up immediately the question of treaties which had been abrogated. The Governments of Belgium, Spain, Portugal, Denmark, Italy, and Japan had all been informed that their treaties with China had expired and that, therefore, plenipotentiaries should be appointed to begin negotiations for the conclusion of new instruments. The Japanese Government, more uncompromising than any of the others, declined to negotiate as long as the attitude of the Nationalist authorities toward the treaty of 1896 remained unchanged. The other powers likewise, with one accord, contested China's right to terminate international agreements by unilateral action. Nevertheless they were disposed to discuss the question of treaty revision. The Italian Government in particular announced that while reserving all rights in respect of the Sino-Italian treaty of October 26, 1866, it was prepared to give sympathetic consideration to the revision of existing treaty relations and to open immediate negotiations on that subject. In notifying Dr. Wang of this decision, the Italian Minister, Mr. Daniele Varé, made the following concrete proposals:[60]

"The Italian Government are prepared to base the new Treaty on the mutual concession of the most favored nation treatment. Therefore, if on the one hand the Italian Government have no objection to open promptly, and in a friendly spirit, negotiations for the revision of the Treaty as a whole, on the other hand they intend that Italian citizens or companies (in respect to Consular jurisdiction) and Italian import and export trade (in respect to Customs tariff) shall not ever receive a treatment less favorable than that enjoyed in China by the citizens and by the trade of any other country. Therefore I must declare . . . that the new instrument

impeachment. There is no exact equivalent in English for the Chinese word "Yuan." It is usually rendered somewhat loosely as "council." M. T. Z. Tyau, *Two Years of Nationalist China*, Shanghai, 1930, p. 39, note.
[59] *China Year Book, 1929-30*, p. 1191.
[60] Note of July 11, 1928, *China Year Book, 1929-30*, p. 865.

should embody a suspending clause to the effect that the stipulations of the Italo-Chinese Treaty about to be concluded will come into force only after all the Powers signatory to the Washington Agreement shall have adjusted on a new foundation the diplomatic instruments which bind them to China."

The first of the expired treaties to be replaced with a new agreement was that with Belgium. At Nanking on November 22, 1928, a Preliminary Treaty of Amity and Commerce was signed between China and the Union of Belgium and Luxemburg.[61] As regards customs and all related matters, it was agreed that the two parties stood on a footing of perfect equality, each being free to regulate such matters exclusively by its own national laws, subject only to the condition that neither party should receive in the territory of the other treatment less favorable than that accorded to any other country. Article II provided that "the nationals of each of the two High Contracting Parties shall be subject, in the territory of the other Party, to the laws and the jurisdiction of the law courts of that Party." It was agreed that negotiations should begin as soon as possible with a view to concluding a Treaty of Commerce and Navigation "based upon the principle of reciprocity and equality of treatment." Appended to the treaty were several notes and a number of declarations.[62] Dr. Wang stated to the Belgian Chargé d'Affaires, Baron J. Guillaume, that Article II of the treaty should be understood to "begin to be operative" on January 1, 1930. Before that date the Chinese Government would make detailed arrangements with the Belgian Government for the assumption by China of jurisdiction over Belgian subjects. Failing such arrangements before the date named, Belgian subjects should thereafter be amenable to Chinese laws and jurisdiction "as soon as the majority of the Powers now possessing extraterritorial privileges in China" should have agreed to relinquish them. The National Government promised that the Civil Code and the Commercial Code in addition to other

[61] *Treaties and Agreements, 1919-1929*, pp. 240-41.
[62] *Ibid.*, pp. 241-43.

Codes and laws then in force, would be promulgated on or before January 1, 1930. The next Declaration, by Dr. Wang, was to the effect that when Belgian subjects in China ceased to enjoy the benefit of consular jurisdiction, the Chinese Government, in view of the fact that Chinese citizens were permitted to live and trade and acquire property in any part of the territories of Belgium and Luxemburg, would permit Belgian and Luxemburg subjects to enjoy the same rights in China, subject to the limitations to be prescribed in its laws and regulations. Finally, Baron Guillaume agreed that Belgian subjects in China should be required to pay such taxes as might be prescribed in laws and regulations duly promulgated by the Chinese Government, provided that the same taxes were paid by the nationals of all the powers having treaty relations with China.

The signature of the Belgian treaty was followed five days later by the signature of a similar agreement with Italy.[63] Article I of this agreement duplicated the provisions of the Belgian treaty with regard to customs matters. By Article II it was agreed that the nationals of each party should be subject, in the territory of the other party, to the laws and jurisdiction of the law courts of that party, to which they should have "free and easy access for the enforcement and defence of their rights." Negotiations were to be started as soon as possible for the purpose of concluding a Treaty of Commerce and Navigation based on "the principles of absolute equality and non-discrimination in their commercial relations and mutual respect for sovereignty." As regards extraterritorial rights, the Belgian precedent was followed except for one minor change. By an exchange of notes annexed to the treaty it was agreed that Article II should become operative on January 1, 1930, before which date the Chinese Government would make detailed arrangements with the Government of Italy for the assumption by China of jurisdiction over Italian subjects. Failing such arrangements on that date, however, Italian subjects were to be amenable to Chinese laws and jurisdiction from a date to be

[63] *Treaties and Agreements, 1919-1929*, pp. 243-6.

fixed by China after an agreement regarding the abolition of extraterritoriality had been reached "with all the Powers signatory of the Washington Treaties," it being understood that this date would be applicable to all such powers. China again promised that the Civil and Commercial Codes would be promulgated on or before January 1, 1930, and promised further that when extraterritoriality had been abolished, Italian subjects would be free to reside and trade and acquire property in the interior of the country.[64] The Italian Minister declared, finally, that the subjects of his government living in China would be required thereafter to pay Chinese taxes.

The conclusion of treaties with Belgium and Italy made it possible for Dr. Wang to sign similar agreements with the diplomatic representatives of Denmark, Portugal, and Spain. The Danish treaty was signed on December 12,[65] that with Portugal on December 19,[66] and that with Spain on December 27, 1928.[67] Each of these, as regards both the treaty itself and the annexes thereto, followed textually the Italian agreement of November 27.[68]

While the work of replacing expired treaties with new instruments was going forward, negotiations with regard to tariff autonomy were proceeding with the powers whose treaties still remained in force. On September 12, 1928, Dr. Wang proposed to the Governments of Norway, Sweden, and the

[64] The provision relating to foreign residence in the interior of China caused Dr. Wang to be subjected to a certain amount of hostile criticism. On December 13 a mob wrecked his official residence and denounced him as a traitor for having signed the Belgian and Italian treaties. Mr. Sun Fo, who, however, did not participate in this demonstration, pointed out that while the provision opening the interior to Belgian and Italian trade and residence was reciprocal in name, it would actually be one sided in effect; Chinese would be unable to utilize such privileges in foreign countries, but at the same time China would be bound to open the entire country to foreign exploitation. *North China Herald*, CLXIX, Dec. 29, 1928, p. 515. The fact that these and similar treaties were later ratified indicated that other members of the National Government did not share Mr. Sun's views.
[65] *Treaties and Agreements, 1919-1929*, pp. 246-9.
[66] *Ibid.*, pp. 252-6.   [67] *Ibid.*, pp. 270-73.
[68] Annexed to the Portuguese treaty in addition was an interpretation of Article I relating to most favored nation treatment in tariff matters, which appeared also as an annex to the Dutch treaty signed the same day.

Netherlands that they enter into tariff agreements with China similar to the agreement which had been concluded with the American Government. Similar proposals were made to the Governments of Great Britain and France.[69]

The first of the new group of tariff treaties was that with Norway, signed at Shanghai on November 12 by Dr. Wang and the Norwegian Chargé d'Affaires, Mr. N. Aall.[70] Except that it was to become effective immediately upon the exchange of ratifications, the Norwegian agreement was identical with the American treaty of July 25. A supplementary exchange of notes dealt with the Treaty of Peace, Amity, and Commerce concluded between China and Norway in 1847. Dr. Wang pointed out that conditions in both countries had changed greatly since the conclusion of this agreement, and suggested the desirability of a new treaty to replace it.[71] The Norwegian Chargé replied that his government had already given proof of its friendship by concluding the tariff treaty. He felt confident, therefore, that the friendly attitude of his government would not be found to have changed when the question of revising the entire treaty of 1847 came up for consideration.[72]

The Netherlands conceded China's right to tariff autonomy in a treaty concluded at Nanking December 19, 1928.[73] The next day a similar treaty was signed by Dr. Wang and the Swedish Chargé d'Affaires, Baron C. Leijonhufvud.[74] Both agreements duplicated the substance and in most respects also the wording of the American and Norwegian agreements.

The tariff treaty with Great Britain was signed at Nanking December 20, 1928.[75] All provisions in existing treaties between the two parties which limited in any way China's right to settle her national customs tariff in such way as she might think fit were abrogated, and the principle of complete national

[69] *China Year Book, 1929-30,* pp. 839, 832, 845.
[70] *Treaties and Agreements, 1919-1929,* pp. 237-8.
[71] Note of November 15, 1928, to Mr. Aall, *Treaties and Agreements, 1919-1929,* p. 239.
[72] Note of November 17, 1928, *ibid.,* p. 239.
[73] *Ibid.,* pp. 249-50.   [74] *Ibid.,* pp. 263-64.   [75] *Ibid.,* pp. 257-8.

tariff autonomy was to apply. China was free also to impose tonnage dues at such rates as might be deemed proper. Reciprocal most favored nation treatment was provided for as regards duties, internal charges, or taxes on goods imported or exported, and also with regard to tonnage dues and all matters connected therewith. The provisions of the treaty were amplified by a supplementary exchange of notes between Dr. Wang and Sir Miles Lampson. Dr. Wang confirmed the understanding of the British Minister that the *ad valorem* rates of duty or the specific rates based thereon in the National Customs Tariff to be adopted by the National Government were to be the same as the rates discussed and provisionally agreed upon at the Tariff Conference of 1926 and that these would be the maximum rates to be levied on British goods; furthermore, that these would remain the maximum rates on such goods for a period of at least one year from the date of enforcement of the tariff. On behalf of his government, Dr. Wang also confirmed the terms of the proclamation issued on July 20, 1927, announcing that it was the intention of the National Government to take as soon as possible the necessary steps effectively to abolish *likin,* native customs dues, coast-trade duties, and other similar taxes on imported goods whether levied in transit or on arrival at destination. It was now the intention of the National Government that "goods having once paid import duty to the Maritime Customs in accordance with the rates imposed in the new or any subsequent national tariff" should be freed as soon as possible from any levies of the nature specified in the proclamation of July 20, 1927.[76] Finally, Dr. Wang stated that it was the intention of his government "to apply the new customs tariff uniformly on all land and sea frontiers of China and that, as from the date of the coming into force of the new tariff," the preferential rates then levied on goods imported or exported by land frontier would accordingly be abolished.[77]

[76] *Treaties and Agreements, 1919-1929,* pp. 261-2.   [77] *Ibid.,* p. 263.

The British treaty was signed at one-fifteen on the morning of December 20. Eight hours later Sir Miles Lampson presented his credentials to the titular head of the government, General Chiang Kai-shek, thus completing British recognition of the National Government of China. While the presentation ceremony was taking place, *H. M. S. Suffolk,* anchored in the Yangtse, fired a salute of twenty-one guns which was immediately returned by the flagship of Admiral S. K. Chen.[78]

Of the 1928 tariff treaties, the last to be signed was that with France, concluded at Nanking on December 22.[79] Except that it was to become operative immediately upon the exchange of ratifications, the French treaty duplicated all of the provisions of the American agreement. Appended was a list of Chinese products with regard to which the minimum French tariff should continue to be applied. The list included Chinese silks, tea, and certain spices. As for other articles for which the Chinese Government desired to obtain the benefit of the minimum French tariff, it was agreed that a separate reciprocal tariff convention would be negotiated.[80] The French Minister, Count D. de Martel, expressed confidence that the National Government would abolish *likin* with the least possible delay after the coming into force of the new tariff, and would also effectively prevent the establishment of provincial taxes designed to replace *likin.* He pointed out also that since interest was not then being paid on certain French loans concluded by the Government of China, the assignment of a part of the additional receipts furnished by the customs for the service of these loans would "constitute a measure appropriate to the active development of Franco-Chinese economic relations. . . ." Dr. Wang merely expressed general agreement with reference to these matters.[81]

While these treaties were being negotiated, the Nanking Government was taking steps to prepare for the enforcement

[78] *North China Herald,* CLXIX, Dec. 29, 1928, p. 514.
[79] *Treaties and Agreements, 1919-1929,* pp. 265-6.
[80] *Ibid.,* p. 267.
[81] *Ibid.,* pp. 268-9.

of the new national tariff law. In taking these preliminary steps, the government had little cause to fear the opposition of any of the powers concerned except Japan. The attitude of the Japanese Government was first revealed during an informal exchange of views which took place in November between Dr. Wang and the Japanese Consul-General at Shanghai, Mr. S. Yada. In addition to tariff autonomy, outstanding Sino-Japanese questions which had to be dealt with were the Nanking, Hankow, and Tsinan Incidents, unsecured loans held by Japanese, and the expired commercial treaty of 1896. Dr. Wang insisted that these matters be discussed together. Mr. Yada, on the other hand, had been instructed to discuss them one at a time, beginning with the Nanking and Hankow Incidents.[82] An agreement regarding procedure might have been reached had not Dr. Wang demanded the withdrawal of Japanese troops from Tsinan prior to the beginning of any formal negotiations whatever. Acting on instructions from Tokyo, Mr. Yada rejected this demand and announced that the troops in question would be withdrawn only after satisfactory guarantees had been given for the maintenance of peace and order in Shantung.[83] Thus the exchange of views between Dr. Wang and the Japanese Consul-General terminated on November 23.

The breakdown of unofficial negotiations at Nanking did not prevent Mr. Yada, on his return to Shanghai, from discussing the question of tariff autonomy with the Minister of Finance, Mr. Soong. Mr. Soong expressed the desire for a simple Sino-Japanese tariff agreement similar to that which he had signed in July with the American Minister. Mr. Yada announced the willingness of his government to acquiesce in the enforcement of the new tariff law provided part of the increased revenues were earmarked for the service of Japanese loans. The grant of full tariff autonomy, however, would necessarily be contingent on the prior liquidation of all Sino-Japanese issues then awaiting settlement.[84] Little progress was made toward recon-

[82] *North China Herald*, CLXIX, Nov. 2, 1928, p. 295.
[83] *Ibid.*, Dec. 1, 1928, p. 339.
[84] *China Weekly Review*, XLVII, Dec. 1, 1928, p. 26.

ciling these opposing points of view, and as a result the
National Government, anticipating favorable action by the other
powers concerned, decided to proceed with the enforcement
of the national tariff law with or without Japanese consent.[85]
On December 8 each of the foreign consuls at Shanghai received a copy of the new tariff schedule which had been promulgated the day before together with an official notification
to the effect that it would become operative on February 1,
1929.[86] At first Mr. Yada declined to receive this communication. Later, however, he was induced to accept it for transmission to his government.[87] That government, after some
hesitation, decided to abandon its opposition to the collection
of the new duties, the State Council at Nanking having announced meanwhile that $5,000,000 from the customs revenues
would be devoted annually to the service of imperfectly secured
domestic and foreign—including Japanese—loans.[88] Under
these circumstances, the new tariff law became effective on
February 1, 1929.[89]

In January, 1929, the Japanese Government was finally compelled to reconsider its entire attitude with regard to China.
The "forward" policy of Premier Tanaka had not yielded the
benefits expected of it. Quite by contrast, that policy had placed
a growing strain on relations between the two countries. An-
gered by the conduct of the Japanese at Tsinan in May, 1928,

[85] The Danish, Dutch, Portuguese, British, Swedish, French, and Spanish
treaties remained to be signed.
[86] The new schedule, including rates ranging from seven and one-half
per cent to twenty-seven and one-half per cent, was practically identical with
the graduated interim schedule agreed upon at the Tariff Conference of
1925-6. The notification of the National Government made it clear that the
new schedule would be enforced for only one year, at the expiration of which
period China would be free to revise the rates. *China Year Book, 1929-30*,
p. 678.
[87] *North China Herald*, CLXIX, Dec. 15, 1928, p. 426. *Ibid.*, CLXX,
Jan. 26, 1929, p. 134.
[88] *North China Herald*, CLXX, Jan. 26, 1929, p. 134. *Ibid.*, Feb. 2,
1929, p. 178.
[89] *North China Herald*, CLXX, Feb. 9, 1929, p. 234. On January 8, the
Ministry of Finance reaffirmed its policy of completing within six months
the abolition of *likin* in the provinces of Kiangsu, Chêkiang, Anhwei, Kiangsi,
and Fukien. *Ibid.*, CLXX, Jan. 12, 1929, p. 49.

the Chinese had revived the boycott against Japanese goods. The effect of this boycott was to intensify the economic stagnation from which Japan had already begun to suffer. Merchants interested in the China trade were beginning to manifest their discontent in a rising chorus of protest, and it was more than likely that this discontent would assume political form in the Diet, due to reassemble on January 21 after its New Year recess, in which the government had only a very slender majority. Moreover, Japan was diplomatically isolated by the fact that the Nanking Government had succeeded in concluding tariff and other agreements with twelve countries. Under these circumstances, the Japanese Minister, Mr. Yoshizawa, was ordered to Nanking for a conference with Dr. Wang.[90]

At their first meeting on January 24, both men agreed that until a settlement had been reached with regard to the Tsinan Incident, it would be impossible to discuss other matters. Dr. Wang demanded that a date be set for the withdrawal of Japanese troops from Shantung. Mr. Yoshizawa declined to name such a date until satisfactory guarantees had been given for the protection of Japanese interests there.[91] The Japanese Minister declined to admit the responsibility of his government for the loss of Chinese lives and the destruction of Chinese property at Tsinan, and insisted on the other hand that the

[90] Aside from the promulgation of the Chinese tariff law, two other developments gave the Japanese Government cause for concern at this time. On December 29, 1928, Chang Hsueh-liang announced his allegiance to the Nanking Government and hoisted the National flag at Mukden. The next day the National Government appointed Marshal Chang as Northeastern Defense Commissioner. *North China Herald,* CLXX, Jan. 5, 1929, p. 5. There was also a renewed outbreak of anti-Japanese feeling at Hankow resulting from the accidental killing of a riksha coolie by a motorcycle operated by a member of the Japanese naval patrol. *North China Herald,* CLXX, Jan. 19, 1929, p. 93.

[91] *China Weekly Review,* XLVII, Feb. 9, 1929, p. 442. In an official statement issued January 19, Dr. Wang had declared that the National Government had consistently adhered to the policy of protecting foreign lives and property in China. Nevertheless, in order to dissipate apprehensions on the part of the Japanese, the National Government would exercise particular caution and provide special measures for further ensuring protection to Japanese lives and property in Shantung as soon as the Japanese Government had expressed its readiness actually to evacuate its troops from that region. *North China Herald,* CLXX, Jan. 26, 1929, p. 134.

National Government pay compensation for the loss of life and destruction of property suffered by Japanese. Dr. Wang then suggested that both sides pay damages, the amount in each case to be fixed by a joint Sino-Japanese commission which would be constituted for the purpose. Acting on specific instructions from Tokyo, the Japanese Minister rejected this proposal.[92] The agreement which was finally signed on March 28 was made possible only by material concessions on both sides. The two governments declared jointly that "while looking upon the incident which occurred at Tsinan on May 3 last as one most unfortunate and even tragic in view of the traditional friendship between Japan and China," they were ready "to dismiss entirely from their minds all discordant feelings attending the incident in the expectation that their future relationship may thereby be greatly improved." [93] The National Government undertook to be solely responsible for the safety of Japanese lives and property in China and the Japanese Government in turn promised to complete the evacuation of its troops from Shantung within two months. With regard to losses suffered by both Chinese and Japanese during the fighting at Tsinan, it was agreed, finally, that a joint commission should be formed to assess the necessary damages after investigation on the spot.[94]

Sino-Japanese differences with regard to the Nanking and Hankow incidents of March and April, 1927, were finally liquidated by an exchange of notes between Dr. Wang and Mr. Yoshizawa on May 2, 1929. The National Government declared that communists had been responsible in both instances, and promised compensation for Japanese losses.[95] Following a subsequent local agreement between the Chinese Commis-

---

[92] *North China Herald,* CLXX, Feb. 23, 1929, p. 302. *China Weekly Review,* XLVIII, March 30, 1929, p. 181. While these negotiations were proceeding, a local agreement was reached on February 13 between the Chinese Ministry of Railways and the Japanese military authorities at Tsinan for the operation of a certain number of freight trains over the Tientsin-Pukow Railway through the Japanese military zone about Tsinan. *China Weekly Review,* XLVIII, Mar. 30, 1929, p. 181.

[93] *China Year Book, 1929-30,* p. 892.

[94] *Ibid.,* pp. 892-3.

[95] Texts of the notes, *Treaties and Agreements, 1919-1929,* pp. 278-9. *China Year Book, 1929-30,* pp. 900-902.

sioner of Foreign Affairs and the Japanese Consul-General at Hankow, Japan withdrew from Hankow the force of marines which had been stationed there since April, 1927. The withdrawal was completed on May 31, 1929, the day before the state funeral of Dr. Sun Yat-sen.[96]

During their negotiations relative to other subjects, Dr. Wang and Mr. Yoshizawa had discussed the matter of a tariff treaty between China and Japan. The Japanese Government was still of the opinion that the commercial treaty of 1896 remained valid. The attempt of the National Government to terminate this agreement by unilateral action was justified neither by the provisions of the treaty nor by the principle of altered circumstances. Expressing the views of his government in the latter connection, Mr. Yoshizawa stated that not only was the so-called principle of altered circumstances "incapable of being regarded as an established rule of law in international relations, but the admission of such a principle would render almost all treaties liable to repudiation at the pleasure of either of the Contracting Parties, thus shaking the very foundations of international law." The Japanese Government was unable to recall a precedent where such a principle had ever received actual application.[97] Nevertheless, should the National Government "consent to regulate Sino-Japanese relations in accordance with the provisions of the existing treaty and on that basis propose its revision, the Japanese Government would be quite prepared to entertain such proposal and enter into negotiations with a view to effecting such revision of the Treaty as [might] be deemed appropriate." [98] In his reply to this note, Dr. Wang declined to enter into further argument concerning the continued validity of the treaty in question, since both Govern-

[96] *North China Herald*, CLXXI, June 1, 1929, p. 341. After impressive ceremonies lasting three days and ending on June 1, the body of Dr. Sun was placed in a magnificent mausoleum on Purple Mountain overlooking the city of Nanking. The ceremonies were attended by the diplomatic representatives of seventeen powers and the Vatican. *North China Herald*, CLXXI, June 8, 1929, p. 379. Two days after the funeral, the Japanese, Italian, and German Ministers presented their credentials to Chiang Kai-shek.

[97] Yoshizawa to Wang, April 26, 1929, *China Year Book, 1929-30*, pp. 837-8.

[98] *Ibid.*

ments had already made their views sufficiently clear. He announced, however, that his Government was ready "immediately and in all sincerity" to enter into negotiations in the hope that within the shortest possible time a new treaty would be concluded on the basis of equality and mutual respect for sovereign rights.[99]

In the fall of 1929, Mr. Sadao Saburi replaced Mr. Yoshizawa as Japanese Minister to China.[100] The appointment of Mr. Saburi seemed to promise the beginning of more friendly relations between Japan and China, for he was known to be particularly sympathetic toward Chinese aspirations. His tragic and untimely death on November 28 prevented the beginning of treaty negotiations. The Japanese Government then announced its intention of appointing Mr. Torikichi Obata as its representative in China. The Chinese Government, remembering Mr. Obata's connection with the Twenty-One Demands of 1915, declined to receive him.[101] After waiting some time in the hope that the Nanking authorities would reconsider their decision, the Japanese Government finally authorized the Consul-General at Shanghai, Mr. M. Shigemitsu, to act as Chargé d'Affaires in negotiations with Dr. Wang.

The delay in negotiating the tariff treaty with Japan prevented the Chinese Government from enforcing full tariff autonomy on February 1, 1930.[102] Meanwhile the growing depreciation in the value of silver compelled the government to announce that beginning February 1, 1930, customs duties on imports would be collected on a gold rather than a silver basis.[103]

The negotiations between Dr. Wang and Mr. Shigemitsu

[99] Note of April 27, 1929, *China Year Book, 1929-30*, pp. 838-9.
[100] The Tanaka government resigned on July 2. In the new ministry, Baron Shidehara resumed office as Minister for Foreign Affairs.
[101] *North China Herald*, CLXXIII, Dec. 21, 1929, p. 457.
[102] Another factor was the failure of the Dutch Government to ratify its treaty of December 19, 1928. The exchange of ratifications did not take place until November 18, 1930. For the dates on which each of the tariff treaties came into effect, see *China Year Book, 1931*, pp. 473-4.
[103] Order of January 15, 1930, issued by Finance Minister Soong. *China Year Book, 1931*, pp. 268-9.

resulted in a tariff treaty which was initialed on March 12, 1930. After receiving the approval of the Japanese Privy Council, this agreement was formally signed at Nanking on May 6, coming into effect ten days later.[104] The two parties agreed that all matters relating to rates of duty on the import and export of articles, drawbacks, transit dues and tonnage dues, should be regulated exclusively by the laws of the country concerned. Reciprocal most favored nation treatment was provided with regard to these and other similar matters. The stipulations contained in the treaty as well as in the notes annexed thereto were to be incorporated in a Treaty of Commerce and Navigation which was to be concluded as soon as possible.

In the notes annexed to the treaty,[105] the Chinese Government agreed to maintain for a period of three years the rates contained in the tariff law of 1929 relative to cotton goods, fishery and sea products, and wheat flour imported from Japan. China likewise agreed not to change for a period of one year the rates of duty on certain innumerated goods of a miscellaneous character. With regard to a few of these items, however, the Chinese Government reserved the right to increase existing rates by not more than two and one-half per cent *ad valorem*, a similar reservation being made at the same time with regard to an excise on imported cotton yarn. On its part the Japanese Government promised that during the ensuing three-year period there would be no increase in the prevailing rates on grass cloth, silk piece goods, and embroidered goods imported from China. With regard to the last two items, Japan agreed furthermore to reduce by thirty per cent the duties then collected on such articles. It was agreed also that at the expiration of four months from the coming into force of the treaty, the reduced rates of the Chinese Customs Tariff collected on articles imported or exported across the land frontiers between China and Japan should be abolished; thereafter full rates specified in the Chinese tariff law should be collected on all such articles. Mr. Shigemitsu asked for and received confirma-

[104] Text, *ibid.*, p. 471.   [105] Texts, *ibid.*, pp. 472-3.

tion of his understanding that it was the intention of the Chinese Government to abolish as soon as possible all such charges as *likin*, native customs duties, coast-trade duty, and transit dues. Dr. Wang stated that his government had already issued a mandate ordering the abolition of *likin* as from October 10, 1930, and had instructed the Minister of Finance to take all measures necessary to carry this order into effect. Finally, Mr. Shigemitsu, referring to the large number of unsecured and inadequately secured obligations of China due to Japanese creditors, suggested that some arrangement be made for the speedy liquidation of such obligations. Dr. Wang, in reply, stated that the Chinese Government had already commenced to set aside the sum of $5,000,000 from the customs revenues for the purpose of consolidating the domestic and foreign obligations of China, and also that a conference would be called on or before October 1, 1930, at which an adequate plan for consolidation would be presented and discussed with a view of devising means (including an increase of the sum above mentioned) for effectuating the consolidation in question.[106]

On May 16, 1930, ten days after the formal signature of the Sino-Japanese Treaty, Dr. Wang signed with the French Minister, Count de Martel, an agreement relating to trade between China and French Indo-China, negotiations for which had gone on intermittently since 1926. As already related, the French trade conventions of 1886, 1887, and 1895 had been denounced by the Peking Government. On July 11, 1928, Dr. Wang informed the French Chargé d'Affaires in Peiping that the Nationalist Government regarded the three conventions as having lapsed on July 7, 1928, and asked that a plenipotentiary be appointed to begin immediate negotiations for a new agreement.[107] M. Cosmé declined to agree that the conventions had lapsed but intimated that his government was ready to examine

[106] Full tariff autonomy, except as qualified by the temporary provisions of the Japanese treaty, became effective with the enforcement of a new tariff law on January 1, 1931. Harold S. Quigley in *Current History*, February, 1931, p. 795. Joseph Gordon, "China Wins Tariff Independence," *Ibid.*, July, 1931, pp. 547-50.

[107] Wang to Cosmé, *China Year Book, 1929-30*, pp. 828-9.

with a representative of the Nationalist Government the question of limited revision in accordance with the express provisions of the conventions.[108] The matter again received consideration at the time the French tariff treaty was signed in December, 1928. Count de Martel informed Dr. Wang that the French Government was prepared to begin immediate negotiations for the conclusion of a new convention to replace the conventions of 1886, 1887, and 1895, it being understood that during the course of the negotiations, no changes would be made in existing arrangements relative to Indo-China. In particular, the existing reductions on duties for imports and exports were to remain in force until the new convention had been completed.[109] Dr. Wang expressed the hope that the proposed negotiations would be satisfactorily completed before March 31, 1929. On that date existing tariff reductions on goods imported or exported across the Indo-Chinese land frontier would be abolished whether or not a new trade convention had been signed.[110] Count de Martel merely acknowledged receipt of this communication "for any useful purposes." [111]

By Article I of the agreement signed on May 16, 1930, the trade conventions of 1886, 1887, and 1895 were expressely abrogated.[112] Chinese Consuls might be stationed at Saigon and at Hanoi or Haiphong in French Indo-China, and the French Government was to continue to enjoy the right to maintain Consuls at Lungchow, in the Province of Kwangsi, and at Szemao, Hokow, and Mengtze in Yünnan. The nationals of China in French Indo-China and French nationals in the above-mentioned Chinese localities were to have the right to reside, travel, and engage in industry or commerce. The treatment accorded them for the exercise of such rights was to be no less favorable than that accorded the nationals of any other power. Chinese goods exported from any Chinese port and transported

[108] Notes to Dr. Wang, July 13 and September 10, 1928, *China Year Book*, 1929-30, pp. 829-31.
[109] Note of December 23, 1928, *China Year Book*, *1929-30*, p. 834.
[110] Note of December 23, 1928, *Ibid.*, pp. 834-5.
[111] Note of December 23, 1928, *Ibid.*, p. 835.
[112] Text, *China Year Book*, 1931, pp. 474-5.

overland through Tonking to the provinces of Yünnan,
Kwangsi, and Kwangtung were to pay a duty of only one per
cent *ad valorem*. Similarly, Chinese goods exported through
Tonking from Yünnan, Kwangsi, and Kwangtung were to be
accorded preferential treatment; certain raw materials were ex-
empted from the payment of all duties, and other goods were
to pay a duty of only one per cent *ad valorem*. Provision was
made for the reciprocal extradition of criminals. The convention was to remain in force for five years, after which period
either party might denounce it after giving one year's notice.[113]

In addition to conducting successful negotiations with powers
already enjoying treaty rights in China, the National Government succeeded also, during 1929 in concluding new treaties,
each on the basis of equality and reciprocity, with three other
powers. The first of these was the Sino-Polish Treaty of Amity,
Commerce, and Navigation signed at Nanking on September
18, 1929.[114] It consisted, in addition to twenty-two articles,
of a Final Protocol comprising three declarations explanatory
of certain stipulations contained in the treaty, and an Annex.
On July 1, 1930, upon the request of the Polish Government,
an Additional Protocol was signed at Nanking to supplement
the treaty with additional explanations. The delay in ratifying
this agreement has been due to the fact that the Polish Parliament has not been in session.[115]

[113] Notes exchanged at the same time that the convention was signed
provided that Chinese nationals in Indo-China should enjoy the same treatment with regard to laws, jurisdiction, and procedure in civil, criminal, fiscal
and other matters, as the nationals of any other country. Regulations governing frontier traffic on the Yünnan Railway were to be revised by agreement
between the two parties. Similarly, existing agreements relative to telegraphic
communications, including wireless telegraphy, between French Indo-China
and the three adjoining Chinese provinces, were to be revised. Texts of the
notes, *China Year Book, 1931*, pp. 475-8.
[114] Dr. M. T. Z. Tyau has said that this day will go down in the diplomatic history of China "as a day on which China proclaimed to the world
that she would now accept nothing less than an equal and independent status
in the Family of Nations. Previous efforts of the Waichiao Pu had been
directed to the removal of the vestiges of the old régime, "but the Sino-
Polish Treaty was the first full expression of a new spirit." *Two Years of
Nationalist China*, p. 119.
[115] *China Year Book, 1931*, p. 478.

The second of these agreements was the Treaty of Amity between China and the Hellenic Republic, signed at Paris on September 30, 1929, by the Chinese and Greek Ministers to France.[116] It provided for the exchange of diplomatic and consular representatives, the former to enjoy the privileges and immunities customarily accorded under international law, and the latter to be treated "with due consideration and regard." The nationals of either party residing in the territory of the other were accorded the right, in conformity with the laws and regulations of the country, to buy, to sell, to travel, and in general to engage in commerce or any other lawful undertaking in any locality where the nationals of any other nation were permitted to do so. They were placed, together with their property, under the jurisdiction of the local tribunals and were required to comply with the laws of the country where they resided. They were not, however, to pay any impost, tax, or contribution higher than those paid by the nationals of the country. Subject to the grant of most favored nation treatment, each party was free to regulate all questions relative to customs matters exclusively by its own domestic legislation. With regard to questions not specifically provided for in the treaty, the principles of equality and mutual respect for territorial sovereignty were to apply. The treaty was to be valid for a period of three years, after which either party might denounce it after giving six months advance notice of its intention to do so.

The treaty with Greece was a mere treaty of friendship. The agreement with Czecho-Slovakia on the other hand, signed at Nanking on February 12, 1930, was a complete Treaty of Amity and Commerce consisting of twenty-one articles.[117] It contained the usual provisions relating to the exchange of diplomatic and consular representatives (Articles II, III). The nationals of each party were to enjoy, in the territory of the

[116] Text, *China Year Book, 1931,* p. 478. A Sino-Greek treaty substantially similar to this was signed at Paris on May 26, 1928, by the Greek and Chinese Ministers to France, the latter representing the Peking Government. Text, *Treaties and Agreements, 1919-1929,* pp. 226-8. Due to the Nationalist capture of Peking a week later, this treaty was never ratified.
[117] Text, *China Year Book, 1931,* pp. 479-80.

other, the full protection of the laws and regulations of the country with regard to their persons and property. They were accorded the right, subject to the laws of the country, to travel, reside, establish firms, acquire or lease property, work and engage in industry or commerce in all localities where the nationals of any other country were permitted to do so (Article V). It was agreed that the nationals of each country in the territory of the other were to be subject, together with their property, to the laws and regulations of the country and to the jurisdiction of its law courts. However, in legal proceedings such nationals were to have free and easy access to the courts as well as liberty to employ lawyers or representatives in accordance with the laws of the country (Article VI). Chinese nationals resident in Czecho-Slovakia, and similarly Czecho-Slovak nationals resident in China, were required to pay taxes, imposts, and charges in accordance with the laws of the country. Such taxes and other charges, however, were not to be other or higher than those paid by the nationals of the country (Article VII). The Eighth Article provided that "The workmen of each of the High Contracting Parties shall, irrespective of their sex, have all the facilities of entry into the territory of the other, and shall, subject to its laws and regulations equally applicable to all foreign workmen, enjoy the same treatment and protection as the workmen of the country." Neither government was to subject the nationals of the other "to any personal or domiciliary search except in accordance with laws and regulations in force" (Article X). Detailed arrangements were made relative to the disposal of property belonging to deceased persons (Article XI). It was agreed that each party should be free to regulate its customs tariff and all matters related thereto in accordance with domestic laws, subject only to the condition that most favored nation treatment should be accorded with regard to the payment of import and export duties, and also to duties, internal charges, and taxes on goods imported or exported (Article XII). Goods, the produce or manufacture of one of the parties, passing in transit through the territory of the other, in conformity with the laws of the country, were to be reciprocally free from all transit duties (Article XIV). Article XV read as follows: "The inland and coastwise navigation in the territory of either of the High Contracting Parties shall be closed to the nationals of the other and their vessels without prejudice to the stipulations of international treaties relating to international rivers." Each party agreed to accord protection to trade marks, designs, and models belonging to nationals of the other (Article XVII). The treaty was to remain in force for three years. Thereafter either party might denounce it after giving six months notice of an intention to do so.[118]

[118] Two other agreements belong to this period. The first was a Sino-American Treaty of Arbitration, signed by Secretary Stimson and Dr. Wu at Washington on June 27, 1930. It provided for the submission of justiciable disputes to the Permanent Court of Arbitration at The Hague or to some other competent tribunal, as might be decided in each case by special agreement. The provisions of the treaty were not to be invoked in respect of any dispute the subject matter of which (a) was within the domestic jurisdiction of either party, (b) involved the interests of third parties, (c) concerned the Monroe Doctrine, or (d) involved the observance of the obligations of China under the Covenant of the League of Nations, *China Year Book, 1931,* pp. 494-5.

The second was a temporary tariff arrangement provided for in an exchange of notes on April 23, 1930, between the Chinese Minister in London, Dr. Alfred Sze, and the Egyptian Chargé d'Affaires, Dr. Hamed Mahmoud. Pending the negotiation of a Treaty of Amity and Commerce between China and Egypt, each government was to accord at once most favored nation treatment to the agricultural and industrial products of the other when imported into its territory. Texts, *China Year Book, 1931,* p. 495.

CHAPTER XI

EXTRATERRITORIALITY, RESIDENTIAL CONCESSIONS,
AND THE CHINESE EASTERN RAILWAY

FIVE of the treaties negotiated by the National Government
of China in 1928 contained clauses relating to the abandonment of extraterritorial rights. The clause in the Belgium treaty
was to become operative on January 1, 1930, or as soon thereafter as a majority of the powers then possessing extraterritorial
privileges in China had agreed to relinquish them. Similar
clauses in the treaties with Italy, Denmark, Spain, and Portugal, were to take effect when like agreements had been reached
with all of the powers originally signatory to the Washington
treaties.

In the spring of 1929, Dr. Wang set to work to secure the
necessary assent of the other powers. On April 27, 1929, notes
on the subject were addressed to the American, Brazilian, British, Dutch, French, and Norwegian envoys in China.[1] Dr.
Wang recalled that the Chinese representatives first at Paris
and then at Washington had expressed the strong desire of their
government for the early removal of limitations on China's
jurisdictional sovereignty. With the unification of the country
and the establishment of a strong national government, a new
era had been inaugurated in the relations between China and
foreign countries through the recent negotiation of tariff
treaties. It was hoped that these treaties would materially

---

[1] The notes to the American, British, and French Ministers were identical. Text, *China Year Book, 1929-30*, pp. 904-5. No notes were sent to
the Governments of Sweden or Switzerland, both having indicated that they
would offer no objection to the revision of extraterritoriality clauses in their
treaties which were due to expire during the current year. *China Weekly
Review*, XLVIII, May 4, 1929, p. 397.

enhance the well-being of all countries concerned. But it was the conviction of the Chinese Government that this material well-being would be promoted still further by the readjustment of existing relations on a basis of friendly equality in matters of jurisdiction. It went without saying that extraterritoriality in China was a legacy of the old régime, which not only had ceased to be applicable to present-day conditions, but had become so detrimental to the smooth working of the judicial and administrative machinery of China that her progress as a member of the family of nations had been unnecessarily retarded. It was a matter for sincere regret that while many governments were eager and persistent in their endeavor to promote genuine friendship and harmony among nations, such anachronistic practices as only tended to mar the friendly relations between the Chinese people and foreign nationals were allowed to exist at a time when justice and equity were supposed to govern the relations among nations.

Dr. Wang stated that China had recently made rapid progress in the reform of her legal and judicial systems. Courts and prisons along modern lines had been and were being established throughout the entire country. In addition to numerous codes and laws already in force, the Civil Code and the Commercial Code had reached the final stage of preparation and would be ready for promulgation before January 1, 1930. Certain countries which had already renounced their extraterritorial privileges were satisfied with the protection afforded to their nationals by Chinese law, and other countries could rest assured that the legitimate rights and interests of their nationals would not be unfavorably affected by their relinquishment of such privileges. The Chinese Government hoped, therefore, that the foreign powers would give immediate and sympathetic consideration to China's desire to have the restrictions on her jurisdictional sovereignty removed at the earliest possible date.

The American, British, French, and Dutch replies to this note were delivered to the Chinese Government on August 10, the Norwegian reply being dated four days later. The American

Government fully appreciated the efforts which were being made in China to assimilate Western juridical principles.[2] It was necessary to point out, however, that there did not exist in China at the moment "a system of independent Chinese courts free from extraneous influence" which was capable "of adequately doing justice between Chinese and foreign litigants." Reference was made to the recommendations upon which the Commission on Extraterritoriality had agreed in 1926. The American Government believed that not until these recommendations had been fulfilled in far greater measure than was then the case would it be possible "for American citizens safely to live and do business in China and for their property adequately to be protected without the intervention of the consular courts." The sudden abolition of the system of protection by American extraterritorial courts in the face of conditions then prevailing in China "would in effect expose the property of American citizens to danger of unlawful seizure and place in jeopardy the liberty of the persons of American citizens." Nevertheless, the American Government, desiring to be helpful, was ready, if the suggestion met with the approval of the Chinese Government, "to participate in negotiations which would have as their object the devising of a method for the gradual relinquishment of extraterritorial rights, either as to designated territorial areas, or as to particular kinds of jurisdiction, or as to both," provided that such gradual relinquishment was paralleled by actual improvements, achieved by the Chinese Government, "in the enactment and effective enforcement of laws based on modern concepts of jurisprudence."

The British Government likewise observed with sympathy the efforts of the Chinese Government to reorganize its judicial and legal system along modern lines.[3] It was pointed out, however, that the promulgation of codes embodying Western legal principles represented only one portion of the task to be accomplished before special arrangements which had hitherto regu-

[2] MacMurray to Wang, *Treaties and Agreements, 1919-1929*, pp. 279-82. *China Year Book, 1929-30*, pp. 905-7.
[3] Lampson to Wang, Text, *China Year Book, 1929-30*, pp. 908-10.

lated the residence of foreigners in China could safely be abandoned. In order that those reforms should become a living reality, it appeared to His Majesty's Government "to be necessary that Western legal principles should be understood and be found acceptable by the people at large, no less than by their rulers," and that the courts which administered these laws "should be free from interference and dictation at the hands, not only of military chiefs, but of groups and associations who either set up arbitrary and illegal tribunals of their own or attempt to use legal courts for the furtherance of political objects rather than for the administration of equal justice between Chinese and Chinese and between Chinese and foreigners." Not until these conditions had been met would it be practicable for British merchants "to reside, trade, and own property throughout the territories of China" with the same guarantees that were accorded to Chinese merchants in Great Britain. Any agreement purporting to accord such privileges to British merchants would remain for some time to come a mere paper agreement to which it would be impossible to give effect in practice. The British Government, therefore, while ready to consider modifications in the prevailing system of extraterritoriality, was not yet prepared to abandon it entirely.

The British note had suggested indirectly that the abolition of extraterritoriality would have to be followed by the abolition of the treaty port system and the consequent opening of the entire country to foreign trade and residence. Both the French and the Netherlands Governments held similar views. Both announced, also, that their abandonment of extraterritorial rights would be contingent on further improvements in the Chinese system of administering justice.[4] The Norwegian Government expressed its readiness to abolish its consular courts as soon as all the other treaty powers had agreed to do so.[5]

The American and British Governments, and less directly

---

[4] Texts of the notes, *China Year Book, 1929-30,* pp. 910-12.
[5] Aall to Wang, *China Year Book, 1929-30,* p. 912.

the French Government also, had indicated a willingness to discuss proposals for the modification of the extraterritorial system. The notes of the Dutch and Norwegian Governments suggested that they intended to follow the lead of the great powers. In September, consequently, Dr. Wang addressed fresh notes, similar in substance, to each of the governments concerned.[6] He reiterated the Chinese view that material benefits would follow the relinquishment of extraterritorial rights and suggested that the Chinese people had already begun to discriminate against the nationals of powers which still retained such rights and to show greater friendliness toward other foreigners who were content to live under the laws of the country. The American, British, and French notes had referred to the report submitted by the Commission on Extraterritoriality. Dr. Wang stated that since the completion of that report, conditions in China had "greatly changed," and in particular both the political and judicial systems had "assumed a new aspect." To pass judgment, therefore, on the existing state of law and judicial administration in China in the light of what was contained in the report of 1926 was "doing no justice to the steadfast policy of the National Government." Dr. Wang recalled that the foreign powers had already agreed to abandon their rights under the Capitulations with Turkey, and declared that the Chinese judicial system did not suffer by comparison with that of Turkey at the time the Capitulations were abolished. Moreover, several other powers had recently concluded treaties with China by which they agreed "to relinquish Extraterritoriality on January 1, 1930." They would not have done so had they not been satisfied that there existed in China "a judiciary capable of rendering justice to their nationals and a body of laws adequate to give protection to their lives and property." The Chinese Government requested, therefore, that the other governments enter into immediate discussions with authorized

[6] For texts of the notes to the American and French Governments, the first dated September 5 and the second September 7, 1929, see *China Year Book, 1929-30*, pp. 912-15.

representatives of the Chinese Government for the purpose of making arrangements for the abolition of extraterritoriality.

After consulting among themselves the American, British, French, and Dutch Ministers in Peiping again announced the views of their governments in notes transmitted to Dr. Wang on October 31.[7] The American Government was ready to commence negotiations for the gradual abolition of extraterritorial rights, but desired first that the Chinese legal codes be completed and enforced. The Government of France expressed its willingness to consider any concrete program for the abolition of consular jurisdiction whenever such a program had been prepared by the Chinese Government.[8]

The National Government's campaign to bring consular jurisdiction to an end received, at this time, the moral endorsement of the Mexican Government.[9] The Mexican treaty of 1899, supplemented by the *modus vivendi* of 1921, expired on November 30, 1928. On October 31, 1929, the Chinese Minister to Mexico, Mr. Frank W. Lee, addressed to the Mexican Foreign Office a note requesting a public declaration to the effect that Mexico had no intention thereafter of seeking extraterritorial rights in China. By such a declaration, made public at a time most advantageous to China, the Mexican Government would express its "complete sympathy with China's aspirations to exercise sovereign jurisdiction as a free and independent state."[10] A favorable response to this request was received on November 12, 1929, from Mr. Genaro Estrada, Under-Secretary for Foreign Affairs. Mr. Estrada stated that "it is not possible to deny to any nation, as it is not denied in this case, the recognition of its complete rights of sovereignty, sustained in the efforts and legitimate aspirations of the respective peoples." Consequently the Mexican Government had no intention of

[7] *North China Herald*, CLXXIII, Nov. 16, 1929, p. 248.
[8] *Ibid.*
[9] According to the Maritime Customs estimate for 1928, there were only eighteen Mexican citizens then living in China. *China Year Book, 1931*, p. 2.
[10] Lee to Estrada, *China Year Book, 1931*, pp. 487-8.

discussing the right of China to adopt the laws that harmonized with her people, nor to demand in the future extraterritorial privileges in that country.[11]

The Chinese Government was determined to announce the end of the extraterritorial régime as from January 1, 1930. The powers concerned were equally determined to permit no interference with treaty rights long enjoyed by their nationals in China. An impending crisis was averted by an exchange of views between the Chinese Minister in London, Dr. Sze, and the British Secretary for Foreign Affairs, Mr. Arthur Henderson. The British Government, said the Foreign Secretary, desired to do its utmost to facilitate negotiations on the subject of extraterritoriality, and disclaimed all responsibility for political conditions in China which had prevented the commencement of serious discussions. Appreciating the fact, however, that the Chinese Government might be faced with difficulties should the date of January 1, 1930, arrive without visible progress having been made regarding the matter, the British Government was willing to agree that January 1 "should be treated as the date from which the process of the gradual abolition of extraterritoriality should be regarded as having commenced in principle," and would not object to any declaration to that effect which the Chinese Government might think it desirable to issue.[12] The Chinese Minister stated that his government regarded this pronouncement "as most timely and conducive to the promotion of friendly feelings" between the two countries.[13]

Under these circumstances, the National Government, on December 28, 1929, issued the following mandate:[14]

"In every full-sovereign State foreigners as well as its nationals are equally amenable to its laws and to the jurisdiction of its tribunals. This is an essential attribute of State sovereignty and a well-established principle of International Law.

[11] Note to Mr. Lee, *China Year Book, 1931,* p. 488. See also *China Critic,* III, Jan. 30, 1930, pp. 114-15.
[12] Aide-Mémoire, Henderson to Sze, December 20, 1929, *China Year Book, 1931,* pp. 486-7.
[13] Sze to Henderson, December 24, 1929, *China Year Book, 1931,* p. 487.
[14] *Ibid.,* p. 487.

"For more than eighty years China has been bound by the system of extraterritoriality, which has prevented the Chinese Government from exercising its judicial power over foreigners within its territory. It is unnecessary to state here the defects and disadvantages of such a system. As long as extraterritoriality is not abolished, so long will China be unable to exercise her full sovereignty. For the purpose of restoring her inherent jurisdictional sovereignty, it is hereby decided and declared that on and after the first day of the first month of the nineteenth year of the Republic (January 1, 1930) all foreign nationals in the territory of China who are now enjoying extraterritorial privileges shall abide by the laws, ordinances, and regulations duly promulgated by the Central and Local Governments of China. The Executive *Yuan* and the Judicial *Yuan* are hereby ordered to instruct the Ministries concerned to prepare as soon as possible a plan for the execution of this Mandate and to submit it to the Legislative *Yuan* for examination and deliberation with a view to its promulgation and enforcement."

The Mandate of December 28 was not intended to terminate, by summary and unilateral action, valid treaty rights of long standing. It was intended rather as a formal announcement to the people of China that their government was in deadly earnest with regard to the abolition of consular jurisdiction. But more than that, it was designed to compel the foreign powers concerned to give immediate and serious consideration to the question of revising, by mutual agreement, such treaties as still provided for the exercise of extraterritorial rights.[15] As such it provoked no unusual concern on the part of either the American or the British Government, both taking the view that January 1 merely marked the beginning of the gradual abandonment of their special privileges in China.[16] The French Government

[15] An official statement issued by Dr. Wang on December 30, 1929, contained the following concluding paragraph: "The Chinese Government, relying on the sympathy already shown and assurances given by the Powers concerned, believes that there is no difference of opinion between those Powers and China regarding the principle involved; and it is prepared to consider and discuss within a reasonable time any representations made with reference to the plan now under preparation in Nanking. In this respect, the issuance of the Mandate of December 28 should be regarded as a step towards removing the cause of constant conflict and at the same time promoting the relations between Chinese and foreigners." *China Year Book, 1931*, p. 487.

[16] *North China Herald*, CLXXIV, Jan. 7, 1930, pp. 1-2. Two incidents, however, both occurring in January, 1930, did give the British and American

entered a formal protest, reserving all of its rights with regard to the existing treaty.[17] The Italian Minister reminded the Chinese Government of the conditions laid down in Annex I of the treaty of November 27, 1928, and announced that Italian consular courts would continue to operate until those conditions had been met.[18] The Brazilian Chargé, Mr. Pedro Soares, informed Dr. Wang that his government had watched with deep appreciation the endeavor of China to reform her laws and judicial organization so that satisfactory protection might be accorded to the lives and property of foreigners. The Brazilian Government, therefore, was ready, in collaboration with other interested powers, to enter into negotiations with the Chinese Government for the purpose of reaching a final settlement relative to the abolition of extraterritoriality.[19]

Governments some cause for concern. On January 23 at Hankow, a motor car driven by Lieutenant Commander McBride, of the British navy, accidentally ran over and killed a Chinese boy. After being arrested by Chinese police, the officer was escorted to the Bureau of Public Safety in the native city. Representations made by British Consular authorities met with a firm refusal to release the officer, the Chinese police stating that they were acting in accordance with instructions from Nanking to the effect that all foreigners were henceforth to be tried in Chinese courts according to Chinese law. McBride was finally released after the British Consul-General had given a written guarantee that he would appear for any inquiry that might be made. *North China Herald,* CLXXIV, Jan. 28, 1930, p. 132. This incident doubtless accounted for an aide-mémoire subsequently handed by Mr. Henderson to Dr. Sze in London. The British Government deemed it of the utmost importance that no untoward incident should imperil the forthcoming negotiations with regard to extraterritoriality. The Chinese Government was asked, therefore, to issue strict orders to all provincial and local authorities to the effect that treaty stipulations affecting the status and privileges of British subjects should continue in full force until modifications had been effected as the result of negotiations. *North China Herald,* CLXXIV, Feb. 11, 1930, p. 205.

The other incident concerned an American missionary, Mr. A. H. Smith, whose motor car killed a Chinese youth at Tungchow, Kiangsu, on January 29. Smith immediately submitted himself for trial to the Chinese court at Tungchow. An American destroyer was sent to the city bearing a consular officer who investigated the affair and sent his findings to the American Legation in Peiping. The missionary was subsequently tried by the Chinese court and fined $100 (silver). The American State Department apparently took the view that Smith was not authorized to submit himself to Chinese jurisdiction except as specified in existing treaties. *New York Times,* Feb. 14 and Feb. 19, 1930.

[17] *North China Herald,* CLXXIV, Jan. 7, 1930, p. 2.
[18] *Ibid.*
[19] Note of January 27, 1930. Text, *Peiping Leader,* Feb. 25, 1930.

During 1930 the Nanking Government continued its efforts to reach some agreement with the British, American, French, and Japanese Governments relative to the relinquishment of extraterritorial privileges. Each of the foreign governments concerned desired the adoption of some plan for the progressive abolition of consular jurisdiction. Concrete proposals along this line were submitted to Dr. Wang by Sir Miles Lampson on September 11, 1930, and on September 18, the Department of State at Washington announced that draft proposals for an agreement relative to the gradual abandonment of American extraterritorial privileges were ready for discussion. The British proposals apparently contemplated the surrender of jurisdiction in civil cases immediately, except in the principal ports, and the surrender of criminal jurisdiction after five years. The American plan, similar to but not identical with that formulated by the British Government, was based in part on the principle of transfer of jurisdiction relative to specified kinds of cases and in part on the principle of such transfer in all but specified areas.[20] Sino-Japanese negotiations were initiated at Nanking on March 12, 1931. Dr. Wang was said to have demanded the immediate and unconditional abolition of Japan's rights of consular jurisdiction. The Japanese Government, according to reports, was willing to proceed with negotiations on the following lines: Jurisdiction to be surrendered over all civil cases and minor criminal cases in Peiping, Tientsin, Hankow, Canton, and Shanghai; a court to be established in which Japanese judges would be permitted to collaborate in cases involving their nationals; cases involving Japanese in the interior to be brought into this mixed court; Japanese to have the same privileges as Chinese in the five cities named in respect of taxation, the leasing of land, the establishment of factories, etc.; Japanese privileges of leasing in special areas—the reference apparently being to Manchuria—to be recognized.[21]

Dr. Wang continued to insist on China's full right to judicial

[20] Harold S. Quigley in *Current History*, December, 1930, p. 477. *Ibid.*, January, 1931, p. 637.
[21] Harold S. Quigley in *Current History*, May, 1931, p. 319.

autonomy and in April, 1931, negotiations with the representatives of the four powers reached a deadlock. In an effort to break this deadlock, and at the same time to win support in the Peoples' Convention which was to meet the next day at Nanking, the National Government on May 4 promulgated regulations for the enforcement of the mandate on extraterritoriality which had been issued on December 28, 1929.[22] The regulations provided that beginning January 1, 1932, all foreigners who had been entitled to extraterritorial rights on December 31, 1929, were to be subject to the jurisdiction of Chinese courts. In the Special Districts of the Three Eastern Provinces, and at Mukden, Tientsin, Tsingtao, Shanghai, Hankow, Chungking, Foochow, Canton, and Yunnanfu, special courts were to be established for the trial of criminal and civil cases involving foreigners. Any foreigner residing in the interior who was a defendant in a civil or criminal suit might ask that the case be tried before the nearest of these special courts. Advisers, who need not necessarily be Chinese, might be attached to each of the special courts by the Ministry of Justice. Such advisers would be allowed to submit to the courts written memoranda outlining their views relative to specific cases, but would not be permitted to interfere with the rendering of judgments. The arrest or detention of foreigners, or the search of their residences or offices, was to be carried out in accordance with provisions of the Chinese Criminal Code. Foreigners charged with a criminal offense were to be handed over to the appropriate court within twenty-four hours after arrest. Arbitration agreements were to be recognized by the court if not contrary to law or morals. Foreigners in civil or criminal cases might appoint Chinese or foreign lawyers to act as their representatives or to conduct their defense. Foreigners charged with violation of certain police regulations were to be tried by local police courts. The punishment in such cases, however, was not to exceed a fine of fifteen dollars. For the detention and imprisonment of

[22] Text, *North China Herald*, CLXXIX, May 5, 1931, p. 148.

foreigners, places were to be designated by a special order of the Ministry of Justice.[22a]

Of some significance in connection with China's desire to assert her jurisdictional sovereignty was the agreement of February 17, 1930, by which the mixed court at Shanghai was restored to Chinese control. A grievance of long standing among the Chinese concerned the fact that beginning in 1911, the foreign consular body at Shanghai assumed the right to appoint the Chinese judges of this tribunal, which was located in the International Settlement. Particular emphasis was given to this grievance during the disturbances of 1925. A year later the consular representatives of the interested powers at Shanghai succeeded in concluding with the Kiangsu Provincial Government an agreement providing for the replacement of the Mixed Court by a Provisional Court and a Court of Appeal, the judges of which were to be appointed by the Provincial Government, then controlled by Marshal Sun Ch'uan-fang.[23] The 1926 agreement, which was to remain in force three years, became operative on January 1, 1927.

On May 8, 1929, Dr. Wang addressed identic notes to the American, Brazilian, British, French, Netherlands and Norwegian Ministers, requesting them to begin immediate negotiations for the reorganization of the Provisional Court at Shanghai.[24] The Dutch Minister, on behalf of his colleagues, replied on June 7 stating that since the court was a strictly local institution, its reorganization should be discussed on behalf of the interested Legations by a commission chosen from among their local representatives together with the representatives of the Chinese Government. Dr. Wang protested on July 3, and in-

[22a] On December 29, 1931, the Nanking Government, wrestling with political disorganization induced by the Japanese military invasion of Manchuria and disastrous floods in the Yangtse Valley, ordered that the enforcement of the Regulations of May 4, 1931, should be "temporarily postponed." Text of mandate, *The Chinese Nation* (Shanghai), III, Jan. 6, 1932, p. 104.

[23] Text, *Treaties and Agreements, 1919-1929*, pp. 169-81.

[24] It is noteworthy that a copy of this note was not sent to the Japanese Minister, nor to the representatives of Belgium, Italy, Denmark, Portugal, or Spain.

sisted on a settlement of the question directly with the Ministers themselves. On August 2, Mr. Oudendijk accepted Dr. Wang's proposal.[25]

Beginning from December 9, 1929, twenty-eight meetings of the commission were held at Nanking, and on February 17, 1930, an agreement was signed by the representatives of the Ministers of the powers concerned, with the exception of the French delegate who signed five days later.[26] The Provisional Court was replaced by a District Court, substantially similar to other Chinese courts of the same grade, and a Branch High Court to which appeals could be taken. Both courts were of course to apply Chinese law, both substantive and procedural. The deputy judge system permitting foreign consular representatives to assist in all cases, was abolished. The clerical force of the court was henceforth to be under Chinese control. The judicial police were to be nominated by the municipal council of the International Settlement but appointed by and subject to removal by the Chinese Government. The Women's Prison and the civil detention quarters were transferred to Chinese control, and other prisons which remained in the possession of the foreign municipal council were to be subject to Chinese inspection.

RESIDENTIAL CONCESSIONS

When the Nationalist Government took over exclusive control of China's foreign relations, negotiations were pending with regard to the retrocession of the Belgian and British Concessions at Tientsin. In January, 1929, the Ministry of Foreign Affairs at Nanking received word that Baron Jules Guillaume, Counsellor of the Belgian Legation, had been appointed as commissioner to negotiate for the return of the Belgian Concession.[27] Formal negotiations which began in May resulted in an agreement which was signed at Tientsin on August 31,

[25] *China Year Book, 1931*, p. 488.
[26] Text, *Ibid.*, pp. 489-91.
[27] *North China Herald*, CLXX, Feb. 2, 1929, p. 178.

1929.[28] Belgium agreed to turn over the Concession which was thereafter to be administered under Chinese laws and regulations and protected by the same. All public properties of the Concession, together with the bank deposits of the municipality, were likewise handed over to the Chinese Government. Title deeds and certificates of private property issued by the Belgian Consulate were to be exchanged for certificates of perpetual lease issued by the Chinese Government. It was agreed that there should be no change in the land tax in the former Concession until the National Government had promulgated a new general law governing land taxation. The Chinese Government agreed to reimburse the Belgian Government for debts of the former municipality amounting to Tientsin Taels 93,826.48.

Negotiations for the rendition of the British Concession at Tientsin were resumed in 1929, and in the middle of that year a draft agreement modifying that which had been concluded in 1927 was signed by the Chinese and British delegates.[29] Meanwhile the Concession was reorganized so as to place the British and Chinese upon an equal footing as regards franchise and representation on the council.[30]

The British Concession at Chinkiang was formally returned to Chinese control on November 15, 1929, following an exchange of notes between Dr. Wang and Sir Miles Lampson.[31] The British Municipal Administration was dissolved. The Chinese Government agreed to issue deeds of perpetual lease in exchange for the certificates of title to the lots of land in the former Concession which had been issued by the British Government. Pending the promulgation by the National Government of a new law governing land taxation throughout China, and until the actual application of that law to the Chinkiang

[28] Text, with Annexes, *China Year Book, 1929-30*, pp. 916-18.
[29] *China Year Book, 1931*, p. 73 note.
[30] Statement of Mr. Arthur Henderson before the House of Commons, January 22, 1930, *Parliamentary Debates*, 5th Series, Vol. 234, pp. 213-14.
[31] Texts of the notes, dated October 31, 1929, *China Year Book, 1931*, pp. 481-2. Actually the police administration of the Concession was in Chinese hands after May 24, 1927, previous to which time Nationalist troops had occupied the city. *Ibid.*, p. 481.

district, the annual land tax paid by former holders of British Crown leases in the Concession was not to be changed. British firms at Chinkiang were to continue to enjoy the right of conveying goods, merchandise, and material across the Bund from warehouses to pontoons or ships in the stream. The Chinese Government agreed to place the sum of $68,000 at the disposal of two commissioners, one to be appointed by itself and the other by the British Government, who would jointly scrutinize claims for losses suffered by British subjects and distribute the necessary amounts. Any balance remaining over after the settlement of all claims was to be returned to the National Government.

Provision was made for the rendition of the British Concession at Amoy in notes exchanged by Dr. Wang and the British Minister on September 17, 1930.[32] As in the case of the Chinkiang Concession, documents of title to land issued by the British Government were to be exchanged for deeds of perpetual lease issued by the Chinese Government, and there was to be no change in the local land tax pending the promulgation and enforcement of a new law governing land taxation throughout China.

Between 1927 and 1930, the Chinese Government recovered full administrative control over the British Concessions at Hankow, Kiukiang, Chinkiang, and Amoy. Less important but no less significant was the reorganization of the local governments in the International Settlements at Shanghai and Kulangsu in such a way as to permit representation of the Chinese rate payers. The International Settlement at Shanghai was governed by a council of nine members elected from among the foreign rate payers. During the disturbances of 1925, demands were made that Chinese be admitted to membership on the Council, the number of Chinese and foreign members to be determined on the basis of the total taxes paid by the Chinese and foreign rate payers, respectively. At the annual meetings of the foreign rate payers in 1926, a resolution was adopted providing for an

[32] Texts, *China Year Book, 1931,* p. 482-3.

increase in the size of the council to permit the election for the first time of three Chinese members. This arrangement was approved by the Ministers of the interested foreign powers, but was not acceptable to the Chinese, the latter contending that since they paid more than half of the taxes in the Settlement they were entitled to representation on that basis.[33] In 1928 a compromise was arranged by the foreign municipal authorities and representatives of the Chinese rate payers. In addition to three Chinese members on the council, six more Chinese were to be allowed to serve on committees of the council having charge of the various administrative departments of the municipality.[34] At the annual meeting of the foreign rate payers in 1930, further action was taken to increase the number of Chinese members on the council from three to five, the number of foreign members meanwhile remaining stationary at nine.[35]

In September, 1926, the Senior Consul at Amoy received from the Diplomatic Body at Peking a telegram authorizing the appointment of three Chinese members to the municipal council of the International Settlement at Kulangsu. Owing to a dispute concerning the meaning of this telegram, no Chinese members were appointed to the council for 1928, the Chinese desiring to limit the size of the council to seven members, of whom three were to be Chinese, while the intention of the interested diplomatic representatives was to increase Chinese (there was already one Chinese member on the council) without reducing foreign representation. In August, 1929, an arrangement was made whereby the council should consist of five foreign and three Chinese members, and, further, that special Chinese committeemen should serve in an advisory capacity on the five committees of the council.[36]

[33] See Anatol M. Kotenev, *Shanghai: Its Municipality and the Chinese*, Shanghai, 1927, Ch. XIII.
[34] *China Year Book, 1929-30*, pp. 101-3.
[35] *Ibid.*, 1931, p. 74. *China Weekly Review*, LII, May 10, 1930, pp. 396, 411.
[36] *China Year Book, 1931*, p. 75. Chinese have representation on the municipal councils of other foreign concessions as follows: British Concession at Tientsin, 5 foreign and 5 Chinese members; French Concession at Tientsin, 3 Chinese and 11 foreign members, including the French consul who serves

Reference has already been made to the unsuccessful negotiations in 1922 and 1924 for the return of the British leased
territory at Weihaiwei. In January, 1930, the British Minister,
Sir Miles Lampson, began a new series of conversations on the
subject with Dr. Wang. The draft Convention and Agreement
which were completed in February were formally signed on
April 18, 1930.[37] The Convention for the lease of Weihaiwei,
concluded on July 1, 1898, was expressly abrogated and the
area, together with all islands in the bay, returned to the Republic of China. The British Government agreed to turn over
without compensation the following properties: all lands and
buildings belonging to it in the former leased territory; the
Chefoo-Weihaiwei cable and certain government stores; the civil
hospitals at Port Edward and Wenchuantang, including land,
buildings and equipment; all land previously owned by the
Chinese Government on the island of Liukungtao; all existing
aids to navigation, including lighthouses, markbuoys and storm
signals. The Chinese Government agreed to maintain so far as
possible existing regulations concerning the land and house tax,
sanitary and building regulations, and policing. All documents
of title to land issued by the British Administration to persons
other than Chinese were to be exchanged for Chinese deeds of
perpetual lease. The area was to remain open for international
residence and trade unless and until the Chinese Government
decided to close the port and use it exclusively as a naval base.
Furthermore, pending the establishment of such a naval base,
the Chinese Government agreed to lease to the British Govern-

as president; French Concession at Shanghai, 5 Chinese and 12 foreign mem-
bers, including the French consul-general who serves as president; French
Concession at Hankow, 2 Chinese and 6 foreign members, including the
French consul-general who acts as chairman. The Chinese have no representation on the municipal councils of the Japanese Concessions at Newchwang,
Tientsin, or Hankow, nor are they represented on the councils of the British
and French Concessions at Canton (Shameen). The Italian Concession at
Tientsin has no council. *China Year Book, 1931,* pp. 73-5. In January 1931
it was reported that France had expressed a willingness to return her Hankow
Concession within five years. Harold S. Quigley, *Current History,* February,
1931, p. 796.
   [37] Text, *China Year Book, 1931,* pp. 483-6. The exchange of ratifications was effected on October 1, 1930, and the transfer of Weihaiwei to
Chinese control took place the same day.

ment free of charge for a period of thirty years, with the option of renewal by the holders, certain designated lands and buildings in the territory for the requirements of the British Consulate and the public interests of the residents. It was agreed that the British Government should be accorded the right to lease as a sanitorium and summer resort for the use of the British navy a certain number of buildings and facilities on the island of Liukungtao for a period of ten years, with the option of renewal on the same terms by agreement or on such other terms as might be agreed upon between the two governments. Ships of the British navy were also to be given the privilege of visiting Liukungtao and its waters during the months of April to October, inclusive, it being understood that in the event of war involving either China or Great Britain, the ships concerned would be withdrawn from such waters.

THE CHINESE EASTERN RAILWAY

Some one has remarked after a study of Chinese diplomatic history that the negotiation of a treaty has usually meant the beginning rather than the end of trouble between China and the power concerned. The remark is particularly apt with regard to the Sino-Soviet agreements of 1924. Two provisions of those agreements provoked unending friction and controversy almost from the moment of their signature. The first was the provision for joint administration of the Chinese Eastern Railway as a commercial enterprise. The second was the clause relating to the dissemination of propaganda inimical to the political and social institutions of either country.

As early as August 1, 1923, before these agreements were negotiated, the Chinese authorities in Manchuria had shown evidence of a desire to control directly such activities of the Railway Company as were not related specifically to railway operations. In the course of many years, the company had acquired much land. Some of this was used in connection with railway construction. The rest was leased to private persons

388   *China's Foreign Relations*

and companies, as the opportunity offered, as part of a general policy of developing the territory adjacent to the railway and thereby increasing its freight revenues. Late in July, 1923, it became known that General Chu Ching-lan, Chief Administrator of the Railway Zone, had received orders from Marshal Chang Tso-lin at Mukden to take over the management of the Railway's Land Department.[38] Russian protests, coupled with remonstrances made about the same time by the consular representatives of Great Britain, France, the United States, and Japan, caused the Mukden Government to reconsider its action. In February, 1924, therefore, that government announced that pending a final adjustment of the matter by agreement between the Chinese and the Soviet Governments, the following regulations would be in effect: such properties as the Railway Company had originally acquired were to remain in its possession; except with regard to lands and buildings directly required for the use of the Company, the drawing up of plans for the establishment of markets, ports, towns or villages, together with all construction work connected therewith, was to be undertaken by the Chinese authorities; before additional lands could be leased, the sanction of the Chinese authorities must first be secured in each instance, and all leasees, both old and new, were required to pay Chinese taxes.[39] Even these regulations did not represent the limit of Chinese interference, and in May, 1925, Mr. Karakhan felt called upon to protest against the actions of the local authorities at Harbin which he denounced as "illegal and intolerable." [40]

Both agreements of 1924 provided for control of the Railway Company by a Board of Directors of ten persons, five to be named by the Chinese Government and five by the Soviet Government. The Board, however, did not function effectively, often not meeting for long periods, and as a consequence real power was concentrated in the hands of the General Manager

[38] *North China Herald,* CXLVIII, Aug. 18, 1923, p. 450.
[39] *China Year Book, 1924,* p. 890.
[40] *China Weekly Review,* XXXII, May 30, 1925, pp. 374-5.

and his assistant, both of whom were Soviet citizens.[41] This fact gave rise to a near crisis in January, 1926, when General Manager Ivanoff, acting on his own responsibility, declined to furnish transportation for troops loyal to Chang Tso-lin until payment therefor had been made in advance. When Ivanoff attempted to prevent the military authorities from operating trains in defiance of his orders, he was placed under arrest.[42] The Soviet Government, aroused by this arbitrary action, gave Chang Tso-lin three days in which to effect Ivanoff's release and to restore normal traffic over the Changchun-Harbin section of the railway.[43] The Mukden dictator deemed it expedient to meet these demands, an agreement having been reached meanwhile for defraying the cost of transporting Chinese troops out of China's share of the railway profits.[44] Subsequently, however, the Soviet Government found it necessary to replace General Manager Ivanoff with a new appointee.[45]

The Mukden authorities next cast covetous eyes upon the fleet of ships belonging to the railway company. For eighteen months these ships had been idle in consequence of a mandate published on January 22, 1925, forbidding any except Chinese vessels to navigate the inland waters of Manchuria.[46] Demands having been made, the fleet was handed over to Chinese control on August 31, 1926, together with the entire shipping department of the railway.[47] When the Russian Government protested, the officials at Mukden pointed to the Soviet seizure, carried out several years before, of barges and terminal facilities

[41] There was also a Chinese Assistant General Manager who seems, actually, to have had little to do.
[42] *North China Herald*, CLVIII, Jan. 30, 1926, p. 178.
[43] *Ibid.*, p. 177.
[44] *Ibid.*, p. 178.
[45] *Ibid.*, CLIX, Apr. 24, 1926, p. 152. *Ibid.*, May 1, 1926, p. 190. In April, 1926, Comrade Serebriakoff, Chief of the Department of Communications at Moscow, was sent to China to negotiate a permanent settlement of the railway question with the Mukden Government. The negotiations which began early in June were broken off after only a few days. *North China Herald*, CLIX, June 12, 1926, pp. 474, 479.
[46] *North China Herald*, CLX, Sept. 4, 1926, p. 439.
[47] *Ibid.*, Sept. 11, 1926, p. 491.

owned by the Chinese Eastern Railway Company at Vladivostok.[48] At the same time the Chinese authorities, despite remonstrances from Moscow, assumed charge of the educational department of the company.[49] Similar action was taken in December, 1928, with regard to the telephone system operated by the company at Harbin.[50]

One of the reasons assigned for the Chinese seizure of the railway's educational department was that the schools were being used to propagate communist ideas and ideals in violation of the 1924 agreements. Marshal Chang Tso-lin had developed a particular hatred of Soviet principles. He believed that the sudden revolt of one of his ablest generals in November, 1925, had been caused by Soviet machinations. He was convinced also that his arch enemy, Marshal Feng Yu-hsiang, was receiving financial and other assistance from the Soviet Government.[51] There was also the fact that the Nationalists to the south were known to be receiving aid from Russia.

In March, 1926, Marshal Chang's determination to rid northern China of communist influence took concrete form in a demand for the recall of the Soviet Ambassador, Mr. Karakhan, who was charged with having instigated student riots and also with having encouraged civil commotion in other ways.[52] This demand was repeated on a number of occasions after the Fengtien capture of Peking. When it became apparent that Mr. Karakhan's usefulness in China had come to an end, the Soviet Government finally, in August, 1926, ordered his return to Moscow where he took up the position of Acting Commissar of Foreign Affairs.[53] His place at Peking was taken by the newly appointed Chargé d'Affaires, Mr. A. S. Chernyk.

In the spring of 1927 Marshal Chang resolved upon far

[48] *Ibid.*, also Sept. 18, 1926, p. 543.
[49] *Ibid.*, Sept. 4, 1926, p. 439.
[50] *China Weekly Review*, XLVII, Jan. 12, 1929, p. 290.
[51] For the text of an alleged agreement between Feng and the Soviet Government dated Mar. 11, 1925, see *North China Herald*, CLVII, Dec. 26, 1925, p. 552.
[52] *North China Herald*, CLIX, Apr. 24, 1926, p. 151.
[53] *Ibid.*, CLX, Sept. 4, 1926, p. 436.

more drastic action in the attempt to curb the spread of Bolshevism—which he was inclined to associate with the progress of his enemies, the Nationalists. On April 6, 1927, a force of Chinese troops and police raided the Soviet Embassy in Peking, thoroughly searched buildings occupied by the Military Attaché, seized a vast quantity of papers and documents, and arrested a number of Russians and Chinese found on the premises.[54] The Soviet Government immediately denounced the raid as "an unprecedented violation of the elementary rules of international law," [55] and presented certain demands which the Chinese Government declined to accept. Thereupon the Russian Chargé asked for and received his passports. Replying to the Soviet protest on April 16, the Foreign Minister, Dr. Koo, defended the action of the Chinese authorities which, he said, was fully justified as a measure of self-defense. The documents taken during the raid abundantly proved that members of the Embassy staff had been engaged in the dissemination of communist propaganda contrary to the stipulations of the Peking agreement.[56]

Despite the withdrawal of the Soviet diplomatic representative, Soviet Consulates in Manchuria and north China remained open until the spring of 1929 [57] when a new crisis was precipitated by a raid on the consulate at Harbin. The Chinese authorities had received word that a regional conference of the Communist Internationale would be held there on May 27, 1929. While the meeting was in progress, Chinese police appeared on the scene, seized two truckloads of papers and documents, and arrested forty-two Russian Consular officials including the Consul-General and Vice-Consul at Harbin and the

[54] *North China Herald*, CLXIII, Apr. 9, 1927, p. 63. For a first-hand account of the raid, see the article by Lawrence Impey in *China Weekly Review*, XL, Apr. 23, 1927, pp. 198-9. Translations of some of the documents seized are given in *Chinese Social and Political Science Review*, XI, July and October, 1927, Public Documents Supplement.

[55] Litvinov to Cheng Yen-chi, Chinese Chargé at Moscow, April 10, 1927, text, *North China Herald*, CLXIII, Apr. 16, 1927, p. 97.

[56] *North China Herald*, CLXIII, Apr. 23, 1927, p. 145.

[57] As already noted, Russian Consulates in southern China were closed by the Nanking Government in December, 1927, following the abortive communist uprising at Canton.

Consul-General at Mukden, and thirty-nine communists from various parts of Manchuria.[58]

Evidence unearthed during the Consulate raid seemed to confirm Chinese suspicions that various Soviet officials of the Chinese Eastern Railway were taking an active part in the spread of Bolshevist ideas. Consequently, on July 10, the authorities at Harbin proceeded to adopt extreme measures. The entire telegraph system of the railway was seized, all Soviet Unions were dissolved, and the offices of the Soviet Mercantile Fleet, the Far Eastern State Trading Organization, and the Naphtha Syndicate were sealed. The next day, Mr. F. Emshanov, General Manager of the railway, was dismissed from office and replaced by a Chinese appointee. Wholesale dismissals, arrests, deportations, and internment of Soviet employees followed.[59]

The Soviet Government was not long in adopting counter measures. On July 14 the Chinese Chargé at Moscow received from Mr. Karakhan a note denouncing the actions of the Harbin authorities as the "most obvious and grossest violations of clear and unequivocal clauses of agreements concluded between the U. S. S. R. and China" which meant in effect the seizure of the railway and an attempt at unilateral cancellation of existing agreements. China was reminded that by the terms of those agreements, all questions upon which the Railway Board of Directors could not agree were to be referred for settlement to the governments of the contracting parties. The Soviet Government then demanded that:

A conference be called immediately to regulate all questions connected with the Chinese Eastern Railway.

The Chinese authorities cancel immediately all arbitrary orders regarding the Railway.

All arrested Soviet citizens be immediately released, and the Chinese authorities cease their persecution of Soviet citizens and Soviet institutions.

[58] *Chinese Social and Political Science Review*, XIII, October, 1929, Public Documents Supplement, pp. 131-136. For translations of some of the documents taken during the raid, see *The Sino-Russian Crisis*, pamphlet issued by International Relations Committee (Nanking, 1929), pp. 42-81.

[59] *China Year Book, 1929-30*, p. 1217.

The Chinese Government was given three days in which to return a satisfactory answer. In case the demands were met, the Soviet Government was prepared to enter into prompt negotiations for the settlement of all railway questions. In case the demands were not accepted, however, the Soviet Government would be compelled "to resort to other means for the protection of the lawful rights of the U. S. S. R." [60]

The reply of the Chinese Government, transmitted to Moscow on July 16, stressed the fact that for years Soviet officials in China had been active in spreading communist propaganda.[61] The search of the Consulate at Harbin and other measures taken with regard to the Chinese Eastern Railway had merely in view "the prevention of sudden occurrences of incidents that are detrimental to the peace and order of the country." The General Manager and other Soviet officials of the railway had been dismissed because on numerous occasions they had "acted illegally and exceeded their lawful authority," thus "making it impossible for the Chinese officials of the Railway to carry out their duties" according to the agreement of 1924. Furthermore, the Soviet members of the railway staff had used their positions to disseminate propaganda, in violation of the terms of that agreement. The National Government then charged that Soviet authorities had arrested more than one thousand Chinese merchants resident in Russia "without any provocation whatsoever." The Chinese note did not refer directly to the demands contained in Mr. Karakhan's communication. But if the Soviet Government would release all Chinese merchants arrested and detained in Russia, and give such adequate protection and facilities as Chinese merchants in Russia were entitled to, the National Government would be ready "at the appropriate time to take similar measures towards the arrested Soviet agents and the closed office buildings." The Chinese Minister, Mr. Chu Shao-yang, would be instructed to make a careful investigation of the situation at Harbin before returning to his post at Moscow. Thereafter all outstanding issues between China and Soviet Russia as well as questions regarding the Chinese Eastern

[60] *China Year Book, 1929-30*, pp. 1217-20.   [61] *Ibid.*, pp. 1220-22.

Railway could be taken up by Minister Chu with the Soviet Foreign Office "in order to secure a justifiable and amicable solution."

The Soviet Government's second note was dated July 18.[62] The Chinese reply was declared to be unsatisfactory in content and hypocritical in tone. Instead of disavowing the unlawful conduct of its agents in Manchuria, the Chinese Government had sanctioned that conduct, thus justifying the arbitrary seizure of the railway. Moreover, instead of discontinuing the unlawful repressions against Soviet citizens and Soviet institutions in China, the National Government sanctioned those repressions and hypocritically attempted to justify them by the false reference to certain mass repressions against Chinese citizens in the U. S. S. R., thus ignoring the known fact that these repressions in the U. S. S. R. were being applied "only against an insignificant group of spies, opium traders, den keepers, smugglers and other criminal elements among the Chinese citizens." The reference of the Chinese Government to propaganda as the cause of the unlawful actions of its officials was hypocritical and false, for the Chinese authorities possessed on their territory "sufficient means to prevent and to stop such activity had it actually taken place, without seizing the Chinese Eastern Railway and severing the Treaty relations existing between China and the U. S. S. R." In view of the above, the Soviet Government declared that the means necessary to settle amicably the controversies and disputes relative to the Chinese Eastern Railway caused by the Chinese authorities and aggravated by the Chinese Government's note of July 17 had been exhausted, and it was necessary therefore to take the following measures:

"To recall all Soviet diplomatic, consular and commercial representatives from the territory of China.

"To recall all persons appointed by the Government of the U.S.S.R. on the Chinese Eastern Railway from the territory of China.

"To suspend all railway communications between China and the U.S.S.R.

"To order the diplomatic and consular representatives of the

[62] *China Year Book, 1929-30*, pp. 1222-23.

Chinese Republic in the U.S.S.R. to leave immediately the territory of the U.S.S.R."

At the same time the Soviet Government reserved all rights arising from the Peking and Mukden agreements of 1924.

Meanwhile, on July 18, the American Secretary of State, Mr. Henry L. Stimson, took steps to remind both the Chinese and the Russian Governments of their obligations under the Kellogg-Briand pact for the renunciation of war.[63] Late in July the local representatives of the Mukden and the Soviet Governments at Harbin exchanged views relative to a possible settlement of the dispute by peaceful means. These negotiations terminated when Marshal Chang Hsueh-liang showed a disinclination to accept Soviet demands for the reinstatement of the Soviet General Manager and his assistant.[64] Following the breakdown of negotiations at Harbin, the German Government tendered its good offices in an endeavor to bring the two parties together, the result being a number of conversations between the Soviet Ambassador and the Chinese Minister in Berlin.[65] The Soviet Government, at first inclined to be conciliatory, later demanded the right to appoint immediately a new general manager of the railway as a condition precedent to the beginning of formal negotiations. The Chinese refusal to accept this demand caused the failure of the German attempt at mediation.[66] When the German Government subsequently suggested that a mutual exchange of prisoners would ease the situation and facilitate a peaceful settlement, the Soviet Government rejected the proposal on the ground that China had no intention of respecting her treaty obligations.[67]

The failure of these attempts to reach a peaceful settlement

[63] Stanley K. Hornbeck, "American Policy and the Chinese-Russian Dispute," *Chinese Social and Political Science Review*, XIV, January, 1930, pp. 56-60. The Chinese Government on September 13, 1928, accepted the American invitation to become a signatory of this treaty. *China Year Book, 1929-30*, pp. 877-8.

[64] Statement of the Soviet Commissariat of Foreign Affairs, August 7, 1929, *China Year Book, 1929-30*, pp. 1225-26.

[65] *China Year Book, 1929-30*, pp. 1226-27.

[66] Manifesto of the Chinese Government sent on October 25 to all the signatories of the Kellogg-Briand Pact. *China Year Book, 1929-30*, pp. 1227-9.

[67] *Ibid.*

provoked the Chinese Government to invite the attention of the world "to the numerous acts of aggression perpetrated by the Soviet Government within Chinese territory." [68] As early as July there was fighting along the Manchurian border. Soviet troops indulged in frequent raids across the Chinese border, ostensibly in retaliation for similar raids into Russian territory by "White Guards." Soviet aeroplanes dropped bombs on Chinese towns and cities adjacent to the frontier. Toward the end of the year these clashes increased in number and intensity, culminating in November in the advance of a Soviet army into the Barga region, at the western end of the Chinese Eastern Railway. The heavy losses suffered by Chinese troops were equaled only by the loss of life and property among the civilian population. [69]

It was quite apparent that the Soviet Government was determined to force matters to a conclusion. What was equally apparent was that the Mukden Government could expect little effective help, either military or diplomatic, from Nanking. [70] Under these circumstances Marshal Chang Hsueh-liang authorized the Commissioner of Foreign Affairs at Harbin, Mr. Tsai Yun-sheng, to get into telephonic communication with Mr. B. N. Melnikov, previously Soviet Consul-General at Harbin, who was then waiting the course of events at Chita. The resulting exchange of views bore fruit in a tentative arrangement concluded at Nikolsk-Ussurissk on December 3 which provided for the restoration of the situation existing prior to the conflict and based upon the Peking and Mukden Agreements. [71] Following these preliminary negotiations, a formal conference opened at Khabarovsk on December 13. The Soviet Foreign Office was represented by Comrade Simanovsky. The Chinese delegate was Tsai Yun-sheng, who was authorized to act on behalf of both

[68] *Ibid.*

[69] *China Year Book, 1929-30,* p. 1229. *Ibid., 1931,* p. 496. Harold S. Quigley, "Kellogg Pact Invoked in Soviet-Chinese Dispute," *Current History,* January, 1930, pp. 758-63.

[70] The Nanking Government was busy during most of this period quelling insurrections in central and northwest China.

[71] Text, Quigley, *op. cit.,* p. 761.

the Mukden and the Nanking Governments. An agreement was signed on December 22.[72] It provided in substance for the immediate restoration of the *status quo ante* with regard to the administration of the Chinese Eastern Railway, on the basis of the 1924 agreements. Each side agreed to the immediate withdrawal of its troops from the territories of the other. Chinese citizens detained by the Soviet Government and Soviet citizens detained in Manchuria were to be released, including Soviet citizens taken in the Harbin Consulate raid. The Chinese authorities were immediately to disarm the Russian White Guard detachments and deport from Manchuria their organizers and leaders. Consular offices were to be reëstablished by China in Siberia, and by the Soviet Union in Manchuria, and the Mukden Government was to guarantee the privileges of Soviet consular officers within its territory. Finally, it was agreed that a conference for the final settlement of outstanding issues between the two governments should meet in Moscow on January 25.

The Nanking Government declined to ratify the Khabarovsk protocol. On February 8 the Ministry of Foreign Affairs issued a formal statement announcing that Tsai Yun-sheng had exceeded his instructions.[73] He had been authorized to discuss questions arising out of the railway dispute together with the question of procedure for holding a formal conference on the subject. The agreement signed, however, contained in addition to a *modus vivendi* relating to issues arising out of the railway dispute, certain proposals of a general character concerning the relations between the two countries. In agreeing to these general proposals, the Chinese delegate had acted *ultra vires*. The National Government was prepared to send a delegate to the Moscow conference for the exclusive purpose of effecting a settlement of questions connected with the railway. On the other hand, should the Soviet Government deem it necessary to negotiate with the National Government relative to questions

[72] Text, *China Year Book, 1931*, p. 497.
[73] Text, *Ibid.*, pp. 497-8.

of a more general character, such as trade and commerce between the two countries, special delegates for that purpose would have to be appointed.

Eventually all of the provisions of the Khabarovsk protocol relating to the restoration of the *status quo* on the railway were carried out. The Soviet Government designated a new general manager to replace Emshanov. A new Chinese president of the railway was likewise appointed, the previous incumbent having been charged by the Soviet Government with responsibility for the original seizure of the railway. The new railway president was Mr. Mo Teh-hui who, on being appointed Chinese delegate to the Moscow conference, left Harbin May 1, 1930. Following his arrival in the Soviet capital, some time was consumed in discussions concerning the scope of the conference. Mr. Mo had been instructed to negotiate only with regard to the railway. Mr. Karakhan, on the other hand, insisted that the discussions should not be limited to railway questions but should deal also with questions concerning trade, the status of Consuls, and other matters of a more general nature. Eventually the Nanking authorities were induced to enlarge Mr. Mo's powers so as to make possible a general discussion of outstanding issues, as desired by the Soviet Government. The first formal session of the conference was held therefore on October 11, 1930.[74]

The second session of the conference was delayed by a controversy over the interpretation of the Peking and Mukden Agreements of 1924 in relation to the Chinese Eastern Railway. Mr. Karakhan insisted that existing conditions on the railway corresponded to the terms and intent of those agreements. Mr. Mo declared on the contrary that the existing status of the railway was not the same as that contemplated by the 1924 agreements.[75] Both delegates finally decided not to argue further concerning this question, but to proceed with negotia-

[74] *China Year Book, 1931,* p. 498.
[75] See the notes exchanged between Karakhan and Mo, November 10, November 17, November 23, November 28 and November 30, 1930, *China Year Book,* 1931, pp. 498-500.

tions. Thus another session of the conference was held on December 4. Twelve days later the conference sessions were again suspended and shortly thereafter Mr. Mo returned to China to consult with authorities at Mukden and Nanking. Meanwhile sub-committees in Moscow proceeded with a consideration of details.[76]

[76] Harold S. Quigley in *Current History,* January, 1931, p. 637; March, 1931, p. 959; April, 1931, p. 157.

CHAPTER XII

CONCLUSIONS

ONE who remembers the treatment meted out to China at Paris, or goes patiently through the official proceedings of the Washington Conference, can scarcely avoid being struck by the change in the attitude of the powers toward China which has taken place in recent years. Equally significant has been the change in the attitude of China toward the powers. Before the World War China was commonly regarded as the disorderly backyard of European politics. She accepted that humiliating status with ill-concealed resentment, but she accepted it. Now she demands the rights of a sovereign nation, and during the past ten years the powers have gone far toward recognizing the justice of her demands.

A number of factors have assisted the Chinese in the struggle for the recovery of their national rights. The first of these has been the general international situation resulting from the World War. The peoples of the West were war weary. They were compelled to grapple with domestic problems of the first magnitude—great loads of debt, heavy taxes, and acute problems of social readjustment. China might evade or even repudiate her international obligations and a few of the powers might be tempted to employ stern measures as a means of forcing recognition of their treaty rights. But there was no certainty that the peoples of the West would support fresh military adventures in distant lands. Military expeditions were costly, and the costs of the last great military adventure remained yet to be paid. It would not do for governments to encourage social unrest by increasing the burdens of the people still further. More than this, there was a moral sentiment abroad in the world which frowned on the habitual use of forcible methods in dealing with the so-called backward peoples.

The second factor favorable to the realization of Chinese aspirations was the growing realization among Western statesmen that something would have to be done to eliminate sources of international friction in the Pacific area. It was for this reason that the Washington Conference gave detailed consideration to the problems of China. That Conference dealt primarily with the reduction of naval armaments. But it was necessary at the same time to grapple with the problems which made naval armaments necessary. Unredressed grievances in the Far East promised to furnish the fuel for another international conflagration. The powers did comparatively little at Washington to remove the restrictions against which the Chinese protested. But they did place limits to the international competition for preferential rights in China, and at the same time they pledged themselves not to interfere while the Chinese made an honest effort to solve their own domestic problems.

In the third place, all of the powers were engaged after the war in a desperate competitive struggle for markets. China offered an unexploited or at least under-exploited market composed of 400,000,000 potential customers which no foreign Government could afford to ignore. Even the most reactionary of Western statesmen hastened to express sympathy with Chinese aspirations when faced with the prospect of a Chinese boycott of goods which their nationals desired to sell in the Oriental market. This factor more than any other, perhaps, has influenced the direction of British policy. With mills idle and the number of unemployed increasing, the British Government, even when controlled by the Conservatives, had to make radical concessions in order to keep open the Chinese market for British wares.

Finally, there was the grim specter of Soviet Russia spreading the gospel of unrest among Asiatic peoples and seeking to enlist the support of those peoples in a war against national and international capitalism. If China's aspirations were not accorded a sympathetic hearing, there was always the danger that she would be driven into the waiting arms of the Bolsheviki. Russia stood ready to utilize to the utmost every mistake made by the powers in dealing with China. And if Chinese resentment flamed up in a revolutionary conflagration, the flames might well spread to India, Korea, and Indo-China, not to mention Java and the Philippines. The urgent necessity of checking the communist advance in the Orient required Western statesmen to tread cautiously when dealing with China's problems.

At the same time, it is very easy to overemphasize the rôle played by Soviet Russia in stirring the Chinese to open rebellion against the treaty régime. Russia established a precedent by repudiating her own international obligations. The Karakhan declarations of 1919 and 1920 were in a sense revolutionary appeals to China to follow the example of her more radical neighbor. Russian willingness to abandon extraterritorial rights, residential concessions, and control over the Chinese tariff earned the gratitude of the Chinese and caused them to ask at the same time why the other powers delayed following suit. Russian aid and comfort given to Asiatic peoples was not, of course, an end in itself. The war against imperialism in Asia was, in Russian eyes, merely a part of the greater war of communism against capitalism. Capitalist pressure on Soviet Russia could be relieved to a certain extent by sapping the strength of Western capitalism in the colonial and semi-colonial countries of the Orient. The attitude of the Soviet leaders toward China was not purely altruistic. That fact was revealed quite definitely first by their Mongolian policy and then by their insistence on a recognition of Russia's rights with regard to the Chinese Eastern Railway.

Communist influence in China took many forms. Joffe, Karakhan, and Borodin, not to mention lesser lights, lost no opportunity to emphasize China's grievances and to attack the unequal treaties both publicly and privately, both directly and by subtle innuendo. The great influence of Joffe and Karakhan among the students and intellectual leaders of north China can be suggested if not exactly measured. In the south, the advice given by Borodin and other Russians influenced the organization, the tactics, and the revolutionary program of the Kuomintang. The party became a closely knit, well-disciplined body of men, committed to the realization of a clearly defined set of principles. Following Borodin's appearance at Canton, revolutionary appeals were made for the first time to the masses of peasants and workers. The development of a national consciousness among these masses of people meant that the battle for treaty revision was half won. It was only later that the fundamental antagonism between Chinese nationalism and Russian communism became apparent. Communism split the nation into warring social classes. Nationalism required the harmonious coöperation of all social classes in a common struggle against foreign imperialism. When this antagonism of aims became clearly evident, the Chinese Nationalists dispensed with the services of their Russian advisers and broke off relations with the Moscow Government.

One significant development during the period covered by the present study has been the growth of a determination among Chinese statesmen to deal with the powers not as a unit but individually. During the nineteenth century, when the powers were actively engaged in wringing concessions, political and economic, from a recalcitrant Government at Peking, coöperation among the powers occasionally worked to the advantage of China. The more reasonable-minded among them could exercise a measure of restraint over the rest. Since the World War, however, the powers have been content for the most part to rest in the enjoyment of their special privileges without demanding new ones. By and large, they were satisfied with the *status quo,* and their several policies, in consequence, were essentially passive in character. It was the Chinese Government, on the other hand, which adopted an active policy. China became more and more insistent on a modification of the *status quo.* At Paris and again at Washington the Chinese delegates asked, not without eloquence and with becoming dignity, for a redress of their country's legitimate grievances. At the first conference they got nothing, and at the second only a little with the promise of more in the indefinite future. In both instances, China had attempted to deal with the Treaty Powers as a unit. The signal failure of that policy was revealed in the meager results attained.

Coöperation among the powers in the twentieth century meant united opposition to changes in the treaties desired by the Chinese Government. Practically all of the treaties contained unconditional most favored nation clauses. Under such circumstances coöperation among the powers had the effect of reducing their common policy toward China to the level of the most reactionary and least enlightened among them. France took the lead at Washington in offering to return her leased territory provided the other powers followed suit. This program was blocked, as astute French statesmen doubtless foresaw that it would be blocked, by British reservations regarding Kowloon and Japanese reservations relative to Kwantung. Furthermore, eight powers agreed at Washington to make concessions by way of satisfying certain legitimate aspirations of the Chinese. One power, however, was able to block the execution of the entire program until extraneous demands had been met which bore no relation to the Washington program.[1] It was

[1] A month prior to the disturbances of 1925, a foreign editorial writer long resident in China expressed the following view: "There is no question but what the actions of France in blocking the fulfillment of the Washington agreements has seriously damaged not only her own prestige in the Orient, but the prestige of all of the Powers, and this undoubtedly has been responsible for much of the anti-foreign propaganda which has swept this land in the past three years." *China Weekly Review*, XXXII, May 2, 1925, p. 238. See also James A. Thomas, "Business Principles in World Politics," *Asia*, XXV, February, 1925, especially p. 101. Some months later another foreign writer expressed somewhat similar views. The French failure to ratify the Washington agreements, he said, had very important bearings upon the subsequent course of events in China. The masses of the Chinese people did not understand the importance of ratification. They knew only that the powers had met at Washington, that they had come to an understanding with regard to China's tariff, and that nothing further had happened. Consequently the Chinese reached the conclusion that the Powers were insincere and that the Washington Conference had been a bluff. This impression was prevalent throughout China and was one of the explanations for the extensive levying of illegal taxation by provincial authorities. *Far Eastern Review*, XXI, September, 1925, p. 586.

quite evident, therefore, that China would have to discover means of breaking the united front of the Treaty Powers if she expected ever to gain a restoration of her full sovereignty.

The chief factors making it possible for the Chinese Government to deal with the powers singly instead of as a unit were the World War and the Russian revolution. The World War enabled China to conclude with Germany the independent agreement of 1921 providing for the abandonment of all special privileges enjoyed by German nationals in the country. The Russian revolution eliminated Russia from the European family of nations and made possible the Sino-Soviet agreement of May, 1924. Two great powers, isolated from the others, had been induced if not forced to abandon extraterritorial rights, residential concessions, and control over the Chinese tariff. Following the conclusion of the German and Russian treaties, seventy-two per cent of the foreign white residents of China were amenable to Chinese laws and Chinese courts.[2]

After 1926 the Chinese Government declined to deal with the treaty powers as a unit, but resorted to individual negotiations on every possible occasion. At Peking the government took up the treaties one by one as they came due for revision. The Nationalist Government first at Canton and then at Hankow compelled Great Britain to bear the brunt of its attacks, seeking thereby to isolate the British and force them to take the lead in the matter of treaty revision. Mr. Chen even declined to acknowledge that the powers had common interests with regard to the Nanking Incident, but insisted on the right of his government to treat with each one separately. The Nanking Government reaped the full benefit of the policy of individual negotiation when it succeeded in concluding separate treaties with the powers providing in all cases for tariff autonomy and in some cases also for the conditional abandonment of extraterritorial rights.

[2] If allowance be made, however, for Japanese enjoying extraterritorial rights, the above figure should be only 27.2 per cent. Maritime Customs figures for 1924, *China Year Book, 1926*, p. 30.

The Chinese Nationalists cannot claim sole credit for the success of the movement for treaty revision. At a time when the Nationalists represented hardly more than a local faction at Canton, widespread sentiment against the foreign control imposed by the treaties existed in all parts of the country. Reflecting this growing sentiment, the Peking Government used the occasion of China's entrance into the World War to abrogate the treaties with Germany and Austria-Hungary. That this action had the cordial endorsement of the other great powers did not change the result: a breach was made in the structure of foreign privileges in China which the powers had taken eighty years to build. The Russian revolution furnished the Peking Government with an opportunity three years later for suspending existing treaties and assuming jurisdiction over all Russians and their interests in China. The foreign policy of the government at this time was characterized by a steadfast determination not to concede extraterritorial and other privileges to any of the newer European powers and at the same time to negotiate treaties of equality with such powers as were willing to enter into agreements on that basis.

The accomplishments of the Peking diplomats are significant when it is remembered how little effective support they had from the militarists and their satellites who manipulated the government to serve their own ends. The worst of the war lords were not above bartering away their country's natural resources in return for loans wherewith to finance their private wars and increase their private fortunes. And even the best of them were frequently either ignorant of or indifferent toward broad questions of foreign policy. The militarists regarded the Peking Foreign Office as a buffer between themselves and the foreign powers, and so long as the Foreign Office continued to serve this purpose, they interfered little with whatever policy it chose to adopt with regard to treaty revision.

During the period of tuchunism, the foreign policy of China was determined almost exclusively by a relatively small group of men well trained in international law, experienced in diplomacy, and not in the least ignorant of conditions in Western countries. Some of them had been educated in mission colleges in China; others had advanced degrees from universities in the United States, England, or Europe. Practically all of them spoke one or more foreign languages. Cabinets and cliques might come and go, and the provinces might be ruled by ex-bandits, but the Foreign Office and the diplomatic service remained in the hands of these younger men of the Returned Student class. They voiced the nation's grievances at Paris and again at Washington. They stood firmly for the principle that China was entitled to equal treatment as a sovereign nation. Thus precedents were established and foundations laid for the work which has been carried to partial completion by the National Government at Nanking.[3]

The authorities in control of the Peking Foreign Office had to bide their time in the expectation that the trend of international events would work to China's advantage. In the south, however, the Kuomintang leaders, unhampered by the proximity of the Legation Quarter, launched a direct attack upon existing treaties and were not afraid to use strikes, boycotts, and occasional riots in their attempt to compel immediate action by the powers. The international significance of the Nationalist movement lay in the fact that its leaders did not shrink from the use of direct action in their determination to achieve practical results. At Peking the Minister of Foreign Affairs was usually compelled to formulate his own policy and to carry it into effect when and where he could without effective support from the elements which controlled the Government. At Nanking, on the other hand, the voice of Dr. Wang was the voice of the entire National Government behind which stood the powerful Kuomintang.

The campaign to remove restrictions on China's freedom of

[3] The statement of Mr. Thomas F. Millard deserves to be quoted in this connection. "It has been said, and justly, that if all branches of the Chinese Government displayed the ability its diplomats usually do, especially in the last decade, China would be one of the leading nations of the world." *Conflict of Policies in Asia*, p. 236.

action has yielded impressive results. Tariff autonomy has become a reality. The German, Russian, Austrian, Belgian, and some of the British residential concessions have been returned. Increasing numbers of foreigners are being brought under the jurisdiction of Chinese officials and Chinese courts. Definite progress has been made in the work of revising existing treaties, and a beginning has been made in the negotiation of new treaties based on principles of equality and mutual respect for sovereign rights. Five men have been chiefly responsible for the attainment of these results. Dr. Sun Yat-sen provided much of the program and most of the driving force. But the men who wrestled with the actual problems of diplomatic intercourse were Dr. W. W. Yen, Dr. V. K. Wellington Koo, Mr. Eugene Chen, and Dr. C. T. Wang. Each of these leaders had the advantage of training in foreign colleges and universities and all were familiar with political and economic conditions abroad. Dr. Yen and Dr. Koo both had diplomatic experience in the West, and Dr. Wang gained an insight into the subtleties of Occidental diplomacy while serving as one of the Chinese delegates to the Versailles Conference. Mr. Chen was born and educated in the British island of Trinidad.

Aside from questions connected with Japan's anomalous and somewhat exceptional position in Manchuria, four problems remain to be dealt with. The first of these, extraterritoriality, has already been the subject of negotiations between the Chinese Government and the governments of the foreign powers directly concerned. The others are the abolition of foreign inland navigation rights in China, the withdrawal of foreign troops, and the retrocession of the remaining foreign residential concessions and settlements, including the Legation Quarter in Peiping. Germs of a major international conflict lurk in the clash between Chinese nationalism and a system of imperialism inherited from the nineteenth century. Foreign recognition of that fact may go far to determine whether China's unsettled problems can or will be settled by peaceful means.

INDEX

Aglen, Sir Francis, 310-11.
Amoy, return of British residential area at, 384.
Anfu-Chihli war, 133.
Anglo-Japanese Alliance, Chinese protests against renewal of, 107-11; abandonment of, 111.
Austria, treaty of commerce, 1925, 308-9.
Austria-Hungary, Chinese declaration of war against, 34-5; conclusion of peace with, 85.

Balfour, Arthur, 214, 228-9, 230, 239.
Barga, 396; see also Hulunbuir.
Belgium, Chinese termination of treaty of 1865, 312-18; appeal to Permanent Court of International Justice, 319; negotiations for new treaty with Peking government, 319-20; treaty of 1928, 351-2; returns Tientsin concession, 382-3.
Bolivia, treaty of 1919, 97.
Borch, Herbert von, 348.
Borodin, Michael, 290, 330, 335, 403.
Boxer indemnity, payment of German share stopped, 20; Chinese proposals for suspension of Allies' share of, 27; suspension of payments 1917, 40; Chinese hope for cancellation, 52; Russian offers to renounce, 127, 130, 136, 185; Gold Franc dispute, 259-62, 264-5; return of to China, 265-6 note.
Boxer Protocol, 1, 2, 19; Chinese proposals for modification, 27, 69.
Boycott, of Japanese goods, 80, 254, 359; of British goods, 266-7, 293, 296.
Brazil, note on extraterritoriality, 378.

Canton, autonomous government, 33, 43-4, 207; demand for separate representation at Washington Conference, 208; Shakee massacre, 267; communist insurrection at, 1927, 336-7.
Chamberlain, Sir Austen, 303.
Chang Chu-sun, 133.
Chang Hsueh-liang, 347, 395-6.
Chang Hsün, 33-4.
Chang Shih-lin, 135.
Chang Tso-lin, 122, 133, 139, 163, 180, 194-6, 203, 205, 244, 248, 276, 278; orders collection of surtaxes on imports, 310; generalissimo, 311; retirement from Peking 1928, 328; interference with Chinese Eastern Railway administration, 388-90; opposition to communism, 390-1.
Chang Tsung-hsiang, 79, 88.
Changchun conference, 170-1.
Chen Chiung-ming, 249.
Chen, Eugene, Acting Minister for Foreign Affairs Canton, 293-4; statement of Nationalist aims, 300-1; Minister for Foreign Affairs Hankow, 301; notes concerning Nanking incident, 305-7; estimate of, 405, 408.
Chernyk, A. S., 390.
Ch'i Hsieh-yuan, 196.
Chiang Kai-shek, commander of Nationalist armies, 295; declaration concerning treaties, 295-6; establishes separate government at Nanking, 331; resignation as commander-in-chief, 334-5; returns to power, 337; pledge to protect foreign property, 346; becomes chairman of State Council, 349.
Chile, desire for commercial treaty with China, 96.
Chin Yun-p'eng, 207, 244.

Index 415

Switzerland, treaty of 1918 signed, 88.

Sze, Sao-ke Alfred, 54; delegate to Washington Conference, 209, 219, 239, 376.

Ta Tsing Liu Li, 3.

T'ang Shao-yi, 30, 249.

Tariff, Chinese, proposals for rate increase, 27; revision 1917; 40; rates for non-treaty nations, 40-1; 72 note; movement for autonomy, 52-3; Chinese statement at Paris Conference, 71-2; Chinese statement at Washington Conference, 214-15; Washington treaty, 215-16; revision 1922, 249-50; conference 1925-6, 270-81; levy of surtax at Canton, etc., 293-4, 310; law of 1929, 358; duties collected on gold valuation, 362.

Tariff autonomy, Chinese demand for at Peking Conference, 271-3; Peking government preparations for, 311; proclaimed by Nanking government 1927, 332-5; recognized by United States, 347-8; in treaties of 1928, 351-2, 354-6; recognized by Japan, 363; becomes effective, 364 note.

Tariff Conference, Peking, 1925-6, proposals of C. T. Wang, 271-2; resolution concerning tariff autonomy, 273-4; Japanese and American proposals for interim tariff rates, 273-5; Chinese declaration concerning taxation of foreigners, 275; proposal to abolish duties on coastwise trade, 275; suspension, 279-80.

Tashkent, 130-1, 134.

Telegraphic installations, foreign, request for withdrawal from China, 70.

Tientsin, negotiations concerning British concession at, 327-8, 383; rendition of Belgian concession, 382-3.

Treaties, Chinese policy concerning new, 88-9; demand for revision 1925, 267-9, 289-90; views of Sun Yat-sen concerning, 293; policy of Peking government toward revi-

sion of, 308, 311-12; *see also* Belgium, France, Spain, Japan; policy of Nanking government toward revision, 331-2, 341-2; Interim Regulations, 342-3.

Trianon, treaty of signed by China, 85.

Troops, foreign in China, request for withdrawal, 69, 221-3.

Ts'ai T'ing-kan, 278, 280, 321.

Ts'ai Yuan-pei, 170.

Tsai Yun-sheng, 396-7.

Tsao Ju-lin, 79-80.

Ts'ao Kun, 133; inaugurated President, 181, 259; 198, 206, 244, 257, 263.

Tsinan incident, 345-6; settlement of, 359-60.

Tuan Ch'i-jui, Premier, 10; favors breach with Germany, 17, 31-2; attempts to unify country, 43; retirement as Premier, 46; heads Frontiers Protection Bureau, 119; Provisional Chief Executive, 198, 263, 271, 276; retirement, 278.

Tuchuns, favor war against Germany, 30-1; demand dissolution of Parliament, 32; lack of interest in foreign affairs, 406.

Twenty-One Demands, Chinese request at Paris for abrogation of 1915 treaties, 62-4; Japanese reply to same, 64-5; discussed at Washington Conference, 231-2, 240-3; Chinese attempt to negotiate regarding 1923, 252-4.

Tyau, Phillip K. C., 243.

Underwood, Oscar W., 215, 227.

Ungern von Sternberg, Baron, 141, 162-3.

United States, urges China to sever relations with Germany, 9-10, 11; advises Chinese factions to compose differences, 32; policy toward Nationalists 1927, 299-300; settlement of Nanking incident, 338-41; tariff treaty 1928, 347-8; treaty of arbitration with China 1930, 369 note; replies to Chinese notes on extraterritoriality, 371-2, 375.

Van Blokland, Beelaerts, 48.